Race, Creed, Color, or National Origin:
A Reader on Racial and Ethnic Identities
in American Society

With the compliments of

F. E. PEACOCK PUBLISHERS, INC.
401 WEST IRVING PARK ROAD
ITASCA, ILLINOIS 60143

race, creed, color, or national origin

A Reader on Racial and Ethnic Identities in American Society

ROBERT K. YIN

THE RAND CORPORATION, WASHINGTON, D.C.
MASSACHUSETTS INSTITUTE OF TECHNOLOGY

F. E. PEACOCK PUBLISHERS, INC., ITASCA, ILLINOIS

Table of Contents

PREFACE

This collection of readings was motivated by the conviction that race and ethnicity have played a much more important role in American society than is generally recognized. Such a conviction may appear to be an understatement in light of the rude awakenings of the 1960s, when racial injustice became a prominent issue. However, we have only recently been able to examine those events with some perspective, and to realize that social inequity is but one of many issues involving racial and ethnic factors. It is only now, for instance, that we are beginning to examine the persistence of ethnic identities, or to appreciate the true impact of immigration trends, or even to analyze more comprehensively the role of race and ethnicity in the American city.

Underlying this conviction are three observations: one sociological, another psychological, and the third policy-related. On the sociological side, the examination of residential, occupational, and other social group patterns reveals consistent (though not always strong) segregation by race and ethnicity; people simply tend to choose to live or to work or to socialize with others of their 'own kind.' As a result, racial and ethnic institutions have not disappeared as quickly as might have been expected. On the psychological side, we identify other people by their names and faces, and as long as the personal relationships remain at an extremely casual level, the racial and ethnic characteristics of the names and the faces will be of some consequence. This may lead to undesired discrimination, to be sure, but the salient feature of our social perceptions is that we are not color blind, and the process of stereotyping individuals aids us in adjusting to our social environment. On the policy side, it appears that for the immediate future at least, racial and ethnic factors will enter into the calculus of such decision-making processes as the hiring of new employees, the awarding of grants and other federal monies, and the selection of members to advisory groups and boards of trustees.

The acceptance of race and ethnicity as important dimensions of American society poses a new set of problems and challenges for social science, however. For a long time, the study of race and ethnicity, as I try to suggest in the introductory essay, has been based on a distinctly different premise: that such characteristics were of declining importance, and that assimilation into the American way of life was the dominant process to be understood. The rush to understand assimilation precluded the development of any pluralistic framework, one that would begin by asking some obvious questions (e.g., what is race? ethnicity? how are they expressed in social institutions? how are they important in American society? why do they persist?), and that would allow for the answers to contribute to an overall social portrait of the country. Ironically, what we might call pluralism today differs in spirit but not in content from what might have been called bigotry in the past.

It is my hope, at any rate, that these readings can provide the sketchy outlines of a social portrait. In this endeavor, I am most indebted to the authors whose works appear here, as well as to Nathan Glazer and Edgar Borgatta, who have continued to provide much food for thought on this topic. I am also grateful to Barbara Fern Yin, who has been an acute observer and a most helpful critic. The responsibility for the final product, however, is mine alone.

R.K.Y.

Washington, D.C.
November, 1972

INTRODUCTION

No single topic has dominated contemporary American society more than race and ethnic group identity. Racial conflict has persisted throughout American history, marked by lynchings, urban riots, and other forms of violent confrontation. Today, a racial emotionalism incorporating the worst forms of fear and mistrust by both blacks and whites is still pervasive. Although the urban riots of the 1960s have subsided, the domestic issues like scatter-site housing and school busing that arouse the greatest emotions remain those related to race. The nation has yet to develop a consistent ideology for dealing with differences among black people and white people; integration, separatism, pluralism, community control and benign neglect have all been tried at different times and in different forms. It is likely that racial tensions will persist until some viable ideology develops.

While black-white relations have always been an important issue in America, there has also been a revived awareness of other racial and ethnic identities. Indians, Mexican-Americans, and Puerto Ricans, for instance, have made their interests known as never before, both independently and in concert with blacks and orientals as part of the Third World peoples. Moreover, a consciousness of differences among white ethnic groups has resurfaced. This has been manifested most clearly perhaps in the popular arts, where a top television show, "All in the Family," promoted bigotry to stardom in the early 1970s, and where such books as *The Unmeltable Ethnics, The Decline of the Wasp,* and *The Ethnic Factor* have appeared with increasing frequency. The arousal of ethnic identities, even among those people whose families have not been recent immigrants, certainly makes one wonder whether such identities were ever lost, or whether indeed they have merely been overlooked until the present time.

Underlying the sensitivity about racial and ethnic identities is the fact that discrimination according to such social groups has formed the basic weave of the entire American social fabric and institutional structure. For example, racially segregated neighborhoods and schools throughout the country are the rule, and not the exception; ethnic group identities, whether based on religion or national origins or both, influence the choice of residence, employment, and life-style, especially in the country's large metropolitan areas. To be sure, there have been other social identities as well: at the end of the 1960s, a new sexist awareness raised important questions about antifeminist discrimination; social opportunities have always been selective by economic class; and new divisions according to age have emerged such as the large-scale development of nursing homes for the elderly and day-care centers for the young.

But race and ethnicity have been the outstanding dimensions for social identities in America. Race has been important because of the unique history of the American black people, a history that includes a severe form of human slavery and continued discrimination by skin color, especially against blacks, but also against yellows, reds, and browns. Ethnicity has been important because of the continued and significant migration of foreign peoples to the United States. In fact, the immigration factor has been so prominent in American history that Oscar Handlin has written, "Once I thought to write a history of the immigrants in America. Then I discovered that the immigrants *were* American history."[1] Though the flow of new immigrants in relation to the native population has decreased in recent years, the character of the recent migration *and* the declining birthrate of the native population still make immigration a critical component of the nation's population growth.

RESEARCH ON RACE AND ETHNICITY

It would be entirely fitting, then, if race and ethnicity were the subject of continuing social inquiry, and if the basic facts of race and ethnic group identity were widely known, even if not well understood. But this has not been the case. In fact, until the last decade, race and ethnicity received relatively little attention from social scientists.[2] One can attempt to blame the paucity of research simply on the lack of financial support by government and other sponsors,[3] or one can attribute the paucity to the narrow interests of scholars themselves. In history, for ex-

---

[1]Oscar Handlin, *The Uprooted* (Boston: Little, Brown and Company, 1951), p. 3.

[2]This sentiment has been echoed in several articles. See Melvin M. Tumin, "Some social consequences of research on racial relations," *American Sociologist,* May 1968, 3:117–23; Rudolph J. Vecoli, "Ethnicity: A neglected dimension of American history," in Herbert J. Bass (ed.), *The State of American History* (Chicago: Quadrangle Books, Inc., 1970), pp. 70–88; Andrew M. Greeley, "Ethnicity as an influence on behavior," in Otto Feinstein (ed.), *Ethnic Groups in the City: Culture, Institutions, and Power* (Lexington, Mass.: D.C. Heath & Co., 1971), pp. 3–16; and L. Paul Metzger, "American sociology and black assimilation: Conflicting perspectives," *American Journal of Sociology,* January 1971, 76:627–47.

[3]This thought is pursued by Melvin Tumin in "Some social consequences," *op. cit.*

ample, few researchers were interested in studying racial or ethnic identities; scholars of white Protestant backgrounds tended to overlook the importance of such identities, and scholars of ethnic backgrounds tried to de-emphasize their personal backgrounds by studying other subjects.[4] But more likely, the failure to study racial and ethnic identities reflected an implicit value orientation maintained within American social science throughout the first half of the century.

During this time, social science thinking was dominated by an assimilationist doctrine, which held that all racial and ethnic groups ultimately lost their separate identities and adopted a unitary American way of life. For Frederick Jackson Turner, the American frontier was the scene of such assimilation; for Robert Ezra Park, the city played a similar role. The symbol of both scenes was the melting pot, a creation of the playwright Israel Zangwill, who fashioned the following lines for a play that opened in this country in 1908:

America is God's crucible, the great Melting Pot where all the races of Europe are melting and re-forming! Here you stand, good folk, think I, when I see them at Ellis Island, here you stand in your fifty groups, with your fifty languages and histories, and your fifty blood hatreds and rivalries. But you won't be long like that, brothers, for these are the fires of God you've come to—these are the fires of God. A fig for your feuds and vendettas! Germans and Frenchmen, Irishmen and Englishmen, Jews and Russians—into the crucible with you all! God is making the American.[5]

Lest anyone underestimate the extent of Zangwill's imagination, even people of the black and yellow races were specifically mentioned as ingredients in the great melting pot. Thus according to the assimilationist doctrine and its melting pot analogy, people of different races, creeds, and national origins were assumed to work their way into American society, eventually to become indistinguishable from the general society. In this manner, the melting pot also served as an ideal symbol for the American democratic ethos; all individuals became equals in the United States.

The works of Turner and Park, though unrelated to each other, both exemplified the tone of research in their respective fields of history and sociology.[6] In sociology especially, interest in Park's race relations cycle and in the process of assimilation stood at the forefront of race and ethnic research, with Simpson and Yinger's *Race Relations* perhaps the most widely used textbook. In both fields, the normative American way

---

[4]Vecoli, "Ethnicity," *op. cit.*

[5]From Zangwill's play, as quoted by Milton M. Gordon, *Assimilation in American Life: The Role of Race, Religion, and National Origins* (New York: Oxford University Press, 1964), p. 120.

[6]Vecoli, "Ethnicity," *op. cit.*

of life drew the main research focus, serving as the standard against which racial and ethnic groups were studied. This meant that few investigators made racial and ethnic institutions the objects of inquiry on their own right.

The assimilationist orientation also led to one unfortunate oversight: little evidence was gathered to determine whether in fact all racial and ethnic groups were assimilating. On the one hand, there was a logical difficulty. If all groups were *eventually* supposed to assimilate, it was difficult to distinguish a genuine counterexample from a case of very slow assimilation.[7] On the other hand, the study of ethnic groups, like the U.S. census of population, simply lost track of ethnic identities after the first generation or two of post-immigration families. This added to the misleading impression that ethnic groups were disappearing, an impression reinforced by the statements of some researchers who actually forecast that ethnic groups had a limited future in the United States, as they were being assimilated so rapidly.[8] Similarly, the study of racial groups failed to recognize the severe racial barriers facing the black citizen, especially as the black population in the cities grew during the 1950s. For instance, two political scientists have noted that in their field, the prevailing pluralist view of community power[9] vastly underplayed the extent of racial (or any other kind of) inequity in the city, and thus provided no hint of the subsequent urban riots. The riots were outward manifestations of conflicts that the pluralists had honestly not perceived.[10]

Only in the last 10 years has research on race and ethnicity finally begun to increase. First came the gradual realization that the melting pot was an inadequate model, oversimplified at best and incorrect at worst. In *Beyond the Melting Pot* (1963), Glazer and Moynihan reviewed the persistence of racial and ethnic identities in New York, and stated simply that "The point about the melting pot . . . is that it did not happen."[11] Second, community researchers discovered strong ethnic enclaves thriving in the city (and resisting urban renewal) and even

---

[7]Amitai Etzioni, "The ghetto: A re-evaluation," *Social Forces,* March 1959, 37:255–62.

[8]W. Lloyd Warner and Leo Srole, *The Social Systems of American Ethnic Groups* (New Haven, Conn.: Yale University Press, 1945), pp. 295–96.

[9]The pluralist view stipulated that in urban politics, there was a relatively wide sharing of power among different groups, and that there was certainly no power elite dominating the decision-making (see Nelson W. Polsby, *Community Power and Political Theory* [New Haven, Conn.: Yale University Press, 1963]).

[10]Stephen M. David and Jewel Bellush, "Introduction: Pluralism, race, and the urban political system," in Bellush and David (eds.), *Race and Politics in New York City: Five Studies in Policy-Making* (New York: Praeger Publishers, Inc., 1971), pp. 3–24.

[11]Nathan Glazer and Daniel Patrick Moynihan, *Beyond the Melting Pot* (Cambridge, Mass.: The M.I.T. Press, 1963), p. v.

sprouting in the suburbs.[12] Third, the 1960s saw the production of several major studies of race and social policy, led by Moynihan's *The Negro Family* (1965), James S. Coleman's *Equality of Educational Opportunity* (1966), and the U.S. Riot Commission Report (1968).

Some of this research still fell into the assimilationist mold. It characterized people of different races as being inherently equal, and therefore gave strong support to a policy of racial integration. Integration, however, implicitly meant the assimilation of black people into white-oriented institutions and society.[13] One scholar actually went so far as to claim the existence of a continuous line of research, beginning with Myrdal's *An American Dilemma* (1944) and culminating with the Moynihan and Coleman reports, that definitively established the major causes and effects of American race discrimination. He went on to suggest that, had government heeded these research findings and promoted a more rapid rate of racial desegregation and integration, some of the subsequent urban riots might have been avoided.[14] But there are several difficulties with this position. First, the early documentation of racial inequality was not sufficient. For instance, few people anticipated the likely dimensions of racial discrimination or conflict in the North; as late as the Civil Rights Act of 1964, it should be remembered, integration was thought to be primarily a problem of creating change in southern institutions.[15] Second, even if the documentation had been sufficient, the research, beginning with Myrdal's study,[16] did little to suggest what courses of action were available to government. (Precisely how one goes about desegregating schools, as we have learned for instance, is not a trivial question.) Third, the line of reasoning gives no consideration to the possibility that there may have been a majority constituency to which government was indeed responding, and that, rightly or wrongly, the majority might not have wished the rapid removal of racial barriers. Finally, it is not even clear that the blacks wanted equality or integration on terms defined solely by white social scientists.

Other investigators during the last 10 years have attempted to frame their research around the unique political and social development of racial and ethnic groups, without regard to questions of integration or

---

[12]The most notable studies were Herbert J. Gans, *The Urban Villagers* (New York: The Free Press, 1962); William M. Dobriner, *Class in Suburbia* (Englewood Cliffs, N.J.: Prentice-Hall, Inc., 1963), especially pp. 65-67, 118; and Albert I. Gordon, *Jews in Suburbia* (Boston: Beacon Press, 1959).

[13]L. Paul Metzger, "Conventional social science and racial integration," in J. David Colfax and Jack L. Roach (eds.), *Radical Sociology* (New York: Basic Books, Inc., 1971), pp. 67–78.

[14]Tumin, "Some social consequences," *op. cit.*

[15]See, for example, Nathan Glazer, "Blacks and ethnic groups: The difference, and the political difference it makes," *Social Problems,* Spring 1971, 18:444–61, for one treatment of northern versus southern differences.

[16]Metzger, "American sociology," *op. cit.*, makes this criticism of Myrdal's work.

assimilation; in fact, the identities of the individual racial or ethnic groups have been consciously preserved. This approach tends to follow the idea of cultural pluralism, first set forth by Horace Kallen in 1915 and later revived by him and Adamic's *A Nation of Nations* (1944).[17] Interestingly, the desire to study racial and ethnic groups in this manner is very similar to the doctrine of cultural relativism espoused in the study of foreign cultures. As described by one eminent anthropologist,

> The principle of cultural relativism has long been standard anthropological doctrine. It holds that any cultural phenomenon must be understood and evaluated in terms of the culture of which it forms part. The corresponding assumption in the organic field is so obvious that biologists have scarcely troubled to formulate it. The difference is that we, the students of culture, live in our culture, are attached to its values, and have a natural human inclination to become ethnocentric over it, with the result that, if unchecked, we would perceive, describe, and evaluate other cultures by the forms, standards, and values of our own . . . [18]

Studies in the mold of cultural pluralism have meant a reexamination of black culture and black family life from the point of view of black society in the United States.[19] The same ethos has led to the recent revival of research on such topics as sickle cell anemia, a disease peculiar to black people, and treatment of which will probably have little impact on the health of white people. The studies have also meant the realization that white American society is not a unitary society, but that it consists of diverse subcultures influencing residential, occupational, marriage, voting, and other social patterns.[20] The very creation of the popularly used acronym "WASP," a term defined by E. Digby Baltzell 15 years ago,[21] is perhaps most symptomatic of the recent differentiation among

---

[17]For a brief discussion of cultural pluralism, see Nathan Glazer, "Ethnic groups in America: From national culture to ideology," in Morroe Berger *et al.* (eds.), *Freedom and Control in Modern Society* (New York: Octagon Books, 1954), pp. 158–73.

[18]Alfred L. Kroeber, *The Nature of Culture* (Chicago: University of Chicago Press, 1952).

[19]For instance, see Robert Blauner, "Black culture: Myth or reality?" in Norman E. Whitten, Jr., and John F. Szwed (eds.), *Afro-American Anthropology: Contemporary Perspectives* (New York: The Free Press, 1970), pp. 347–66; and Robert Staples, "Towards a sociology of the black family: A theoretical and methodological treatment," *Journal of Marriage and the Family,* February 1971, 33:119–38.

[20]For instance, see Andrew M. Greeley, *Why Can't They Be Like Us? America's White Ethnic Groups* (New York: E.P. Dutton & Co., Inc., 1971); and Murray Friedman, "Is white racism the problem?" *Commentary,* January 1969, pp. 61–65.

[21]Baltzell used the term in *The Protestant Establishment: Aristocracy and Caste in America* (New York: Random House, Inc., 1964). Vance Packard, writing in 1962, gave Baltzell the credit for defining the term. See Vance Packard, *The Pyramid Climbers* (New York: McGraw-Hill Book Co., 1962), p. 35. Packard himself used the term in *The Pyramid Climbers,* but not in his earlier work, *The Status Seekers* (New York: McGraw-Hill Book Co., 1959), suggesting that the term came into existence around the turn of the decade.

white ethnic groups. Finally, one investigator has even carried the pluralistic approach so far as to suggest modifications in the application of majority rule in the United States.[22]

The general resurgence of research in the last 10 years, however, has only slowly begun to yield sufficient information about race and ethnicity. Moreover, because of the heightened social conflict over matters of race, poverty, and war, much of the recent research has been overly (if understandably) concerned with the social problems created by race and ethnicity. In reviewing the research, one group of scholars has written that studies of race and ethnicity have generally fallen into three categories: (a) studies of individual racial and ethnic groups, with Thomas and Znaniecki's *The Polish Peasant in Europe and America* (1918) serving as a prototype; (b) studies of social interaction among racial and ethnic groups, typically concerned with race relations; and (c) studies of racial and ethnic groups from the point of view of social problems, e.g., job discrimination.[23] If we accept this typology, then it seems that while the earlier research on race and ethnicity was dominated by studies on assimilation and therefore fell into the social interaction category, the more recent research has been dominated by the social problems approach.[24] One is hard pressed, however, to find many studies in the remaining category, i.e., studies on individual racial and ethnic groups. (In fact, one is hard pressed to cite other major works in the tradition of *The Polish Peasant*.) A solid core of research on racial and ethnic group life in the United States has yet to develop.[25]

The fundamental concern underlying studies in all three categories, however, is the same; it involves an understanding of racial and ethnic identities. In other words, the investigation of race relations, of social problems related to race and ethnicity, and of different racial and ethnic groups all presume prior information about the definition of racial or ethnic group identity, about the formation, maintenance, and dissolution of such identities, and about the importance of such identities in American society. Put simply, we need to know what constitutes racial and ethnic differences, and why such differences are important. Unfortu-

[22]Herbert J. Gans, "We won't end the urban crisis until we end 'majority rule'," *The New York Times Magazine,* August 3, 1969.

[23]John Harding *et al.,* "Prejudice and ethnic relations," in Gardner Lindzey and Elliot Aronson (eds.), *The Handbook of Social Psychology* (2d ed.; Reading, Mass.: Addison-Wesley Publishing Co., Inc., 1969), Vol. 5, pp. 1-76.

[24]I have previously written about the shortcomings of the social problems approach in relation to urban studies. See Robert K. Yin, "Introduction," in *The City in the Seventies* (Itasca, Ill.: F. E. Peacock Publishers, Inc., 1972), pp. ix–xvii. The basic shortcoming is that the problems are defined by their societal context, and rarely in a theoretical context. For an elaboration, see Herbert Blumer, "Social problems as collective behavior," *Social Problems,* Winter 1971, 18: 298–306.

[25]Although there are now summary textbooks of the existing research. See the two multi-volumed series, "Ethnic groups in comparative perspective," ed. by Peter I. Rose, published by Random House, Inc., and "Ethnic groups in American life," ed. by Milton M. Gordon, published by Prentice-Hall, Inc.

nately, many studies of race and ethnicity have not dealt with these issues explicitly. The main purpose of *Race, Creed, Color, or National Origin* is to assemble a collection of articles that begins to address the question of race and ethnic group identity.

UNDERSTANDING RACIAL AND ETHNIC IDENTITIES

As in the study of the individual in society, there are two basic aspects in analyzing race and ethnic group identity: the characteristics of the identities themselves, and the societal context within which the identities are important. To the extent that either there were no separate identities (e.g., all people looked and behaved alike), or there were separate identities but they were unimportant in the institutional structure of society (e.g., people looked or behaved differently, but were nevertheless treated equally), racial and ethnic group identities would be a less important matter. To be sure, these two aspects are only distinguishable in an analytic sense, for identities are often defined in terms of the societal context, and conversely, the context can be defined as a composite of all group identities. Nevertheless, questions of identity can be treated somewhat apart from questions of societal context.

Turning first to the question of the identities themselves, one would have to claim that the most important characteristic of these identities is that they are *group* identities. Simple as it may sound, the point needs to be made explicitly to counter the popular myth that we are a nation of individuals.[26] Far more important than the image of the United States as a nation of immigrants, for instance, is the fact that the United States has been a nation of *immigrant groups*. This is because immigration has not been a random process, composed of individuals entering each year in equal proportions from other countries; it has been more of a wavelike process, with immigrants from certain countries dominating certain periods of time. Second, the immigrant groups came from countries that were at different stages of their nation-state development, so the groups had different preconceptions and aspirations upon arriving in the United States.[27] Third, the immigrants have not randomly scattered upon their arrival in the United States, either, but have settled in groups, with residential enclaves often surviving for several generations.

The distinction between group and individual identity leads to another observation: the assimilation process may be different for

---

[26]The myth, and the denials by people like Woodrow Wilson that minorities existed in American society, are described by Friedman, "Is white racism the problem?" *op. cit.*

[27]Nathan Glazer, "Ethnic groups in America," Some groups, like the Germans, can even be further differentiated into separate waves of people of different economic class. See Theodore Huebener, *The Germans in America* (Philadelphia: Chilton Book Co., 1962), p. 136.

groups than it is for individuals. For instance, the mechanisms for individual assimilation might include intermarriage, a rising income, residential relocation, and a legal change of surname. Group assimilation, however, might include Milton Gordon's critical distinction between cultural and structural assimilation (groups may culturally assimilate by adopting American tastes and habits, but at the same time may resist structural assimilation by maintaining strong within-group social relations);[28] group identification as a function of generational differences (the third generation after immigration may show *more* identification with its Old World past than the second generation);[29] and the effects of U.S. diplomatic relations on ethnic group status (e.g., a rise of ethnic pride among Chinese-Americans may accompany the expansion of Sino-American diplomatic relations).[30] One suspects that the processes of individual and group assimilation are indeed considerably different, and we need to know a great deal more about both.

Turning to the societal context, racial and ethnic group discrimination and segregation have been American facts of life. First, even if it were true that all individuals in the country were treated equally, it would not follow that all groups would have received equal treatment.[31] This paradox is most evident in the recent surge of concern over institutional racism,[32] whereby equal treatment of individuals (as, say, in the admissions procedures of a university) can result in systematic discrimination among certain groups of people (Chinese and Jews might be favored, while blacks and Mexican-Americans might be disfavored). The major objection to institutional racism is that it automatically reinforces group discriminations and unfairly maintains a status quo in American society, allowing those groups in power to remain in power. What makes institutional racism difficult to deal with is that it can take place even though individual people may be acting in good faith and in a nondiscriminatory manner.

Second, in actual fact neither individuals nor groups have been treated equally in American society. If judged by history, this conclusion is quite clear. Black people were enslaved and simply never meant to be covered by the original tenets of the U.S. Constitution. Only the 14th Amendment, ratified in 1868 and reversing the Dred Scott decision, first

---

[28]Gordon, *Assimilation in American Life,* pp. 60–83.

[29]According to Nathan Glazer, the phenomenon wasn't discussed until Marcus L. Hansen's "The problem of the third generation immigrant," in 1938. See Glazer, "Ethnic groups in America," *op. cit.*

[30]For a description of the situation in New York City, see *The New York Times,* March 12, 1972.

[31]Nathan Glazer, "The limits of social policy," *Commentary,* September 1971, pp. 51–58.

[32]For example, see Louis L. Knowles and Kenneth Prewitt (eds.), *Institutional Racism in America* (Englewood Cliffs, N.J.: Prentice-Hall, Inc., 1969).

spelled out citizenship and civil rights for black people.[33] However, the 15th Amendment, ratified in 1870, was needed to override existing state laws (including those of several northern states) and to establish that no citizens would be denied the right to vote on account of "race, color, or previous condition of servitude." These amendments did not signal the automatic cessation of racial discrimination. Rather, states promulgated the use of poll taxes, literacy tests, "grandfather" clauses, and other residence requirements to prevent blacks from voting; to make sure that the point got across, lynchings were also used as a form of intimidation, with the peak year being 1892, when 162 blacks were lynched.[34] The problems involved in establishing basic civil rights for black people have continued to the present day, with key court decisions and new legislative acts, e.g., *Plessy* v. *Ferguson* (1896), *Brown* v. *Board of Education of Topeka* (1954), and the Civil Rights Act of 1964 all playing important roles.

Other groups have also been the subject of overt discrimination in American society. The Immigration Laws of 1921 and 1924, for instance, established immigration quotas according to the immigrants' country of origin.[35] Since the quotas were calculated according to the proportion of people of various national origins already in the United States, many of the less represented groups received only token quotas. Moreover, these Immigration Laws were not the first to exclude people because of their country of origin. The Chinese had been the first to suffer from American exclusionary policies, with Chinese migration to the United States eliminated by the Chinese Exclusion Act of 1882, an act that was extended twice before being finally repealed in 1943.[36] Within the United States, institutions have also been highly discriminatory. Perhaps the most overt examples of such discrimination were the quotas first established for Jewish students enrolled in institutions of higher

---

[33]For general reviews of the historical documents pertinent to the civil rights of black people, see Albert P. Blaustein and Robert L. Zangrando (eds.), *Civil Rights and the Black American: A Documentary History* (New York: Washington Square Press, 1968); Stanley Feldstein (ed.), *The Poisoned Tongue: A Documentary History of American Racism and Prejudice* (New York: William Morrow & Co., Inc., 1972); and Edgar A. Toppin, *A Biographical History of Blacks in America Since 1528* (New York: David McKay Co., Inc., 1971).

[34]Toppin, *A Biographical History,* pp. 143–147.

[35]For a description of the events leading to these pieces of legislation, see Oscar Handlin, *Race and Nationality in American Life* (Boston: Little, Brown and Company, 1957), pp. 77-110.

[36]See Jethro K. Lieberman, *Are Americans Extinct?* (New York: Walker & Co., 1968), pp. 9, 15–18. For a long time, the anti-Chinese sentiment was thought to be merely a regional prejudice, centered around the California area where Chinese workers were potentially a disruptive economic force. Recent investigations, however, have challenged this "California thesis," and have found evidence of strong national sentiments in favor of excluding the Chinese. See Stuart Creighton Miller, *The Unwelcome Immigrant: The American Image of the Chinese, 1785-1882* (Berkeley, Calif.: University of California Press, 1969).

learning during the 1920s. These quotas were sometimes concealed behind a number of subterfuges (e.g., the desire for equitable distribution among geographic regions), but in the case of at least one major university, they were the subject of open debate.[37]

American society, then, has continually defined basic human rights and economic and social opportunities according to racial and ethnic identities. Moreover, our discussion has stuck mainly with overt discrimination, and has not even touched upon the more covert and subtle practices of American businesses and institutions. The more caustic observer may claim that America has in fact been a blatantly racist society. Such an observer might cite the well-known racial prejudices of egalitarian heroes like Thomas Jefferson and Abraham Lincoln as evidence for his view.[38] He might also claim that virtually every egalitarian measure, like Lincoln's Emancipation Proclamation,[39] has been motivated by political or economic expedience, and not by considerations of racial injustice. The more optimistic observer can argue that racial and ethnic discriminations, though serious, are nevertheless diminishing. He could cite Franklin D. Roosevelt's landmark executive order on employment practices in 1941, which incidentally first used the phrase ". . . regardless of race, creed, color, or national origin"; the Civil Rights Act of 1964, whose equal employment provisions were the first to add reference to discrimination by sex; and the Immigration Act of 1965, which eliminated the national origins quota system.[40] Both observers have correctly stated the past. The question is, what shall the future be like?

These two major aspects of racial and ethnic identities—the identities themselves and the societal context—form the two parts of *Race, Creed, Color, or National Origin*. Part One, "Racial and Ethnic Identities," attempts first to trace the unique American heritage that has produced the diversity of racial and ethnic groups in our society. Second, it attempts to deal with the definition of the identities themselves (e.g., what is a racial group? an ethnic group?), and with the question of how such identities are maintained, focusing mainly on the role of the family. Part

---

[37]For a full discussion of the topic, see Stephen Steinberg, "How Jewish quotas began," *Commentary*, September 1971, pp. 67–76.

[38]Jefferson's "Notes on the State of Virginia" show that he personally considered blacks to be inferior to whites (cited by Feldstein, *The Poisoned Tongue*, pp. 46–53). In spite of these views, Jefferson appears to have promoted an antislavery provision in the Declaration of Independence, though the provision was eventually eliminated at the Continental Congress (see Blaustein & Zangrando, *Civil Rights and the Black American*, pp. 42–44). Lincoln's personal views on white superiority over blacks are documented in the Lincoln-Douglas debates in 1858 (see Blaustein and Zangrando, *Civil Rights and the Black American*, pp. 162–72).

[39]Blaustein and Zangrando, *Civil Rights and the Black American*, pp. 191–201.

[40]On Roosevelt's executive order and the Civil Rights Act, see Blaustein and Zangrando, *Civil Rights and the Black American*, pp. 356–59 and 524–50; on the new immigration act, see Edward M. Kennedy, "The Immigration Act of 1965," *The Annals*, September 1966, 367: 137–49.

Two, "Identities in Contemporary American Society," attempts to answer the question of why such identities have been important, first examining racial and ethnic differentiation in the metropolis and in institutions, and then raising some of the issues of likely public concern in the future.

Necessarily, the readings are selective, and cover only a few of the many relevant subjects. A conscious prejudice has been to focus on the role of race and ethnicity in the public sector, i.e., on matters dealing with government and public services. This seems justifiable because the public sector has become so dominant in American society, and because questions of race and ethnicity have been so clearly important to areas of public subsidy like housing, urban development, education, health care, and employment. Conversely, only a few articles raise issues regarding the role of religion, reflecting the apparent decline of the traditional church in American society. Another major omission is attributable to the organization of the book. Because of the emphasis on general questions of racial and ethnic identities and their societal context, there is only minimal coverage of the special circumstances of any specific racial or ethnic group. Other topics knowingly given too much or too little attention have been described in the introductory passages to each section. The main goal throughout has been to inform the reader and to arouse his curiosities about the role of racial and ethnic identities in our society.

PART ONE

Racial and Ethnic Identities

A. AMERICAN HERITAGE

Race and ethnicity have been important social identities throughout American history. Three separate races, the Indian, the black, and the white, existed from the earliest colonization of North America. For instance, the first blacks came to Jamestown in 1619, and the colonies were over 15 percent black by 1776. And from the very beginning, the major social differences among the three races were readily apparent. Moreover, the races remained segregated into three separate castes. Alexis de Tocqueville, in his classic *Democracy in America,* wrote extensively about the situation of the three races. De Tocqueville's account captures quite lucidly the relationship among the three races, including the contrast between the Negro and Indian reactions to subservience by the white man, and a portion of his remarks are presented in the first article of this reader (Selection 1).

The segregation of blacks from white people, of course, was mainly accomplished through the unique institution of North American slavery.[1] While not all black people were enslaved, the American slavery system consisted of one of the severest forms of human bondage the world has ever known, with the residual effects on Americans still being felt today. For instance, the effects of slavery on black culture and the black family have frequently been noted.[2] However, less attention has been given to the question of how and why slavery arose in the first place. Stanley Elkins (Selection 2) suggests that the origins of slavery, as with so many other institutions in American history, were related not just to the crop economy of the South, but to the very nature of the American capitalist enterprise. The postslavery plight of the blacks, and their only gradual attainment of basic civil rights, has already been discussed.[3]

The main reason for the rise and persistence of ethnic group iden-

---

[1]There were strong variations in the form that slavery took in different parts of the Americas. See Frank Tannenbaum, *Slave and Citizen: The Negro in the Americas* (New York: Alfred A. Knopf, Inc., 1946).

[2]For instance, see E. Franklin Frazier, *The Negro Family in the United States* (Chicago: University of Chicago Press, 1939), Chap. 2.

[3]See the Introduction of this reader. For an excellent and readable account of the Civil Rights movement during the crucial decade of 1954 to 1964, see Anthony

tifications, on the other hand, has been the pattern of large-scale immigration to the United States. People of all countries migrated freely to the United States until the late 19th century. Then, the immigration laws became progressively exclusionary according to national origin (itself interesting—they could have become exclusionary according to some other criterion), beginning with the Chinese Exclusion Act of 1882, and culminating with the passage of the Immigration Acts of 1921 and 1924. The last two acts established immigration quotas according to national origin, with the size of the quota determined by the number of people of various national origins already in the United States.[4] The late President Kennedy took a personal and strong interest in revoking the exclusionary law, and his actions ultimately resulted in the abolition of the national origins quota system and a new Immigration Act of 1965. In Selections 3 and 4, Kennedy first traces the development and effect of the older laws of 1921 and 1924, and then Bill Kovach, a reporter for *The New York Times,* highlights the impact of the newer law of 1965.[5] As Kovach notes, the new law has resulted in an increasing immigration of Asians, southern Europeans, and Central Americans. Only time will tell whether the increase also means that groups like the Chinese will now develop social patterns and problems (e.g., juvenile delinquency) that the older immigrant groups like the Irish have already experienced.

Immigration has had a profound effect on the American population, if only because of the relatively high proportion of immigrants. As late as the decade from 1901 to 1910, for instance, the total immigration was about 10 percent of the existing U.S. population. Today, the proportion is much lower. However, because the native birthrate is declining, immigration accounts for a significant and growing percentage (over 20 percent in 1970) of the total population growth.[6] Max Lerner (Selection 5) captures some of the cultural diversity that these immigration patterns have produced. It is interesting to note that different immigrant groups have maintained their separate identities as part of the American heritage even in places like Hawaii, where the common image is one of a high rate of intermarriage and assimilation.[7]

Lewis and The New York Times, *Portrait of a Decade: The Second American Revolution* (New York: Random House, Inc., 1964).

[4] See also the Introduction of this reader.

[5] For other accounts of the changes in immigration laws and the immigration patterns themselves, see Helen F. Eckerson, "Immigration and national origins," *The Annals,* September 1966, 367:4–14; Edward M. Kennedy, "The Immigration Act of 1965," *The Annals,* September 1966, 367:137–39; and Charles B. Keely, "Effects of the Immigration Act of 1965 on selected population characteristics of immigrants to the United States," *Demography,* May 1971, 8:157–69.

[6] Richard Irwin, "Changing patterns of American immigration," *International Migration Review,* Spring 1972, 6:18–31.

[7] See, for example, Lawrence H. Fuchs, *Hawaii Pono: A Social History* (New York: Harcourt, Brace & World 1961).

The immigration experience has raised a major question in relation to the more recent migration of blacks from the rural South into American cities. Some have claimed that the urban blacks are merely undergoing the same process of assimilation as the European immigrants underwent 50 years ago.[8] Oscar Handlin, among others, has stated that the differences between blacks and ethnic groups are ones of degree, and not of kind.[9] William Taylor (Selection 6) argues, however, that the analogy is inappropriate because of the unique experience of the blacks in being victims of American slavery and because of continued racial discrimination in American society.[10] In a more recent article, Nathan Glazer has differentiated between the blacks' experience in the North as opposed to the South, and claims that the analogy between blacks and other immigrant groups may indeed be valid in the North.[11] This debate will not be easily settled, but an increasingly important factor is that black people themselves consider their experience to be unique, and this perception must dominate any academic debate.

In the final article of this section, Milton Gordon (Selection 7) summarizes three different models of assimilation that have been used to explain the immigrant experience in America. Gordon suggests that the first two models, Anglo-conformity and the melting pot (and even the variant "triple melting pot"[12]), have become less relevant and increasingly inadequate, and the third model, cultural pluralism, may be more appropriate in describing the contemporary American scene. At the end of the article, Gordon also discusses briefly his distinction between cultural (behavioral) assimilation and structural assimilation. His main suggestion here is that different immigrant groups may readily adopt the habits and tastes of the "American" culture, but the groups may still retain strong ethnic and racial identities by a high degree of residential segregation and intramarriage.

---

[8]For example, see Irving Kristol, "The Negro today is like the immigrant yesterday," *The New York Times Magazine,* September 11, 1966.

[9]Oscar Handlin, "The goals of integration," in Talcott Parsons and Kenneth B. Clark (eds.), *The Negro American* (Cambridge, Mass.: Houghton Mifflin Co., 1966), p. 663.

[10]For other reasons against the analogy, see the *Report of the Advisory Commission on Civil Disorders* (New York: Bantam Books, Inc., 1968), Chap. 9.

[11]Nathan Glazer, "Blacks and ethnic groups: The difference, and the political difference it makes," *Social Problems,* Spring 1971, 18:444–61.

[12]The "triple melting pot" hypothesis claims that there are three melting pots, defined by the major religions (Catholic, Jewish, and Protestant), within which a high degree of assimilation (intermarriage) occurs, rather than a single melting pot in which assimilation occurs among all ethnic groups. The hypothesis has been popularly discussed and given much credence, although it is highly suspect on statistical grounds. Simply stated, higher rates of intermarriage would normally be expected among larger groups (e.g., the three religions) than among smaller groups (e.g., various ethnic groups) for purely numerical reasons. See Paul H. Besancency, "On reporting rates of intermarriage," *American Journal of Sociology,* May 1965, 70:717–21.

1. The present and probable future condition of the three races

ALEXIS DE TOCQUEVILLE

The principal task that I had imposed upon myself is now performed: I have shown, as far as I was able, the laws and the customs of the American democracy. Here I might stop; but the reader would perhaps feel that I had not satisfied his expectations.

An absolute and immense democracy is not all that we find in America; the inhabitants of the New World may be considered from more than one point of view. In the course of this work my subject often led me to speak of the Indians and the Negroes, but I have never had time to stop in order to show what place these two races occupy in the midst of the democratic people whom I was engaged in describing. I have shown in what spirit and according to what laws the Anglo-American Union was formed; but I could give only a hurried and imperfect glance at the dangers which menace that confederation and could not furnish a detailed account of its chances of survival independently of its laws and manners. When speaking of the united republics, I hazarded no conjectures upon the permanence of republican forms in the New World; and when making frequent allusions to the commercial activity that reigns in the Union, I was unable to inquire into the future of the Americans as a commercial people.

These topics are collaterally connected with my subject without forming a part of it; they are American without being democratic, and to portray democracy has been my principal aim. It was therefore necessary to postpone these questions, which I now take up as the proper termination of my work.

. . . . .

The territory now occupied or claimed by the American Union spreads from the shores of the Atlantic to those of the Pacific Ocean. On the east and west its limits are those of the continent itself. On the south it advances nearly to the tropics, and it extends upward to the icy regions of the north.

The human beings who are scattered over this space do not form, as in Europe, so many branches of the same stock. Three races, naturally distinct, and, I might almost say, hostile to each other, are discoverable among them at the first glance. Almost insurmountable barriers had been raised between them by education and law, as well as by their ori-

Reprinted from Alexis de Tocqueville, *Democracy in America* (New York: Alfred A. Knopf, 1945), Volume 1, pp. 343–347. Copyright © 1945 by Alfred A. Knopf, Inc. Originally published in 1835 and 1840.

gin and outward characteristics; but fortune has brought them together on the same soil, where, although they are mixed, they do not amalgamate, and each race fulfills its destiny apart.

Among these widely differing families of men, the first that attracts attention, the superior in intelligence, in power, and in enjoyment, is the white, or European, the MAN preeminently so called; below him appear the Negro and the Indian. These two unhappy races have nothing in common, neither birth, nor features, nor language, nor habits. Their only resemblance lies in their misfortunes. Both of them occupy an equally inferior position in the country they inhabit; both suffer from tyranny; and if their wrongs are not the same, they originate from the same authors.

If we reason from what passes in the world, we should almost say that the European is to the other races of mankind what man himself is to the lower animals: he makes them subservient to his use, and when he cannot subdue he destroys them. Oppression has, at one stroke, deprived the descendants of the Africans of almost all the privileges of humanity. The Negro of the United States has lost even the remembrance of his country; the language which his forefathers spoke is never heard around him; he abjured their religion and forgot their customs when he ceased to belong to Africa, without acquiring any claim to European privileges. But he remains half-way between the two communities, isolated between two races; sold by the one, repulsed by the other; finding not a spot in the universe to call by the name of country, except the faint image of a home which the shelter of his master's roof affords.

The Negro has no family: woman is merely the temporary companion of his pleasures, and his children are on an equality with himself from the moment of their birth. Am I to call it a proof of God's mercy, or a visitation of his wrath, that man, in certain states, appears to be insensible to his extreme wretchedness and almost obtains a depraved taste for the cause of his misfortunes? The Negro, plunged in this abyss of evils, scarcely feels his own calamitous situation. Violence made him a slave, and the habit of servitude gives him the thoughts and desires of a slave; he admires his tyrants more than he hates them, and finds his joy and his pride in the servile imitation of those who oppress him. His understanding is degraded to the level of his soul.

The Negro enters upon slavery as soon as he is born; nay, he may have been purchased in the womb, and have begun his slavery before he began his existence. Equally devoid of wants and of enjoyment, and useless to himself, he learns, with his first notions of existence, that he is the property of another, who has an interest in preserving his life, and that the care of it does not devolve upon himself; even the power of thought appears to him a useless gift of Providence, and he quietly enjoys all the privileges of his debasement.

If he becomes free, independence is often felt by him to be a heavier burden than slavery; for, having learned in the course of his life to submit to everything except reason, he is too unacquainted with her dictates to obey them. A thousand new desires beset him, and he has not the knowledge and energy necessary to resist them: these are masters which it is necessary to contend with, and he has learned only to submit and obey. In short, he is sunk to such a depth of wretchedness that while servitude brutalizes, liberty destroys him.

Oppression has been no less fatal to the Indian than to the Negro race, but its effects are different. Before the arrival of white men in the New World, the inhabitants of North America lived quietly in their woods, enduring the vicissitudes and practicing the virtues and vices common to savage nations. The Europeans, having dispersed the Indian tribes and driven them into the deserts, condemned them to a wandering life, full of inexpressible sufferings.

Savage nations are only controlled by opinion and custom. When the North American Indians had lost the sentiment of attachment to their country; when their families were dispersed, their traditions obscured, and the chain of their recollections broken; when all their habits were changed, and their wants increased beyond measure, European tyranny rendered them more disorderly and less civilized than they were before. The moral and physical condition of these tribes continually grew worse, and they became more barbarous as they became more wretched. Nevertheless, the Europeans have not been able to change the character of the Indians; and though they have had power to destroy, they have never been able to subdue and civilize them.

The lot of the Negro is placed on the extreme limit of servitude, while that of the Indian lies on the uttermost verge of liberty; and slavery does not produce more fatal effects upon the first than independence upon the second. The Negro has lost all property in his own person, and he cannot dispose of his existence without committing a sort of fraud. But the savage is his own master as soon as he is able to act; parental authority is scarcely known to him; he has never bent his will to that of any of his kind, nor learned the difference between voluntary obedience and a shameful subjection; and the very name of law is unknown to him. To be free, with him, signifies to escape from all the shackles of society. As he delights in this barbarous independence and would rather perish than sacrifice the least part of it, civilization has little hold over him.

The Negro makes a thousand fruitless efforts to insinuate himself among men who repulse him; he conforms to the tastes of his oppressors, adopts their opinions, and hopes by imitating them to form a part of their community. Having been told from infancy that his race is naturally inferior to that of the whites, he assents to the proposition and is ashamed of his own nature. In each of his features he discovers a trace of slavery, and if it were in his power, he would willingly rid himself of everything that makes him what he is.

The Indian, on the contrary, has his imagination inflated with the pretended nobility of his origin, and lives and dies in the midst of these dreams of pride. Far from desiring to conform his habits to ours, he loves his savage life as the distinguishing mark of his race and repels every advance to civilization, less, perhaps, from hatred of it than from a dread of resembling the Europeans. While he has nothing to oppose to our perfection in the arts but the resources of the wilderness, to our tactics nothing but undisciplined courage, while our well-digested plans are met only by the spontaneous instincts of savage life, who can wonder if he fails in this unequal contest?

The Negro, who earnestly desires to mingle his race with that of the European, cannot do so; while the Indian, who might succeed to a certain extent, disdains to make the attempt. The servility of the one dooms him to slavery, the pride of the other to death.

. . . . .

2. The dynamics of unopposed capitalism

STANLEY M. ELKINS

How had Negro slavery in the United States come into being? There was nothing "natural" about it; it had no necessary connection with either tropical climate or tropical crops: in Virginia and Maryland, where the institution first appeared and flourished, the climate was hardly tropical, and the staple crop—tobacco—might have been grown as far north as Canada. It had nothing to do with characteristics which might have made the Negro peculiarly suited either to slavery or to the labor of tobacco culture. Slavery in past ages had been limited to no particular race, and the earliest planters of colonial Virginia appear to have preferred a laboring force of white servants from England, Scotland, and Ireland, rather than of blacks from Africa. Nor was it a matter of common-law precedent, for the British colonists who settled the areas

Abridged and edited from Stanley M. Elkins, *Slavery: A Problem in American Institutional and Intellectual Life* (Chicago: University of Chicago Press, 1959), pp. 37–52. Copyright © 1959 by The University of Chicago Press. Reprinted by permission. Footnotes enlarging upon the author's text have been omitted.

The author is Professor of History, Smith College, Northampton, Mass.

eventually to be included in the United States brought with them no legal categories comparable to that of "slave," as the term would be understood by the end of the seventeenth century. "Slavery," considered in the abstract as servile bondage, had existed elsewhere for centuries; indeed, the natives of Africa had known it intimately. Yet nothing was inherent, even in the fact of *Negro* slavery, which should compel it to take the form that it took in North America. Negro slavery flourished in Latin America at that same period, but there the system was strikingly different. In certain altogether crucial respects slavery as we know it was not imported from elsewhere but was created in America—fashioned on the spot by Englishmen in whose traditions such an institution had no part. American slavery was unique, in the sense that, for symmetry and precision of outline, nothing like it had ever previously been seen.

An important essay by Oscar and Mary Handlin has focused new attention upon these facts.[1] Although the first shipload of twenty Negroes had arrived in Virginia in 1619, it was not until the 1660's that the key item in the definition of their status—term of servitude—was clearly fixed in law. It was apparently possible for the earliest Negroes to fall into the various servant categories long familiar to the common law of England, none of which in a practical sense included perpetual and inherited chattel bondage. The bulk of agricultural laborers coming into the colonies at this period were white servants whose terms, as time went on, were to become more and more definitely fixed by indenture, and the Negroes, so far as the law was concerned, could be regarded as "servants" like the rest; there was no articulated legal structure in the colonies to impede their becoming free after a term of service and entering society as artisans and holders of property. Indeed, it was still assumed that the profession of Christianity should itself make a difference in status. Manumission, moreover, for whatever reason, was a practice common enough to be taken for granted and was attended by no special legal restrictions.

Yet all this began changing drastically with the 1660's. The very need for new colonists to people the country, and the very preference of planters for English-speaking whites rather than African savages as laborers, had already set into motion a trend to define in law the rights of white servants. To encourage the immigration of such servants and to counteract homeward-drifting rumors of indefinite servitude under desperate conditions, it was becoming more and more the practice to fix definite and limited terms of indenture—five or six years—as a guaranty that a clear future awaited the white man who would cast his lot with the colonies. The Negro, as the Handlins put it, "never profited from these

---

[1]See Oscar and Mary F. Handlin, "Origins of the Southern Labor System," *William and Mary Quarterly,* 3d Series, VII (April 1950), 199–222.

enactments. Farthest removed from the English, least desired, he communicated with no friends who might be deterred from following. Since his coming was involuntary, nothing that happened to him would increase or decrease his numbers." In short, every improvement in the status of the white servant, in widening the gulf between his condition and that of the Negro, served to dramatize the deepening significance of color and in effect to depress the black ever closer to a state of perpetual slavery. This tendency was ultimately recognized by the legislatures of Maryland and Virginia, and they were led to embody in law what had already become fact. "All negroes or other slaves within the province [according to a Maryland law of 1663], and all negroes and other slaves to be hereafter imported into the province, shall serve *durante vita*; and all children born of any negro or other slave, shall be slaves as their fathers were for the term of their lives."[2] Such was the first legal step whereby a black skin would itself ultimately be equatable with "slave."

Now there is not much doubt that in actual practice the Negro in Virginia and Maryland had become a slave long before this time. There were precedents in English colonial practice—if not quite in law—that might have been drawn from Barbados any time after the 1630's. In all likelihood the delay in defining Negro status may be ascribed to the fact that their numbers prior to the 1660's were never very great and hardly warranted special legislation. But there is much significance simply in the fact that a state of legal indeterminacy existed for some forty years. During that period there are just enough examples of Negro suits for freedom, Negro ownership of property (with the legal incidents thereof), and so on, to convince one that even so small a margin between automatic lifetime slavery and something else made all the difference—considering what plantation slavery, both in law and in fact, would be a generation later. It meant a precious margin of space, not to be discounted, for the conservation of traditional human rights. However, once the initial step had been taken, and once Negroes began arriving in appreciable numbers—as they did in the years following the Restoration—there was, as it turned out, little to impede the restless inclination of the law to remove ambiguities. A further course of legislation in the colonies—to which by then had been added the Carolinas—was inaugurated in the period roughly centering upon the turn of the seventeenth

---

[2]Quoted in John Codman Hurd, *The Law of Freedom and Bondage in the United States* (Boston: Little, Brown & Co., 1858), I, 249. A Virginia act of the year before had assumed and implied lifetime slavery. It provided special punishments for servants who ran away in the company of "negroes who are incapable of making satisfaction by addition of a time." Helen T. Catterall, *Judicial Cases concerning American Slavery and the Negro* (Washington, D.C.: Carnegie Institution, 1926 ff.), I, 59. The matter was made explicit when in 1670 it was enacted that "all servants not being Christians, imported into this colony by shipping, shall be slaves for their lives. . . ." Hurd, *Law of Freedom and Bondage*, I, 233.

century; this legislation began suppressing, with a certain methodical insistence, whatever rights of personality still remained to the Negro slave. It was thus that most of the features marking the system of American slavery, as the nineteenth century knew it, had been stamped upon it by about the middle of the eighteenth.

Yet before reviewing in greater detail the legal aspects of this servitude, we should note that the most vital facts about its inception remain quite unaccounted for. The reasons for its delay have been satisfactorily explained—but why did it occur at all? Why should the drive to establish such a status have got under way when it did? What was the force behind it, especially in view of the prior absence of any sort of laws defining slavery? We may on the one hand point out the lack of any legal structure automatically compelling the Negro to become a slave, but it is only fair, on the other, to note that there was equally little in the form of such a structure to prevent him from becoming one. It is not enough to indicate the simple process whereby the interests of white servants and black were systematically driven apart: what was its dynamic? Why should the status of "slave" have been elaborated, in little more than two generations following its initial definition, with such utter logic and completeness to make American slavery unique among all such systems known to civilization?

Was it the "motive of gain"? Yes, but with a difference. The motive of gain, as a psychic "fact," can tell us little about what makes men behave as they do; the medieval peasant himself, with his virtually marketless economy, was hardly free from it. But in the emergent agricultural capitalism of colonial Virginia we may already make out a mode of economic organization which was taking on a purity of form never yet seen, and the difference lay in the fact that here a growing system of large-scale staple production for profit was free to develop in a society where no prior traditional institutions, with competing claims of their own, might interpose at any of a dozen points with sufficient power to retard or modify its progress. What happens when such energy meets no limits?

Here, even in its embryonic stages, it is possible to see the process whereby capitalism would emerge as the principal dynamic force in American society. The New World had been discovered and exploited by a European civilization which had always, in contrast with other world cultures, placed a particularly high premium on personal achievement, and it was to be the special genius of Englishmen, from Elizabeth's time onward, to transform this career concept from its earlier chivalric form into one of economic fulfilment—from "glory" to "success." Virginia was settled during the very key period in which the English middle class forcibly reduced, by revolution, the power of those standing institutions—the church and the crown—which most directly symbolized society's traditional limitations upon personal success and mobility. What the return of the crown betokened in 1660 was not so much "reaction" as the fact that all society had by then somehow made terms with the Puritan Revolution. Virginia had proven a uniquely appropriate theater for the acting-out of this narrower, essentially modern ideal of personal, of *economic,* success. Land in the early days was cheap and plentiful; a ready market for tobacco existed; even the yeoman farmer could rise rapidly if he could make the transition to staple production; and above all there was a quick recognition of accomplishment, by a standard which was not available in England but which was the only one available in Virginia: success in creating a plantation.

The decade of the 1660's, inaugurated by the restoration of the Stuart monarchy, marked something of a turning point in the fortunes of the colony not unrelated to the movement there and in Maryland to fix irrevocably upon the Negro a lifetime of slavery. It was during this decade that certain factors bearing upon the colony's economic future were precipitated. One such factor was a serious drop in tobacco prices, brought on not only by overproduction but also by the Navigation Acts of 1660 and 1661, and the market was not to be fully restored for another twenty years. This meant, with rising costs and a disappearing margin of profit, that commercial production on a small-scale basis was placed under serious disabilities. Another factor was the rise in the slave population. Whereas there had been only about 300 in 1650, by 1670 there were, according to Governor Berkeley, 2,000 slaves in a servant population of 8,000. This was already 25 per cent of the servants, and the figure was even more significant for the future, since the total white servant population in any given period could never be counted on to exceed their average annual immigration multiplied by five or six (the usual term in years, of their indenture), while the increase of slaves over the same period would be cumulative. Such a development would by now be quite enough to stimulate the leaders of the colony—virtually all planters—to clarify in law once and for all the status of life-time Negro servitude. The formation in 1662 of a Royal Company of Adventurers for the importation of Negroes symbolized the crown's expectation that a labor force of slaves would be the coming thing in the colonies.

It was thus in a period of relatively hard times that it became clear, if the colony of Virginia were to prosper, that capitalism would be the dynamic force in its economic life. "Success" could no longer be visualized as a rise from small beginnings, as it once could, but must now be conceived as a matter of substantial initial investments in land, equipment, and labor, plus the ability to undertake large annual commitments on credit. With the fall in tobacco prices, and with the tiny margin of profit that remained, the yeoman farmer found it difficult enough to eke out a bare living, let alone think of competing with the large planter or of purchasing slaves' or servants' indentures. Success was still possible, but now its terms were clearer, and those who achieved it would be fewer in numbers. The man who managed it would be the man with the large holdings—the man who could command a substantial force of laborers, white or black—who could afford a sizable yearly investment in the handling of his crop: in short, the capitalist planter.

. . . . .

What meaning might all this have had for the legal status of the Negro? The connection was intimate and direct; with the full development of the plantation there was nothing, so far as his interests were concerned, to prevent unmitigated capitalism from becoming unmitigated slavery. The planter was now engaged in capitalistic agriculture with a labor force entirely under his control. The personal relationship between master and slave—in any case less likely to exist on large agricultural units than on smaller ones—now became far less important than the economic necessities which had forced the slave into this "unnatural" organization in the first place. For the plantation to operate efficiently and profitably, and with a force of laborers not all of whom may have been fully broken to plantation discipline, the necessity of training them to work long hours and to give unquestioning obedience to their masters and overseers superseded every other consideration. The master must have absolute power over the slave's body, and the law was developing in such a way as to give it to him at every crucial point. Physical discipline was made virtually unlimited and the slave's chattel status unalterably fixed. It was in such a setting that those rights of personality traditionally regarded between men as private and inherent, quite apart from the matter of lifetime servitude, were left virtually without defense. The integrity of the family was ignored, and slave marriage was deprived of any legal or moral standing. The condition of a bondsman's soul—a matter of much concern to church and civil authority in the Spanish colonies—was here very quickly dropped from consideration. A series of laws enacted between 1667 and 1671 had systematically removed any lingering doubts whether conversion to Christianity should make a difference in status: henceforth it made none. The balance, therefore, involved on the one side the constant pressure of costs, prices, and the problems of management, and on the other the personal interests of the slave. Here, there were no counterweights: those interests were unsupported by any social pressures from the outside; they were cherished by no customary feudal immunities; they were no concern of the government (the king's main interest was in tobacco revenue); they could not be sustained by the church, for the church had little enough power and influence among its own white constituencies, to say nothing of the suspicion its ministers aroused at every proposal to enlarge the church's work among the blacks. The local planter class controlled all those public concerns which most affected the daily life of the colony, and it was thus only in matters of the broadest and most general policy that this planter domination was in any way touched by bureaucratic decisions made in London. The emergent institution of slavery was in effect unchallenged by any other institutions.

The result was that the slave, utterly powerless, would at every critical point see his interests further depressed. At those very points the drive of the law—unembarrassed by the perplexities of competing interests—was to clarify beyond all question, to rationalize, to simplify, and to make more logical and symmetrical the slave's status in society. So little impeded was this pressure to define and clarify that all the major categories in law which bore upon such status were very early established with great thoroughness and completeness. . . .

3. Immigration policy

JOHN F. KENNEDY

From the start, immigration policy has been a prominent subject of discussion in America. This is as it must be in a democracy, where every issue should be freely considered and debated.

Immigration, or rather the British policy of clamping down on immigration, was one of the factors behind the colonial desire for independence. Restrictive immigration policies constituted one of the charges against King George III expressed in the Declaration of Independence. And in the Constitutional Convention James Madison noted, "That part of America which has encouraged them [the immigrants] has advanced most rapidly in population, agriculture and the arts." So, too, Washington in his Thanksgiving Day Proclamation of 1795 asked all Americans "humbly and fervently to beseech the kind Author of these blessings . . . to render this country more and more a safe and propitious asylum for the unfortunate of other countries."

Yet there was the basic ambiguity which older Americans have often shown toward newcomers. In 1797 a member of Congress argued that, while a liberal immigration policy was fine when the country was new and unsettled, now that America had reached its maturity and was fully populated, immigration should stop—an argument which has been repeated at regular intervals throughout American history.

Abridgement of "Immigration policy" from *A Nation of Immigrants* (New York: Harper & Row, 1964), revised and enlarged edition, by John F. Kennedy. Copyright © 1964 by Anti-Defamation League of B'nai B'rith. Reprinted by permission.

The fear of embroilment in the wars between Britain and France helped the cause of the restrictionists. In 1798 a Federalist Congress passed the Alien Act, authorizing the expulsion of foreigners "dangerous to the peace and safety of the United States" and extending the residence requirement for naturalization from five to fourteen years. But the Alien Act, and its accompanying Sedition Act, went too far. Both acts were allowed to expire in 1801; the naturalization period went back to five years; and President Thomas Jefferson expressed the predominant American sentiment when he asked: "Shall we refuse to the unhappy fugitives from distress that hospitality which the savages of the wilderness extended to our fathers arriving in this land? Shall oppressed humanity find no asylum on this globe?"

But emotions of xenophobia—hatred of foreigners—and of nativism —the policy of keeping America "pure" (that is, of preferring old immigrants to new)—continued to thrive. The increase in the rate of immigration in the 1820's and 1830's set off new waves of hostility, directed especially against the Irish, who, as Catholics, were regarded as members of an alien conspiracy. Even Ralph Waldo Emerson could write to Thomas Carlyle about "the wild Irish element . . . led by Romanish Priests, who sympathize, of course, with despotism." Samuel F. B. Morse, the painter and inventor of the telegraph, wrote an anti-Catholic book entitled *A Foreign Conspiracy Against the Liberties of the United States*. Some alarmed Americans believed that every Catholic was a foreign agent dispatched by the Pope to subvert American society. In 1834 a mob burned down the Ursuline Convent school in Charlestown, Massachusetts. Though the leading citizens of Boston promptly denounced this act, anti-Catholic feeling persisted.

In the 1850's nativism became an open political movement. A secret patriotic society, the Order of the Star-Spangled Banner, founded about 1850, grew into the American party, whose members were pledged to vote only for native Americans, to demand a twenty-one-year naturalization period and to fight Roman Catholicism. When asked about their program, they were instructed to answer, "I know nothing about it," so people called them the Know-Nothings. Coming into existence at a time when the slavery issue was dissolving the older party allegiances, the Know-Nothings for a moment attracted considerable support. They elected six state governors and seventy-five Congressmen in 1854 and got almost 25 percent of the vote for their candidate, former President Millard Fillmore, in 1856. But soon they, too, were split by the slavery issue, and the party vanished as quickly as it had appeared.

. . . . .

. . . In 1882, recognizing the need for a national immigration policy, Congress enacted the first general legislation on the subject. The most important aspect of this law was that, for the first time, the government undertook to exclude certain classes of undesirables, such as lunatics, convicts, idiots and persons likely to become public charges. In 1891 certain health standards were added as well as a provision excluding polygamists.

From time to time additional laws were added. The only deviation from the basic policy of free, nondiscriminatory immigration was the Oriental Exclusion Act.

Under a special treaty arrangement with China, nationals of that country had been guaranteed free and unrestricted immigration to the United States. At the peak of that immigration, in 1882, there were only forty thousand arrivals; even in 1890 there were but 107,000 Chinese in America. Most of them lived in California and had proved good and useful workers and citizens. Although they had originally been welcomed to America for their services in building railroads and reclaiming the land, the conviction began to grow that Chinese labor was undermining the standards of "American" labor. This became virtually an obsession with many people. In the early 1870's anti-Chinese agitation in California became organized and focused under the leadership of Denis Kearney, who was, ironically, an immigrant from Ireland. A campaign of organized violence against Chinese communities took form, and the hysteria led to political pressure too violent to be resisted. President Hayes vetoed an act of Congress restricting Chinese immigration, but he did force renegotiation of the Burlingame Treaty under which the government of China agreed to restrict emigration voluntarily. Not satisfied with this remedy, Congress then enacted and the President signed into law a series of measures shutting off almost completely immigration from China.

Shameful as these episodes were, they were, however, only an exception to the prevailing policy. A more serious warning of things to come was sounded in 1897 when Congress, for the first time, provided a literacy test for adult immigrants. President Cleveland vetoed the measure. Presidents Taft and Wilson vetoed similar bills on the ground that literacy was a test only of educational opportunity and not of a person's ability or his potential worth as a citizen. In 1917, with tension high because of the war, Congress overrode President Wilson's veto and the literacy test became law.

The twenty-year fight over the literacy test can now be seen as a significant turning point in immigration policy. Indeed, many saw it as such at that time. Finley Peter Dunne, creator of the immortal Mr. Dooley, devoted one of Mr. Dooley's dissertations in 1902 to the subject of the test and immigration. With magnificent irony the Irish bartender says, "As a pilgrim father that missed the first boat, I must raise me claryon voice again' the invasion iv this fair land be th' paupers an' arnychists in Europe. Ye bet I must—because I'm here first. . . . In thim days America was th' refuge iv th' oppressed in all th' wurruld. . . . But as I tell ye, 'tis diff'rent now. 'Tis time we put our back again' th' open dure an' keep out th' savage horde."

But there is no denying the fact that by the turn of the century the opinion was becoming widespread that the numbers of new immigrants should be limited. Those who were opposed to all immigration and all "foreigners" were now joined by those who believed sincerely, and with some basis in fact, that America's capacity to absorb immigration was limited. This movement toward restricting immigration represented a social and economic reaction, not only to the tremendous increase in immigration after 1880, but also to the shift in its main sources, to Southern, Eastern and Southeastern Europe.

Anti-immigration sentiment was heightened by World War I, and the disillusionment and strong wave of isolationism that marked its aftermath. It was in this climate, in 1921, that Congress passed and the President signed the first major law in our country's history severely limiting new immigration by establishing an emergency quota system. An era in American history had ended; we were committed to a radically new policy toward the peopling of the nation.

The Act of 1921 was an early version of the so-called "national origins" system. Its provisions limited immigration of numbers of each nationality to a certain percentage of the number of foreignborn individuals of that nationality resident in the United States according to the 1910 census. Nationality meant country of birth. The total number of immigrants permitted to enter under this system each year was 357,000.

In 1924 the Act was revised, creating a temporary arrangement for the years 1924 to 1929, under which the national quotas for 1924 were equal to 2 percent of the number of foreign-born persons of a given nationality living in the United States in 1890, or about 164,000 people. The permanent system, which went into force in 1929, includes essentially all the elements of immigration policy that are in our law today.[1] The immigration statutes now establish a system of annual quotas to govern immigration from each country. Under this system 156,987 quota immigrants are permitted to enter the United States each year. The quotas from each country are based upon the national origins of the population of the United States in 1920.

The use of the year 1920 is arbitrary. It rests upon the fact that this system was introduced in 1924 and the last prior census was in 1920. The use of a national origins system is without basis in either logic or reason. It neither satisfies a national need nor accomplishes an international purpose. In an age of interdependence among nations such a

---

[1] [Editor's note: This article was written before the Immigration Act of 1965, which radically changed the national origins system. For further comments, see p. 3. See also the following article by B. Kovach, "Eased laws alter U.S. ethnic profile," pp. 19–22.]

system is an anachronism, for it discriminates among applicants for admission into the United States on the basis of accident of birth.

Because of the composition of our population in 1920, the system is heavily weighted in favor of immigration from Northern Europe and severely limits immigration from Southern and Eastern Europe and from other parts of the world.

To cite some recent examples: Great Britain has an annual quota of 65,361 immigration visas and used 28,291 of them. Germany has a quota of 25,814 and used 26,533 (of this number, about one-third are wives of servicemen who could enter on a nonquota basis). Ireland's quota is 17,756 and only 6,054 Irish availed themselves of it. On the other hand, Poland is permitted 6,488, and there is a backlog of 61,293 Poles wishing to enter the United States. Italy is permitted 5,666 and has a backlog of 132,435. Greece's quota is 308; her backlog is 96,538. Thus a Greek citizen desiring to emigrate to this country has little chance of coming here. And an American citizen with a Greek father or mother must wait at least eighteen months to bring his parents here to join him. A citizen whose married son or daughter, or brother or sister, is Italian cannot obtain a quota number for them for two years or more. Meanwhile, many thousands of quota numbers are wasted because they are not wanted or needed by nationals of the countries to which they are assigned.

In short, a qualified person born in England or Ireland who wants to emigrate to the United States can do so at any time. A person born in Italy, Hungary, Poland or the Baltic States may have to wait many years before his turn is reached. This system is based upon the assumption that there is some reason for keeping the origins of our population in exactly the same proportions as they existed in 1920. Such an idea is at complete variance with the American traditions and principles that the qualifications of an immigrant do not depend upon his country of birth, and violates the spirit expressed in the Declaration of Independence that "all men are created equal."

One writer has listed six motives behind the Act of 1924. They were: (1) postwar isolationism; (2) the doctrine of the alleged superiority of Anglo-Saxon and Teutonic "races"; (3) the fear that "pauper labor" would lower wage levels; (4) the belief that people of certain nations were less law-abiding than others; (5) the fear of foreign ideologies and subversion; (6) the fear that entrance of too many people with different customs and habits would undermine our national and social unity and order. All of these arguments can be found in Congressional debates on the subject and may be heard today in discussions over a new national policy toward immigration. Thus far, they have prevailed. The policy of 1924 was continued in all its essentials by the Immigration and Nationality Act of 1952.

There have been some minor amendments to that Act. In 1957 legislation was passed to reunite families being separated by restrictive provisions of the immigration legislation. Under it approximately eighty thousand persons have been admitted. Among them are the wives, husbands, parents or children of American citizens, or escapees and refugees from Communist persecution. In 1958 the immigration laws were amended to give the Attorney General added discretionary powers to adjust the status of people admitted as aliens. A 1959 amendment further facilitated the reunion of families, and a 1960 amendment provided for United States participation in the resettlement of certain refugee-escapees. In 1961 a special status was granted orphans coming to this country for adoption by American parents.

4. Eased laws alter U.S. ethnic profile

BILL KOVACH

. . . There is a new Fall River in the making as a result of shifting immigration patterns that are adding new features to the profile of the American population.

Lured by earlier settlements from the Old World, Portuguese immigrants are flocking to southeastern Massachusetts in numbers exceeding 4,000 a year. Since the immigration laws were liberalized in 1965, the Portuguese have overwhelmed older groups from Northern European countries and now form the predominant ethnic group of the region.

Fall River is only one among many cities in the United States undergoing a radical shift in ethnic makeup because of the liberalized immigration laws.

Los Angeles and other West Coast cities have developed entirely new communities of Filipinos; The Boston Globe carries a weekly column in Spanish for thousands of new Spanish-speaking residents; Greek and Middle Eastern restaurants are opening in a number of towns across the country.

Indeed, the Immigration Act of 1965, which allowed for the first time large-scale immigration from countries outside Northern Europe, is changing America fast.

The Census Bureau recently reported that nonwhite immigration reached significant proportions for the first time from 1960 to 1970—accounting for nearly 14 per cent of all immigrants—for a total of half a million people. Immigration accounted for about 20 per cent of the total population growth of the United States—a total of 3.9 million people—in the decade.

Fall River, which is 15 miles southeast of Providence, R.I., typifies the new immigration patterns.

A few years ago, to serve the needs of the changing population of southeastern Massachusetts, the Roman Catholic Church entered into an agreement with the family of Luciano J. Pereira, a young native of St. Michael Island in the Portuguese-owned Azores. The church, it was agreed, would educate young Luciano (public education was provided by the Government only through the third grade) if he would agree to serve the needs of the church.

An assistant at St. Michael Church here, Father Pereira administers to the growing community of Portuguese immigrants.

When Father Pereira came to perform his service to the Portuguese-American community, he was dealing with a small band of people. The Azores had served as a station of cheap labor for the New Bedford and Fall River ships. Some settled here and each generation lured others to work in cordage factories and later in the textile factories that saved the region from economic ruin in the face of steamship competition.

Twentieth-century immigration from the Azores and the Cape Verdean Islands—as well as the mainland of Portugal—was miniscule, however, under the National Origins Act of 1924, which favored Northern Europeans almost to the exclusion of the Southern and Eastern Europeans and Asians.

In 1965, the last year that the quota system begun by the 1924 law was in operation, 42 Portuguese immigrants came to Fall River. In 1970, there were 700.

The Immigration Act of 1965, which became fully operative in 1968, abolished the old National Origins quota system, which tried to keep the same ethnic balance in immigration that was reflected in the population census of 1920.

QUOTAS BY NATIONS

Quotas were allocated by nations before 1965; Britain, Germany and Ireland accounted for 70 per cent of all immigrant visas issued for Europe, Asia and Africa. Southern and Eastern Europeans, Orientals and Africans were admitted only in tightly controlled dribbles.

By 1965, a Democratic party campaign for a more equitable system bore fruit. The act passed that year put all potential immigrants on a first-come, first-served basis. Europe, Asia and Africa were granted 170,000 immigrant visas each year; Canada and Latin America were

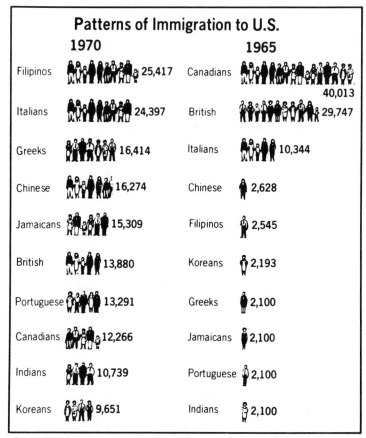

Patterns of Immigration to U.S.

1970

Filipinos	25,417
Italians	24,397
Greeks	16,414
Chinese	16,274
Jamaicans	15,309
British	13,880
Portuguese	13,291
Canadians	12,266
Indians	10,739
Koreans	9,651

1965

Canadians	40,013
British	29,747
Italians	10,344
Chinese	2,628
Filipinos	2,545
Koreans	2,193
Greeks	2,100
Jamaicans	2,100
Portuguese	2,100
Indians	2,100

allocated 120,000. No national quotas were imposed and the only limit set was a ceiling of 20,000 from any one country in a year.

At the same time, the law gave a clear priority to relatives of United States residents seeking immigration visas.

The result was like opening a flood gate for those countries whose entry had been restricted. Italians, Chinese, Filipinos and others formerly curbed streamed in.

The results are graphically shown in comparisons of the country of origin of immigrants in 1965 and 1970. The Philippines and Italy replaced Canada and Britain by 1970 in the top three countries sending new citizens to America.

Ireland, France, the Netherlands, Russia, Sweden, and Norway dropped out of the list of the top 25 nations by 1970 to be replaced by countries such as Jamaica, Portugal, and India.

Indian and Portuguese communities are springing up in cities that once had Irish and German colonies; Yugoslavs are filling restaurant jobs once dominated by Frenchmen; Spanish is the first language with more and more residents of New York, Boston and Chicago.

PROBLEMS, TOO

The sudden shift in the character and size of immigration to the United States has created a number of problems, including the following:

> • Chinatown in San Francisco is bursting at the seams because of immigration that reached a peak of 10,000 in 1969. The new immigrants do not fit into the traditional life style set by the long-time residents.
> • Chicago's schools are filling with Spanish-speaking and Chinese-speaking youngsters attempting to cope with little in the way of special programs in language training.
> • Hawaii is receiving unskilled Filipinos and Orientals who compete with local labor and force wage rates down.

Such problems are magnified in places like Fall River, a city of 50,000 population.

Clustering around churches like St. Michael and St. George, named for the home islands and serving communities from those islands, the Portuguese have spread across Fall River, dominating the north and east arms of the city.

Names like Silva, Cabral and Escobar predominate. Restaurants feature povo (octopus), couves (kale soup) and de bulho (a mixture of tripe and liver).

Inside neat frame houses that reflect the pride in ownership that drove most of the immigrants to invest their first American money in homes, scenes of rediscovery are common. Scenes like the one at 139 Merchant Street, where 72-year-old José M. Silva, tears streaming from his eyes, was reunited with his sisters for the first time in 50 years.

A scene so frequent as to be characteristic of Fall River these days is that of a middle-aged or elderly Portuguese couple, carefully dressed in a dark suit or dress, being led through stores and offices by a young, dark-haired 12-year-old. The youngster, testing his still-imperfect English, is necessary as an interpreter for the newly arrived relatives.

In supermarkets and employment offices, the young one transmits information back and forth as his elders begin to cope with the job of becoming Americanized.

John R. Correiro, who in 1967 organized the English as a Second Language Center here to help immigrant children move more smoothly into the school system, has studied the problem in detail.

"Primarily," he said, "it is a problem of rapid adjustment with little or no help. Most come directly from farms, many never wore shoes. Can you imagine the shock? One day you leave a peasant culture by airplane and the next day you're in the middle of a complex, dizzy city."

. . . . .

5. Is there an American stock?

MAX LERNER

Every traveler in the tropics comes away with an unforgettable sense of the pervasive jungle enclosing him. America's jungle is its ethnic environment of a myriad of peoples. In such a tropical luxuriance every ethnic type is present, everything grows fast and intertwines with everything else, anything is ethnically possible.

The best vantage points for observing the variety of American ethnic strains are on a subway in New York or a San Francisco street or at an Army induction center. Each is a broad channel through which the human material of America streams. Every people in Europe, most of the varied stocks of European and Asian Russia; peoples from Israel and the Arabs of the Middle East; peoples from China and Southeast Asia, from the Philippines, Hawaii, Australia, from the farthest reaches of India, from Liberia and Nigeria, from the Gold Coast and the Ivory Coast, from Kaffirland and the Witwatersrand, from every country in South and Central America, from every Caribbean island, from British and French Canada, from Greenland and Iceland—there is scarcely a stock on the ethnic map of the world that is not represented in America.

Let me make my use of terms clear. I use "stock" rather than "race," and "ethnic" rather than "racial," because in both cases I mean something in which race is only one ingredient. I have in mind a compound of influences from race, nationality, language, religion, region or subregion —any recognizable strain which not only by its common descent but by its length of living on the same soil, under the same sky, and in the same community has formed a relatively stable biopsychological and cultural type.

Is any one of these ethnic stocks more "American" than the others? To say of someone that "he is of American stock" has come to mean that he is white, probably Protestant and of Anglo-Saxon descent, and that his forebears emigrated to America some generations back. But there is little of solace here for the distinction-hunters. In most civilizations the conquering stock has tried to set itself off on the one hand from the conquered natives, on the other from the newcomers who may want to get in on the power and the glory. In America this has been difficult on several scores: the natives were too few and were so ruthlessly stripped of land, home, and livelihood that the deed trailed little glory behind it. If "American stock" is to mean descent from those who were most im-

Abridged from Max Lerner, *America as a Civilization* (New York: Simon & Schuster, Inc., 1957), Volume I, pp. 77–81. Copyright © 1957 by Max Lerner. Reprinted by permission of Simon and Schuster, Inc.

mediately in on the kill, the leaders of the Great Predation, it would carry a guilt of which many would be gladly rid. The real conquest of America was not a military conquest, to deck out a boast that the strength of killers flows in one's blood: it was a conquest of forest and plain, of mountain and valley and river, of new technologies and new social forms; and in it every wave of immigrants took part. Although the largest single group came from the British Isles, there was no one stock that pre-empted the glory of settling America: even in the early decades of the Republic, there was a variety of stocks shaping the amalgam of "this new man, the American." Finally, the leveling force of the democratic idea has resulted in a crossbreeding and mingling of stocks which have made the task of the racial purist a hopeless one.

This effort to pre-empt the term "American" for a single strain out of many, and exclude from it all the others, is a familiar device in the technique of prescriptive prestige. Whatever meaning it may have in the case of a more inbred and homogeneous people, in America it is meaningless. Yet there are some who recoil from racism but regard the length of settlement as a crucial distinguishing mark. "Wouldn't European stocks which have been here longer," a friend writes me, "be more 'American' than the recent ones? Isn't a Lowell or a Roosevelt, for example, likely to be more 'American' than my Chinese laundryman's son?" By the test of time the most "American" stocks would be the American Indians, the descendants of the Pilgrims, and the descendants of the early Negro slaves—which is not exactly what was meant. The idea that European stocks are more "American" not by the fact of long settlement but by the fact of being European (West European, not Mediterranean or Slavic), is an idea easy to succumb to. Its strength derives from the fact that the English, Scottish, French Huguenot, and Dutch influences are interwoven with early American history. It is easier and more natural to think of a Lowell or Roosevelt as American than of a recent Chinese immigrant or a descendant of an early Indian or Negro family, but this is because the West Europeans have run the show in America since early times and have therefore made the rules and set the admission price. They feel more at home and have made others feel less at home.

Our thinking will be clearer if we say that there are three levels of meaning attached to "American": the links of family and stock with American history over time; the equal or unequal claims to rights and privileges under the law; the sense of commitment to American life. Only on the first level does the question of stock enter, however irrationally. On the second level there can be no discrimination between a Lowell or Roosevelt and the Chinese laundryman's son. On the third level the problem is one of individuals, not of stock: Americans belonging to the newer stocks may be as committed to the obligations and meanings of the American experience as the older ones, and many have enriched it greatly.

Yet in the world's most notable ethnic democracy there remains a hierarchy of prestige depending partly on stock—black, yellow, brown, and red at the bottom, white Protestant, West European on top, with the lines between the rest drawn partly in terms of closeness to Colonial descent, partly of geographic closeness to the British center of origin of the early settlements. A roughly chronological chart of the sequence of waves of immigration—English, Dutch, German, Scotch-Irish, French, Scandinavian, Irish, Mediterranean, Jewish, Balkan, Slavic, Mexican and Latin American, Filipino, Middle Eastern, Oriental—would correspond roughly to the descending scale of prestige in the ethnic hierarchy. The big divergences are that the Indians, who came first, are not at the top but toward the bottom of the pyramid; and the Negroes, who were brought over early, are not near the top but at the very bottom. On the prestige chart of the ethnic hierarchy, one could superimpose a residence map showing which stocks are distributed in slum areas, in tolerable living quarters, in middle-class districts, in residential areas. Over that one could draw an occupational chart of the functions to which the ethnic groups have been more or less specialized.

This is fluid, but the correspondences are roughly there. Making allowance for the constant breaking of the mold and the emergence of many Negroes as doctors, lawyers, teachers, ministers, businessmen, it remains true that in the South the Negroes have done and still do the heavy labor in the fields, and everywhere the dirty jobs in the factories and on the roads and wharves, in digging ditches and laying tracks and building tunnels, while their women are domestics. The Chinese, Filipinos, and Puerto Ricans are also still specialized to do domestic and routine jobs. The Mexicans (or "Spanish-speaking Americans") work at sweated labor in the factories of the Southwest and as migratory workers on the farms of the Southwest and California. The Poles, Czechs, Magyars, and Slovaks are in the coal mines of Pennsylvania, West Virginia, and Illinois, in the steel mills and at the open-hearth furnaces of Gary and Pittsburgh and Buffalo. The Scandinavians are farmers in the Midwest and loggers in the lumber camps. The Irish of the later immigration are policemen, saloonkeepers, and bartenders in New York and Boston, but also day laborers and building-trades workers, transport workers, longshoremen. The Italians and the Jews work in the garment trades of New York and the other Eastern centers; the Italians are also barbers and shoeshine boys and musicians, and they work the truck gardens in New Jersey and the vineyards of California, as do the Japanese; while the Jews move from the sweatshops into the small trades and the middlemen functions, and into medicine, law, dentistry, teaching, and the entertainment world.

But in the fluid life of America, the specialization does not stick. Cutting across the ethnic occupation map is the fact that it is the new arrivals of most stocks who do the menial and dirty work and drift to the peripheral occupations, while the earlier and resourceful ones break out of their cultural molds, buy farms and houses, get university training, attain skills, and move up to become members of the middle class. The epithets do often stick—"Wop," "Dago," "Sheeny," "Kike," "Nigger," "Norske," "Mick," "Spick," "Polack," "Hunkie," "Bohunk," "Chink," "Jap," "wetback," "greaser"—betraying a class and xenophobe animus as well as a racist one.

Sometimes, in overcompensation for this prevalent animus, one is tempted to ask whether we can in fact distinguish stock from stock, or whether there are not simply *individuals* in a rich and bewildering variety?

It is true that the differences between the stocks are not clear-cut, that one could find within one of them—say the Jews—wider differences of physiognomy, height, bone structure, skull structure, temperament, than between particular Jews on the one hand and particular Italians or Irish or Portuguese or Syrians on the other. It is also true that ethnic differences do not carry with them the differences of superiority or inferiority that the racists ascribe to them. Although there are no supermen in America, there are Americans who hunger for a cult of the blond Anglo-Saxon gods; although there are no sub-men in America, there are whites who cling to their color out of a panic sense of emptiness and who pant to assign Negroes or Puerto Ricans or Mexicans or Chinese to the category of inferior men. There are no Americans who belong to radically different branches of the human family, in the sense that their blood is of a different genus, or that some are closer to apes and others closer to gods, some born to work and others to lord it over them. There is not even an ethnically pure group in America (unless we speak of ethnic subpockets like the Hutterites from Russia who settled in South Dakota and have been almost completely endogamous) for at this point in history the chromosomes of any group contain also some genes from most of the others.

Yet it would be foolish to deny the reality of ethnic stocks in America and the differences between them. Those who came to America came from relatively stable ethnic groups. They brought with them obvious physical hereditary differences and habits of life that set them off from the others, and the social hostility they encountered often made them huddle together in more or less isolated ethnic communities. Many of them thus retained and even froze their sense of separateness, while others kept themselves open to every influence from other groups, including interbreeding. If we recognize that there is no stigma to membership in any one of the ethnic stocks of America the whole question of stock can be taken with realism and without passion.

The fact is that America is more than an agglomerate of individuals jumbled in hopeless confusion. America is a myriad of stocks, each with some identity maintained from the earliest to the latest migration. What gives America its biological richness is that it is a mingling of ethnic strains. What gives America its cultural richness is that it is a mingling of traditions and temperaments. Unless the stocks had brought an identity of their own, it would be meaningless to talk of their mingling. Unless those identities were changed and dissolved in the process, shaped and reshaped, caught up in the ever-flowing stream of the life of all of them together, it would be meaningless to talk of America.

. . . . .

6. The immigrant myth

WILLIAM L. TAYLOR

The black city dweller, at long last, has begun to shed his cloak of anonymity. For years, most white Americans seemed determined to treat Negroes in the cities as invisible men—people whose presence was hardly to be acknowledged, much less the circumstances in which they lived and their feelings understood. But events have conspired to deprive whites of this cheerful ignorance of their darker city neighbors. For one thing, in most cities there are simply too many of them now to be overlooked. Then, too, in almost every major city, Negroes have made known their despair and anger by sending up smoke signals that even in Los Angeles could hardly be mistaken for smog. And, while urban ghettos remain physically and psychologically isolated from white society, the reporting of television and newspapers has conveyed a picture of the conditions of life for people who are poor and black.

Thus, most white people now are aware that Negro families in the central city live in dilapidated and deteriorating housing; that their neighborhoods are infested by rats; that their children do not have an adequate diet and lack warm clothing in the winter.

Awareness of these facts of ghetto life, however, does not necessarily import an understanding of causes or agreement upon remedy. On these questions, most white people appear to have reached conclusions that

Reprinted from William L. Taylor, *Hanging Together: Equality in an Urban Nation* (New York: Simon & Schuster, Inc., 1971), pp. 48–56. Copyright © 1971 by William L. Taylor. Reprinted by permission of Simon and Schuster, Inc.

rob the problems of a sense of urgency and divest the white community of any responsibility for their creation or solution, instead shifting the entire burden to Negroes themselves.

The touchstone of this set of conclusions is the widely held belief that the situation in which black people now find themselves in the cities is closely analogous to that faced by European and Asian immigrants who came to this nation in the late nineteenth and early twentieth centuries. In this view, the Negro as a migrant to the city is simply the latest in a long line of racial and ethnic groups—Germans, Irish, Orientals, Jews, Italians—in search of opportunity. As the most recent arrival, it is natural that he should be low man on the totem pole, struggling for the least desirable jobs, living in slum housing, and falling prey to a variety of social ills. But this is viewed as a temporary situation; other immigrant groups made their way into American society by dint of hard labor, sacrifice, and perseverance. If the Negro pursues the same course, the analysis runs, there is no reason to doubt that he too will eventually receive his reward. Or, alternatively, it is argued that the reason that Negroes have not yet extricated themselves from urban poverty is that they have failed to apply themselves in the same rigorous way that earlier groups did. The fault, then, is largely theirs.

The immigrant analogy is a popular one. It has enabled many among the millions of white Americans whose parents or grandparents came to the United States in humble circumstances to say in substance, *"We made it on our own, why can't they?"* Support for the analogy is not infrequently found in popular journals[1] (one such piece that appeared in *The New York Times Magazine* a couple of years ago was illustrated by a cartoon that depicted a Negro family actually getting off the boat behind little old ladies wearing babushkas and men carrying their belongings in knapsacks). And, curiously, some black separatists who would reject out of hand the parallels drawn between the history of Negroes and of immigrant groups are nonetheless ready to invest their hopes in proposals for remedies—e.g., the establishment of small business and other self-help enterprises and the accumulation of political power through control over local party machinery—that essentially grow out of the immigrant experience.

The appeal of the immigrant analogy is not difficult to understand. There are many surface parallels, beginning with the fact that the migration of Negroes in recent years from the rural South to the cities of the North and West constitutes a mass movement of people outranked in our history only by the waves of European immigrants at the turn of the century. (Although Negroes began leaving the South in some numbers soon

---

[1]See, e.g., Irving Kristol, "The Negro today is like the immigrant yesterday," *The New York Times Magazine,* September 11, 1966, p. 50.

after the Civil War, the movement has reached a peak only in recent years; from 1940 to 1966 the net out-migration of black people from the South was about 3.7 million. From 1901 to 1921, approximately 14.5 million immigrants entered the United States.[2]) Other similarities between the situation of immigrants and Negroes include their predominantly rural peasant origins and the persecution they suffered before leaving them, their physical and psychological confinement in ghettos once they reached America's cities, and the ill-treatment both groups received at the hands of the majority society. The awareness that immigrant groups were verbally mistreated and abused, while perhaps a potentially sobering lesson about the dangers of stereotyping, may also help some whites to alleviate feelings of guilt about expressions of racist sentiment against Negroes. After all, it is argued, the Irish were once reviled as being lazy and drunk, Jews as being clannish and dirty, Italians and Poles as being ignorant, and each group overcame these prejudices. One may question, then, the seriousness of similar abuse directed against Negroes; it may be regarded as little more than the hazing of the new boy on the block that is quickly forgotten once he has proved his worth and entered the club. Recourse to the immigrant analogy is, finally, comforting; in the optimistic American tradition it promises a happy ending to a story full of strife and bitterness.

But appealing as it may be to draw parallels between the experience of immigrant groups and black people, it is submitted that the analogy is wrong and dangerous. The analogy is wrong because (1) it ignores fundamental differences between the character of the oppression suffered by Negroes and that suffered by immigrant groups, and (2) it overlooks major distinctions between the nature of American society of sixty or seventy years ago and the far more complex, technological society of the 1960s and 1970s, and the barriers that each presented to the advancement of minority groups. The analogy is dangerous because it leads to complacency and to a misreading of what must be done and how much effort is required to create genuine opportunity for black people and to establish harmonious relations between the races.

Many Irish immigrants arrived in this country as refugees from famine and exploitation. Jews from eastern Europe came to escape pogroms that were only the most recent chapter in a history of persecution that had once included bondage. Immigrants from southern Italy came here to escape the terrible privations of a semifeudal society.

Yet none of these evils could compare in their impact upon the individual to those that the system of chattel slavery imposed in America. Slavery in this country systematically destroyed the Negro family. In

---

[2] *Report of the National Advisory Commission on Civil Disorders* (Washington, D.C.: U.S. Government Printing Office, 1968), p. 117.

law, marriages between slaves had no standing. Adopted as a device to remove any impediment to transactions that would break up slave families, the doctrine also meant that marriages could be dissolved at will, that Negro fathers had neither authority nor responsibility in the raising of their children, that children had no legal protection against the forced separation of their parents.[3] Add to this the fact that women slaves could be sexually exploited because the law recognized few crimes against the Negro except those that would impair his value as his master's property and the strangulation of any real possibility of family life became complete.[4]

Nor did the peculiar institution of slavery in the United States allow much possibility for the Negro to better his condition. By law and by tradition, Negroes were not allowed to learn to read and write, on the theory that they did not have the capacity to absorb an education, that it would be useless to them and that it would only make them rebellious. Restraints against the education of Negroes were not limited to the slaveholding South. During the eighteenth and much of the nineteenth century, most of the free states of the North either excluded Negroes altogether from the public schools or allowed them to attend only vastly inferior segregated institutions.[5] Nor could Negroes in any significant numbers acquire the kinds of skills that might stand them in good stead after the abolition of slavery. They did not have the opportunity as slaves or even as freed men to acquire and practice the skills of artisans or tradesmen, a fact that made slavery in this country even more repressive than similar institutions in Latin American countries.[6]

It is difficult, of course, to measure the contemporary impact upon opportunities for black citizens of these not so ancient evils. It is possible that, as deeply destructive as many slave practices were, their effects might have been all but eradicated today were it not for the continuance of discrimination against Negroes during the century since emancipation. One suspects, for example, that the continued instability of family life among poor black people may be traced at least as much to the per-

---

[3]Arnold Sio, "Interpretation of slavery: The slave status in the Americas," in Allen Weinstein and Frank O. Gattell (eds.), *American Negro Slavery* (New York: Oxford University Press 1968), pp. 314–15. See also Stanley Elkins, "Slavery and Negro personality," in Weinstein and Gattell (eds.), *American Negro Slavery*, p. 245.

[4]Sio, *op. cit.*, pp. 321–22.

[5]Leon F. Litwack, *North of Slavery* (Chicago: University of Chicago Press, 1961), pp. 113ff.

[6]Herbert S. Klein, "The slave economies of Cuba and Virginia," in Weinstein and Gattell (eds.), *American Negro Slavery, op. cit.*, pp. 112–128. In the view of some historians, such as Elkins and Tannenbaum, slavery in the United States was in many other ways a far more repressive institution than Latin-American slavery, but this is a conclusion on which not all agree. A summary of some of the varying views appears in Sio, *op. cit.*

sistent denial of job opportunities to Negro men and to welfare policies that have made the break-up of families the price of receiving government assistance as to the lasting effects of slavery. While no neat slide-rule calculation will provide the answer to such questions, there is a danger in ascribing too much weight to historical practices, no matter how severe, as the source of current deprivation. Such an emphasis lends credence to the prevalent belief among whites that distinctive "cultural characteristics" of the Negro people provide the principal explanation for their deprived status. There is a major difference, of course, in the fact that many of those who subscribe most avidly to theories of cultural difference tend conveniently to forget the vicious practices that may have given rise to these presumed differences. But, whether or not stress upon cultural differences includes an awareness of the impact of slavery, the result may be the same—a preoccupation with changes in Negro family life and values, rather than with changes in external conditions, as the key to progress. So, for example, it appears to be widely assumed among white people that Negro parents place less value upon obtaining a good education for their children than other racial and ethnic groups, a conclusion which tends to exculpate public school systems of blame for the failure of black students. If this were so, it might be explained, without any implication of racial inferiority, as a legacy of the suppression of education during slavery. But the evidence does not support this assumed difference in values; in fact, extensive interviews conducted by the U.S. Commission on Civil Rights in the ghettos of some of our major cities have convinced this observer, at least, that black parents are as concerned as any other group about the education of their children.[7]

If, however, there is risk in relying too heavily upon the practices of slavery as an explanation for the present status of Negroes, it would be equally a mistake to discount them entirely. For, in stripping Negroes of any opportunity for family life, education, and the acquisition of skills, slavery robbed them of resources that would be of crucial importance after emancipation. Many immigrant groups arrived in this country without visible means of support. But each had intangible assets of considerable value. Jews had a long-standing attachment to scholarship that helped them to enter the professions and a reservoir of business acumen that aided in the establishment of small enterprises. The Japanese had similar ties to education and strong family bonds that helped to sustain them through periods when they, like Negroes, were made the victims of racial legislation. The great wave of Irish immigrants had been preceded by a smaller, educated group which had prospered and was in a position

---

[7] A summary of some of the testimony of Negro parents at public hearings held by the Commission in several cities appears in U.S. Commission on Civil Rights, *A Time to Listen . . . A Time to Act* (Washington, D.C.: U.S. Government Printing Office, 1967), pp. 41–49.

to aid in establishing the Catholic Church as a powerful instrument for self-help. Italian immigrants, like others, had close family bonds and some of the skills that would prove useful in building the cities. Even late arrivals, like the Puerto Ricans, came with some assets that distinguished their situation from that of Negroes. Puerto Ricans, unlike Negroes, came to the cities from a place where they were not regarded as a lower caste and, especially during the 1950s, some arrived with skills that had ensued from rapid industrialization of the island (assisted by American investments, subsidies, and tax exemptions).[8]

If slavery had been a less tyrannical institution, perhaps a colorable case could be made for the immigrant analogy. But it was not; Negroes emerged from bondage without the reserves that other groups had to sustain them through the long fight for survival in the cities.

To maintain a belief in the immigrant analogy, another crucial difference must be ignored—the contrast in character and impact between *foreign* and *domestic* oppression.

The immigrant from Europe may have been driven to America by poverty, economic exploitation, or political persecution rather than attracted by the promise of riches; he may have sustained the shock of being uprooted and of finding himself in new and alien surroundings. But he had left behind his foreign oppressor and in that simple fact there lay hope. Even after he had experienced discrimination in the new world, had been shunned and isolated, relegated to dirty jobs and slum housing, hope could not be completely extinguished. He was not, after all, a member of a small minority; most around him were poor or had recently been poor. And there was solid evidence to support a belief that if he worked hard and persevered, he too might win a place in society.

In contrast, the Negro at any stage in history could hardly maintain the belief that he had escaped from foreign oppression. Perhaps in the days immediately following the Civil War, Negroes journeying to northern cities could imagine themselves entering a new land ruled by a different breed of people. But they soon found themselves subject to laws and policies which disfranchised them and refused them access to public schools, the courts, and other public facilities. Although these laws yielded gradually to the new constitutional amendments, their repeal was not accompanied by much practical improvement in the status of black people. They still were denied the opportunity to acquire skills and a useful education and they found themselves displaced from even the menial positions they occupied by later-arriving groups of white immigrants.[9] And with the Compromise of 1877 which resulted in the withdrawal of Federal troops from the South, the North became a

---

[8]See Nathan Glazer and Daniel Moynihan, *Beyond the Melting Pot* (Cambridge, Mass.: The M.I.T. Press, 1963).

[9]Litwack, *op. cit.*, pp. 162–66.

partner in the subjugation of the southern Negro, further dispelling any concept of separate nations.[10]

The later Negroes arrived in northern cities, the more difficult the illusion of a "new world" became. By the time the greatest wave of migration came in the 1940s, most immigrant groups had achieved a measure of economic success and the Negro found himself relatively alone in his poverty and confinement. And then, the employer who refused him a job, the landlord who denied him an apartment, the policeman who abused him, and the merchant who cheated him destroyed any remaining illusion that Northerners were very different from other white Americans of his experience—plantation bosses and southern sheriffs. Given the whole history of northern segregation codes and racial policies directed toward Negroes and of restrictions upon education and economic advancement, black people could scarcely hold a different view. The white immigrant might have looked upon the ghetto as the first rough harbor from a foreign storm; for most Negroes it was simply another mark of their lowly place in American society.

In addition to the pivotal differences already cited, one additional factor should be noted—the inevitable distinction between the character and durability of *racial* as against *ethnic* types of discrimination. For European immigrants and especially for their children, one of the principal routes to success in American society was assimilation. They could drop their foreign ways, perfect American speech, if necessary change their names, and become indistinguishable from the mass of long-settled American citizens. True, it is fashionable these days to conclude that in practice this theory of the "melting pot" has failed, by noting the considerable extent to which ethnic groups have maintained separate interests.[11] In their zeal to make this point some writers have distorted the focus, turning their spotlight almost exclusively on the central city and the still substantial number of older, first-generation Americans who reside there, and away from the increasing ranks of later generations who are located in suburbia. But whatever the perspective from which the problem is viewed, the major point is that for immigrants the melting pot was and is the prevailing dogma, and the measure always has been how close we have come or how far we have fallen short of its promise.

For Negroes (and for the much smaller ranks of other racial minorities) the melting pot theory has never applied. The black person has not had the option of securing equality of treatment by becoming physically indistinguishable from the mass of American citizens. Nor has

---

[10]See U.S. Commission on Civil Rights, *Freedom to the Free* (Washington, D.C.: U.S. Government Printing Office, 1963), pp. 51 ff. The concessions were made to the South by Republicans in order to secure the election of their candidate, Rutherford B. Hayes, in the disputed Presidential election of 1876.

[11]See, for example, Glazer and Moynihan, *op. cit.*

this even been viewed as a long-range solution, because sexual taboos, no longer enshrined in law but still prevalent, inhibit interracial marriage.

Thus, for Negroes, in contrast to white immigrants, there are no bypaths to full citizenship. Their progress is always measured and limited by the extent to which prejudice and discrimination are overcome. More than a century and a half ago, Tocqueville recognized the importance of this distinction. Looking beyond what he regarded as the inevitable abolition of slavery, he wrote:

> There is a natural prejudice that prompts men to despise whoever has been their inferior long after he has become their equal; and the real inequality that is produced by fortune or by law is always succeeded by an imaginary inequality that is implanted in the manners of the people. But among the ancients this secondary consequence of slavery had a natural limit; for the freedman bore so entire a resemblance to those born free that it soon became impossible to distinguish him from them.
>
> . . . When I remember the extreme difficulty with which aristocratic bodies, of whatever nature they may be, are commingled with the mass of the people, and the exceeding care which they take to preserve for ages the ideal boundaries of their caste inviolate, I despair of seeing an aristocracy disappear which is founded upon visible and indelible signs.[12]

Tocqueville's despair may have been premature, but the salient fact is that the experience of more than one hundred years since the abolition of slavery has yet to prove him wrong. This alone should give pause to those who have embraced the immigrant analogy and all its comfortable implications.

7. Assimilation in America: Theory and reality

MILTON M. GORDON

Three ideologies or conceptual models have competed for attention on the American scene as explanations of the way in which a nation, in the beginning largely white, Anglo-Saxon, and Protestant, has absorbed over 41 million immigrants and their descendants from variegated

---

[12]Alexis de Tocqueville, *Democracy in America* (New York: Knopf, Inc., 1945), Vol. I, pp. 371–73.

Abridged and edited from Milton M. Gordon, "Assimilation in America: Theory and reality," *Daedalus,* Spring 1961, pp. 263–85. Reprinted by permission of *Daedalus,* Journal of the American Academy of Arts and Sciences, Boston, Mass. *Ethnic Groups in American Life.*

The author is Professor of Sociology, University of Massachusetts, Amherst.

sources and welded them into the contemporary American people. These ideologies are Anglo-conformity, the melting pot, and cultural pluralism. They have served at various times, and often simultaneously, as explanations of what has happened—descriptive models—and of what should happen—goal models. Not infrequently they have been used in such a fashion that it is difficult to tell which of these two usages the writer has had in mind. In fact, one of the more remarkable omissions in the history of American intellectual thought is the relative lack of close analytical attention given to the theory of immigrant adjustment in the United States by its social scientists.

. . . . .

ANGLO-CONFORMITY

"Anglo-conformity"[1] is a broad term used to cover a variety of viewpoints about assimilation and immigration; they all assume the desirability of maintaining English institutions (as modified by the American Revolution), the English language, and English-oriented cultural patterns as dominant and standard in American life. However, bound up with this assumption are related attitudes. These may range from discredited notions about race and "Nordic" and "Aryan" racial superiority, together with the nativist political programs and exclusionist immigration policies which such notions entail, through an intermediate position of favoring immigration from northern and western Europe on amorphous, unreflective grounds ("They are more like us"), to a lack of opposition to any source of immigration, as long as these immigrants and their descendants duly adopt the standard Anglo-Saxon cultural patterns. There is by no means any necessary equation between Anglo-conformity and racist attitudes.

It is quite likely that "Anglo-conformity" in its more moderate aspects, however explicit its formulation, has been the most prevalent ideology of assimilation goals in America throughout the nation's history. As far back as colonial times, Benjamin Franklin recorded concern about the clannishness of the Germans in Pennsylvania, their slowness in learning English, and the establishment of their own native-language press.[2] Others of the founding fathers had similar reservations about large-scale immigration from Europe. In the context of their times they were unable to foresee the role such immigration was to play in creating the later greatness of the nation. They were not at all men of unthinking

---

[1]The phrase is the Coles's. See Stewart G. Cole and Mildred Wiese Cole, *Minorities and the American Promise* (New York: Harper & Brothers, 1954), Chap. 6.

[2]Maurice R. Davie, *World Immigration* (New York: The Macmillan Co. 1936), p. 36, and (cited therein) "Letter of Benjamin Franklin to Peter Collinson, 9th May, 1753, on the condition and character of the Germans in Pennsylvania," in Jared Sparks, *The Works of Benjamin Franklin, with Notes and a Life of the Author* (Boston, 1828), Vol. 7, pp. 71–73.

prejudices. The disestablishment of religion and the separation of church and state (so that no religious group—whether New England Congregationalists, Virginian Anglicans, or even all Protestants combined—could call upon the federal government for special favors or support, and so that man's religious conscience should be free) were cardinal points of the new national policy they fostered. "The Government of the United States," George Washington had written to the Jewish congregation of Newport during his first term as president, "gives to bigotry no sanction, to persecution no assistance."

. . . . .

Anglo-conformity received its fullest expression in the so-called Americanization movement which gripped the nation during World War I. While "Americanization" in its various stages had more than one emphasis, it was essentially a consciously articulated movement to strip the immigrant of his native culture and attachments and make him over into an American along Anglo-Saxon lines—all this to be accomplished with great rapidity. To use an image of a later day, it was an attempt at "pressure-cooking assimilation." It had prewar antecedents, but it was during the height of the world conflict that federal agencies, state governments, municipalities, and a host of private organizations joined in the effort to persuade the immigrant to learn English, take out naturalization papers, buy war bonds, forget his former origins and culture, and give himself over to patriotic hysteria.

After the war and the "Red scare" which followed, the excesses of the Americanization movement subsided. In its place, however, came the restriction of immigration through federal law. Foiled at first by presidential vetoes, and later by the failure of the 1917 literacy test to halt the immigrant tide, the proponents of restriction finally put through in the early 1920's a series of acts culminating in the well-known national-origins formula for immigrant quotas which went into effect in 1929. Whatever the merits of a quantitative limit on the number of immigrants to be admitted to the United States, the provisions of the formula, which discriminated sharply against the countries of southern and eastern Europe, in effect institutionalized the assumptions of the rightful dominance of Anglo-Saxon patterns in the land. Reaffirmed with only slight modifications in the McCarran-Walter Act of 1952, these laws, then, stand as a legal monument to the creed of Anglo-conformity and a telling reminder that this ideological system still has numerous and powerful adherents on the American scene.

THE MELTING POT

While Anglo-conformity in various guises has probably been the most prevalent ideology of assimilation in the American historical experience, a competing viewpoint with more generous and idealistic overtones has had its adherents and exponents from the eighteenth century onward. Conditions in the virgin continent, it was clear, were modifying the institutions which the English colonists brought with them from the mother country. Arrivals from non-English homelands such as Germany, Sweden, and France were similarly exposed to this fresh environment. Was it not possible, then, to think of the evolving American society not as a slightly modified England but rather as a totally new blend, culturally and biologically, in which the stocks and folkways of Europe, figuratively speaking, were indiscriminately mixed in the political pot of the emerging nation and fused by the fires of American influence and interaction into a distinctly new type?

. . . . .

Eventually, the melting-pot hypothesis found its way into historical scholarship and interpretation. While many American historians of the late nineteenth century, some fresh from graduate study at German universities, tended to adopt the view that American institutions derived in essence from Anglo-Saxon (and ultimately Teutonic) sources, others were not so sure.[3] One of these was Frederick Jackson Turner, a young historian from Wisconsin, not long emerged from his graduate training at Johns Hopkins. Turner presented a paper to the American Historical Association, meeting in Chicago in 1893. Called "The Significance of the Frontier in American History," this paper proved to be one of the most influential essays in the history of American scholarship, and its point of view, supported by Turner's subsequent writings and his teaching, pervaded the field of American historical interpretation for at least a generation. Turner's thesis was that the dominant influence in the shaping of American institutions and American democracy was not this nation's European heritage in any of its forms, nor the forces emanating from the eastern seaboard cities, but rather the experiences created by a moving and variegated western frontier. Among the many effects attributed to the frontier environment and the challenges it presented was that it acted as a solvent for the national heritages and the separatist tendencies of the many nationality groups which had joined the trek westward, including the Germans and Scotch-Irish of the eighteenth century and the Scandinavians and Germans of the nineteenth. "The frontier," asserted Turner, "promoted the formation of a composite nationality for the American people. . . . In the crucible of the frontier the immigrants were Americanized, liberated, and fused into a mixed race, English in neither nationality nor characteristics. The process has gone on from the early days to our own." And later, in an essay on the role of the Mississippi Valley, he refers to "the tide of foreign immigration which has

---

[3]See Edward N. Saveth, *American Historians and European Immigrants, 1875–1925* (New York: Columbia University Press, 1948).

risen so steadily that it has made a composite American people whose amalgamation is destined to produce a new national stock."[4]

It remained for an English-Jewish writer with strong social convictions, moved by his observation of the role of the United States as a haven for the poor and oppressed of Europe, to give utterance to the broader view of the American melting pot in a way which attracted public attention. In 1908, Israel Zangwill's drama, *The Melting Pot,* was produced in this country and became a popular success. It is a play dominated by the dream of its protagonist, a young Russian-Jewish immigrant to America, a composer, whose goal is the completion of a vast "American" symphony which will express his deeply felt conception of his adopted country as a divinely appointed crucible in which all the ethnic divisions of mankind will divest themselves of their ancient animosities and differences and become fused into one group, signifying the brotherhood of man. In the process he falls in love with a beautiful and cultured Gentile girl. The play ends with the performance of the symphony and, after numerous vicissitudes and traditional family opposition from both sides, with the approaching marriage of David Quixano and his beloved. During the course of these developments, David, in the rhetoric of the time, delivers himself of such sentiments as these:[5]

America is God's crucible, the great Melting Pot where all the races of Europe are melting and re-forming! Here you stand, good folk, think I, when I see them at Ellis Island, here you stand in your fifty groups, with your fifty languages and histories, and your fifty blood hatreds and rivalries. But you won't be long like that, brothers, for these are the fires of God you've come to—these are the fires of God. A fig for your feuds and vendettas! Germans and Frenchmen, Irishmen and Englishmen, Jews and Russians—into the Crucible with you all! God is making the American.

Here we have a conception of a melting pot which admits of no exceptions or qualifications with regard to the ethnic stocks which will fuse in the great crucible. Englishmen, Germans, Frenchmen, Slavs, Greeks, Syrians, Jews, Gentiles, even the black and yellow races, were specifically mentioned in Zangwill's rhapsodic enumeration. And this pot patently was to boil in the great cities of America.

Thus around the turn of the century the melting-pot idea became embedded in the ideals of the age as one response to the immigrant receiving experience of the nation. Soon to be challenged by a new philosophy of group adjustment (to be discussed below) and always competing with the more pervasive adherence to Anglo-conformity, the

---

[4]Frederick Jackson Turner, *The Frontier in American History* (New York: Henry Holt, 1920), pp. 22–23, 190.

[5]Israel Zangwill, *The Melting Pot* (New York: The Macmillan Co., 1909), p. 37.

melting-pot image, however, continued to draw a portion of the attention consciously directed toward this aspect of the American scene in the first half of the twentieth century. In the mid-1940's a sociologist who had carried out an investigation of intermarriage trends in New Haven, Connecticut, described a revised conception of the melting process in that city and suggested a basic modification of the theory of that process. In New Haven, Ruby Jo Reeves Kennedy[6] reported from a study of intermarriages from 1870 to 1940 that there was a distinct tendency for the British-Americans, Germans, and Scandinavians to marry among themselves—that is, within a Protestant "pool"; for the Irish, Italians, and Poles to marry among themselves—a Catholic "pool"; and for the Jews to marry other Jews. In other words, intermarriage was taking place across lines of nationality background, but there was a strong tendency for it to stay confined within one or the other of the three major religious groups, Protestants, Catholics, and Jews. Thus, declared Mrs. Kennedy, the picture in New Haven resembled a "triple melting pot" based on religious divisions, rather than a "single melting pot." Her study indicated, she stated, that "while strict endogamy is loosening, religious endogamy is persisting and the future cleavages will be along religious lines rather than along nationality lines as in the past. If this is the case, then the traditional "single-melting-pot" idea must be abandoned, and a new conception, which we term the "triple-melting-pot" theory of American assimilation, will take its place as the true expression of what is happening to the various nationality groups in the United States."[7] The triple melting-pot thesis was later taken up by the theologian, Will Herberg, and formed an important sociological frame of reference for his analysis of religious trends in American society, *Protestant-Catholic-Jew*.[8] But the triple melting-pot hypothesis patently takes us into the realm of a society pluralistically conceived. We turn now to the rise of an ideology which attempts to justify such a conception.

CULTURAL PLURALISM

Probably all the non-English immigrants who came to American shores in any significant numbers from colonial times onward—settling either in the forbidding wilderness, the lonely prairie, or in some accessible urban slum—created ethnic enclaves and looked forward to the preservation of at least some of their native cultural patterns. Such a

---

[6]Ruby Jo Reeves Kennedy, "Single or triple melting-pot? Intermarriage trends in New Haven, 1870-1940," *American Journal of Sociology*, 1944, 49:331–39. See also her "Single or triple melting-pot? Intermarriage in New Haven, 1870-1950," *American Journal of Sociology*, 1952, 58:56–59.

[7]Kennedy, "Single or triple melting-pot? . . . 1870–1940," *op. cit.*, p. 332 (author's italics omitted).

[8]Will Herberg, *Protestant-Catholic-Jew* (Garden City, N.Y.: Doubleday Publishing Co., 1955).

development, natural as breathing, was supported by the later accretion of friends, relatives, and countrymen seeking out oases of familiarity in a strange land, by the desire of the settlers to rebuild (necessarily in miniature) a society in which they could communicate in the familiar tongue and maintain familiar institutions, and, finally, by the necessity to band together for mutual aid and mutual protection against the uncertainties of a strange and frequently hostile environment. This was as true of the "old" immigrants as of the "new." In fact, some of the liberal intellectuals who fled to America from an inhospitable political climate in Germany in the 1830's, 1840's, and 1850's looked forward to the creation of an all-German state within the union, or, even more hopefully, to the eventual formation of a separate German nation, as soon as the expected dissolution of the union under the impact of the slavery controversy should have taken place.[9] Oscar Handlin, writing of the sons of Erin in mid-nineteenth-century Boston, recent refugees from famine and economic degradation in their homeland, points out: "Unable to participate in the normal associational affairs of the community, the Irish felt obliged to erect a society within a society, to act together in their own way. In every contact therefore the group, acting apart from other sections of the community, became intensely aware of its peculiar and exclusive identity."[10] Thus cultural pluralism was a fact in American society before it became a theory—a theory with explicit relevance for the nation as a whole, and articulated and discussed in the English-speaking circles of American intellectual life.

. . . . .

... Early in 1915, there appeared in the pages of *The Nation* two articles under the title "Democracy *versus* the Melting-Pot." Their author was Horace Kallen, a Harvard-educated philosopher with a concern for the application of philosophy to societal affairs, and, as an American Jew, himself derivative of an ethnic background which was subject to the contemporary pressures for dissolution implicit in the "Americanization," or Anglo-conformity, and the melting-pot theories. In these articles Kallen vigorously rejected the usefulness of these theories as models of what was actually transpiring in American life or as ideals for the future. Rather he was impressed by the way in which the various ethnic groups in America were coincident with particular areas and regions, and with the tendency for each group to preserve its own lan-

---

[9]Nathan Glazer, "Ethnic groups in America: From national culture to ideology," in Morroe Berger, Theodore Abel, and Charles H. Page *(eds.), Freedom and Control in Modern Society* (Princeton, N.J.: D. Van Nostrand Co., Inc., 1954), p. 161; Marcus Lee Hansen, *The Immigrant in American History* (Cambridge, Mass.: Harvard University Press, 1940), pp. 129–140; John A. Hawgood, *The Tragedy of German-America* (New York, G.P. Putnam's Sons, 1940), *passim.*

[10]Oscar Handlin, *Boston's Immigrants (rev. ed.; Cambridge, Mass.: Harvard University Press, 1959), p. 176.*

guage, religion, communal institutions, and ancestral culture. All the while, he pointed out, the immigrant has been learning to speak English as the language of general communication, and has participated in the over-all economic and political life of the nation. These developments in which "the United States are in the process of becoming a federal state not merely as a union of geographical and administrative unities, but also as a cooperation of cultural diversities, as a federation or commonwealth of national cultures,"[11] the author argued, far from constituting a violation of historic American political principles, as the "Americanizers" claimed, actually represented the inevitable consequences of democratic ideals, since individuals are implicated in groups, and since democracy for the individual must by extension also mean democracy for his group.

. . . . .

Within the next decade Kallen published more essays dealing with the theme of American multiple-group life, later collected in a volume.[12] In the introductory note to this book he used for the first time the term "cultural pluralism" to refer to his position. These essays reflect both his increasingly sharp rejection of the onslaughts on the immigrant and his culture which the coming of World War I and its attendant fears, the "Red scare," the projection of themes of racial superiority, the continued exploitation of the newcomers, and the rise of the Ku Klux Klan all served to increase in intensity, and also his emphasis on cultural pluralism as the democratic antidote to these ills. He has since published other essays elaborating or annotating the theme of cultural pluralism. Thus, for at least forty-five years, most of them spent teaching at the New School for Social Research, Kallen has been acknowledged as the originator and leading philosophical exponent of the idea of cultural pluralism.

. . . . .

CONCLUSIONS

In the remaining pages I can make only a few analytical comments which I shall apply in context to the American scene, historical and current. My view of the American situation will not be documented here, but may be considered as a series of hypotheses in which I shall attempt to outline the American assimilation process.

First of all, it must be realized that "assimilation" is a blanket term which in reality covers a multitude of subprocesses. The most crucial

---

[11]Horace M. Kallen, "Democracy *versus* the melting-pot," *The Nation,* 18 and 25 February 1915; reprinted in his *Culture and Democracy in the United States* (New York: Boni and Liveright, 1924); the quotation is on p. 116.

[12]Kallen, "Democracy *versus* the melting-pot," *ibid.*

distinction is one often ignored—the distinction between what I have elsewhere called "behavioral assimilation" and "structural assimilation."[13] The first refers to the absorption of the cultural behavior patterns of the "host" society. (At the same time, there is frequently some modification of the cultural patterns of the immigrant-receiving country, as well.) There is a special term for this process of cultural modification or "behavioral assimilation"—namely, "acculturation." "Structural assimilation," on the other hand, refers to the entrance of the immigrants and their descendants into the social cliques, organizations, institutional activities, and general civic life of the receiving society. If this process takes place on a large enough scale, then a high frequency of intermarriage must result. . .

. . . . .

[M]y point is that while *behavioral assimilation* or acculturation has taken place in America to a considerable degree, *structural assimilation,* with some important exceptions has not been extensive.[14] The exceptions are of two types. The first brings us back to the "triple melting pot" thesis of Ruby Jo Reeves Kennedy and Will Herberg. The "nationality" ethnic groups have tended to merge within each of the three major religious groups. This has been particularly true of the Protestant and Jewish communities. Those descendants of the "old" immigration of the nineteenth century, who were Protestant (many of the Germans and all the Scandinavians), have in considerable part gradually merged into the white Protestant "subsociety." Jews of Sephardic, German, and Eastern-European origins have similarly tended to come together in their communal life. The process of absorbing the various Catholic nationalities, such as the Italians, Poles, and French Canadians, into an American Catholic community hitherto dominated by the Irish has begun, although I do not believe that it is by any means close to completion. Racial and quasi-racial groups such as the Negroes, Indians, Mexican-Americans, and Puerto Ricans still retain their separate sociological structures. The outcome of all this in contemporary American life is thus pluralism—but it is more than "triple" and it is more accurately described as *structural pluralism* than as cultural pluralism, although some of the latter also remains.

My second exception refers to the social structures which implicate intellectuals. There is no space to develop the issue here, but I would argue that there is a social world or subsociety of the intellectuals in America in which true structural intermixture among persons of

---

[13]Milton M. Gordon, "Social structure and goals in group relations," in Morroe Berger, Theodore Abel, and Charles H. Page (eds.), *Freedom and Control in Modern Society* (Princeton, N.J.: D. Van Nostrand Co., Inc., 1954), p. 151.

[14]See Erich Rosenthal, "Acculturation without assimilation?" *American Journal of Sociology,* 1960, 66:275–88.

various ethnic backgrounds, including the religious, has markedly taken place.

My final point deals with the reasons for these developments. If structural assimilation has been retarded in America by religious and racial lines, we must ask why. The answer lies in the attitudes of both the majority and the minority groups and in the way these attitudes have interacted. A saying of the current day is, "It takes two to tango." To apply the analogy, there is no good reason to believe that white Protestant America has ever extended a firm and cordial invitation to its minorities to dance. . . .

With regard to the immigrant, in his characteristic numbers and socioeconomic background, structural assimilation was out of the question. He did not want it, and he had a positive need for the comfort of his own communal institutions. The native American, moreover, whatever the implications of his public pronouncements, had no intention of opening up his primary group life to entrance by these hordes of alien newcomers. The situation was a functionally complementary standoff.

The second generation found a much more complex situation. Many believed they heard the siren call of welcome to the social cliques, clubs, and institutions of white Protestant America. After all, it was simply a matter of learning American ways, was it not? Had they not grown up as Americans, and were they not culturally different from their parents, the "greenhorns?" Or perhaps an especially eager one reasoned (like the Jewish protagonist of Myron Kaufmann's novel, *Remember Me To God,* aspiring to membership in the prestigious club system of Harvard undergraduate social life) "If only I can go the last few steps in Ivy League manners and behavior, they will surely recognize that I am one of them and take me in." But, alas, Brooks Brothers suit notwithstanding, the doors of the fraternity house, the city men's club, and the country club were slammed in the face of the immigrant's offspring. That invitation was not really there in the first place; or, to the extent it was, in Joshua Fishman's phrase, it was a " 'look me over but don't touch me' invitation to the American minority group child."[15] And so the rebuffed one returned to the homelier but dependable comfort of the communal institutions of his ancestral group. There he found his fellows of the same generation who had never stirred from the home fires. Some of these had been too timid to stray; others were ethnic ideologists committed to the group's survival; still others had never really believed in the authenticity of the siren call or were simply too passive to do more than go along the familiar way. All could now join in the task that was well within the

---

[15]Joshua A. Fishman, "Childhood indoctrination for minority-group membership and the quest for minority-group biculturism in America," in Oscar Handlin, (ed), *Group Life in America* (Cambridge, Mass.: Harvard University Press, forthcoming).

realm of the sociologically possible—the buildup of social institutions and organizations within the ethnic enclave, manned increasingly by members of the second generation and suitably separated by social class.

. . . . .

With the racial minorities, there was not even the pretense of an invitation. Negroes, to take the most salient example, have for the most part been determinedly barred from the cliques, social clubs, and churches of white America. Consequently, with due allowance for internal class differences, they have constructed their own network of organizations and institutions, their own "social world." There are now many vested interests served by the preservation of this separate communal life, and doubtless many Negroes are psychologically comfortable in it, even though at the same time they keenly desire that discrimination in such areas as employment, education, housing, and public accommodations be eliminated. However, the ideological attachment of Negroes to their communal separation is not conspicuous. Their sense of identification with ancestral African national cultures is virtually nonexistent, although Pan-Africanism engages the interest of some intellectuals and although "black nationalist" and "black racist" fringe groups have recently made an appearance at the other end of the communal spectrum. As for their religion, they are either Protestant or Catholic (overwhelmingly the former). Thus, there are no "logical" ideological reasons for their separate communality; dual social structures are created solely by the dynamics of prejudice and discrimination, rather than being reinforced by the ideological commitments of the minority itself.

Structural assimilation, then, has turned out to be the rock on which the ships of Anglo-conformity and the melting pot have foundered. To understand that behavioral assimilation (or acculturation) without massive structural intermingling in primary relationships has been the dominant motif in the American experience of creating and developing a nation out of diverse peoples is to comprehend the most essential sociological fact of that experience. It is against the background of "structural pluralism" that strategies of strengthening intergroup harmony, reducing ethnic discrimination and prejudice, and maintaining the rights of both those who stay within and those who venture beyond their ethnic boundaries must be thoughtfully devised.

B. IDENTITY DEFINITION AND MAINTENANCE

At first glance, both the concepts of race and ethnicity would seem to be easy to define. If nothing else, one could give several examples of ethnic groups in America: the Irish, Italians, Jews, Mexicans, and Puerto Ricans. Race would seem to be a simple matter of distinguishing among the three major races of mankind (the Mongolian, the Negro, and the Caucasian), although theorists until the early 20th century would have claimed the existence of many more racial groups, each of which "explained" individual temperament and group culture.[1] Both ethnicity and race would thus appear to have simple determinants, with ethnic groups being composed of people from other countries, and racial groups being composed of people with certain biological characteristics. Further examination, however, shows that these initial definitions are inadequate.

First of all, some ethnic groups (e.g., the Jews before 1948) need not share a country of origin. What is important is that they share a *sense* (real or imagined) of common political and cultural origins, generally linked with some country but also including some if not all of the following: a common religion, a common language, similar physical attributes among the people, and shared behaviors and customs.[2] Furthermore, what is important is that the ethnic group itself and some other group *both* consider the ethnic group to have these common characteristics. An ethnic group identity, in other words, is composed not merely of the characteristics themselves, but also of a *social relationship* between two or more groups (classically, an ingroup versus an outgroup relationship). More often than not, the social relationship involves a difference in power status, in which the ethnic group usually has a minority

---

[1]For a brief history of the idea of "race," see Thomas F. Gossett, *Race: The History of an Idea in America* (New York: Schocken Books, Inc., 1965).

[2]Max Weber, "Ethnic groups," in Talcott Parsons *et al.* (eds.), *Theories of Society* (single vol. ed.; New York: The Free Press, 1965), pp. 305–09; and Melvin M. Tumin, "Ethnic group," in J. Gould and W. L. Kolb (eds.), *A Dictionary of the Social Sciences* (New York: The Free Press, 1964), pp. 243–44.

or less powerful status. Louis Wirth (Selection 8) explores the intricate nature of this relationship, pointing out how minority groups do not have the same opportunities as the majority group. In addition, he makes the interesting observation that a minority group need not be a statistical minority, nor need it be an alien group.[3]

Similarly, the apparently straightforward biological basis for racial distinctions has also turned out to be a weak one. Ashley Montagu (Selection 9) first provides a brief history of the use of the term "race" and then claims that it has no conceptual relationship to the genetic nature of man. Montagu suggests that the aggregates of physical characteristics (e.g., skin color, hair type, hair color, and facial features) that appear to distinguish different "races" of people are not linked genetically as fixed complexes. Rather, the physical characteristics we normally associate with "race" must be treated individually as separate traits, controlled by separate genes. It is thus difficult to make any case for dividing or classifying man into different races on biological grounds. What this implies is that the concept "race," to the extent that it has any meaning, is dominantly a *social* identification. In other words, our culture defines certain people as belonging to a given "race" mainly on the basis of some social identification. And in the United States, as C. Eric Lincoln (Selection 10) points out, the characteristic of skin color has usually served as the single trait by which "race" has been identified. The student of race identification must therefore be highly wary of studies, for instance, comparing blacks and whites along socioeconomic, behavioral, or other variables. Since there is no consistent cluster of biological traits distinguishing the black group from the white group, the distinction generally boils down to a difference in skin color. Moreover, because of intermarriage, even the single trait of skin color does not usually exist as a pure trait, but includes a wide variety of hybrids.[4]

Given these definitions of ethnicity and race, another important question can be raised about American blacks: Are they merely a racial group or are they also an ethnic group? Since the definition of ethnicity, as we have seen, includes a sense of common political and cultural heritage recognized both by the ethnic group itself and by some other group, there have been several inquiries about the existence of a separate black heritage in the United States.[5] Up until the 1950s, the consensus of

---

[3]There have been many analyses of majority-minority relations. For example, see Stanley Lieberson, "A societal theory of race and ethnic relations," *American Sociological Review,* December 1961, 26:902–10; J. Milton Yinger, *A Minority Group in American Society* (New York: McGraw-Hill Book Co., 1965); and Hubert Blalock, *Toward a Theory of Minority Group Relations* (New York: John Wiley & Sons, Inc., 1967).

[4]For an example of an analysis of specific genetic traits and race, see T. Edward Reed, "Caucasian genes in American Negroes," *Science,* August 1969, 165:762–68.

[5]These inquiries and major issues are discussed in Robert Blauner, "Black culture:

opinion might have been that blacks had no separate heritage. More recently, however, following the Civil Rights movement and the urban riots, black people themselves have promoted a more separatist attitude, and the development of Afro-American studies and militant separatist groups have helped to uncover the distinctive features of the black American heritage.[6] Blacks may thus be considered an ethnic group as well as a racial group. At the same time, this does not mean (and this is the main point of those who object to the definition of blacks as an ethnic group) that the experience of black Americans has been or will necessarily be similar to those of other ethnic groups.

The next group of articles in this section deals with the maintenance of different ethnic and racial identities. There are many ways of preserving such identities, e.g., religious customs and rites, different languages, special schools, and continued travel to and identification with a foreign land.[7] The most important institution in transmitting and preserving ethnic and racial identities, however, is the family. The family environment provides the child with a specific set of cultural values and practices, and these reflect the experience and upbringing of the parents. If the parents both share the same ethnic and racial heritage, then that heritage is likely to be passed down in some form (even negatively) to the child. If the parents are of different backgrounds, as in interethnic or interracial marriages, then the original heritage of either or both parents is likely to be substantially modified.[8] Florence Kluckhohn (Selection 11) develops a theoretical framework for analyzing the value systems of families, and then suggests the major differences among value

---

Myth or reality?" in Norman E. Whitten, Jr., and John F. Szwed (eds.), *Afro-American Anthropology: Contemporary Perspectives* (New York: The Free Press, 1970), pp. 347–66.

[6]A recent investigation has countered the notion that extreme separatism (i.e., into distinct geographic subareas) is supported only by blacks. In fact, the investigation showed more support for this extreme separatism among white people. See Joe R. Feagin, "White separatists and black separatists: A comparative analysis," *Social Problems,* Fall 1971, 19:167–80.

[7]These ways emphasize the ingroup behavior that leads to identity maintenance. However, equally if not more important is the behavior of outside groups, whose discrimination or prejudice also helps to maintain racial and ethnic identities. For analyses of the outgroup behavior, see for example, Gordon W. Allport, *The Nature of Prejudice* (Garden City, N.Y.: Doubleday & Co., Inc., 1958); Robin M. Williams, Jr., *Strangers Next Door: Ethnic Relations in American Communities* (Englewood Cliffs, N.J.: Prentice-Hall, Inc., 1964); and John-Harding *et al,* "Prejudice and ethnic relations," in Gardner Lindzey and Elliot Aronson (eds.), *The Handbook of Social Psychology* (2d ed.; Reading, Mass.: Addison-Wesley Publishing Co., Inc.; 1969), Vol. 5, pp. 1–76. For a brief article on the role of verbal labels in outgroup identification, see Erdman B. Palmore, "Ethnophaulisms and ethnocentrism," *American Journal of Sociology,* January 1962, 67:442–45.

[8]For surveys of intermarriage patterns, see Albert I. Gordon, *Intermarriage: Interfaith, Interracial, Interethnic* (Boston: Beacon Press, 1964); and Joseph P. Fitzpatrick, "Intermarriage of Puerto Ricans in New York City," *American Journal of Sociology,* January 1966, 71:395–406.

systems of three groups: Italian-Americans, Irish-Americans, and middle-class Americans. Her analysis identifies several of the critical dimensions along which ethnic and racial differences are likely to exist in family life.

Families of different ethnicity and race also display different demographic and behavioral characteristics. Peter Uhlenberg (Selection 12) relates the demographic differences between Mexican-American and Japanese-American families to differences in the economic and educational achievement motives of these two groups, while Zena Smith Blau (Selection 13) presents a compassionate portrait of one of the most famous ethnic characters in American history, the Jewish mother. Blau describes the values that were cherished by the Jewish mother, and suggests the various means by which these values were transmitted to the children of the family.

The black family, of course, has received the most (if still sparse) attention among all racial and ethnic groups.[9] A great controversy regarding the effects of the broken family was created by the Moynihan report, which suggested that the instability of the black family was responsible for the poor social conditions of the urban black American.[10] Andrew Billingsley (Selection 14) attempts to counter the Moynihan argument by pointing out that social scientists have paid far too much attention to the pathological aspects of black family life, and have overlooked the vast majority of unbroken families. Furthermore, Billingsley makes the more basic point that American scholarship has generally ignored the black family, and that much more needs to be understood about the black family as an institution on its own right, rather than as a deviant from white family norms.

As a partial summary for this section, Andrew Greeley (Selection 15) reviews the definition of ethnic groups and identifies a totally new group that appears to satisfy this definition: the American intellectual community. By extending the definition of ethnicity to its limits, Greeley effectively outlines the critical dimensions of ethnicity. At the same time, his observations about the intellectual community form an excellent commentary on one aspect of contemporary American culture.

---

[9]For a recent review, see Robert Staples, "Towards a sociology of the black family: A theoretical and methodological assessment," *Journal of Marriage and the Family,* February 1971, 33:119–38.

[10]Lee Rainwater and William L. Yancey, *The Moynihan Report and the Politics of Controversy* (Cambridge, Mass.: The M.I.T. Press, 1967). For a more recent study of race and family stability, see Reynolds Farley and Albert I. Hermalin, "Family stability: A comparison of trends between blacks and whites," *American Sociological Review,* February 1971, 36:1–17.

8. The problem of minority groups

LOUIS WIRTH

. . . . .

We may define a minority as a group of people who, because of their physical or cultural characteristics, are singled out from the others in the society in which they live for differential and unequal treatment, and who therefore regard themselves as objects of collective discrimination. The existence of a minority in a society implies the existence of a corresponding dominant group enjoying higher social status and greater privileges. Minority status carries with it the exclusion from full participation in the life of the society. Though not necessarily an alien group the minority is treated and regards itself as a people apart.

To understand the nature and significance of minorities it is necessary to take account of their objective as well as their subjective position. A minority must be distinguishable from the dominant group by physical or cultural marks. In the absence of such identifying characteristics it blends into the rest of the population in the course of time. Minorities objectively occupy a disadvantageous position in society. As contrasted with the dominant group they are debarred from certain opportunities—economic, social and political. These deprivations circumscribe the individual's freedom of choice and self-development. The members of minority groups are held in lower esteem and may even be objects of contempt, hatred, ridicule, and violence. They are generally socially isolated and frequently spatially segregated. Their subordinate position becomes manifest in their unequal access to educational opportunities and in their restricted scope of occupational and professional advancement. They are not as free as other members of society to join the voluntary associations that express their interests. They suffer from more than the ordinary amount of social and economic insecurity. Even as concerns public policy they are frequently singled out for special treatment; their property rights may be restricted; they may not enjoy the equal protection of the laws; they may be deprived of the right of suffrage and may be excluded from public office.

Aside from these objective characteristics by which they are distinguished from the dominant group and in large measure as a result of them, minorities tend to develop a set of attitudes, forms of behavior, and other subjective characteristics which tend further to set them apart. One cannot long discriminate against people without generating in them a sense of isolation and of persecution and without giving them a conception of themselves as more different from others than in fact they are. Whether, as a result of this differential treatment, the minority comes to suffer from a sense of its own inferiority or develops a feeling that it is unjustly treated—which may lead to a rebellious attitude—depends in part upon the length of time that its status has existed and in part upon the total social setting in which the differential treatment operates. Where a caste system has existed over many generations and is sanctioned by religious and other sentiments, the attitude of resignation is likely to be dominant over the spirit of rebellion. But in a secular society where class rather than caste pervades the stratification of people, and where the tradition of minority status is of recent origin, minorities, driven by a sense of frustration and unjustified subordination, are likely to refuse to accept their status and their deprivation without some effort to improve their lot.

When the sentiments and attitude of such a disadvantaged group become articulate, and when the members become conscious of their deprivations and conceive of themselves as persons having rights, and when they clamor for emancipation and equality, a minority becomes a political force to be reckoned with. To the individual members of such a group the most onerous circumstance under which they have to labor is that they are treated as members of a category, irrespective of their individual merits. Hence it is important to recognize that membership in a minority is involuntary; our own behavior is irrelevant. Many of us are identified with political, social, and intellectual groups which do not enjoy the favor of the dominant group in society, but as long as we are free to join and to leave such groups at will we do not by virtue of our membership in them belong to a minority. Since the racial stock from which we are descended is something over which we have perhaps least control and since racial marks are the most visible and permanent marks with which we are afflicted, racial minorities tend to be the most enduring minorities of all.

It should be noted further that a minority is not necessarily an alien group. Indeed, in many parts of the world it is the native peoples who constitute the minority, whereas the invaders, the conquerors, or the newcomers occupy the status of dominant groups. In the United States the indigenous Indians occupy the position of a minority. In Canada the earlier French settlers are a minority in relation to the more recent English migrants. In almost all colonial countries it is the "foreigners" who are dominant and the indigenous populations who are subordinate.

Nor should it be assumed that the concept is a statistical one. Although the size of the group may have some effect upon its status and upon its relationship to the dominant group, minorities are not to be judged in terms of numbers. The people whom we regard as a minority may actually, from a numerical standpoint, be a majority. Thus, there are many parts of the South in the United States where the Negroes are the overwhelming majority of the inhabitants but, nevertheless, are an unmistakable minority in the sense that they are socially, politically, and economically subordinate.

It may even be true that a people may attain the status of a minority even though it does not become the object of disesteem, discrimination, and persecution. If it considers itself the object of such inferior treatment, an oppression psychosis may develop. If a group sets itself apart from others by a distinctive culture and perpetuates itself in this isolated condition long enough, the social distances between itself and others may grow so great as to lead to the accumulation of suspicion and non-intercourse which will make it virtually impossible for members of these groups to carry on a truly collective life. Lack of intimate knowledge of and contact with others may in the course of time generate an incapacity for mutual understanding and appreciation which allows mental stereotypes to arise which the individual cannot escape. What matters, then, about minorities is not merely their objective position but the corresponding patterns of behavior they develop and the pictures they carry around in their heads of themselves and of others. While minorities more often than not stand in a relationship of conflict with the dominant group, it is their nonparticipation in the life of the larger society, or in certain aspects thereof, that more particularly marks them as a minority people and perpetuates their status as such.

. . . . .

In Europe and in America there are today vast differences between the status of different ethnic groups from country to country and from region to region. In pre-war Poland under the Czarist regime the Poles were a distinct ethnic minority. When they gained their independence at the end of the first World War, they lost their minority status but reduced their Jewish fellow Poles to the status of a minority. As immigrants to the United States the Poles again became themselves a minority. During the brief period of Nazi domination the Sudeten Germans of Czechoslovakia reveled in their position of dominance over the Czechs among whom they had only recently been a minority. The European immigrants to the United States from such dominantly Catholic countries as Italy and Poland, for instance, find themselves reduced from a dominant to a minority group in the course of their immigration. It is not the specific characteristics, therefore, whether racial or ethnic, that mark a people as a minority but the relationship of their group to some other group in the society in which they live. The same characteristics may at one time and under one set of circumstances serve as marks of dominant status and at another time and under another set of circumstances symbolize identification with a minority.

It is much more important, therefore, to understand the nature and the genesis of the relationship between dominant group and minority group than it is to know the marks by the possession of which people are identified as members of either. Once we know that almost any distinctive characteristics, whether it be the physical marks of race, or language, religion, and culture, can serve as criteria of membership in a minority we will not be inclined to construct a typology of minorities upon the marks by which they are identified. A fruitful typology must rather be useful in delineating the kinds of relationships between minorities and dominant groups and on the kinds of behavior characteristically associated with these types of relationships.

An adequate typology of minorities must, therefore, take account of the general types of situations in which minorities find themselves and must seek to comprehend the *modus vivendi* that has grown up between the segments of those societies in which minority problems exist. There are a number of axes alongside of which the problems of minorities range themselves. Among these are: (1) the number and size of distinct minorities in the society in question; (2) the degree to which minority status involves friction with the dominant group or exclusion from participation in the common life of the society; (3) the nature of the social arrangement governing the relationship between minority and dominant group; and, (4) the goals toward which the minority and dominant groups are striving in quest of a new and more satisfactory equilibrium. A survey of historical and contemporary minority problems along these lines will probably not cover the whole range of minority problems and to that extent the typology will be partial. At the same time it should be understood that as long as the relations between minority and dominant group are fluid—and wherever they do not rest upon long-accepted and settled premises—any rigid typology will prove unsatisfactory. Conversely where the minority's relationship to the dominant group is definitely structuralized and embedded in the mores, laws, and institutions a typological approach may be highly rewarding.

The number of minorities that a country has appears to have a significant effect upon minority-dominant group relations. Where there is just one minority the attitudes of the dominant group are molded by the unique characteristics of that particular minority. This tends to bisect the country into two contending groups. This happens to be the case in Belgium where the Flemings and Walloons stand in relationship of dominant and minority group, respectively, to each other. The situation is quite different in the United States, where aside from the Negro, the Indian, and the Oriental, who constitute our leading racial minorities, we have many ethnic minorities, consisting of our European immigrant groups and their descendants and such religious minorities as Catholics, Jews, and Mormons in a predominantly Protestant country. A singular and unique minority must absorb all of the anxieties, frustrations, fears, and antipathies of the dominant group. But if dominant group attitudes are directed toward a number of minorities, some of these may escape relatively easily and often at the expense of the others. There is little doubt but that the Negro in the United States has become the principal shock absorber of the antiminority sentiment of the dominant whites. The Negro in this country has been so clearly our leading minority that in comparison with his status the ethnic minorities have occupied a relatively dominant position. Indeed the attitude of the ethnic minorities toward the Negro differs little from the attitude of the long-established white Protestant settlers. Where there are several distinct minorities in a country the dominant group can allow itself the luxury of treating some of them generously and can at the same time entrench itself and secure its own dominance by playing one minority against another.

Similarly, the extent to which a minority differs from the dominant group conditions the relations between the two. Where the groups differ widely in race and culture and are thus easily distinguishable in appearance and behavior, the lines separating them tend to persist without much overt effort. Where the dominant group is the bearer of an advanced civilization and the subordinate group is without modern technology and is characterized by a folk culture, as is the case in colonial situations, the dominant group can maintain its superior position simply by manipulating the military and administrative machinery. Where, however, the respective groups are of the same racial stock but differ only as regards language, religion, or culture, the tension between them becomes more marked, and the attempts at domination of the minority become more evident. The segregation of minority groups may be relatively complete or only partial, and their debarment from rights and privileges may be negligible or severe. Much depends upon their relative numerical strength and the extent to which they are believed to constitute a threat to the existing order.

The nature of the social relationships existing between the dominants and the minorities comes closer than either of these factors to illuminating the problems that arise. When the relationship between the two groups is that of master and slave, of rulers and ruled, of exploiters and exploited, the conflicts that arise are those characteristic of situations of super-and subordination. They become essentially power relationships involving on the part of the dominant group resort to the sanctions of custom, law, and force, whenever persuasion, prestige, and the manipulation of economic controls do not suffice. Where the minority occupies the position of a caste the sanctions of religion and custom may be quite adequate, but in secular societies the perpetuation of a group in minority status requires the manipulation of public opinion and of economic and political power, and, if these fail, the resort to violence.

Thoroughgoing differences and incompatibilities between dominant and minority groups on *all* fronts—economic, political, social, and religious—or consistent and complete separation and exclusion of the minority from participation in the life of the larger society have tended toward more stable relationships between dominant and minority groups than similarity and compatibility on merely *some* points, and the mere segmental sharing of life on a few frontiers of contact. The granting of some political and civil rights to hitherto submerged groups has inevitably led to the claim for the full rights of citizenship and of equality of opportunity in other respects. Slavery as an institution in the Western World was moribund as soon as the religions of the white man invested the Negro with a soul.

While the above criteria might give us a basis for the classification of minorities, they do not come as close to the actual minority problems that plague the modern world as we can come by analyzing the major goals toward which the ideas, the sentiments, and the actions of minority groups are directed. Viewed in this way minorities may conveniently be typed into: (1) pluralistic; (2) assimilationist; (3) secessionist; and (4) militant.

. . . . .

9. The meaninglessness of the older anthropological conception of "race"

ASHLEY MONTAGU

It is said that when the theory of evolution was first announced it was received by the wife of the canon of Worcester Cathedral with the remark, "Descended from the apes! My dear, we will hope it is not true. But if it is, let us pray that it will not become generally known."

The attempt to deprive the classical anthropologist of his belief in "race" may by some be construed as a piece of cruelty akin to that which sought to deprive the canon's wife of her belief in the doctrine of special creation. Indeed, the older anthropological conception of "race" and the belief in special creation have much in common, for "race" is, to a large extent, the special creation of the anthropologist. Most anthropologists have until recently taken it for granted that "race" corresponds to some sort of physical reality in nature. Indeed, the concept of "race" is one of the fundamental ideas with which the anthropologist has habitually worked. To question the validity of this basic concept upon which he was intellectually nurtured as if it were an axiom is something which scarcely occurred to him. One doesn't question the axioms upon which one's science and one's activity in it are based—at least, not usually. One simply takes them for granted.

But in science, as in life, it is a good practice to attach from time to time a question mark to the facts one takes most for granted, to question the fundamental postulates or facts which require no demonstration; for a fact as a postulate is largely the opinion of those who should know— and those who should know are but human, and therefore liable to err. In science such questioning is important, because without it there is a very real danger that certain erroneous or arbitrary ideas, which may originally have been used merely as a convenience, may become so fortified by technicality and so dignified by time that their original infirmities may eventually be wholly concealed.

So with the older or classical anthropological conception of "race." It was, indeed, nothing but a whited sepulcher, a conception which in the light of modern field and experimental genetics proved utterly erroneous and meaningless; "an absolutist system of metaphysical beliefs," as it has been called.[1] As such, it has been suggested that the term be dropped from the anthropological as well as from the popular vocabulary, for it is a tendentious term which has done an infinite amount of harm and no good at all.

The development of the anthropological conception of "race" may be traced from the scholastic naturalization of Aristotle's doctrine of the predicables of genus, species, difference, property, and accident. From the Middle Ages through the seventeenth century it may be followed to the early days of the Age of Enlightenment, when Linnaeus, in 1735, took over the concepts of class, genus, and species from the theologians to serve him as systematic tools.[2]. . . the term *race* was first introduced into the literature of natural history by Buffon in 1749. But Buffon did not use the term in a classificatory sense; this was left to Blumenbach.

As used by Blumenbach, the term "race" merely represented an extension of the Aristotelian conception of species; that is to say, it was a subdivision of a species. Like Buffon, Blumenbach recognized that all human beings belong to a single species, as did Linnaeus, and he considered it merely convenient to distinguish between certain geographically localized groups of man. Thus, when with Blumenbach, in the late eighteenth century, the term assumed a classificatory value, it was under-

---

[1]Myrdal, *An American Dilemma: The Negro Problem and Modern Democracy* (New York: Harper & Row, Publishers, 1944), p. 116.

[2]Linnaeus, *Systema naturae.*

stood that that value was purely arbitrary and no more than a simple convenience. It had no other meaning than that.

The Aristotelian conception of species, the theological conception of special creation, and the natural history of the Age of Enlightenment, as represented particularly by Cuvier's brilliant conception of unity of type, namely, the idea that animals can be grouped and classified upon the basis of assemblages of structural characters which, more or less, they have in common—these three conceptions fitted together extremely well and yielded the idea of the fixity of species, an idea which, in spite of every indication to the contrary in the years which followed, was gradually extended to the concept of "race."

The Darwinian contribution showed that species were not so fixed as was formerly believed and that under the action of natural selection one species might give rise to another; that all animal forms might change in this way. It is, however, important to remember that Darwin conceived of evolution as a process involving continuous materials which, without the operation of natural selection, would remain unchanged. Hence, under the Darwinian conception of species it was still possible to think of species as relatively fixed and immutable, with the modification that under the slow action of natural selection they were capable of change. For the nineteenth-century anthropologist, therefore, it was possible to think of "race" or "races," not as Blumenbach did in the eighteenth century, as an arbitrary convenience in classification, but as Cuvier did at the beginning of the nineteenth century for all animals, as groups which could be classified on the basis of the fact that they possessed an aggregate of common physical characters, and, as Darwin later postulated, as groups which varied only under conditions of natural selection, but which otherwise remained unchanged.

This is essentially a scholastic conception of species with the one fundamental difference that a species is considered to be no longer fixed and immutable. As far as the older anthropological conception of "race" is concerned, a few anthropologists, still unaware of the significance of the findings of modern genetics, continue to think of "race" as the scholastics thought of species, as a knowable, even though mutable, fixed whole, the essence of which could be defined *per genus, species, propria, differentia, et accidens.*

In fact, the anthropologist had simply taken over a crude eighteenth-century notion which was originally offered as a general term with no more than an arbitrary value—a convenient aid to the memory in discussing various groups of mankind—and, having erected a tremendous terminology and methodology about it, deceived himself in the belief that he was dealing with an objective reality.[3]

An illuminating reflection of a persisting anthropological viewpoint

---

[3]As Boas remarked, "we talk all the time glibly of races and nobody can give us a

occurs in an attractive book by a student of anthropology. In explaining the object of her investigations, she writes: "The purpose of these anthropometric measurements is the establishment of various physical types. The more generalized characteristics of any one locality can be determined, the resemblances to and differences from their near and remote neighbours, the ideal being to discover the various strains which are there combined. In anthropology there is as much information to be gathered from these physical measurements as from the study of social habits and customs."[4] This represents a fair statement of the older anthropological viewpoint: "the purpose of these anthropometric measurements is the establishment of various physical types."

For more than a century anthropologists have been directing their attention principally toward the task of establishing criteria by means of which "races" of mankind might be defined—a diverting parlor game in which by arbitrarily selecting the criteria one could nearly always make the "races" come out exactly as one thought they should. As Boyd writes, "Those of the proposed criteria which were adopted are evidently those which were found to give 'reasonable results'—that is, they brought home the bacon; so that in cases where the anthropologist was convinced race differences ought to exist, these criteria proved that they did. Unobliging criteria which seemed to show no differences between races 'obviously' distinct, or which indicated differences within groups 'obviously' homogeneous, have been tactfully relegated to the scrap heap."[5] In this observation we probably have the crux of the whole problem. Only those methods of "race" classification which indicated the "right sort" of "race" differences were encouraged and utilized.

Most anthropologists took completely for granted the one thing which required to be proved, namely, that the concept of "race" corresponds with a reality which can actually be measured and verified and descriptively set out so that it can be seen to be a fact[6]—in short, that the an-

---

definite answer to the question what constitutes a race." Speaking of his earliest days as a physical anthropologist, Boas says: "When I turned to the consideration of racial problems I was shocked by the formalism of the work. Nobody had tried to answer the questions why certain measurements were taken, why they were considered significant, whether they were subject to other influences." Boas, "History and Science in Anthropology: A Reply," *American Anthropologist,* Vol. XXXVIII (1936), 140.

[4]Crockett, *The House in the Rain Forest,* p. 29.

[5]William C. Boyd, *Genetics and the Races of Man* (New York: John Wiley & Sons, 1950), p. 195.

[6]T.H. Huxley, in his essay, published in 1865, "On the Methods and Results of Ethnology" (reprinted in *Man's Place in Nature,* Ann Arbor: University of Michigan Press, 1959), refused to use the terms "stocks," "varieties," "races," or "species" in connection with man, "because each of these last well-known terms implies, on the part of its employer, a preconceived opinion touching one of those problems, the solution of which is the ultimate object of the science; and in regard to which, therefore, ethnologists are especially bound to keep their minds open and their judgments freely balanced."

thropological conception of "race" is true, which states that in nature there exist groups of human beings comprised of individuals each of whom possesses a certain aggregate of characters which individually and collectively serve to distinguish them from the individuals in all other groups.

Stated in plain English, this is the conception of "race" which most anthropologists have held and practically everyone else, except the geneticist, accepts. When, as in recent years, some anthropologists have admitted that the concept cannot be strictly applied in any systematic sense, they have thought to escape the consequences of such an admission by calling the term a "general" one and have proceeded to play the old game of blindman's buff with a sublimity which is almost enviable. For it is not vouchsafed to everybody completely to appreciate the grandeur of the doctrine here implied. The feeling of dissatisfaction with which the older anthropologists had viewed the many laborious attempts at classification of human groups had not, on the whole, succeeded in generating the disloyal suspicion that something was probably wrong somewhere. If there was a fault, it was generally supposed, it lay not with the anthropologist, but with the material, with the human beings themselves who were the subject of classification, and who always varied so much that it was difficult to put them into the group where they were conceived properly to belong. This was definitely a nuisance, but, happily, one which could be overcome by the simple expedient of "averaging"—the principal occupation of the student of "race."

The process of averaging the characters of a given group, of knocking the individuals together, giving them a good stirring, and then serving the resulting omelet as a "race" was, until recently, essentially the anthropological process of race-making. It may have been good cooking, but it was not science, since it served to confuse rather than to clarify. When an omelet is done it has a fairly uniform character, though the ingredients which have entered into its making have been varied. So it was with the anthropological conception of "race." It was an omelet which corresponded to nothing in nature: an indigestible dish conjured into being by an anthropological chef from a number of ingredients which were extremely varied in character. This omelet conception of "race" had no existence outside the statistical frying pan in which it had been reduced by the heat of the anthropological imagination.

It is this omelet conception of "race" which is so meaningless—meaningless because it is inapplicable to anything real. When, recently, anthropologists began to realize that the proper description of a group does not consist in the process of making an omelet of it, but in the analysis and description of the character of the variability of the elements entering into it—its ingredients—they discovered that the fault lay not with the materials but with the conceptual tool with which they had approached their study.

That many differences exist between different groups of human beings is obvious; but the older anthropological conception of these was erroneous, and the classical anthropological approach to the study of their relationships was unscientific and pre-Mendelian. Taxonomic exercises in the classification of assemblages of phenotypical (external) characters will never succeed in elucidating the relationships of different groups of mankind to one another, for the simple reason that it is not assemblages of characters which undergo changes in the formation of the individual and the group but the single units which are physiologically associated with those characters. One of the great persisting errors involved in the anthropological conception of "race" has been due to the steady refusal to recognize this fact. The fact is that it is not possible to classify the various groups of mankind by means of the characters which the older anthropologists customarily used, because those characters do not behave as the pre-Mendelian anthropologists thought they should behave, namely, as complexes of characters which are relatively fixed and are transmitted as complexes, but instead they behave in a totally different manner, as the expression of the many independent units, linked and unlinked, which have entered into their formation.

The parallel in the history of biology is striking here and has been well illustrated by Dobzhansky, who writes: "Many studies on hybridization were made before Mendel, but they did not lead to the discovery of Mendel's laws. In retrospect, we see clearly where the mistake of Mendel's predecessors lay: they treated as units the complexes of characteristics of individuals, races, and species, and attempted to find rules governing the inheritance of such complexes. Mendel was first to understand that it was the inheritance of separate traits, and not complexes of traits, which had to be studied. Some of the modern students of racial variability consistently repeat the mistakes of Mendel's predecessors."[7]

The materials of evolution are not represented by continuous aggregates of characters, but by discontinuous packages of chemicals, each of which is more or less independent in its action and may be only partially responsible for the expression of any character. These chemical packages are the genes, situated mostly within the chromosomes, structures with which many anthropologists were until recently scarcely on terms of a bowing acquaintance. The genes retain both their independence and their individual character more or less indefinitely, although probably they are all inherently variable and, in time, may undergo mutation. For these reasons any conception of "race" which operates as if inheritance were a matter of transmitting gross aggregates of characters is both erroneous and meaningless. To quote Dobzhansky once more:

---

[7]Dobzhansky, *Genetics and the Origin of Species*, 3rd ed. (New York: Columbia University Press, 1951), p. 78.

"The difficulty . . . is that . . . the concept of race as a system of character averages logically implies a theory of continuous, rather than of par-
ticulate, germ plasm. Such a concept is obviously outmoded and incapable of producing much insight into the causative factors at work in
human population. Although the genic basis of relatively few human
traits is known, it seems that following up the distribution of these traits
could tell us more about the 'races' than a great abundance of
measurements."[8]

The principal agencies of evolutionary change in man are primarily
gene variability and gene mutation. Evolutionary changes are brought
about through the rearrangements in the combinations of genes in
consequence of the operation of many secondary factors, physical and
cultural, and changes in the character of genes themselves. In order to
appreciate the meaning of the variety presented by mankind today it is
indispensably necessary to understand the manner in which these
agencies work. Thus, in man it is practically certain that some forms of
hair and skin color are due to mutation, while still other forms are due
to various combinations of these mutant forms with one another, as also
with nonmutant forms. The rate of mutation for different genes in man
varies. It has been calculated that the gene for normal clotting mutates,
for example, to the gene for hemophilia in one out of less than 10,000
individuals per generation. It is highly probable, for example, that such
a mutation occurred in the person of Queen Victoria's father,[9] a fact
which in the long run may perhaps constitute both his and her chief
claim to fame. The rate of mutation of the blood group genes, however
appears to be low.[10] Mutation of skin-color genes also is infrequent,
while mutation of hair-form genes is somewhat more frequent.

If anthropologists are ever to understand how the different groups of
mankind came to possess such characters as distinguish the more geographically isolated of them, and those of the less isolated, more recently
mixed, and therefore less distinguishable groups, it should be obvious
that they must cease making omelets of the very ingredients, the genes,
which it should be our purpose to isolate and to map. What must be
studied are the frequencies with which such genes occur in different
groups of populations. The gene frequency method for the study of the
distribution of human genes is a simple one and has now been available
for some time,[11] as likewise has been the method for the study of genetic

---

[8]*Ibid.*, p. 359.

[9]J.B.S. Haldane, *Heredity and Politics* (New York: W.W. Norton & Co., 1938), p.
88.

[10]See Montagu, *Human Heredity*.

[11]For a clear exposition of the facts see Boyd, *Genetics and the Races of Man;* C.
Stern, *Principles of Human Genetics* (San Francisco: W.H. Freeman & Co., 1960);
Strandskov, "The distribution of human genes," *Scientific Monthly,* LII (1942),
203–15, and "The genetics of human populations," *American Naturalist,* LXXVI
(1942), 156–64.

linkage in man.[12] If, roughly speaking, one gene be arbitrarily assigned to every component of the body, it should be fairly clear that as regards the structure of man we are dealing with many thousands of genes. In the fruit fly *Drosophila melanogaster,* in which there are four pairs of chromosomes, it has been estimated that there are no less than 5,000 genes. Man has 23 pairs of chromosomes; if we award him the same number of genes as *Drosophila* may be assumed to have on each chromosome, namely, 1,250, then man has at least 28,750 genes in the chromosomes of his sex cells. But altogether apart from this in a single mating the theoretical possible combinations between the 23 chromosomes of the male and those of the female are 8,388,608, or 2 raised to the 23rd power, and the chance of any one such combination being repeated more than once is one in 70,000,000,000,000, or 2^{23} x 2^{23}. It will be seen that the different combinations that a 30,000-gene system can take reach a stupendous figure. This is on a purely numerical basis. By totally different methods Spuhler has arrived at the figure of about 34,000 genes in man,[13] and Evans at an estimate of between 10,000 and 100,000 genes in man.[14] If we consider the newer concepts, which recognize that the adult individual represents the end point in the interaction between all these genes, under the influence of the environments in which they have undergone development, the complexities become even greater.[15] The morphological characters which anthropologists have relied upon for their "racial" classifications have been few indeed, involving a minute fraction of the great number of genes which it would actually be necessary to consider in attempting to make any real —that is to say, genetically analytic—classification of mankind.

To sum up, the indictment against the older, or classical, anthropological conception of "race" is that: (1) it is artificial, (2) it does not correspond with the facts, (3) it leads to confusion and the perpetuation of error, and finally, (4) for all these reasons it is meaningless, or rather, more accurately, such meaning as it possesses is false. Based as it is on unexamined facts and unjustifiable generalizations, it were better that the term "race," being so weighed down with false meaning, be dropped altogether from the vocabulary.

If it be agreed that the human species is one and that it consists of a group of populations which, more or less, replace each other geographically or ecologically and of which the neighboring ones intergrade or

[12]Finney, "The detection of linkage," *Journal of Heredity,* XXXIII (1942), 156–60; Kloepfer, "An investigation of 171 possible linkage relationships in man," *Annals of Eugenics,* XIII (1946), 35–71; Mather, *The Measurement of Linkage in Heredity.*

[13]Spuhler, "An estimate of the number of genes in man," *Science,* CVIII (1948), 279.

[14]Evans, "Quantitative inferences concerning the genetic effects of radiation on human beings," *Science,* CIX (1949), 299–304.

[15]See Montagu, *The Biosocial Nature of Man;* Montagu, *Prenatal Influences.*

hybridize wherever they are in contact, or are potentially capable of doing so,[16] then it should be obvious that the task of the student interested in the character of these populations must be to study the frequency distribution of the genes which characterizes them—not entities which are purely imaginary.

Physical anthropologists must recognize that they have unwittingly played no small part in the creation of the myth of "race," which in our time has assumed so dangerous a form. It is encouraging to be able to say that since the appearance of the first edition of this book in 1942 most anthropologists have seen their responsibility clearly and are taking active steps to exorcise the monster of "race" and deliver the thought and conduct of mankind from its evil influence.[17] Dr. G. M. Morant, in delivering the address on physical anthropology at the centenary meeting of the Royal Anthropological Institute, said: "It seems to me that the time has come when anthropologists must fully recognize fundamental changes in their treatment of the problem of racial classification. The idea that a race is a group of people separated from all others on account of the distinctive ancestry of its members is implied whenever a racial label is used, but in fact we have no knowledge of the existence of such populations to-day or in any past time. Gradations between any regional groups distinguished, and an absence of clear-cut divisions, are the universal rule. Our methods have never been fully adapted to deal with this situation."[18]

---

[16]Mayr, "Speciation phenomena in birds," *Biological Symposia,* II (1941), 66, and *Systematics and the Origin of Species,* pp. 154 ff.; Mayr, *Animal Species and Evolution.*

[17]For a cogent criticism, by a cultural anthropologist, along similar lines, see the chapter on "race" in Ralph Linton, *The Study of Man* (New York: Appleton-Century-Crofts, Inc., 1936), pp. 22–45. See also Krogman, "The concept of race," in Linton (ed), *The Science of Man in the World Crisis* (New York: Columbia University Press, 1945), pp. 38–62.

[18]Morant, "The future of physical anthropology," *Man,* XLIV (1944), 17.

10. Color and group identity in the United States

C. ERIC LINCOLN

Mary had a little lamb
Its fleece was white as snow
And everywhere that Mary went
That little white lamb could go.

Mary had another lamb
Its fleece was black, you see
They thought he was a "you-know-what"
And hung him from a tree.[1]

In the United States where the enduring problem in social relations is between whites and Negroes, skin color is probably the most important single index for uncritical human evaluation. It is paradoxical that this is so, for color is notoriously unreliable as a tool for determining any substantial qualities of an individual, particularly his "race." And it is with race that the question of color is ultimately concerned. Despite this obvious unreliability, color is made to function as a cultural index for racial determination whenever it is conceived of as a valid external symbol of supposedly intrinsic qualities. The presence or absence of these qualities determines whether a person belongs to an "inferior" or "superior" social group, and whether his life chances are circumscribed or maximized in terms of his group membership.

In social relations in the United States, color is often read as a signal to denigrate, to discriminate, to segregate. It takes on the characteristics of a cultural norm, so much so that a complex of rewards, punishments, and the strictest taboos have grown up around it. American children, both Negro and white, very early develop behavior patterns and adopt value systems based on color, and American adults are seldom free from its connotations. That a racial determination on the basis of color can only be approximate and for a limited spectrum of individuals at best does not seem to impair its credibility as a legitimate index for human evaluation. Nor does it seem to diminish the apparent *need* for identifying persons by race. On the surface this would seem to indicate that

Abridged and edited from C. Eric Lincoln, "Color and group identity in the United States," *Daedalus,* Spring 1967, pp. 249–63. Reprinted by permission of *Daedalus,* Journal of the American Academy of Arts and Sciences, Boston, Mass. Spring 1967, *Color and Race.*

The author is Professor of Sociology and Religion, Union Theological Seminary, New York, N.Y.
[1]From "Joe Jipson," *The Autobiography of a Southern Town;* an unpublished manuscript by C. Eric Lincoln.

America's cultural concern about color is essentially nominal. The need to make decisions on a racial basis is perhaps psychologically atavistic, a tribal anachronism rooted in the dim past when everyone not a member of the tribe threatened its well-being.

Thousands of Negroes "pass" permanently into the white race each year. This cannot be effectively prevented so long as there are interracial unions, with or without benefit of law or clergy. Thousands of others pass whenever it provides social or economic opportunities not readily available outside the majority group. Reliable estimates on the basis of three hundred and fifty years of miscegenation and passing suggest that there are several million "Caucasians" in this country who are part Negro insofar as they have Negro blood or Negro ancestry.[2] Since there are few Negro Americans who do not have some white blood, the continuing preoccupation with racial identification by color would seem to be of little reward—the more crucial facts having already been established by a countervailing proclivity.

Nonetheless, American society has troubled itself considerably to detect by various supplementary devices—sometimes refined, but more often of a cruder sort—what may be undetectable to the uncritical eye. It thus reaffirms its apparent need (and the quality of its commitment) for the establishment of racial identity as a crucial factor in social intercourse. A generation ago when strict segregation followed identification, some of the night clubs, hotels, and other places of entertainment and public accommodation in Chicago and other cities hired "spotters" to point out light-skinned Negroes who sought to pass for white and enter the segregated establishments. Since the operating premise of the white proprietors was that "one coon can recognize another," the spotters were always Negroes, some of whom were themselves light enough to pass. The system broke down during the depression years when few Negroes, light-skinned or otherwise, had enough money to bother about trying to spend it in places where they had to run a color gauntlet. Having nobody to spot, the "spotters" felt their jobs in jeopardy and began to ask their friends to come by occasionally in the interest of the survival of the profession. The whole sordid arrangement collapsed when the supply of friends of "passable" skin color ran low, and the ersatz "Caucasians" became darker and darker with hair that was fuzzier and fuzzier. Reduced to spotting the obvious, the spotters were soon dispensed with.

This absurd practice demonstrates the near pathological obsession with race and color Americans have exhibited. It is *e pluribus unum*— one out of a multitude. In the illustration given, those most anxious about color and identity were Caucasian, which is to say, white. But in a

---

[2]Sociologist Robert P. Stuckert of Ohio State University estimates: "Over 28 million white persons are descendants of persons of African origins"—about 21 per cent of the Caucasian population of the United States.

well-known southern city a leading Negro church for years discouraged the attendance of would-be worshipers who were darker than a *café au lait* stripe painted conveniently on the doorjamb of the sanctuary.

In its American manifestations, the fundamental problem of color and group identity derives in large measure from the desire of the established white hegemony, particularly the former slave-owning class, to distinguish itself by all means available from the blacks, who, whether as slaves or freedmen, had little status and no power.[3] As long as the vast majority of the blacks were of unmixed African descent, the problem was minimized. Their distinctive visibility made their racial origins unmistakable. In fact, the very first significance of color was the early development of a rationale in the colonies that made it possible to hold a black bondservant for life, to make him a slave, while a white bondservant could be held only for a term of years.[4]

From the date that blacks could, as a matter of course, be held in legal servitude for life, color became an important index of race and, hence, of prestige and status.[5] A ban against intermarriage was immediately instituted. Theretofore, intermarriage between black bondsmen from Africa and white bondswomen from England and Ireland had been common. Social acceptability was measured in terms of class, which could be transcended, rather than in terms of race, which was immutable. In the context of a distribution of status and power that implied the freedom of all white men and the susceptibility to chattel slavery of all Negroes, color became the visual rule of thumb for the assignment of "place" or status.

· · · · ·

The problem of negative associations with blackness goes deeper than aesthetics. American culture associates Negroes with darkness, an extremely negative quality. In the innocent and painful prattle of Negro children heard a scant generation ago, *"Black is evil!"* was a retort intended to account for behavior one disapproved of in a playmate.[6] In the

---

[3]In a larger sense, the problem of color and identity in America is related to the general ascendancy of the West, which is to say white Europeans, since the fifteenth century, and the subsequent colonization of Asia, Africa, and the New World. In his book, *Caste, Class and Race* ([Garden City, N. Y., 1948], p. 346), Oliver Cox makes the signal observation that "since the belief in white superiority—that is to say white nationalism—began to move over the world, no people of color have been able to develop race prejudice independent of whites."

[4]See John Hope Franklin, *From Slavery to Freedom* (New York, 1947), p. 70ff.

[5]This was first practiced in Virginia in 1661; Maryland followed in 1663. A Virginia law of 1670 fixed the status of Negroes and Indians respectively by decreeing that "all servants not being Christians" (that is, not being "white") coming into the colony by sea, "shall be slaves for their lives." Those "coming by land" (Indians) could be bound for a term of years.

[6]In Boston, the author was once physically attacked by a white child with no other explanation than, "I don't like you because you're black!"

rural areas, black people were frequently associated with sorcery and voodoo.[7] Everywhere black people were pitied, for deep in the soul of even the whitest Negro was an erosive *self*-pity, even a self-hatred that gnawed at his vitals, questioned his manhood, and excused his failures in a way he did not want them to be excused. There was something inherent in being black that marked a man; something sinister that mocked a man.

The crucial question has always been the question of identity. Who *is* this Negro whose identifying characteristic is his color and what is his status in the world? *Whence does that status derive?* Is he African—an involuntary expatriate? Is he, in fact, "just a nigger"—a monster, blackened by God, broken in servitude, and inherently incapable of human excellence? How should he designate himself? By what name should he identify himself before the world and serve notice of what he conceives himself to be?

There has been little unanimity in the Negro's search for his identity. The Negro slaves came from many tribes and many cultures. Even though the experience of slavery reduced them all to a common denominator, it did not fuse them into an ideological unit. Only attractive ideas and persuasive leadership could do that; the nature of slavery in America left little room for the development of either.

The confusion of identity is vividly expressed in the names by which Negroes have chosen at various times to designate themselves: "persons of color," "colored people," "Negroes," "colored Americans," "Black Anglo-Saxons," "Americans," "Afro-Americans," "Afra-Americans," "Negro Americans"; and, more recently: "black men," "black Americans," "black people." Widely used by white writers, but commonly rejected by Negro intellectuals and black nationalists is the term *American Negroes*. This eristic term allegedly carries the stamp of something "made in America" and is the inverse of the designations commonly applied to other ethnic groups—"German Americans," for instance.[8] "That we are called 'American Negroes,' " a prominent Negro writer has said, "is a concession of courtesy on the part of our Caucasian brothers. In translation, 'the American Negro' can only mean 'our nigger.' "

Despite some improvements in the Negroes' position as a major ethnic group pressing for a larger share of the common values of the society, the question of color and identity has in some sense become more in-

---

[7] A belief possibly reinforced by once popular "jungle" films and stories; but possibly a recollection of a fragmentary cultural experience having to do with tribal religious rites or witchcraft.

[8] The implication, say the critics, is that the Negro has no prior nationality or culture, that he is in fact a creation of the white man, "something made in America." Only the Indian should have "American" placed before his ethnic name, it is argued.

volved and more intricate than before. There have been changes in the way Caucasians and Negroes see each other, and profound changes in the way Negroes see themselves. These newly developing attitudes have not always found mutual acceptance, nor are they necessarily consistent with one another. The de-escalation of color as an index of social standing in the Negro sub-society immeasurably strengthened and unified the factions previously contending for leadership and prestige. Forced to more diligently prepare themselves, the descendants of the less-favored field hands of plantation days have at least caught up. Today, education, wealth, high social status, and leadership are distributed fairly evenly across the color spectrum of the Negro community.

If anything, the light-skinned Negro is at a disadvantage. In the old days, color meant (at least nominal) privilege, for it bespoke the presence of the master's blood. Today, as the Negro develops an increasing appreciation of his own accomplishments and shares vicariously the accomplishments of other non-whites, the premium on "the master's blood" is signally diminished. Anyone whose light skin color is thought to be of recent derivation is exposed to a degree of censure and disapproval not known in former times.

As far as the larger society is concerned, the presence of white blood in a Negro does not bridge the chasm between castes any more today than it did formerly. In personal relations, Caucasians have, since the plantation days, usually been less threatened by blacks who were thought of as "knowing their places" than by mulattoes or "yellow niggers" who were always suspect. This white attitude can be explained in part, of course, by guilt feelings deriving from a covert recognition of kinship, which could never be openly admitted without violating the strictest taboos. But there was also the deep-seated belief that too much white blood transformed the stereotyped docile, accommodating Negro into a dissatisfied, potential trouble-maker. Hence, enduring bonds of affection and qualified respect frequently developed between whites and darker Negroes, a felicitous relationship from which light-skinned Negroes were generally excluded. In quite recent times, this tradition has undergone some interesting changes that reflect the inconsistencies of a color differential.

When civil rights legislation first required the employment of Negroes in major industry, wherever possible the "instant Negroes"[9] hired were of very fair complexions. Negroes serving as clerks and saleswomen in department stores or as route salesmen were frequently mistaken for white by their customers and sometimes by their co-workers. This was, of course, precisely what their employers had hoped for. In hiring

---

[9] Negroes hired in token numbers merely to comply with the law.

Negroes who could "pass," they complied with the law without appearing to have done so. They thus reduced the supposed threat of customer and white employee reaction against being served by or working with Negroes. This policy was discontinued in favor of hiring highly visible Negroes and placing them in the most conspicuous assignments when compliance officials could discover no change in hiring policies, and Negro leaders protested that their followers wanted to "see their people on the job without having to look for them."

There are signs that the civil rights movement as a supporting thrust to a certain degree of Negro "readiness" in terms of education, accomplishment, and demonstrated potential has successfully breached the wall separating Negroes and whites into two castes. The breach is certainly not general, but for the first time in American history, Negroes enjoy some degree of lateral mobility. There is *some* social movement across color lines. Perhaps the sudden recognition of this fact contributed in no small degree to the amazing "pull-back" on the part of large numbers of whites who had been heavily involved in the civil rights movement so long as it was limited to civil rights—and concentrated in the South. The white retreat would seem to buttress other evidence that white America in general, despite some fits and starts, is not yet ready to accept Negroes on equal terms so long as they remain Negroes. Arnold Toynbee's observations of thirty years ago are still valid:

> The . . . [Negro] may have found spiritual salvation in the White Man's faith; he may have acquired the White Man's culture and learnt to speak his language with the tongue of an angel; he may have become adept in the White Man's economic technique, and yet it profits him nothing if he has not changed his skin.[10]

A few, select, individual Negroes have been able to approach the American main stream with varying degrees of marginality. In doing so, they run the inevitable risk of becoming as alienated from the nether culture from which they came as they are likely to remain in reference to the culture they seek to enter. But change *is* occurring.

Even as the machinery of caste is being dismantled and discarded, the color-caste psychology persists. It is not difficult to understand the continuing frustrations of the black masses. A universal system of *apartheid* has, in effect, been exchanged for a selective system of *apartheid*. This may be progress, but it is not progressive enough to satisfy the present-day needs of the black millions who are still beyond the pale. The color computer has been programmed to extend to selected Negroes of high accomplishment selected categories of privileges previously withheld from all Negroes. An "integrated" society in which the common values

---

[10]Arnold J. Toynbee, *A Study of History,* Vol. 1 (London, 1935), p. 224.

of that society will be freely accessible to the general population regardless of color has not been realized, nor does it seem to be rapidly approaching.

Taking no comfort from what they perceive as an *entente cordiale* between the white establishment and the Negro leadership class, the black *lumpen proletariat* seethes with hostility and resentment. Despite modifications of law and practice produced by the efforts of the civil rights movement, the black masses are unimpressed because they are unaffected. Critical selectivity functions at the top; the tortured masses at the bottom feel no tremor of change.

The Great Society has spent millions of dollars in the interest of the poor and the disinherited. In doing so, the government created yet another clique of petty bureaucrats and interposed them between the people and the help they need. By day the black ghetto is resplendent with sleek, fat professionals—Negro and white—striving mightily to re-mold the people in images they reject and despise; by night—the professionals having fled home to the suburbs—the people gather on the street corners to contemplate the probabilities of black power, or the ecstasy of long, hot summers. Despite the ministrations of the professionals, the people are as hungry, as unemployed, and as hostile as before.

As their frustrations multiply, the black masses become more and more alienated from the larger society and from the tiny Negro middle class that hopes to cross the chasm eventually and to enter the American main stream. The problem of color and identity takes on crucial meaning in this context. The term *Negro,* which has for so long aroused mixed emotions even among those who accepted it, has for the militant[11] masses become an epithet reserved for the Negro middle class, particularly those suspected of desiring to be integrated into the white society.

Neither the traditional black nationalists nor the advocates of "black power," which is a new form of militant black nationalism, accept integration as being either possible or desirable under existing conditions. Integration is interpreted as a one-way street. It means to those not impressed by its possibilities the abandonment of traditional values and styles of life on the off-chance of being accepted by a group "which never appreciated you for what you were, and resents you for what you are trying to become." Stokely Carmichael declares:

> Integration . . . speaks to the problem of blackness in a despicable way. As a goal it has been based on complete acceptance of the fact [*sic*] that in order to have a decent house or education, blacks must move into a white neighborhood or send their children to a white school.

---

[11]The greater portion of the black masses can still be classified as "quiescent," although they are certainly more susceptible to sporadic activities than ever before.

This reinforces, among both black and white, the idea that "white" is automatically better and "black" is by definition inferior. This is why integration is a subterfuge for the maintenance of white supremacy.[12]

To the black masses, the Negro integrationists and integrationist leaders seem to take on the characteristics of "collaborators with the enemy," and need to be labeled distinctly as such. Hence, the black militants have resurrected the connotation of "Negro" as being a thing, a puppet, a creation of the white man, finding it peculiarly applicable to the Negro middle class and its leadership.[13]

Like the Garveyites and the Black Muslims before them, the new black militants—particularly those in the Student Non-Violent Coordinating Committee—do not see themselves in the image of the white American. They dress unaffectedly and wear their hair *à la mode Africaine*—combed, but unstraightened. They refer to themselves and to all other non-integrationist-minded black Americans as "black people." The term is deliberately chosen as a symbol of racial polarization. It intends to imply the solidarity of the black masses, here and abroad; to disavow any necessary commitment to white values or deference to the white establishment; to distinguish the masses from the integrationists; and to exploit new feelings of black nationalism and *négritude* that have taken hold in the Negro community since World War II. It answers, at least for the time being, all the important questions of identity and color. Many middle-class Negroes, remembering the negative stereotypes formerly associated with blackness, cannot bring themselves to speak of Negroes as "black people." Neither can many whites for that matter.[14] The stereotypes die too hard.

The new SNCC strategy aims at organizing a power base from which black people can influence decisions within the existing political arrangement without being subject to review by white monitors. Implied is a fundamental rejection of reliance upon the white man's integrity, a point to which all black nationalist groups must come by definition. The synonym for black nationalism is black ethnocentrism, and ethnocentrism always implies a suspicion of some other peoples' integrity, their values, and their truth.

---

[12]Stokely Carmichael, "What we want," *The Boston Sunday Herald,* October 2, 1966.

[13]In conversation, the word may be sarcastically pronounced with excessive stress on the first syllable ("NEE-gro"), recalling readily to the ingroup mind the slurred pronunciation of some Southerners that renders the word "Negra," which to sensitive ears is a covert way of saying "nigger."

[14]In a graduate seminar on minority relations, a young white student protested to a Negro classmate: "Why do you call yourself 'black'? I could never call you black. There is something not right about it. Besides, I think you're a nice guy." "You can't call me 'black,' " the Negro student answered, "and that is your guilt. I can call myself 'black,' " and that is my freedom."

In the conventional interpretation of human confrontation, belief is always preceded by doubt. Not so with the Negro in America. He believed first and has but lately learned to doubt. It is a tragedy that doubt was even necessary, since the faith he had required so little to fulfill. But America is now forever beyond the point of naïveté and innocence, and is unlikely to pass that way again. The lessons that have been learned cannot be forgotten, and there are new teachers to interpret old experiences. Elijah Muhammad justifies his all-black Muslim organization on the grounds that "You can't whip a man when he's helping you," thus surreptitiously but unequivocally identifying the enemy as the white man. The SNCC rationale is more adroit. SNCC wants its white supporters to work among prejudiced whites "who are not accessible" to its Negro agents. The net result is the same: the effective removal of white individuals, however well-intentioned, from sensitive strategy and policy-making areas where racial loyalties may jeopardize the pursuit of the black man's program.

Traditional black nationalism has been oriented toward separatism— or, at best, toward a pluralistic society. The "black-power" syndrome recognizes the substantial existence of a plural society already and intends to capitalize on it. Like the integrationists, SNCC wants power within the existing political structure, but unlike more moderate organizations, SNCC is impatient with indirect power and suspicious of contingent or shared power. "Black power" is conceived as palpable, manipulatable, black-controlled power that carries with it a sense of dignity for black people and a feeling of security from white caprice. An organized, voting black minority with a substantially unified ideological orientation could conceivably produce such power. Whether it can be produced on the basis of color alone is debatable.[15]

The question is not whether black people are capable of leadership and self-direction or of making the sacrifices that may be needed. They have demonstrated their capabilities in all these areas, and more. The more fundamental question is whether color alone is a unifying force sufficient to weld together in a monolithic (or, better, monochromatic) sociopolitical movement a black minority exhibiting an immense spectrum of needs, wants, desires, and intentions based on conflicting systems of value. The question of identity has not been resolved. Color alone does not answer satisfactorily the questions about the self one needs to have answered as the basis for intelligent decision-making about oneself and others. Negroes in America still do not know who they are. Not having resolved this elemental problem, they approach all other

---

[15]Malcolm X saw color as the only possible basis of unification. He attempted to eclipse the problem of white ancestry so obvious in many Negroes, himself included, by declaring: "We are all black, different shades of black, and not one of us means any more to a white cracker than any other one."

problems in human relations with predictable ambivalence and uncertainty. That is why they fight bravely in the far off places of the world, march peacefully in Washington, and die cravenly in Mississippi and Alabama. This, too, is why they sing "Black and White Together" by day, and "Burn! Baby, Burn!" by night.

The Negro's experiences in America have produced in him a mass social neurosis that can only become more morbid as the frustrations of trying to cope with the problem of color and identity are intensified by education and increased marginality at the top of the social pyramid, and by increasing poverty and the concomitant loss of personhood at the bottom. Involuntary servitude did not shatter the psyche of the Negro. He could overcome servitude—slavery if you insist—just as countless other peoples of different races and cultures had. Slavery was not a unique experience. Still, although it existed for centuries in Africa as well as elsewhere, nowhere but in America was it accompanied by such devastation of personality. It was not the slavery *per se,* but the pitiless obliteration of the history and the culture of a people, the deliberate distortion of that history and culture. It was the casual pollution of a race without the compassion and responsibility of acknowledgment. It was, above all, the snide rejection of the Negro's claim to be "American." Less deserving people from all over the world could come to America and claim that identity so long as they were white. The Negro could never claim it because he was black.

The trauma of this rejection polarizes the color crisis between the races and keeps alive the anxieties of identification and color within the Negro sub-group. Charles Silberman is probably right: "Consciousness of color is not likely to disappear unless color itself disappears or unless men lose their eyesight."[16] But consciousness of color, like consciousness of kind, is not a reasonable basis upon which to project a system of group relations. Nor has it ever been.

11. Variations in the basic values of family systems
FLORENCE ROCKWOOD KLUCKHOHN

For many years, my own interest has been centered on the variations of the quite universal institution commonly called The Family. And the still broader perspective has been the variations in basic value—value

---

[16]Charles E. Silberman, *Crisis in Black and White* (New York, 1964), p. 166.
Reprinted from Florence Rockwood Kluckhohn, "Variations in the basic values

orientations—found both between cultures and within cultures. Therefore, it is from this point of view that I wish to approach the problems of diagnosing and treating disturbances in family relations.

Psychologically speaking, it is well known that the developing personalities of children are greatly affected by the kinds of relationships they have with a mother, a father, and siblings. Sometimes, but not very often, in the analyses of family patterns made in this country, the influences of grandparents and collateral relatives are considered. But even when these are considered, not much attention has been given to the differing effects of culturally variable family patterns upon the relationships themselves and the kinds of personalities which result from them.

One of the factors needing attention, then, is the cultural one, or—I would prefer to say—the value orientation factor. We are concerned with finding out both what kinds of strains are common to families and particular cultures or subcultures and what additional ones are to be expected when a family is in process of acculturation.

Basic values are not superficial phenomena. The value orientations (the term I prefer) of a people are deeply rooted, are mainly unconscious, and are also so pervasive that they markedly affect the patterns of behavior and thought of a people in all areas of activity. Let me quote a statement from Clyde Kluckhohn:

> There is a "philosophy" behind the way of life of every individual and of every relatively homogeneous group at any given point in their histories. This gives, with varying degrees of explicitness or implicitness, some sense of coherence or unity to living both in cognitive and affective dimensions. Each personality gives to this "philosophy" an idiosyncratic coloring, and creative individuals will markedly reshape it. However, the main outlines of the fundamental values, existential assumptions, and basic abstractions have only exceptionally been created out of the stuff of unique biological heredity and peculiar life experience. The underlying principles arise out of, or are limited by, the givens of biological human nature and the universalities of social interaction. The specific formulation is ordinarily a cultural product. In the immediate sense, it is from the lifeways which constitute the designs for living of their community or tribe or region or socioeconomic class or nation or civilization that most individuals derive their "mental-feeling outlook."[1]

The anthropologist, dealing with quite different cultures the world around, has concerned himself mostly with a demonstration of the often

of family systems," *Social Casework*, February-March 1958, 39:63–72. Copyright © 1958 by the Family Service Association of America. Reprinted by permission.
    [1]Clyde Kluckhohn *et al.,* "Values and value-orientations in the theory of action," in Talcott Parsons and Edward A. Shils (eds.), *Toward a General Theory of Action* (Cambridge, Mass.: Harvard University Press, 1952), Part IV, chap. ii, pp. 409–10.

dramatic differences between cultures. What I wish now to present is a classification of values and some ideas about variation which allow us to analyze both this kind of difference and the other kind which I call intracultural variation.

Three major assumptions underlie both the classification system of value orientations[2] and the conceptualization of aspects of variation in value orientations.

First, it is assumed that there is a limited number of common human problems for which all peoples at all times must find some solution. This is the universal aspect of value orientations because the common human problems to be treated arise inevitably out of the human situation.

But however universal the problems, the solutions found for them are not the same; hence the next consideration is the degree of relativity or, better, the range of variability. The second assumption is that while there is variability in solutions of all the problems, it is neither limitless nor random but is definitely variable within a range of possible solutions.

The third assumption, which provides the key to the later analysis of variation in value orientations, is that all variants of all solutions are in varying degrees present in all societies at all times. Thus, every society has, in addition to its dominant profile of value orientations, numerous variant or substitute profiles. And in both the dominant and the variant profiles, there is always a rank ordering of value orientations emphases rather than a single emphasis.

Five problems have been tentatively singled out as the crucial ones common to all human groups. These problems are stated here in the form of questions, and in each case there is a parenthetical designation of the name that will be used hereafter for the range of orientations relating to the question:

1. What is the character of innate human nature? (Human-Nature Orientation)

2. What is the relation of man to nature (supernature)? (Man-Nature Orientation)

3. What is the temporal focus of human life? (Time Orientation)

---

[2]For a fuller discussion of this classification scheme and the theory of variation in value orientations, see two articles by the author, "Dominant and substitute profiles of cultural orientations: Their significance for the analysis of social stratification," *Social Forces,* 1950, 28(4): 276–93; and "Dominant and variant value orientations," in Clyde Kluckhohn, Henry A. Murray and David M. Schneider (eds.), *Personality in Nature, Society, and Culture* (2d ed.; New York: Alfred A. Knopf, 1953), pp. 342–57.

A still more complete version of the theory, as well as the results of testing it in five cultures, appears in *Variations in Value Orientations* (Evanston, Ill.: Row, Peterson & Co., 1961), a monograph written by the author in collaboration with Fred L. Strodtbeck and others.

4. What is the modality of human activity? (Activity Orientation)

5. What is the modality of man's relationship to other men? (Relational Orientation)

. . . . .

1. Human Nature Orientation.—To the question of what innate human nature is, there are the three logical divisions of Evil, Good and Evil, and Good. Yet it may be argued that the category of Good *and* Evil is not one but two categories. There certainly is a significant difference between the view that human nature is simply neutral and the view of it as a mixture of the good and bad. Moreover, the subprinciples of mutability and immutability increase the basic threefold classification to six possibilities. Human nature can, for example, be conceived to be Evil and unalterable or Evil and perfectible; as Good and unalterable or Good and corruptible; as an invariant mixture of the Good and Evil or as a mixture subject to influence.

Few will disagree that the orientation inherited from Puritan ancestors and still strong among many Americans is that of a basically Evil but perfectible human nature. According to this view, constant control and discipline of the self are required if any real goodness is to be achieved, and the danger of regression is always present. But some in the United States today, perhaps a growing number, incline to the view that human nature is a mixture of the Good and Evil. These would say that although control and effort are certainly needed, lapses can be understood and need not always be severely condemned. This latter definition of basic human nature would appear to be a more common one among peoples of the world, both literate and non-literate, than the one held to in the historical past of this country. Whether there are any total societies committed to the definition of human nature as immutably Good is to be doubted. Yet the position is a possible one, and it certainly is found as a variant definition within societies.

2. Man-Nature (-Supernature) Orientation.—The three-point range of variation in the man-nature orientation—Subjugation to Nature, Harmony with Nature, and Mastery over Nature—is too well known from the works of philosophers and culture historians to need much explanation. Mere illustrations will demonstrate the differences between the conceptions.

Spanish-American culture in the American Southwest gives us an example of a very definite Subjugation-to-Nature orientation. The typical Spanish-American sheep herder in a time as recent as fifteen years ago believed firmly that there was little or nothing a man could do to save or protect either land or flocks when damaging storms descended upon them. He simply accepted the inevitable. In Spanish-American attitudes toward illness and death one finds the same fatalism. "If it is the Lord's will that I die, I shall die," is the way they express it, and many a

Spanish-American has refused the services of a doctor because of this attitude.

If the conceptualization of the man-nature relationship is that of Harmony, there is no real separation between man, nature, and supernature. One is simply an extension of the other, and the conception of wholeness derives from their unity. This orientation, little understood in this country since it is third-order one, seems to have been the dominant one in many periods of Chinese history, and it is strongly evident in Japanese culture at the present time as well as historically. It is also the orientation attributed to the Navaho Indians by Clyde Kluckhohn.

The Mastery-over-Nature position is the first-order one of most Americans. Natural forces of all kinds are to be overcome and put to the use of human beings. Rivers everywhere are spanned with bridges; mountains have roads put through and around them; new lakes are built, sometimes in the heart of a desert; old lakes get partially filled in when additional land is needed for building sites, roads, or airports; the belief in man-made medical care for the control of illness and the lengthening of life is strong to an extreme; and all are told early in life that "the Lord helps those who help themselves." The view in general is that it is a part of man's duty to overcome obstacles; hence the great emphasis upon technology.

3. *Time Orientation.*—The possible cultural interpretations of the temporal focus of human life break easily into the three-point range of Past, Present, and Future. Far too little attention has been given to the full range of major variations in the time orientation.

Obviously, every society must deal with all the three time problems; each one has its conceptions of the past, the present, and the future. Where societies differ is in the rank order emphasis given to each; a very great deal can be told about the particular society or part of a society being studied, and much about the direction of change within it can be predicted, if one knows what the rank order emphasis is.

Illustrations of the variations in temporal focus are also easily found. Spanish-Americans, who have been described as taking the view that man is a victim of natural forces, are also a people who give a first order position to Present-Time. They pay little attention to what has happened in the past and regard the future as a vague and most unpredictable period. Planning for the future or hoping that the future will be better than either present or past simply is not their way of life.

Historic China was a society that gave first order value preference to Past-Time. Ancestor worship and a strong family tradition were both expressions of a Past-Time orientation. So also was the Chinese attitude that nothing new ever happened in the present or would happen in the future; it had all happened before in the far distant past.

Americans, more strongly than most peoples of the world, place an emphasis upon the future—a future that is anticipated as "bigger and better." This does not mean they have no regard for the past or thought of the present. But it certainly is true that no current generation of Americans ever wants to be called "old-fashioned." The ways of the past are not considered good just because they are past, and truly dominant Americans are seldom content with the present. This view results in a high evaluation of change, providing the change does not threaten the existing value order—the American way of life.

4. *Activity Orientation.*—The modality of human activity is the fourth of the common human problems giving rise to a value-orientation system. The range of variation in solutions suggested for it is the three-fold one of Being, Being-in-Becoming, and Doing.

In the Being orientation, the preference is for the kind of activity which is a spontaneous expression of what is conceived to be "given" in the human personality. In some sense, this orientation is a spontaneous expression in activity of impulses and desires; yet care must be taken not to make this interpretation a too literal one. In no society, as Clyde Kluckhohn has commented, does one ever find a one-to-one relationship between the desired and the desirable. The concrete behavior of individuals in complex situations and the moral codes governing that behavior usually reflect all the orientations simultaneously. A stress upon the "isness" of the personality and a spontaneous expression of that "isness" is not pure license, as we can easily see if we turn our attention to a society or segments of a society in which the Being orientation is the first order preference. Mexican society illustrates this preference well in its widely ramified patterning of *fiesta* activities. Yet never in the *fiesta,* with its emphasis on spontaneity, is there pure impulse gratification. The value demands of some of the other orientations make for codes which restrain the activities of the individuals in very definite ways.

The Being-in-Becoming orientation shares with the Being a great concern with what the human being is rather than what he can accomplish, but here the similarity ends. The idea of development, so little stressed in the Being orientation, is paramount in the Being-in-Becoming one. Erich Fromm's conception of "the spontaneous activity of the total integrated personality" is close to but not identical with the Being-in-Becoming mode.

The Doing orientation is so characteristically the dominant one in American society that there is little need for an extensive discussion of it. Its most distinguishing feature is a demand for the kind of activity that results in accomplishment achieved by acting upon persons, things, or situations. What the individual does, and what he can or will accomplish, are almost always the primary questions in the American's scale of appraisal of persons. "Getting things done" and "Let's *do* something about it" are stock American phrases.

Fromm also considers this orientation to be different from the one he defines in his concept of spontaneity, but he does not accord it an equally favored position. Instead, he actually condemns it as a fertile source of neurotically compulsive behavior. Although few would disagree that the Doing orientation of Americans makes for a competition with others which is often extreme and intense, it has not as yet been demonstrated that such competition customarily leads to or reflects compulsiveness in the technical sense of the term.

5. *Relational Orientation.*—The last of the common human problems to be treated is the definition of man's relation to other men. This orientation has three subdivisions: the Lineal, the Collateral, and the Individualistic.

Individual autonomy is always found even in the most extreme types of *gemeinschaft* societies—that is, folk societies. The like-mindedness and behavioral similarities of individuals in "homogeneous" groups have been overstressed. It is usually, if not always, the case that considerable leeway is permitted for individuality within the confines of the definitely fixed customs which *gemeinschaft* groups require for the ordering of human relationships. Individuality and individualism are both results of attention being given to the autonomy of the individual, but they are vastly different concepts, and significant nuances of meaning are lost when, as is so often the case, they are either confused or equated. There is actually less opportunity for a truly spontaneous individuality of expression in an individualistic society than in other more fixed and firmly regulated social orders. But, on the other hand, the man in an individualistic society need not remain in a fixed position and need not so often bow his head in acceptance of a dominating authority. He is much more "free to be like everyone else."

Collaterality also is found in all societies. The individual is not a human being except as he is a part of a social order, and one type of inevitable social grouping is that which results from laterally extended relationships. These are the more immediate relationships in time and space. Biologically, sibling relationships are the prototype of the Collateral relationship.

In addition, all societies must take into account the fact that individuals are biologically and culturally related to each other through time. There is, in other words, always a Lineal principle in relationships which is derived both from age and generational differences and from cultural continuity.

There will always be a variability, within systems and sub-systems as well as between them, in the primacy and the nature of goals which is in accord with variable stressing of the three principles. When the Individualistic principle is dominant, individual goals have primacy over the goals of specific Collateral or Lineal groups. This in no sense means that there is license for the individual to pursue selfishly his own interests and in so doing disregard the interests of others. It is simply that each individual's responsibility to the total society and his place in it are in terms of goals (and roles) which are defined and structured as autonomous ones in the sense of being independent of particular Lineal or Collateral groupings.

A dominant Collateral orientation calls for a primacy of the goals and welfare of the laterally extended group. The group in this case is always moderately independent of other similar groups, and the problem of a well-regulated continuity of group relationships through time is not highly critical. The Navaho extended families and the loosely articulated combinations of these in what Clyde Kluckhohn calls an "outfit" are illustrations of such groups. One also finds collaterality dominant in Italian culture. And although the individual Navaho or Italian always has some autonomous roles and some individualistic goals, and always also has some roles and goals that relate to a wider system viewed as continuous in time, the roles and goals that have primacy for him are those that are representative of his extended household group or "outfit."

If it is the Lineal principle that is dominant, it is again group goals that have primacy, but there is the additional factor that one of the most important of those group goals is continuity through time. *Continuity* of the group through time and ordered positional succession within the group are both crucial issues when Lineality dominates the relational system. Although other patterns are possible, it appears that the most successful means of maintaining a Lineal emphasis are either those based squarely upon hereditary factors such as primogeniture or those that are assimilated to a kinship structure.

To delineate the value-orientation profiles of three groups [within American Society], histories, novels, and other sources were used. It is possible to test directly for the ranking of the orientations, but we have not as yet been able to do this for our sample.[3] These profiles are now given in Table 1, but given with the warning that "ethnic labels" can be dangerous. For example, some Italians and some Irish-Americans, most certainly variants in their homeland, were more attuned to dominant American middle-class values at the time they arrived

---

[3]In the research done on five subcultures in the American Southwest—Zuni, Navaho, Spanish-Americans, Mormons, and Texans—a research instrument was developed for a direct testing. The instrument and the results obtained with it appear in *Variations in Value Orientations*.

in this country than are many Old Yankees after several hundred years of participation in United States culture. But we need the modal (typical) orientation profiles as a base line for the analysis of the difference between the problems expected and those found. Therefore, in the following table the modal profiles of the dominant Middle-class American, the Italian-American, and the Irish-American are drawn to the extent that we feel much certainty about them. For both the Italians and the Irish, the positions stated are those to which it is assumed a majority of the two groups held when they came to the United States.

As for the American middle-class case, I shall not take time to cite more than a few of the well-known facts. Parents are much concerned with the performance of their children, and training is ideally for independence of action and a show of initiative. Property gets classified as "mine and thine." Competitive behavior is rewarded and success acclaimed. The child is also quite typically the hope of the future for many families, most especially those where parents have not themselves gone as far as they had hoped to go. The family is quite individualized, and relations with relatives of the extended family, either Lineal or Collateral, are not usually strong. Extended relations certainly are not held to if the holding is regarded as detrimental to the social mobility of the particular nuclear family.

Of all known types of families, this one is probably the best suited to our highly rationalized economic system and other spheres of our na-

Table 1
Culture

Orientation	Middle-class American	Italian-American	Irish-American
Relational	Ind > Coll > Lin	Coll > Lin > Ind	Lin > Coll > Ind
Time	Fut > Pres > Past	Pres > Past > Fut	Pres > Past > Fut (but some indication of an earlier Past > Pres > Fut)
Man-Nature	Over > Subj > With	Subj > With > Over	Subj = With > Over (doubt about first order here and some doubt that there is a clear-cut first order preference)
Activity	Doing > Being > Being-in-Becoming	Being > Being-in-Becoming > Doing	Being > Being-in-Becoming > Doing
Human Nature	Evil > Mixed > Good Mixed Evil and Good > Evil > Good	Mixed Good and Evil predominantly	Most definitely an *Evil* basic nature with perfectibility desired but problematic.

tional life. It does produce achievement-minded, independent, and future-oriented individuals who are largely free of ties that bind them in time and place. Critics of the American family all too often forget to consider the wider social system and the meshing of family and other institutions.

But the critics are correct in pointing to the numerous strains on individuals which are more or less endemic in such a family. There are many strains on women as wives and mothers, on men as husbands and fathers, and these, separately and in relation to each other, inevitably have effects upon developing children. Much has been written on all the strains and their effects. Erik Erikson, for one, has provided us with a most penetrating analysis in the chapter on "The American Identity" in his *Childhood and Society*.[4] Many books and articles have been devoted to the analysis of the American feminine role, to the American mother-child relationship, and some even to the roles men play as husbands and fathers.

In illustrating our use of the value-orientation theory for a diagnosis and interpretation of family relations, I shall first discuss some aspects of the Italian patterns. If one turns back to the table that lists the orientations of all three cultures, it is easily noted that there is a wide-range difference between the value preferences of the typical Italian and the middle-class American on all orientations. In each case, if the Italian is to become a thorough-going middle-class American in his basic values, he must move from his own first order preferences to what has been in the past his third order and least favored value choices. This is no easy move for any people to make and certainly not one that can be made quickly without creating problems. It has long been my contention that the assimilation process for peoples coming into this country will vary in accord with the degree of goodness of fit between the value orientations they brought with them and the dominant values of the society. When people have markedly different value preferences on all the orientations, the process will be slower and more fraught with difficulties than if there were agreement on some one or two. And the most difficult change of all is the radical shift to value positions that formerly had been the least favored of all.

All the Italian families [that we have interviewed as part of our study] are in process of movement away from typical Italian values to those of the dominant culture, but there are differences in both rate and kind of movement between the "sick" and "well" families. The most critical difference seems to be the order of change by orientation. In the "sick" families there has been, for one reason or another, a breakdown

----

[4]Erik H. Erikson, *Childhood and Society* (New York: W. W. Norton & Co., 1950).

of the Collateral *relational* ties, whereas in the "well" families these ties are still quite strong. It is one thing to try to change from a non-planning Present-Time and Being oriented position when one has the "cushion" of ramified family ties to support and sustain one in case of failures, but quite another thing when these are lacking. The pacing of change and the cognitive grasp of the difference between goals and the means of attaining them and the relation of means to goals are the other striking criteria by which the two kinds of families can be differentiated.

In the Italian families defined as "sick" the Collateral ties have been partially or wholly destroyed, and there is not as yet in any of them a sufficient understanding of an Individualistic relational orientation for them to operate successfully as "isolated nuclear" families. They are stranded and confused, virtually in a void as far as relations with others are concerned. They also all show small ability to instrument their plans and desires for the material things or other of the goals of middle-class culture which they have come to consider important goals. The well families, in contrast, have maintained quite good Collateral ties on both sides of the family—and relative both to goals set and the means of attaining them, they are far more "realistic."

All these families have problems, many of them very similar in origin, in nature, and in degree. It is the handling of them which varies so greatly. In the well families there is, in addition to the more realistic grasp of the relation of means to ends, a greater ability on the part of the parents to look problems in the face and communicate with each other about them. The parents in the sick families have poor communication with each other, and they characteristically deny that there are tensions between them or that they are in any way to blame for the problems they face. They project onto the outside world, but more important still they also have found a focus for projection within the family itself—a particular child.

Let me illustrate from two cases ever so briefly. In one of these—one where we have had little success in the treatment of the family—the father and mother have both had troubles with their extended families, and they feel that in no way can they count on the relatives to help them out; they also, partly because of these same relatives, are a "looked down upon" family in the community (largely Italian) in which they live. There is a great deal of friction between themselves which scarcely ever comes out into the open. In fact, one of the main reasons for the failure of therapy in this family was that, every time the therapist of the father or the mother came close to bringing to the fore the problems between them, there was a withdrawal on the part of one or both. The father in particular was extremely reluctant to co-operate if co-operation meant any discussion of himself or his relationships.

Teachers of their children, the doctors whom they sought out in great variety, employers, and neighbors whom they accused of spying upon them were frequent targets for their feelings of failure and frustration. But it was their first child, a little girl of ten years with a low level of intelligence, who was the main target for the projection of their problems. They constantly assigned to this child the implicit and informal roles of "the bad girl," "the girl who was and would always be a disgrace to them," "the child who was a cross to bear." The child is, indeed, a difficult case. Not only is her intelligence low, but she is the closest to being an atypical child of any.that we had in our sample. But one may, and we did, question how much of her most bizarre behavior and her lack of ability to perform in school were effects of the roles that both the father and mother have assigned to her. Certainly it is a fact that the parents have been (1) strongly resistant to facing the possibility that the main problems are in themselves rather than in this one child and (2) almost equally resistant to agreeing to anything that might really help the child. In other words, her aberrant behavior, which they certainly in some part induce, seems to be necessary for the maintenance of what family equilibrium does exist.

In another case, not dissimilar in general outline, we were more successful in treatment but only after a very long period of time. This family, too, was cut off from ties with the extended families of both father and mother, and there was an even greater feeling of isolation relative to the community in which they lived. Here the child singled out as a problem child upon whom many kinds of frustrations and anxieties could be projected was a little girl, the second of the family, who again was less bright than her siblings. But another factor in the focusing of attention upon this particular child was that after a long siege of rheumatic fever that she had had, her doctors, all middle-class Americans, had insisted that special attention be accorded her. She was to have a room to herself, a special kind of bed, and other attentions that did not fit in at all well with the Collateral patterning of Italian families. This special treatment increased resentment toward her and made her the better target for all kinds of tensions. And here again the informal and implicit roles assigned to her were that she was untrustworthy, irresponsible, and would always be a probable source of disgrace to the family in the wider community. The additional one was that she was demanding in a way "good" Italian children should not be.

Obviously, in these and all our other cases, the factor of value conflict is only one of many to be considered. But its importance becomes most apparent when one compares families that are so very similar in many ways but very different in the degree to which acculturation is a problem for family equilibrium.

The significance of the value factor is made even more obvious when the acculturation processes of different groups are compared. In the

Irish-American group, for example, one finds different problems because the shifts in value positions which the Irish have had to make, if and when they become assimilated, are different from those Italians must make.

But rather than give the details of this comparison, I wish to illustrate from the Irish-American case another use of the value-orientation theory in the analysis of family problems. This use is the prediction of the kinds of strains one is likely to find common in a system because of the particular combination of basic values adhered to in a culture and the further strains that are produced when acculturation occurs.

In our analysis of the culture of rural Irish, we were especially struck by the possibilities for much intracultural strain because of the juxtaposition in the total value system of a very strong first-order Lineal relational orientation[5] and a dominant human-nature orientation which is a more extreme version of the Evil but perfectible position than even that adhered to by New England Puritans. This particular combination of value orientations requires on the one hand a training of persons for dependent behavior and a low degree of individual responsibility, but on the other keeps them ever conscious of an evil nature which they *themselves* must control. The Yankee Puritan whose dominant relational orientation was Individualism was not caught in this dilemma of contradictions. Thus, we expected to find, fairly typically, in the Irish group strong denial and escape mechanisms. More concretely, we predicted that members of the group would commonly deny responsibility for happenings, including consequences of their acts, but that they also would have intensive guilt feelings. It was further predicted that escape patterns would be prevalent—most especially in cases where men in their occupational roles had been thrown too much and too soon into situations demanding much individual responsibility and quite independent action. Conversely, it was expected that there would be fewer instances of either of these defense mechanisms in cases where men had found employment in organizations, governmental or otherwise, which were quite Lineal in character. It was also expected that sexuality would be a source of great anxiety to this group.

On the whole, our findings have accorded well with our expectations. The prevalence of the denial and escape defense mechanisms has been striking indeed. Treatment of the "sick" Irish-American families has been greatly handicapped because issues and problems are so often and so strongly denied. Moreover, it has been our experience that it is difficult to keep Irish-American families in treatment.

---

[5]The best single source of information on the lineal *relational* structure of modern rural Ireland is Conrad M. Arensberg and Solon T. Kimball, *Family and Community in Ireland* (Cambridge, Mass.: Harvard University Press, 1940).

These few illustrations must serve to indicate how we have found the factor of basic values—value orientations—critical to the analysis of family relations.

12. Demographic correlates of group achievement: Contrasting patterns of Mexican-Americans and Japanese-Americans

PETER UHLENBERG

As increasing attention is focused upon the disadvantaged Mexican-American population in the Southwest, the recurring question of why some groups fail economically while others succeed becomes salient once again. One approach to answering this question, and currently the more popular, is to examine the American social structure to discover barriers to achievement by minorities. But clearly this approach yields only a partial answer, for some minorities (most noticeably Jews and Japanese-Americans) have achieved remarkable upward mobility in face of severe opposition from the larger society. Another approach to understanding the success or failure of a particular group is to investigate the internal social structure of that group itself. To the extent that the behavior of individuals in different groups varies in more than superficial ways, one must anticipate differences in levels of group achievement. Yet in studies of social stratification of minorities in the United States, the role of variations between groups in demographic behavior has been seriously neglected. This paper will indicate some demographic correlates of group achievement by focusing upon two minorities—Mexican-Americans and Japanese-Americans. The apposition of these two populations is especially revealing because, starting with quite similar positions after World War I, Japanese-Americans achieved rapid

Abridged and edited from Peter Uhlenberg, "Demographic correlates of group achievement: contrasting patterns of Mexican-Americans and Japanese-Americans," *Demography*, February 1972, 9:119–128. Copyright © 1972 by the Population Association of America. Reprinted by permission.

The author is Assistant Professor, Department of Sociology, University of North Carolina, Chapel Hill, North Carolina.

upward social mobility while Mexican-Americans experienced minimal mobility.

. . . . .

SIMILARITIES AND DIFFERENCES IN
SOCIAL EXPERIENCES

Compared to Mexicans, no other immigrant group to the United States has encountered more similar conditions than Japanese. The migration experience itself is a first area of parallel. Both groups arrived in large numbers only after 1900, both settled almost exclusively in California and the Southwest, both found initial employment primarily in agriculture, and both began at the bottom of the status hierarchy. Furthermore, both Mexican-Americans and Japanese-Americans encountered a variety of barriers to achievement in the United States, and neither developed political power at a national level. The potential problems associated with linguistic differences were greater for Japanese since differences between Japanese and English are greater than between Spanish and English. Schools, however, have offered Japanese children even less special attention than they have Spanish-speaking children. The greater physical distinctiveness of Japanese provides another potentially greater handicap.

Above all, experiences of prejudice and discrimination by the two groups must be compared because these are frequently alleged as sufficient explanations of the relative deprivation of Mexican-Americans (see Uhlenberg, 1971, pp. 36–72). A large amount of information has been assembled to document the existence of discrimination against Mexican-Americans in areas of housing, education, and employment, although in recent years discrimination has substantially receded (McWilliams, 1948; Grebler, 1970, pp. 585–88). However, the intensity of discrimination against Japanese-Americans during the first half of the twentieth century greatly exceeded that encountered by Mexican-Americans (Kitano, 1969; Thomas, 1946). In California in the early 1900's there were laws prohibiting intermarriage with Japanese and segregating oriental school children. Laws were passed making it impossible for Japanese immigrants to become naturalized citizens, and then legislation in California prohibited "aliens ineligible for citizenship" from owning agricultural land. Hostility toward Japanese-Americans resulted in the total exclusion of Japanese immigrants to the United States after 1924, and it was not until 1952 that token immigration quotas were again given to Japan.

The most extreme example of discrimination occurred in 1942 when all Japanese-Americans living on the West Coast were incarcerated in "relocation centers" merely on the ground that they were of Japanese descent. Over two-thirds of the 110,000 Japanese-Americans incarcerated were American citizens, having been born in the United States. The relocation camps, in which a majority of Japanese-Americans lived for over three years, were extremely austere with only communal dining and toilet facilities available for families (Yatsushiro, 1944). Large financial losses associated with the evacuation from homes and properties left the Japanese in a weak economic position following the war. Thus if one accepts the argument that discrimination by the larger society is sufficient to account for a minority's level of achievement, then he is forced to predict a very low socio-economic position for Japanese-Americans in 1960, one below that of Mexican-Americans.

Despite the obstacles encountered in American society, Japanese-Americans have been able to succeed educationally and economically, and now occupy a position in the status hierarchy substantially above that of Mexican-Americans. In fact, the educational achievement of Japanese-Americans exceeds that of the total white population. The exceptionally high educational attainment of Japanese-Americans compared to native whites and Mexican-Americans is shown in Table 1.

Table 1

Percent distribution by number of school years completed for Spanish surname, Japanese-American and native white males aged 25 to 44 years old, 1950

Years of school completed	Japanese-American	Native-white	Spanish surname
8 or fewer	11.3	32.3	58.1
9-11	11.7	21.8	17.9
12 or more	76.9	45.8	23.9
16 or more	12.8	9.5	3.8

Source: U.S. Bureau of the Census. Census of Population: 1960. Subject Reports. Educational Attainment. PC(2)-5B, Table 1 and 2; and Persons of Spanish Surname. PC(2)-1B, Table 3.

(Following the practice of the Census Bureau, the Mexican-American population is represented by the Spanish surname population living in the five Southwestern states. For a justification see Uhlenberg, 1971, pp. 212–218). Among males aged 25 to 34 in 1960, 82 percent of Japanese-Americans were high school graduates, compared to 57 percent of native whites and 26 percent of Mexican-Americans. More than five times as many Japanese-Americans as Mexican-Americans in this age category were college graduates.

We turn now to a comparison of the demographic patterns associated with the upwardly mobile Japanese-American and the relatively non-mobile Mexican-American populations. Three areas of behavior are examined: family size, family stability, and timing of family formation.

FAMILY SIZE

The differentiation between Mexican-Americans and Japanese-Americans on the family size variable can best be seen by comparing the percent of children reared in families of various sizes (see Table 2).

Table 2

Distribution of Spanish surname, Japanese-American and native white children born to women 40 to 49 years old in 1960 by children ever born to their mothers

Number of children ever born to mother	Number and percent of children					
	Spanish surname		Native white		Japanese-American	
	Children	Percent	Children	Percent	Children	Percent
1	16,360	2.8	1,660,106	7.4	3,803	6.1
2	43,658	7.4	4,851,342	21.7	15,288	24.4
3	58,029	9.8	4,891,809	21.9	18,966	30.3
4	67,144	11.3	3,686,168	16.5	12,584	20.1
5	60,445	10.2	2,403,755	10.8	4,970	7.9
6	65,628	11.1	1,571,016	7.0	3,978	6.3
7+	281,473	47.5	3,274,906	14.7	3,083	4.9
Total children	592,737	100.0	22,339,102	100.0	62,672	100.0

The census report combines Spanish surname women with 5 and 6 children. The distribution of these women according to whether they had 5 or 6 was assumed to be the same as for nonwhite women aged 40-44 in rural, non-farm areas (since their fertility schedule was very similar to Spanish surname women).
Source: Derived from U.S. Bureau of the Census. U.S. Census of Population: 1960. Subject Reports. Women by Number of Children Ever Born. Final Report PC(2)-3A, Tables 8 and 11.

One of every two Mexican-American children, in contrast to one of every seven native white and only one of 20 Japanese-American children, is born into a family in which the mother will bear at least seven children. Except for the negligible effect of infant and childhood mortality, the data in Table 2 accurately reflect the number of siblings children in the various groups have, siblings with whom they must share the attention, affection, and resources of parents. Only 29 percent of Mexican-American children are reared in families in which the mother has fewer than five children, while 67 percent of other white children and 81 percent of Japanese-American children live in such families. Japanese-Americans clearly have adopted a small family size pattern while the Mexican-American minority has retained a large family size pattern.

For Mexican-Americans, large families and low incomes combine to produce extensive overcrowding, as shown in Table 3. Nearly half of the Mexican-American youth, in contrast to less than one-tenth of all white children, are living in households with more than 1.5 persons per room. To visualize what a density of this order actually means, consider a family with seven members, which would be allowed four rooms. Assuming

Table 3

Percent Distribution of white and Spanish surname children by persons per room in their household, by age, 1960

Density and group	Age	
	0-5	6-17
Spanish surname		
1.00 or less	33.0	29.3
1.01-1.50	20.9	24.3
1.51 or more	46.1	46.3
Total	100.0	100.0
White*		
1.00 or less	67.0	71.1
1.01-1.50	23.5	20.3
1.51 or more	9.5	8.6
Total	100.0	100.0

*Total white population of the U.S.
Source: U.S. Bureau of the Census. U.S. Census of Population: 1960. Subject Reports. Persons by Family Characteristics. Final Report PC(2)-4B, Table 3; and calculations from the one-in-one-thousand sample from the 1960 Census.

a kitchen and living room, the seven individuals would have available only two bedrooms. Similarly a family of nine would be forced to share three bedrooms. Seven out of ten other white children live in households with a density of 1.0 or fewer persons per room, but only three out of ten Mexican-American children are in this advantaged category.

The data in Tables 2 and 3 refer to the entire Mexican-American population, and hence conceal important variations within the group. The pattern of large families applies to those with low levels of education and low incomes, but it does not characterize the segment of the Mexican-American minority that has achieved middle-class status and no longer closely identifies with the ethnic group. Among families in which both husband and wife have attended less than eight years of school and the husband earns less than $3000 per year (in 1959), women average 6.1 children each (calculated from the one-in-one-thousand sample from the 1960 census). In contrast, the average number of children per woman in families where both husband and wife are high school graduates and the husband earns over $5000 annually is only 2.0. The large family size for the group as a whole reflects the high concentration of Mexican-Americans in the lower income and education categories. One consequence of this gross differential in fertility by social class is to increase the proportion of children being reared in homes able to provide the fewest economic and educational advantages. For example, if there was no fertility difference by education of mothers, 20.0 percent of the children born to women aged 35 to 54 in 1960 would have high school educated mothers, instead of the 11.1 percent who do under existing circumstances.

FAMILY STABILITY

The extent of family instability for Japanese-Americans, Mexican-Americans, and other whites is presented in Table 4. The percent of ever-married women aged 45 to 64 still living with their first husbands gives an approximate indication of how many families survive intact through the childbearing stage. Only 57 percent of the Mexican-American females are seen to fall into this most stable marriage pattern. Using percent of females who are divorced, separated, or remarried as a measure of family disorganization, Japanese-Americans are seen to have greatest stability. About 15 percent of the Japanese-American females aged 45 to 64 are in these categories, compared to 20 percent of other whites, and 25 percent of Mexican-Americans.

Furthermore, it should be noted that a trend toward increasing instability is developing among Mexican-Americans. Most studies of Mexican-Americans have commented upon the stability of families in the

Table 4
Percent distribution of ever-married Spanish surname, Japanese-American, and other white women by marital status and age, 1960

Group and marital status	Age	
	35-44	45-64
SPANISH SURNAME		
Husband present:		
Married once	71.1	57.0
Married more than once	13.5	13.6
Widowed	3.9	17.8
Other*	11.5	11.6
Total	100.0	100.0
JAPANESE-AMERICAN		
Husband present:		
Married once	87.1	65.3
Married more than once	5.7	8.8
Widowed	1.9	20.1
Other*	5.2	5.8
Total	100.0	100.0
OTHER WHITES		
Husband present:		
Married once	78.0	65.3
Married more than once	12.3	12.2
Widowed	2.7	14.9
Other*	7.0	7.6
Total	100.0	100.0

*Divorced, separated, or husband absent.
Source: U.S. Bureau of the Census. U.S. Census of Population: 1960. Subject Reports. Persons of Spanish Surnames. Final Report PC(2)-1B, Table 7; Marital Status, Final Report PC(2)-4E, Table 1; and Non-white Population by Race. Final Report PC(2)-1C, Tables 19 and 21.

group. Sociologist John Burma for example writes that among Mexican-Americans, "family ties are usually strong and divorce and desertion are more rare than among Anglo families" (Burma, 1954, p. 84). This greater stability is clearly no longer the case, and a comparison of different generations reveals that Mexican-Americans born in the United States have less stable families than do the foreign-born. Among third generation Mexican-Americans in urban areas of California, for example, less than half of all first marriages are still intact for females aged 45 to 64, and 37 percent of the women are divorced, separated, or remarried. The very rapid growth of the urban Mexican-American population in California is contributing to the trend of increasing numbers of children in this minority being reared in broken homes.

FAMILY FORMATION

In the period of life from adolescence to young adulthood most individuals are forced to make several important decisions, including decisions about marriage and birth of children. As with the other variables examined, the Japanese-American population follows a very different pattern during this stage of the life cycle than does the Mexican-American population. To a much greater extent than the rest of the population, Japanese-Americans extend their period of education and delay their ages at marriage. In 1960, 65 percent of all Japanese-Americans aged 18 or 19 years old were enrolled in school, compared to 43 percent for all whites of this age, and twice as many Japanese as whites were enrolled at ages over 22. Comparing marital patterns, . . . the median age at which Japanese-Americans marry is three to four years older than that for members of the dominant society. Although they delay their marriages, nearly the same proportion of Japanese-Americans as whites eventually marry. Thus Japanese-Americans have developed a pattern which does not weaken the importance of the family, but delays age at which the new family is formed in order to permit individuals to obtain greater educational preparation.

Age at marriage for the total white population followed a downward trend after World War II and is currently very low for an industrialized country, but Mexican-Americans marry at even younger ages. Among those aged 25 to 34 in 1960, 28 percent of third generation Mexican-American females, compared to 17.5 percent of all white females, married when they were 17 years or younger, i.e., before the normal age for completion of high school. Two years later, before they were 20 years old, 52.9 percent of the Mexican-American females were married, compared to 10.0 percent of Japanese-Americans. Third generation Mexican-American males are following a similar pattern of early age at marriage, with 21 percent marrying while in their teens and 43 percent by age 21. Furthermore, childbearing tends to follow shortly after these relatively early marriages. Among third generation Mexican-American males aged 20 to 24 who are married, 77 percent have produced at least one child. A consequence of this pattern is to reduce to a minimum for Mexican-Americans the interval of time between leaving families in which they are reared and forming new families through marriage and procreation.

LINKING DEMOGRAPHIC BEHAVIOR
TO GROUP ACHIEVEMENT

This comparison of Mexican-Americans and Japanese-Americans leads to a conclusion that individuals in the two groups encounter extremely different demographic environments. Compared to Japanese-Americans, the Mexican-American population has a demographic system characterized by young ages at marriage, young ages at beginning of childbearing, high rates of reproduction, and high rates of marital instability. Another striking difference between these groups was noted earlier: the much greater educational and economic achievement of Japanese-Americans. Existing research on determinants of individual achievement provides clues related to why the above demographic variables are correlated with levels of group achievement.

A group's demographic system most strongly affects social behavior through the institution of the family. Very different family milieus are related to different demographic systems, and these differences in family patterns have important consequences for individual members of the groups. In particular, family size and family stability significantly influence future achievement of children, and pattern of family formation affects future achievement possibilities of adolescents.

Family size affects the ability of children to achieve through its effect upon possible investment per child in the family and through its effect upon the socialization experience. At any level of family income, an increase in family size reduces per capita income. Since a high level of capitalization, particularly in education, is required to prepare young people for future positions that will be highly rewarding, the greater resources available to children in small families give them a decided advantage over children from large ones. For groups with most of their families in low income categories, such as both Mexican-Americans and Japanese-Americans in the early 1900's, a pattern of large family size restricts the opportunities of the maturing generation to acquire the requisite skills for upward social mobility. The socialization experience of a child is also affected by the size of his family, because the more siblings present in the family the less opportunity each has for parent-child interaction. A lack of parental stimulation appears to diminish achievement motivation in children, and this lower achievement motivation results in lower educational and occupational attainment. Bernard Rosen, among others studying this relationship, has found the effect of family size to be very important. In tests of achievement motivation, he found that children from small families scored, on average, twice as high as those from large families (Rosen, 1961). A recent study of the relationship between family structure and college attendance for young persons concluded:

> Sibship size is an important factor related to educational chances, those from large families being substantially less likely to have attended college than those from smaller families (Adams, 1968, p. 238).

Another large study found a similar relationship.

> The number of children of the head is a major factor influencing the level of education expected for children ... Other things being equal, girls and boys in families with one or two children are expected to obtain a substantially higher level of education than those who are members of families having five or more children (David, 1961, p. 68).

Thus large families are seen to impede achievement of children both by restricting opportunities for obtaining skills and by reducing motivation to achieve.

Among those with low income, large families additionally retard the progress of children by producing crowded home environments. A careful study investigating effects of housing upon physical and mental health found that morbidity among children is strongly influenced by housing conditions, and that independent of other factors, school adjustment and educational advancement by children are positively associated with better housing (Wilner, 1962). Therefore, by producing deleterious physical environments for young people, large families further contribute to the low achievement of many children.

Stability of the family in which a child is reared is another important variable affecting his future life chances. While precise measures of the consequence of family stability are lacking, there is little doubt that, other things being equal, children reared in stable home environments have advantages over those from broken homes (see Willie, 1967; Landis, 1960). In their recent study of occupational success Duncan and Duncan conclude, "The indication that an intact-family background facilitates occupational success is quite compelling." (Duncan and Duncan, 1969; p. 285). Reasons for the detrimental consequences for children of broken homes can be found both in the economic consequences and the socialization experiences associated with family instability. Particularly among low income families, the absence of a male head in the household leaves family members in a precarious economic position. Negative consequences accruing from socialization of children in homes lacking a father further add to the importance of this variable (Herzog, 1968). Thus research has sufficiently established the deleterious consequences for children resulting from disorganized families, so that one can predict that high rates of marital instability will adversely affect the achievement level of a group.

The final variable affecting achievement examined here relates to decisions regarding the formation of new families through marriage and birth of children. To maximize potential for future advances an individual can postpone entrance into marriage and parenthood until after he has acquired an extended education and become established in an occupation. Particularly for males who lack access to resources which permit them to continue preparation for employment after marriage, early assumption of the responsibilities associated with being head of a family greatly restricts opportunities for future advances. For females early marriage and motherhood generally limit opportunities for education at an advanced level, work outside of the home, and engagement in other non-familial activities which might produce lasting interests outside the family. For both males and females, early marriage and early childbearing reduce opportunities to acquire a different approach to childbearing than the one they experienced as children.

In summary, family size, family stability, and timing of family formation are all seen to influence social behavior related to achievement. While members of a group do not consciously develop a particular demographic system, their aggregated behavior on these variables does result in sharp differentiation between groups. Thus there exists a reason to anticipate some correlation between a group's overall demographic behavior and its relative level of achievement in society.

CONCLUSION

The above analysis of contrasting demographic patterns of Mexican-Americans and Japanese-Americans demonstrates the significance that alternative demographic systems have for these two populations. The Japanese-American minority has adopted a pattern that is consistent with upward social mobility for its members, while the demographic behavior of Mexican-Americans tends to obstruct their upward mobility. To continue the study of demographic correlates of group achievement it would be valuable to examine in a similar way the patterns characteristic of other American minorities (e.g., Jews, Puerto Ricans, Negroes, Italians, Greeks, etc.). If a consistent and strong relationship between demographic behavior and achievement level is established, it would seem useful to further relate this topic to theory on the social stratification of minorities.

REFERENCES

Adams, Bert N., and Meiden, Miles T. Economics, family structure, and college attendance. *American Journal of Sociology*, 1968, 74:230–239.

Burma, John H. *Spanish-Speaking Groups in the United States*, Durham, N. C.: Duke University Press, 1954.

Clausen, John A. Family Size and Birth Order as Influences upon Socialization and Personality: Bibliography and Abstracts. Committee on Socialization and Social Structure, Social Science Research Council, 1965.

David, Martin, *et al*. Educational Achievement—Its Causes and Effects. Ann Arbor: Survey Research Center, Monograph No. 23, 1961.

Davis, Kingsley. *Human Society*. New York: Macmillan Press, 1949.

Duncan, Beverly, and Duncan, Otis Dudley. Family stability and occupational success. *Social Problems*, 1969, 16:273–285.

Grebler, Leo, Moore, Joan W. and Guzman, Ralph C. *Mexican-American People*. New York: The Free Press, 1970.

Herzog, Elizabeth, and Sudia, Cecelia E. Fatherless homes: A review of research. *Children*, 1968, 15:177–182.

Kitano, Harry. *Japanese-Americans*. Englewood Cliffs, N.J.: Prentice-Hall, Inc., 1969.

Landis, Judson T. The trauma of children when parents divorce. *Marriage and Family Living*, 1960, 22:7–13.

McWilliams, Carey. *North from Mexico*. Philadelphia: J. B. Lippincott Company, 1948.

Moynihan, Daniel Patrick. Employment, income, and the ordeal of the Negro family. *Daedalus*, 1965, 94:745–770.

Rosen, Bernard C. Family structure and achievement motivation. *American Sociological Review*, 1961, 26:574–585.

Thomas, Dorothy Swaine, and R. Nishimoto. *The Spoilage*. Berkeley: The University of California Press, 1946.

Uhlenberg, Peter. Demography of Relative Deprivation: An Analysis of Mexican-Americans. Unpublished Ph.D. dissertation, University of California, Berkeley, 1971.

Willie, Charles V. The relative contribution of family status and economic status to juvenile delinquency. *Social Problems*, 1967, 14:326–335.

Wilner, Daniel M., *et al*. *The Housing Environment and Family Life*. Baltimore: The Johns Hopkins Press, 1962.

Yatsushiro, Tosio, *et al*. The Japanese-American looks at resettlement. *Public Opinion Quarterly*, 1944, 8:188–201.

13. In defense of the Jewish mother

ZENA SMITH BLAU

A widespread belief in America shared by Jews as well as non-Jews, is that Jews are "smart but neurotic." The Jew's intellectual aptitudes are usually attributed to the cultural values transmitted by Jewish fathers for whom learning and study were traditionally a religious obligation. As for the neurosis, that of course is blamed on the Jewish mother.

That Jews are "smart" is confirmed by the available empirical evidence. Whatever indices have been employed to measure achievement—I.Q. scores, school grades, years of schooling, occupational level, and social mobility—Jews, on the average, exhibit higher levels of performance than the non-Jews to whom they have been compared.[1] But the proposition that neurosis is significantly more widespread among Jews than among non-Jews is not supported by the admittedly limited empirical studies of the subject. A study comparing the prevalence of emotional disorder among Protestants, Catholics, and Jews—based on a sample of 1660 respondents in midtown Manhattan [2]—found that neurotic symptoms were common in all three groups: respondents rated as "well" constituted only 20.2% of Protestants tested, 17.4% of the Catholics, and 14.5% of the Jews. And when the authors classified people according to the *severity* of their symptoms and the degree to which these interfered with their ability to carry on normal activities, they discovered that *impairing* forms of emotional disorder were significantly lower among Jews (17.2%) than among either Protestants (23.5%) or Catholics (24.7%). Further, Jews were concentrated in the mental health category of "mild symptom formation," exhibiting far fewer cases of incapacitating disorder than Protestants and Catholics. Interestingly,

Reprinted from Zena Smith Blau, "In defense of the Jewish mother," *Midstream,* February 1967. Copyright © 1967 by Midstream. Reprinted by permission.

The author is Associate Professor of Sociology, Northwestern University, Evanston, Illinois.

[1]See, for example, Gerald S. Lesser, Gordon Fifer and Donald Clark, "Mental abilities of children from different social-class and cultural groups," *Monographs of the Society For Research in Child Development,* 1965, 30(4):82–83; also, Fred L. Strodtbeck, "Family interaction, values and achievement," in David McClelland and Associates, *Talent and Society* (Princeton, N.J.: D. Van Nostrand Co., Inc., 1958), pp. 135–94; and, Ben B. Seligman and Aaron Antonovsky, "Some aspects of Jewish demography," and S. Joseph Fauman, "Occupational selection among Detroit Jews," in Marshall Sklare (ed.), *The Jews: Social Patterns of an American Group* (Glencoe, Ill.: Free Press, 1958), pp. 83–6 and pp. 119–137.

[2]Leo Srole, Thomas Langner *et al., Mental Health in the Metropolis* (New York: McGraw-Hill Book Co., 1962), Vol. 1, pp. 305–6. This study is of special interest because it sampled a *general* population, instead of only psychiatric patients as previous studies had done, and its findings are therefore unaffected by the fact that some groups, like the Jews, are more favorably disposed to psychiatry than others and more readily seek treatment even for problems of a relatively mild sort.

the Jewish immunity from psychological impairment was most pronounced among respondents from working-class families, where mental illness is generally most prevalent.

If Jewish mothers are to be blamed for their children's psychological problems, should they not also receive some credit for their relative strengths? Indeed this article will suggest that the child-rearing practices of immigrant Jewish mothers contributed significantly to the remarkable educational and occupational attainments of second generation Jews, and could provide an important model for scientific study and emulation.

I feel that I can speak with some authority on the subject of the Yiddishe Mameh, not only as a sociologist concerned with the comparative study of family structures and patterns of socialization, but also as a second generation Jew, who has known many Yiddishe Mamehs—my own mother, her friends, and the mothers of my friends—and who remembers well the social context of Jewish immigrant life in which my generation was raised. I do not suggest, of course, that all Jewish immigrant women exhibited identical maternal behavior, but there can be little question that the constellation of maternal traits commonly referred to as "the Yiddishe Mameh" was the modal maternal pattern among Jewish immigrants from Eastern Europe and that it was different from the typical maternal behavior found among non-Jews in America.[3]

Yiddishe Mamehs were active, responsible, stable, expressive and verbal women for whom *naches fun die kinder* represented the highest form of self-fulfillment and achievement for a woman. They perceived the child as a fragile creature whose body and spirit needed to be carefully and assiduously nurtured and protected not only in infancy but throughout childhood and even adolescence. They went to inordinate trouble and expense to provide their children with the "best and freshest" food, the best medical care, the warmest clothing, at considerable sacrifice of other needs and wants. That their high standards of child care were effective is attested to by the fact that infant and child mortality rates were lower among Jews than in the rest of the American population during the earlier decades of this century, despite the fact that the majority of Jewish immigrants were in the working class where the mortality risks are greatest.

Strong bonds of love and mutual dependency between mother and child are traditional among Jews. For most of their history they have occupied the position of a beleaguered minority exposed to hostility, as well as to the pressure to abandon their faith and take up the ways of the

---

[3]A striking similarity exists between the mode of maternal behavior of the Yiddishe Mameh and that found among women in the new middle class in contemporary Japan, who, like the Jews, are strongly committed to high educational attainment for their children. (Ezra Vogel, *Japan's New Middle Class* [Berkeley: University of California Press, 1963].)

majority. Various practices evolved among diaspora Jews to strengthen and fortify the child to cope with these pressures. The responsibility for establishing the bulwark of this fortification system was assigned to the mother, and the task began at birth of building a healthy body, a strong ego and a strong primary identification with the mother which was perceived as the essential *motivating* force for learning the ways of Jews and for adhering to them, even under adverse conditions.

In America, Yiddishe Mamehs appeared far more permissive, indulgent and self-sacrificing than the typical Anglo-Saxon mother, at least in the years prior to the nineteen-forties. For example, they were a good deal more tolerant of whining and crying, and of dependency behavior generally. They exerted little pressure on their children to control explosions of feeling and temper, and demanded only that they refrain from engaging in physical forms of aggression—*nit mit die hendt,* was a common admonishment in the Jewish home. Toward their fathers and other grown-ups Jewish children were expected to behave with respect, but toward their mothers they were allowed considerably more leeway to express negative as well as positive feelings. Yiddishe Mamehs erected no status distance between themselves and their children. They did not stand on ceremony; they did not protect their pride or their self-respect. With no other human being did the Jewish child develop as close, as trusting, as free and fearless a relationship as with his mother, and therein lay the secret of her power to gain his compliance ultimately in those areas of behavior in which she chose to exert pressure during the entire period of maturation.

Identification with the mother became the cornerstone of the entire socialization process, and Yiddishe Mamehs understood that once it was firmly established, but not before, it became possible to gain the *voluntary* compliance of their children to those basic social norms to which they as Jews were committed, and to which they were determined their children should also permanently adhere, whatever later pressures they might encounter to deny or violate them. That Jews as a rule retain their Jewish identity, and have done so over the centuries, however ambivalently, is largely due, although not entirely, of course, to the strength of the primary identification with the Yiddishe Mameh, and to the profound fear of the guilt that denial of her would engender. The well-known ambivalence of the Jew toward his mother, then, is part and parcel of his ambivalence about remaining a Jew.

Yiddishe Mamehs seemed singularly unconcerned with "discipline" and "independence training." They allowed their children a greater degree of liberty at home than was customary among Gentiles, and readily acknowledged that their children were *zelosen,* that is, pampered, demanding, spoiled, not well-behaved the way Gentile children seemed to be in the presence of their mothers. The Anglo-Saxon code of stoic endurance and suppressed emotion was alien to the Eastern European

Jew. Of course, Yiddishe Mamehs had their boiling point, which varied a good deal depending upon their individual temperament, but generally they preferred controlling their children *mit guten* that is, by explanation, reasoning, distraction, and admonishment. As a rule, they were naggers or screamers rather than disciplinarians. They gained compliance by entreaties repeated so often that finally the child would comply voluntarily, albeit wearily, to their requests. The Yiddishe Mameh avoided methods of control that aroused fear of herself in the child, and regarded such methods as morally wrong as well as inexpedient for cultivating inner controls in her children.

Not that Yiddishe Mamehs endured all misbehavior with perfect equanimity. They were volatile, expressive women, who, if other methods of control failed, would flare up, scream at their children, and occasionally slap them, usually taking care to avoid the region of face and head. But they didn't nurse their anger. The outbursts quickly subsided, the child was embraced and comforted, and peace was restored. Such scenes were commonplace in Jewish homes, and added to the liveliness of the atmosphere.

Jewish fathers as a rule were more controlled and reserved in their dealing with their children, but they were usually not any more harsh with them. However, their silence when they became angry with a child created more discomfort and readier compliance than the mother's outburst. But in both cases it was the discomfort—anxiety and guilt—that parental disapproval induced rather than fear of coercion that led Jewish children at a relatively tender age to internalize those norms of behavior which are of paramount importance to Jews.

But if the Yiddishe Mameh was permissive with respect to the acting out of willfulness, anger, tension, fearfulness in children—appreciating, perhaps, the cathartic uses of such behavior—she was not at all permissive on the question of moral training.

Teaching of the basic precepts of Judaism began virtually in infancy for Jewish children whether they were brought up in religious or in secular homes. The kind of appeal that Yiddishe Mamehs employed to motivate their children to eat, for example, was often couched in normative terms. They didn't simply impress on their children that eating was an act of self-interest—that by doing so they would grow up big and strong —but they also invested this mundane activity with moral significance and transformed it into an act of altruism by urging the child to eat *for others*—for mama, for poppa, for other members of the family, and inevitably, the appeal was made to eat for "the poor, starving children in Europe." Similarly, as their children grew older Mameh represented learning as not only being in the child's own self-interest but also as a means to fulfill his obligations to his parents, to his people, and to humanity.

For all their warmth and indulgence Yiddishe Mamehs were

demanding, determined women who spared neither themselves nor their husbands and children. Their standards and expectations were extremely high, and they insisted on "the best" whether they were shopping for food or selecting a doctor. If you paid them a compliment on the excellence of their gefilte fish or chopped liver they would protest, for *they* could always find something wrong that a less discerning person would, of course, miss. Their ambition for the future achievements of their children was anything but modest. When her son began to make the first feeble sounds on his violin a Yiddishe Mameh already envisioned another Elman or Heifetz. If he showed scientific proficiency she foresaw another Einstein. At any signs of flagging effort or undue interest in activities that might divert their children from serious pursuits, Jewish mothers would inquire with withering contempt, "So what you want? To be a nothing?" In public, however, Jewish women shamelessly bragged about the achievements of their children, and took enormous pride in them.

The scholastic and occupational achievements of their children were, in fact, a major area of status competition among Jewish immigrant women, and there was no social activity that they carried on with more liveliness and zest than bragging about their children to each other. Even relatively diffident, quiet, modest women felt constrained to engage in this pattern of bragging: *Berimen sich mit die kinder.* To say nothing about the accomplishments of their own children when others did so was tantamount to admitting publicly that there was nothing extraordinary about them, which to a Yiddishe Mameh was unthinkable. This ubiquitous social pattern served two important functions in the Jewish immigrant community. First it was a highly effective mechanism for diffusing information and knowledge about paths of achievement and mobility open to Jewish youth. Immigrants had little knowledge initially about the American occupational structure and even those men who possessed extensive religious learning did not, as a rule, have the secular education necessary to enter professional and managerial positions. Fathers, therefore, could not draw on their own experience to prepare their children for occupational ascent. In this kind of a context the gossip that Jewish mothers exchanged about the educational achievements and career plans of their children became an important informational resource in the Jewish immigrant community. The mothers with older children transmitted information about career lines to the mothers with younger children, who, in turn, relayed it to their husbands and children. Every distinction that a Jewish child earned, every step that he traversed in his educational career, every career decision, and every advancement was duly reported by his mother to her circle of friends and acquaintances, and she, in turn, brought back their reports to her own family.

This vast information exchange, operated primarily by mothers in the

Jewish immigrant community, not only bolstered parental ambitions and reinforced the pressure on their children to strive for high educational and occupational goals, but also served to disseminate concrete and realistic knowledge among both generations concerning the barriers, the costs, and the sacrifices involved in the achievement of these lofty goals. The triumphant accounts circulated by proud mothers of the rewards won by their sons through long, arduous educational preparation even in the face of widespread anti-Semitism, encouraged the spread of optimism tempered by realism among the Jewish masses. A Jew, parents would repeatedly remind their children, had to be twice as qualified as a Gentile in order to achieve the same rewards, and it was this kind of hard-headed realism that led them to stress educational attainment and excellence so heavily, and not simply their respect for learning.

Jewish immigrants were no better off economically when they settled in America than other immigrants; they lived in the same squalid neighborhoods; their children attended the same schools and learned from the same teachers but, as a rule, they exhibited a greater aptitude for learning and a greater will to learn than non-Jewish children. Learning, of course, has traditionally commanded respect even among the Jewish masses who, as a rule, had only a meagre amount of secular or religious education. Every indication of intellectual curiosity and verbal precocity in their children was received with pleasure and delight by Jewish parents and long before their formal schooling began Jewish youngsters understood that there was no more effective way to win approval and praise from adults. Even an impudent question or a naughty remark, if clever, was received with amused tolerance by parents and proudly relayed to friends and relatives as evidence of *chochma,* which is the Hebrew word for wisdom, but also is used colloquially to denote brightness, cleverness or wit.

Another stimulus to intellectual aptitude was the talkativeness of the Jewish home. It is now recognized that exposure to this factor in their early formative years increases the learning readiness of children, and it has long been known that verbal skill is an important component of I.Q. and achievement test performance. That Yiddishe Mamehs, in particular, were talkative, any Jewish male will ruefully confirm, but it is not generally recognized that this notorious attribute of theirs gave their children a head start in learning. Whatever Yiddishe Mamehs did for their children—and they did a great deal—was accompained by a flow of language, consisting of rich, colorful, expressive words and phrases. Their vocabulary of endearments alone could fill a modest sized paperback, but they also had a superb store of admonishments, curses, imprecations, explanations, songs and folksayings that they effortlessly invoked as they went about ministering to the needs of their children and their husbands. The freedom that they exhibited with the spoken word invited a similar response from their children and it carried over into school despite the fact that Yiddish, and not English, was their mother tongue. This helps account for the fact that learning aptitude was demonstrated not only by Jewish children whose fathers had extensive religious learning but also by those from homes where learning and cultivation were largely absent.

The determined struggle of Jewish mothers to delay the emotional emancipation of their children is well-known and often criticized but it was nevertheless a significant factor in the high educational attainment of second generation Jews in America. It is to their credit, I think, that they recognized that the basic conditions required to fashion a talmudic scholar are very much the same as those needed to achieve any other career requiring a high order of intellectual skill. In both cases, a prolonged period of time and arduous work must be spent in acquiring a complex body of knowledge, during which time the child must be provided encouragement and emotional support as well as protection from outside influence which might lure him into abandoning long-run plans for more immediate pleasures and rewards. Yiddishe Mamehs achieved this by denying the legitimacy of their children's declarations of independence. *Mainst as du bist shoin a ganzer mensch* (You only think you are a responsible human being), was their stock retort to youthful emancipation proclamations. They employed every stratagem to remain as indispensable to their children in later childhood and adolescence as they had been earlier in life. The concept of early independence training was foreign to their thinking. According to their view a child was a child whether he was five or fifteen and required much the same order of care, devotion and protection in adolescence as in childhood. With respect to learning and intellectual matters generally they encouraged the development of self-reliance and autonomy, but they were reluctant to grant their children other forms of independence or to impose any serious responsibility on them until they had completed their education and were ready to assume the obligations of marriage and a career.

A signal of their readiness to relinquish control was the application of pressure on their sons to find "a nice Jewish girl" and marry her. But until they saw their mission safely accomplished they doggedly resisted their children's perennial attempts to assert their independence. My generation learned to value independence not by being pressured to become self-reliant but by struggling against these formidable adversaries to loosen the bonds that tied us to them. We lost a good many skirmishes with our mothers, but we ultimately won the war, just as they intended.[4]

---

[4]A commonplace criticism of Jewish mothers is that they were overprotective, and overprotection, many people believe, has adverse effects on children, but the little

Perhaps further motivating the sustained protectiveness of Yiddishe Mamehs and their determination to delay the emotional emancipation of their children was their fear that the children would fall prey to the social influence of Gentile friends, particularly those from poor, immigrant families with rural origins in which parents did not value education. Non-Jewish immigrants generally wanted their children to grow up quickly, to get out and earn a living so that they might help relieve the family burden of poverty. In this setting, Jewish parents did not encourage their children to seek the companionship of these other children, preferring that their children pursue solitary pastimes at home rather than have the freedom of the streets.

There is some grim humor in the fact that these efforts by Jewish mothers to insulate their children from bad influences were aided and reinforced by the anti-Semitism that was so widespread in those days in Gentile society. The hostility of Gentiles and exclusion from their fun and games led Jewish youth, either as a matter of preference or because they had no other option, to seek the fellowship of other Jews, with whom they could feel at ease not only because they were Jews but because they shared the same aspirations, the same values and interests, and the same need to submerge the consciousness of the social rejection that each individually had experienced at the hands of the Gentiles. If their "clannishness" violated the democratic ideal it also operated to sustain and reinforce their mother's influence, which is to say their Jewish identification and commitment to learning. In alliance with the right friends, the Jewish mother could make successes, and Jews, of her children.

The unquestionable success of the Jewish mother in educating her children and immunizing them from severe emotional disorders warrants serious study by those interested in the way maternal strategies affect intellectual achievement. It is one thing for a parent to stress the importance of education as the means of escaping poverty; it is quite another, as the Jewish mother knew, to implement these objectives. Most lower class parents who stress the value of education (one thinks of many Negro parents today) must contend with the fact that their children's friends and associates undervalue education, so that a parent who (a) values education and (b) encourages early independence (as most lower

---

empirical research that exists suggests that just the opposite may be the case. David Levy's well-known study, for example, of twenty "over-protected" children first seen at about the age of ten and followed up in late adolescence (*Maternal Overprotection*, New York: Columbia University Press, 1943) reports that they were better than average in their pattern of physical growth, their freedom from accidents, serious illness, eneuresis, and in their heterosexual development, classroom adjustment and scholastic ability, and that, almost without exception, they outgrew the behavior problems—acting out at home, eating problems, and difficulties in forming friendships—they had exhibited in childhood.

class families do) is caught up in contradictory strategies. Children trained to be independent at an early age only become independent of parental influence and more dependent upon their peers.

Middle class families too could learn from the Jewish example. The trend here is toward more permissive, more love-oriented strategies of socialization, especially in the areas of weaning, toilet training, and sex behavior, but at the same time many parents fear that permissiveness will breed dependency and that dependency will hinder successful "adjustment." The child is pressured into doing things for himself and *also* "getting along" with other children. Thus a policy of encouraged early independence results in excessive dependence upon the peer group. This is one of the roots of conformism, the "other-directedness" so often observed in American character.

In the lower classes the tendency to encourage independence almost from birth is often a matter of economic necessity; in the middle-class it is more a matter of ideology. According to this view the prototype of the healthy, wholesome, normal child is one who is happy, extroverted, free of tension, sociable, athletic, and popular. Parents view with amused tolerance their children's preoccupation with keeping abreast of "the other kids" and their conformity to every fatuous fad of teenage culture. They are reluctant to impose limitations on their children's participation in these social rituals for fear that doing so might interfere with their social adjustment and their happiness. By the time their children reach adolescence and are confronted with decisions concerning school, career and marriage, many middle class parents discover that in their haste to establish early independence and good social adjustment they have abdicated to the culture of the young the power that was rightfully theirs. Mediocrity and conformism often ensue.[5]

There are no independent children—except autistic ones, perhaps—but the child whose dependency needs are met in the *home* has less need to turn to his *peers* for protection and emotional support. And just because he needs his mother's approval, the young child will work harder to develop the skills *she* values and be more resistant to the influence of "the other kids." By the time he matures he will have internalized the motivation and goals that make autonomy and excellence possible. The cultivation of this kind of autonomy calls for a strategy of socialization not greatly different, I suspect, from that of the Jewish Mother.[6]

---

[5]A number of studies indicate that high scholastic achievers exhibit less need for social affiliation and lower conformity to peer group standards than less successful students. (David E. Lavin, *The Prediction of Academic Performance* [New York; Russell Sage Foundation, 1965] pp. 64–121.)

[6]Skepticism about the efficacy of independence training seems to be growing among behavioral scientists as the result of recent research. For example, Sears,

14. The treatment of Negro families in American scholarship

ANDREW BILLINGSLEY

. . . . .

FAMILY STUDIES

It would seem most logical that studies of the American family include some reference to Negro family life. However, a recent antholo- gy containing fifty-two family studies has only one which treats the Negro family, and that one is Frazier's, written in 1939. It is not simply that only one article is devoted exclusively to Negro families; one reads all the other articles in vain (some of which are not bound by ethnic focus) looking for any reference to Negro families as part of the general discussion of American family patterns.[1]

An equally extensive, highly respected, and widely used compendium of case studies in family law has only one paper devoted to Negro fami- lies, and that one is focused almost exclusively on the problem of illegiti- macy.[2] These two volumes are unusual in giving even that amount of at- tention to Negro families. Two tendencies, then, are current in studies of American families. The first, and most general, is to ignore Negro fami- lies altogether. The second is to consider them only insofar as they may be conceived as a social problem. In a symposium on The Negro Family at the University of California at Berkeley a few years ago, after a na- tionally known sociologist referred repeatedly to the "problem of the Negro family," a Negro wife and mother rose and took him to task.

Maccoby and Levin, *Patterns of Child Rearing* (Evanston, Ill.: Row, Peterson, 1957) report that the more negatively mothers responded to dependency behavior in their five and six year old children, the more dependent they were likely to be; on the other hand, when mothers exhibited a sympathetic attitude or responded positively to dependency demands, dependency did *not* increase. Rosen and D'Andrade ("The psychosocial origins of achievement motivation," *Sociometry*, 1959, 22:185–218), report experimental evidence that high achievement motivation in boys is positively related to maternal warmth and pressure for high achievement but *negatively* related to independence training.

Abridged and edited from Andrew Billingsley, *Black Families in White America*, pp. 197–207, © 1968. Reprinted by permission of Prentice-Hall, Inc., Englewood Cliffs, New Jersey.

The author is Vice President for Academic Affairs, Howard University, Washing- ton, D.C.

[1]Norman W. Bell and Ezra F. Vogel (eds.), *A Modern Introduction to the Family* (New York: The Free Press, 1960).

[2]Caleb Foote, Robert J. Levy, and Frank E. A. Sander, *Case Studies and Materi- als on Family Law* (Boston: Little, Brown and Company, 1966).

"Why do you always consider us a problem?" she demanded. "I don't consider myself a problem." The sociologist was undaunted. He didn't know why she needed to be so defensive. Thus, despite the fact that the vast majority of Negro families are stable, conforming, and achieving, and cause no problems to anybody, the tendency to view them in negative terms persists. The Negro historian Benjamin Quarles recently observed that "When we pick up a social science book, we look in the index under 'Negro,' it will read, 'see Slavery,' 'see Crime,' 'see Juvenile Delinquency,' perhaps 'see Commission on Civil Disorders'; perhaps see anything except the Negro. So when we try to get a perspective on the Negro, we get a distorted perspective."[3]

Perhaps the greatest symbol of this kind of distortion in recent years is the widely read and even more widely discussed Moynihan Report. Moynihan and his staff examined the 1960 national census data and found that nearly a quarter of all Negro families were headed by females, and that nearly a quarter of all Negro babies that year were born out of wedlock. These are facts which Negroes, social workers, and students of the Negro family have been aware of and concerned about for some time. These statistics alarmed Mr. Moynihan. He concluded, quite incorrectly, that the Negro family in this country is falling apart and failing to prepare Negro children to make their way in the world. According to this view, the Negro community is being destroyed at least as much by its own family structure as by the indifferent and often hostile society around it. While his own data showed quite the contrary, Moynihan concluded that "At the heart of the deterioration of the fabric of Negro society is the deterioration of the Negro family. It is the fundamental source of the weakness of the Negro community at the present time."[4]

Because the 25 per cent of Negro families headed by females was so much higher than the proportion of white families headed by females, Moynihan paid very little attention to the fact that 75 per cent of Negro families met his criteria of stability. There are a number of methodological and substantive problems with the Moynihan report.[5] A major distortion was his singling out instability in the Negro family as the causal factor for the difficulties Negroes face in the white society. It is quite the other way round. But coming just at the time the nation was trying to find a single cause of the Watts riots, Moynihan's thesis struck

[3]Benjamin Quarles, *Jet Magazine,* December 28, 1967, 33(12):32.

[4]Daniel P. Moynihan, *The Negro Family: The Case for National Action* (Washington, D.C.: U. S. Department of Labor, Office of Planning and Research, March 1965), p. 1.

[5]Lee Rainwater and William L. Yancey, *The Moynihan Report and the Politics of Controversy* (Cambridge, Mass.: The M.I.T. Press, 1967).

a responsive chord in the collective American breast. ". . . At the center of the tangle of pathology," he concluded,

> is the weakness of the family structure. Once or twice removed, it will be found to be the principal source of most of the aberrant, inadequate, or antisocial behavior that did not establish, but now serves to perpetuate, the cycle of poverty and deprivation.

He could come to such faulty and inverse conclusions in part because he had no theoretical framework to guide him in the analysis of his statistical data, and in part because his data were limited.

Another serious shortcoming of the whole report was the tendency, common among liberal social scientists, to compare Negroes with whites on standardized objective measures which have been demonstrated to have meaning only in the white, European subculture. Many statistical studies which compare Negroes and whites fall into the almost inevitable position of characterizing the Negro group as deviant. If all a study can describe about Negro family life is what it simultaneously describes about white families, it cannot tell us very much about Negro family life. Moynihan compounded this error, however, by his failure to take into account two very important aspects of the Negro experience: social class and social caste.

. . . . .

But those very social scientists who insist that Moynihan's only sin was that he ignored social class are themselves guilty of ignoring even more powerful definers of the conditions facing Negro families in this country. Negro family life in America is circumscribed by a complex set of social conditions which shape the family in various ways. The Moynihan report is only a more recent and popular example of studies which do not take cognizance of these complexities. For now, however, the question is, how did American scholarship come to provide such a distorted perspective on Negro family life? Reference to the historical development of American family studies provides at least part of the answer.

Family sociology in America was born in the late nineteenth century when social Darwinism held sway.[6] During this period the focus was not on contemporary family life at all, but on earlier more primitive forms. The underlying assumption was that contemporary European family forms represented a natural evolution and had reached a certain stage of perfection. The idea was to search among primitive peoples for the earlier forms of family life, so that the evolutionary process could be traced and the sources of such perfection established. Scholars argued about

---

[6]Bell and Vogel, *A Modern Introduction to the Family, op. cit.,* pp. 3–5.

whether original family relationships were monogamous or polygamous, and found evidence for both in historical documents and oral traditions. They were concerned with whether earlier forms of family structure had been essentially matriarchal or patriarchal, and again found evidence for both.

However vigorously scholars pursued the study of the natural evolution of the family, and however vehemently they argued among themselves, it is strikingly clear that there was no room in such scholarship for concern with Negro family life. For in the United States in the latter part of the nineteenth century, the Negro family had no recognized institutional existence. Freshly released from slavery, the Negro people were struggling to find a place in the wider society, with various degrees of help and obstruction from that society. The dominant focus was on politics and economics in the most basic sense, with no appreciable concern for social integration in any form, and certainly none for family integration. Both Negroes and whites were concerned mainly with survival— the survival of the Negro people, the survival of the southern way of life, and the survival of the republic.

Because there was almost no focus on contemporary family life, and because the Negro people, as a free people, were considered to be extremely contemporary, it is little wonder that Negro family life was so completely ignored. And if some scholars saw that the origin of man was somewhat bound up with the origin and development of group life as represented by the family, it would certainly be the origin and development of the white man which would be studied, and not that of the "primitive" black people in their midst. For in the late nineteenth century, whatever the contribution of the abolitionists, the Civil War victors, and the reconstructionists, none of these liberal groups succeeded in comprehending the essential humanness shared by black and white people alike. All of "the liberals" proceeded on the assumption that the black people was another people, quite apart from the rest of society, though deserving of special help and a certain, though limited, degree of freedom.

A second phase of family studies, stimulated by conditions of *poverty,* focused on the conditions of life faced by contemporary families. These studies grew out of the early twentieth century liberal humanitarian movements, and are represented by the studies of Roundtree and the Webbs of England. Many surveys were conducted to document the conditions of "life and labor" of the working classes in the cities of Europe and America. Such studies were continued in the United States, particularly as economic adversity struck the industrial communities of America, which were being peopled by immigrant families from Europe.

While earlier family studies had focused on primitive groups, these focused on poverty groups and were almost exclusively concerned with economic conditions affecting family life. No attention was paid to the broader set of relationships between family life and community life, or to the place of family life in the wider society. These studies concentrated on the urban poor and consequently ignored Negro family life, for around the turn of the century Negroes were still not an urban industrial force. They were essentially rural peasants located in the deep South.

In many respects, many of the studies of family life conducted during this period were predecessors of some of the current commentary on Negro families. They depended on secondary rather than on first-hand data and were usually statistical in form. Moreover, they concentrated on various forms of deviant behavior which were believed to be results of breakdown in family life. These included divorce rates, crime rates, illegitimacy rates, death rates, and various health statistics. There are indeed some striking parallels between those early poverty studies focused on other ethnic minorities and current studies focused on Negroes.

The 1920s ushered in a third phase of family studies. Poverty seemed somewhat under control, or at least it was pushed from the headlines by the burgeoning prosperity. Scholars of family life began to turn their attention to some of the problems faced by *middle class families*. This period of inquiry may be termed the psychological phase, for many of these studies were concerned with the dominant themes of "adjustment" and "individual happiness." Despite the growth of the middle class in America, economic well-being was not sufficient to guarantee these psychological values. Middle class families began to discover that they had problems of personal—and particularly sexual—adjustment. The study of family life shifted dramatically during this period to the study of middle class family life, and the problems of psychological functioning associated with these families. Not only Freud, but also the social psychological studies of George H. Mead and the sociological studies of Ernest W. Burgess reflected this concern.

Again, Negro families were left out. For while they were becoming increasingly urban after the great migrations of 1914 to 1918, and while they were indeed concentrated in industrial towns and cities of the South and North, the industrial poverty phase of family studies had passed. The new thing was to study the problems of family life among the middle classes, and Negroes, alas, were not yet middle class in any appreciable numbers. Furthermore, and not unrelated to this fact, they were not yet perceived as having psychological and sexual problems to the extent and degree of refinement that white middle class families had them. The European emigrants had discovered that neither a certain degree of assimilation nor economic well-being solved all the problems of existence and family life. Native whites made a similar discovery, thanks to the insights of psychoanalysis. But Negroes were not yet to be admitted into these private circles of family life education lectures, private psychiatric treatment, and studies of family structure and function. For Negroes were still engaged in the struggle for economic survival, and students of family life had already passed through this stage, along with the more prosperous white segments of the society.

The years 1930 to 1940 were the golden age for studies of Negro life; the best studies of Negro family life available today were done during that period. These were years of tremendous political activity. For the first time in nonwar years, what happened in Washington vastly affected every segment of American life. For the first time since Reconstruction, Negroes became an important political force. Negroes were now so transplanted from the rural South and so concentrated in key industrial areas they could not be ignored in the political efforts to save American society from the economic disaster ushered in with 1929. Consequently, as the eyes of the nation turned to a reconstruction of the whole society, including the Negro elements, scholarship turned in a similar direction. Students of family life thus discovered the Negro family.

If the first factor which accounts for this discovery is broadly social—in the sense that the whole society, including all of its important elements, was in trouble and deserved to be studied—the second factor was the emergence of Negro scholars, who could not ignore the Negro family precisely for the same reasons that white scholars could and did. It was during these years, with generous support from white institutions, that Negro scholars, sometimes in active collaboration with white scholars, produced some of the most important studies of Negro family life. Chicago was the focus of sociological inquiry during this period, and from there arrived E. Franklin Frazier's study of *The Negro Family in Chicago*,[7] to be followed toward the end of the decade by his *The Negro Family in the United States*.[8] A few years later there appeared the monumental study of Drake and Cayton, *Black Metropolis*,[9] which has large sections on Negro family life. In addition, the comprehensive series of studies on Negro youth commissioned by the American Council on Education[10] has not since been equaled. These studies, conducted in

---

[7]E. Franklin Frazier, *The Negro Family in Chicago* (Chicago: University of Chicago Press, 1932).

[8]E. Franklin Frazier, *The Negro Family in the United States* (Chicago: University of Chicago Press, 1939).

[9]St. Clair Drake and Horace R. Cayton, *Black Metropolis* (rev. ed.; New York: Harper & Row, Publishers, 1962).

[10]Allison Davis and John Dollard, *Children of Bondage* (New York: American Council on Education and Harper & Row, Publishers, 1940). Other studies in this series are: E. Franklin Frazier, *Negro Youth at the Crossway* (1940); Charles S. Johnson, *Growing up in the Black Belt* (1941); W. Lloyd Warner, Buford H. Junker,

each of the major sections of the country, developed a great body of information on Negro family life. In addition to his work with the American Council on Education, Charles S. Johnson conducted a long series of studies of Negro life in rural America, making a significant contribution to the study of family life among Negroes.[11]

Thus during this period a handful of Negro social scientists, including W. E. B. DuBois, Charles S. Johnson, Allison Davis, St. Clair Drake, Horace Cayton, E. Franklin Frazier, and Ira Reid, joined by a dozen or so white scholars centered mainly around Chicago, including Louis Wirth, Munro Edmonson, John H. Roehr, Robert E. Park, John Dollard, Burleigh B. Gardner, Marx R. Gardner, and W. L. Warner, produced the bulk of social science scholarship about Negro family life.

But in the period running roughly from 1940 to 1960, students of American society had other matters demanding their attention. There was the war to explain, the unprecedented industrialization, the accompanying bureaucratization of society. Along with this, there was the new psychoanalytic revolution, a new and growing prosperity, social class considerations, mental health, and large interest in child rearing practices in the American family. Consequently, it was only with the new emphasis on poverty ushered in during the early 1960s that social scientists again discovered the Negro family. Now they became increasingly aware that not only war and prosperity, but poverty as well, seemed destined to be fixed factors in our social life. The incongruity of it all forced a reexamination, both of the social fabric of the larger and now international society and of the inner workings of our own pluralistic society.

When we took a fresh look at poverty, we observed that Negroes were conspicuous among the poor, though they constituted less than a third of the total poor people in this country. But by now we were armed with statistical techniques which helped us to see that Negroes were overrepresented among the poor. We therefore focused on them, and searched for explanations. By now we also knew the connections between family life and the broader social context, including economic, political, and educational advancement.

It is perhaps a peculiarly American quality to look for single causes of complex phenomena. It was amazingly convenient to explain poverty by ignoring the total poverty picture and explaining only Negro poverty, for in this way one could avoid some of the more troubling aspects of the Negro experience, aside from poverty—namely, persistent prejudice and discrimination based on race. Seeking to explain only *Negro* poverty, one could conveniently ignore the mass of causal factors and focus on

and Walter A. Adams, *Color and Human Nature* (1941); Ira De Augustine Reid, *In a Minor Key: Negro Youth in Story and Fact* (1940).

[11]Charles S. Johnson, *Shadow of the Plantation* (Chicago: University of Chicago Press, 1934).

the Negro people themselves, their leadership, their psychological motivation and aspirations, their family structure, and, in a flash of superficial enlightenment, their history of slavery. The Negro family, therefore, came in for some scholarly attention. But this attention has been directed to only that "half" of Negro families in the lower class, and even more specifically, that "third" of Negro families below the poverty line, or that "quarter" of Negro families headed by women, or that "tenth" of Negro families with illegitimate children, or that even smaller proportion of Negro families which combine these three conditions and are supported by public welfare.

For it must be said with all candor that the social scientists who have recently discovered the Negro family have not yet produced a study of that 75 per cent of Negro families who have stable marriages, or that half of Negro families who have managed to pull themselves into the middle class, or that 90 per cent of all Negro families who are self-supporting, or that even larger portion who manage to keep out of trouble, often despite the grossest kinds of discrimination and provocation. It would be very instructive indeed to know how two-thirds of all Negro families with less than $2,000 annual income in 1966 could manage to hold themselves together and meet the American test of family stability. For surely that is the statistic which needs explaining, rather than the minority of poor families where the man disappears in order to let the family survive economically. In addition, some understanding of how this majority of Negro families manages can help provide clues for the rehabilitation of other families, and at the same time can enlighten the society about the problems these Negro families still face.

The major reason for this selective focus on the negative aspects of Negro family life is that scholars do not yet seem to be interested in the Negro family as an institution for its own sake, and for what an understanding of it can tell us about our society. Studies so far which have focused on Negro family life in the lower class, problem-ridden sectors are not concerned at all with Negro family life. They are concerned, instead, with poverty, family breakdown, and illegitimacy, and somehow tie these phenomena to the Negro experience. This seems to obviate, for a time at least, the urgent need to explain these phenomena in the larger white society, where they are far more numerous. Perhaps if it can be said convincingly enough that people are in these conditions because they have been enslaved and still have a slave mentality, and because they have been discriminated against because of their race—all of which are true enough—then scholars and social reformers can avoid, for a few more years, looking for causes of these phenomena in the normal workings of our society—particularly in the workings of the upper reaches of our financial, industrial, military, educational, political, and religious institutions. This can postpone, for a time, the possible revelation that these pathologies may be endemic to our society, and are therefore normative and structural—not merely functions of individual, psychological, and subcultural hangups.

Fortunately, there is already emerging a small but growing literature on Negro families which takes these families seriously in their own right and does not treat them essentially as deviants from white norms. Outstanding among this new literature is the work of Jessie Bernard,[12] Hylan Lewis and his associates,[13] Lee Rainwater and his associates in St. Louis,[14] Joan Gordon in Harlem,[15] and a number of unpublished works.

15. Intellectuals as an ethnic group

ANDREW M. GREELEY

It is the custom for intellectuals to write biographies of politicians. They generally criticize politicians for lacking the skills which are appropriate to intellectuals. One wonders what would happen if politicians should write biographies of intellectuals.

Professor Arthur Mann

America's intellectual elite, normally secure from criticism, has been taking some lumps lately—and not just from Spiro Agnew. Writing in *The Nation,* John McDermott has accused lower-level members of the

[12]Jessie Bernard, *Marriage and Family among Negroes* (Englewood Cliffs, N.J.: Prentice-Hall, Inc., 1966).

[13]Hylan Lewis, "Changing perceptions of race, class, culture, and social welfare." Paper presented at Institute on Research toward Improving Race Relations, Airlie House, Warrenton, Va., August 1967. See also Lewis's introduction to Camille Jeffers' *Living Poor* (Ann Arbor, Mich.: Ann Arbor Publishers, 1967), and Elliott Liebow, *Tally's Corner* (Boston: Little, Brown and Company, 1966).

[14]Lee Rainwater, "Crucible of identity: The Negro lower-class family," *Daedalus,* Winter 1966.

[15]Joan Gordon, *The Poor of Harlem: Social Functioning in the Underclass* (New York: Office of the Mayor, Interdepartmental Neighborhood Service Center, July 31, 1965).

Abridged and edited from Andrew M. Greeley, "Intellectuals as an ethnic group," *The New York Times Magazine,* July 12, 1970. Copyright © 1970 by The New York Times Company. Reprinted by permission.

The author is Director, Center for the Study of American Pluralism, National Opinion Research Center, Chicago, Illinois.

elite of thinking of themselves as missionaries bringing culture to the heathens, and Michael Lerner, in *The American Scholar,* anticipated Agnew with the suggestion that the intellectual leaders may be snobs. Culture is indeed missionaried at some of the working-class institutions (state colleges are what I have in mind) at which exiled members of this elite are forced to teach to earn their daily bread, and snobbery is as present among this elite as among other groups of human beings.

I would like to suggest a way to understand the split which columnist Joseph Kraft has called "the most dangerous in American society—that between better-educated America and middle America." I propose that we can best judge the relationship between the intellectual elite and the rest of society if we perceive that the intelligentsia is, in fact, an ethnic group. Once we accept this, we begin to see the present tension between this ethnic group and other ethnic groups in its proper perspective.

There are six characteristics which delineate an ethnic group:

(1) A presumed consciousness of kind rooted in a sense of common origin.

(2) Sufficient territorial concentration to make it possible for members of the group to interact with each other most of the time and to reduce to a minimum interaction with members of other ethnic groups.

(3) A sharing of ideals and values by members of the ethnic group.

(4) Strong moralistic fervor for such ideals and values, combined with a sense of being persecuted by those who do not share them and hence are not members of the ethnic group.

(5) Distrust of those who are outside the ethnic group, combined with massive ignorance of them.

(6) Finally, a strong tendency in members of an ethnic group to view themselves and their circle as the whole of reality, or at least the whole of reality that matters. Thus, many primitive tribes use the same word for "human being" as they do for members of the tribe. Those who are outside the group, even if they are conceded some sort of human status, are, nonetheless, not considered terribly important.

Few probably will disagree that the first two characteristics apply to members of the American intellectual elite. Although the common origin of these elitists is not based on common biological ancestors, they are still united by a powerful "consciousness of kind." Their spiritual ancestors are the same, they have attended the same universities, and they know one another rather well—through personal contact at the upper levels of the group and through reading the approved journals at the lower levels. Further, they are highly concentrated in certain ethnic enclaves—in New York, Washington, Boston, Hyde Park in Chicago, the San Francisco area. The University of Chicago scholar, for example, who has attended the Laboratory School, the college and a graduate department at the university and now serves on its faculty, is not likely to leave Hyde Park any more frequently than would a member of a Polish ethnic group leave the Northwest Side of Chicago. And when he does leave, it is to go to similar enclaves where he will be just as effectively isolated from other ethnic groups.

I will content myself, then, with discussing the application of the final four characteristics. First, however, it is necessary to try to define "intellectual elite." It is as hard to arrive at a definition of this elite as of any other ethnic group. Some men and women are clearly a part of it—the editorial staffs of the ethnic journals, the faculties of five or six major universities, the most influential commentators of the mass media—but the boundaries of the group are vague and permeable. Who is "in" and who is "out" of the group are matters for controversy. (One is reminded of the debate in Israel about how to define a Jew.) Perhaps one could say that a member of the intellectual ethnic group can be identified by the journals he reads. Subscriptions to any two of the following are sufficient to guarantee one membership at least on the margins of this ethnic group: *The New York Times, Commentary, Partisan Review, Saturday Review, The New York Review of Books, The Atlantic* (but not *Harper's*), *Dissent, The New Republic* and *The Nation.* In cases of doubt, a subscription to *The New York Review of Books* alone will suffice.[1]

Members of this ethnic group, like all ethnics, are conscious of great differences within their group and are astonished to discover that those on the outside seem quite unaware of these. Thus, the intellectual ethnics are horrified to be told that from the outside Rennie Davis, Irving Howe, Arthur Schlesinger and Joseph Alsop seem to have far more in common with one another than they do with anyone who is not an intellectual ethnic. All one can do in response to their astonishment is to ask whether they know about the deep and basic differences that separate the Polish National Alliance and the Polish Roman Catholic Union. Members of other ethnic groups will forever be convinced that a Harvard man, no matter how fierce his revolutionary rhetoric, how wild his beard, how bizarre his dress, is still at root a Harvard man. If it is legitimate to use Pole (or Irish or Italian or Jew or Swede or Chinese) as a general category without adverting to the differentiations within the group (of course, members of the intellectual ethnic group do this constantly), then there seems no real reason why those who speak of the intellectual elite (perhaps even calling it "intellectual Establishment")

---

[1]Since I am on the staff of a large elite university and read most of the above journals I would, under normal circumstances, be accorded membership in the ethnic group. But I am a dubious case since, in addition to being Irish (a highly suspect quality at best), I am also of the clergy. I think both of these characteristics would be forgiven me if I should marry (which, by the way, I have no intention of doing). Currently an Irish clergyman can make it into the ethnic group by seeking a wife, just as an Irish politician can by being assassinated.

should be concerned with the differentiations that those inside the group consider so terribly important.[2]

First of all, we must investigate the values shared by the members of the intellectual ethnic group. The most basic value is the conviction that the articulation of ideas is the most dignified form of human activity; and closely related is the notion that those whose role it is in society to articulate ideas are not only the most superior members of that society, but also the only ones really qualified to run it. It is taken for granted that there are few problems facing society which intelligence and goodwill could not resolve and, therefore, if problems remain, it is because of the absence of either intelligence or goodwill on the part of those who are responsible for governing the society. It is taken as axiomatic, then, that the mistakes, the tragedies, the confusions, the animosities, the unresolved conflicts, the disasters which affect the society are to be attributed either to ignorance or to malice.[3]

From there, it is one further step to see, if not a conspiracy, at least some sort of implicitly organized plot to prevent social progress and to frustrate the accomplishment of those intelligent programs for social progress which the intellectual ethnic group has devised. Given the superiority of the members of the group and the unquestioned validity of their solutions, they do not need to be paranoid to sniff a plot. Quite the

---

[2]Occasionally a member of the intellectual ethnic group ventures forth to a work situation where other ethnics are to be found, gets a job in such a situation for a rather brief period of time and then reports back to the members of his own group about the fascinating and bizarre behavior in which other ethnics engage—much as Marco Polo reported on China. Such reports are inevitably fascinating since they combine the joys of voyeurism with the pleasures of slumming. The writer feels that he is "telling it like it is" and the ethnic readers are reassured about their own moral and intellectual superiority. Elinor Langer's account in *The New York Review of Books* of her adventures at the New York Telephone Company is a classic example of this variety of literature. The other ethnics ("Polish, Jewish, Italian, Irish, black, Puerto Rican") are typical members of the consumer society. "Packaging is also important: the women will describe not only the thing, but also the box or wrapper it comes in" (how strange and fascinating of them!) . . . "they are especially fascinated by wigs" (just like Marco Polo's Chinese with their pigtails) . . . "The essence of wiggery is escapism" (what else?).

Miss Langer is more perceptive than most such amateur anthropologists. She realizes that she may have been dishonest with her subjects: "I have a strong feeling of bad faith to have written this at all." But, having thus candidly confessed her feelings, she frees herself and her readers from any awkward feelings of guilt and concludes with the marvelously ethnocentric message of her former coworkers: "Perhaps the intellectual and political values of my life by which I was judging yours make equally little sense. Perhaps the skills which give me leverage to do it allow me only to express alienation and not to overcome it; perhaps I should merely be thankful that I was raised an alpha and not a beta."

[3]In matters of "thou shalt not kill," "thou shalt not steal" and "thou shalt not bear false witness," intellectual ethnics are as stern as their Puritan ancestors. However, most of the traditional violations of "thou shalt not commit adultery" are considered, if not praiseworthy, at least understandable, in terms of the offender's childhood. No attempt to justify political corruption, for example, in terms of the politician's childhood experience is likely to be listened to.

contrary, it seems to be the only logical explanation for the fact that they have not yet been given a chance to make society a better place by implementing all of their programs. Therefore, when they rail against "the system" or "the establishment" or "the power elites" or "the structure," they do so with perfect conviction and sincerity, even though to one who is not a member of their ethnic group it seems clear enough that if there is an establishment or a power elite or a structure or a system, then the intellectuals are the ones who run it.

So strong, indeed, is this conviction of the superiority of intelligence and the frustration of this superiority by dark forces, that many of these ethnics do not even see the occasional contradictions in their own behavior. Thus, Theodore Roszak can rail against "the technological establishment" and advocate his own "nontechnological counterculture" in a book mass-produced by a very technological printing press, published by a very establishment publishing house and marketed by the most sophisticated kinds of establishment advertising techniques.

Within the context of these twin basic convictions of the superiority of intelligence and the conspiracy against it, the precise positions this ethnic group takes on specific questions may change, though rarely is this change explicitly acknowledged. However, a number of the group's more generalized positions can usually be identified:

(1) Schools are the most appropriate place to accomplish social reform.

(2) Marxism, whatever its weaknesses may or may not be, is the most effective way of creating social progress—at least outside the United States.

(3) Youth is the hope of the future and thus the intellectual ethnic group must be profoundly concerned with what is happening among the young. Note the obsession, for example, in *The New York Times Magazine* with articles on youth culture. Note also the resolute refusal to face the fact that the youthful protest movement, in its political, psychedelic, communitarian and rock-music manifestations, represents only a small minority even of the college population, to say nothing of the total population under thirty.[4]

(4) There exists somewhere a group called "the people." This group—be it noted, quite distinct from "the silent majority"—is not nearly so well-educated as the intellectuals but does share their values and can be counted on to supply the "muscle" for whatever fantasies about grass-root support the intellectual ethnic group finds itself in need of. The composition of "the people" changes; in the 1930's it was the working class, particularly trade-union members; more recently, this group has

---

[4]Rennie Davis will probably not dance on Judge Hoffman's grave, but there is a good chance that George Wallace will dance on Davis's—and perhaps a lot of other people's, too.

been "the blacks," "the poor" and "the Third World." The mythology of "the people" requires, of course, that all or most of the members of these particular categories be assumed to be part of "the people." However, those presently permitted into "the people" should be wary. Membership is not permanent and can be revoked whenever the evidence becomes irrefutable that substantial elements admitted to "the people" in fact do not share the values of the intellectual ethnic group. My own hunch is that the position of the blacks is quite precarious because at some time in the reasonably near future the intellectual ethnics are going to discover that the black militants and black radicals do not speak for the overwhelming majority of the new black middle classes—or upper black working class, either, for that matter.

Like all ethnic groups, the intellectual elite realizes that to some extent it is separated from and threatened by the rest of society. It therefore becomes necessary to invest its convictions with strong moral force, both to assure allegiance to the values by those inside the group and to provide a weapon for denouncing those who are outside of it. The nineteenth century Irish-American's concern about freedom for Ireland and the twentieth century Slavic-American's commitment to the sanctity of the neighborhood are easily matched by the intellectual's conviction of the morality of his own tradition.

The strong moralism in the intellectual ethnic is reinforced by two other factors. For one, the intellectual's roots in the Puritan Protestant and Jewish messianic past would incline him toward moralism even if there were none so bold as to disagree with him. For another, convinced as he is of his superior intelligence, the intellectual has no trouble in concluding his superior moral rectitude: he is both right and righteous. One need only read through the editorials, the book reviews and the letters columns of any of the ethnic group journals to discover the absolute and unshakable conviction of the typical intellectual ethnic about his own moral righteousness. The long and by now tiresome debate between Noam Chomsky and Arthur Schlesinger is a classic example of this righteousness. Rarely, if ever, does one encounter in any of the journals the slightest hint that anyone thinks that he might not have all the information or be mistaken in his judgments or that his opponents, either inside the group or outside of it, might possibly be men of intelligence and sincerity.[5]

. . . . .

---

[5]Chomsky is obviously at an advantage in his debate with Schlesinger, because Chomsky has never been part of the political administration as Schlesinger has, and, hence, has never had his moral purity tainted by political decision making. Yet one wonders about Chomsky's morality. If really convinced that American society is as imperialistic and demoralized as he claims, why would he continue to accept income from M.I.T., which is about as much a part of the American establishment as an institution possibly could be?

The intellectual is quite capable of compassion—for the poor and the black, especially, but also for drug addicts, terrorists, arsonists, rioters, Russians, Chinese, Arabs and the Vietcong. All these compassions do him great credit, but he is singularly selective in his compassion and in his willingness to understand sympathetically and defend members of other ethnic groups. He finds it difficult, if not impossible, to experience compassion or sympathy, or even understanding, for the United States of America, and particularly for its middle-class and working-class citizens —especially if they are over thirty. This is the "silent majority," the fascist mass, the white backlash and the white ethnic racist. These are the kinds of people whom *Harper's* (a journal that caters to those on the fringe of the intellectual ethnic group) has been examining with aloof and clinical wit in the quasianthropological reports of Marshall Frady and others. See how amusing these Texans or Californians or Gary Hoosiers are—how quaint, how droll, how boorish, how fascist!

One of the reasons for the contempt and disdain directed at members of other American ethnic groups is that they don't demonstrate the required amounts of guilt. They don't feel guilty for their white racism. They don't feel guilty for the massacres at Songmy. They don't feel guilty about being members of the American middle class. If they were the morally righteous people that the intellectual ethnics are, they would feel guilty when the intellectuals insist that they should feel guilty. After all, every American white person is, by definition, a white racist and, as an editorial writer in *Trans*-action recently observed, those Americans who voted for Richard Nixon are as bad as those Germans who voted for Adolf Hitler. And Judson Jerome, writing in *Change,* engages in an orgy of personal guilt feeling because he was shocked when one of his students admitted that he felt perfectly free to steal other people's property since he was no longer hung up on the "private property" bag. Heaven only knows how guilty Jerome would have felt if the student was also stealing his wife, since he was no longer hung up on the adultery bag.

It might be thought that such contempt for the middle class or the working class is a bit premature. The American electorate did resoundingly reject Barry Goldwater. American public opinion did force the deescalation of the Vietnamese war, the first time in history that a major power has been forced by public opinion to settle for something less than victory in armed combat. Further, the American public also solidly supported most of the social reforms that the elite intellectual ethnic group has promoted over the last forty years; it forced President Johnson out of office, it has paid, with only relatively minor protests, for the world commitments which previous generations of intellectual elites got it into, and it has even provided a broad consensus for racial integration (a consensus which may, despite the mythology of white backlash, persist even to the present time).[6] If the support of middle America for the intellectual ethnic group has waned in recent years, it may well be because the intellectual ethnics have tried to force down the throat of middle America social reforms (like school busing) whose effectiveness is questionable.

The intellectuals enthusiastically embraced the militant minorities of the black and youthful populations and their denunciation of middle America on the grounds that the militant minorities were "morally superior." Historians of the future may look on the 1960's as a time not when middle America deserted the intellectual ethnic group, but rather as a time when the intellectual ethnic group deliberately turned its back on its own mass population support and began a flirtation with radical groups whose ability to bring about social change was dubious, but whose moral rectitude—at least from the intellectual elite's viewpoint—was beyond question.

It must be emphasized that this is behavior that is perfectly understandable within the context of ethnic group analysis. It is almost inevitable that an ethnic group be unaware of what is happening in other ethnic groups and project into the other groups its own fears, frustrations and disappointments. American intellectuals are profoundly frustrated by the ambiguities, injustices and seemingly disastrous trends afflicting American society. Their superior intelligence and moral rectitude tell them what the correct answers to these difficulties are; the absence of a positive response from other ethnic groups leads them to a rigid and doctrinaire position not much different in style but considerably different in substance from that of Slavic homeowners who cannot understand why other Americans are offended by the fierce loyalty with which they try to protect their neighborhoods. The Slavic ethnic cannot understand the intellectual's assumption that he has the morally correct answer; and the intellectual is quite incapable of understanding the affection for social turf which is so powerful in the life of the Slavic ethnic. Neither side is able to have much compassion for the other, though, to the credit of the Slav, it may be said that at least he doesn't pretend to be compassionate.

Of course there is, within the intellectual ethnic group, plenty of room

---

[6]One looks in vain in the history of the human race for a situation where a major power has been forced to withdraw from a war because a large segment of its people (and not simply a tiny minority of vocal demonstrators) would not support the war. One further looks in vain for a military establishment which would bring charges against senior officers (including generals) for an atrocity committed in a war, especially when that war was still going on. The intellectual ethnic group copes with this unexpected display of national morality by claiming credit for it. The other ethnics can't win: If they are moral, the intellectual ethnics assume that they are the ones who are responsible for the morality.

for dissent so long as it is the approved kind of dissent. Radical Abbie Hoffman's right to dissent will be vigorously defended, but not Nixon-aide Daniel Patrick Moynihan's (even though Moynihan's alleged dissent is, for the most part, made up of phrases snatched out of context). Drug-touter Timothy Leary is to be supported, but not race-I.Q. comparer Arthur Jensen.[7]

M. I. T.'s "new-politician" Noam Chomsky has the right to academic tenure, but ex-Johnson-aide W. W. Rostow has no right to return to M. I. T. Mayor Lindsay's mistakes are to be defended and sympathized with; Mayor Daley's mistakes are to be used to continue the myth that he is a monster—even though Lindsay was able to win the support of only 45 percent of the city of New York, and Daley 75 percent of the city of Chicago (including in excess of 85 percent of the blacks of that city). Every possible attempt was made by the intellectual elite to justify the mistakes of Israeli political leadership,[8] but no possible justification is seen for the moral behavior of Irish Catholic political leaders.

Like all ethnic groups, intellectuals have their own particular combat rhetoric, which may change more quickly than it does in other groups. It was only after long years that the Irish abandoned their hatred of "the dirty A.P.A.'s" (members of the American Protection Association), and Poles are probably still convinced that their biggest enemies in the United States are "Irish Catholic politicians and bishops." The currently favorite word of the intellectual ethnic group is "revolution." Even though the movements among the young and the black are in fact anything but revolutions in any sense that this word normally conveys, it is still absolutely necessary that the movements be described as "revolution"; never mind that for there to be a revolution the revolutionaries must have at least the passive support of the majority of the population; never mind that only a tiny minority of the nation supports either the student or the women's movements, and only a minority of the blacks supports the most militant kind of black protest.

Never mind that when the minority attempts to force its will on the majority, what one has is not revolution but fascism; never mind even that some of the young and more radical members of the intellectual ethnic group, confusing the slogan of revolution with tactics of revolu-

---

[7] I am persuaded by the essay of Professor Arthur Stinchcombe in the *Harvard Educational Review* (1969) that Jensen's research on the biological roots of racial differences in I.Q. scores is inaccurate, but from inaccuracy it does not follow that he is a racist.

[8] One of the more interesting developments within the intellectual ethnic group is increasing sympathy for the Arabs. Such sympathy is particularly fashionable among young Jewish radicals who combine support for the Arabs with justification for black anti-Semitism in the belief that Jewish merchants do indeed victimize the black poor.

tion (logically enough from their viewpoint), hurl bombs, revolution is the word still to be used. And if other ethnic groups are offended by such rhetorical excess, it is merely proof of their moral inferiority.[9]

Finally, the members of the intellectual ethnic group, like all ethnics, are only vaguely aware of what goes on in other ethnic groups; they do not trust members of the out-groups and seldom, if ever, encounter them with any sort of serious conversation—save in taxicabs or in Stanley Kauffmann's theater. Normally speaking, it is not necessary to be concerned about what members of other ethnic groups think because "everybody" that matters is already part of one's own ethnic group.[10]

In his own way, Spiro Agnew was right when he suggested that a relatively small group of men in the mass media have immense control over the circulation of ideas in American society. Agnew was wrong on two counts, however. There is no conscious conspiracy in this control and, secondly, it has rather less impact than either the Vice President or the intellectual ethnics would like to think. There has been practically no room for dissent either in the leading ethnic journals or in the large-circulation media from the "official" account of the Chicago convention or the Chicago conspiracy trial. Most elite ethnics are convinced that "everyone" was horrified by the behavior of the Chicago police and of Judge Hoffman because *everyone they know* was horrified and because all the right journals say that we *ought* to be horrified. It turns out that the overwhelming majority of the American public approved the behavior of the police at the convention and equally approved the conviction of the Chicago Seven. These data can be dismissed as a sign of the fascism of the masses.[11]

[9]In the last four years the rhetoric and the tactics of the New-Left wing of the intellectual ethnic group have suffered one of the most complete defeats in the history of American politics. Seventy percent of those who favored immediate withdrawal from Vietnam approved the way the Chicago police responded to the convention protest. The Vietnam moratoriums strengthened rather than weakened President Nixon's policy (and sentiment in favor of withdrawal went up from 21 to 35 percent after the New Left was driven into retreat by the silent majority talk). At most, only 10 percent of the country approves of the New Left (whose shouts of "Power to the People" indicate a very strong death urge; if the "people" had their way, most of the New Left would be behind bars), and New Left tactics are the kiss of death for any program or candidate. Despite the abysmal failure of the New Left and its playing into the hands of those who oppose social progress, the intellectual ethnic group has not asked why the New Left failed, nor even really acknowledged that it has in fact failed, save by expressing fear of a "reaction," when a more appropriate fear would be that a New Right might use the New Left's tactics—and with far more effectiveness.

[10]A good way to define an intellectual ethnic is to say that he thought that Norman Podhoretz really "made it" when he became editor of *Commentary*.

[11]It is not my intention to side with the silent majority on either of these issues. The point I wish to make, however, is that if the intellectual ethnic group were a little less concerned with its own rectitude and moral purity and a little more concerned about understanding what was going on in the United States and providing broad consensus for social change, it might begin to ask itself whether the members

Because they are ignorant of and unconcerned about other ethnic groups, the intellectual ethnics are confused and frightened when they detect a change of behavior among the members of other groups. Just as they betrayed ignorance of other groups by assuming that every new scheme which was alleged to improve the conditions of the poor and the blacks would be accepted by the white majority because the scheme was sanctioned by the elite as the only moral one, so they display equal ignorance in overestimating the so-called white backlash. Despite the past records of the middle majority, the intellectual alternates between paying no attention at all to it and being terrified of it. The terror is real enough, but it does not necessarily correspond to some reality which ought to generate terror. The intellectual who shivers with delight at the fantasy of a Polish storm trooper kicking in his door at four o'clock in the morning has the same contact with reality as does the Polish home-owner on the Northwest Side of Chicago who thinks that Black Panthers are lurking in his corner drugstore. Both have created terrors for their own entertainment and delight; both are completely unaware of what really is going on in other ethnic groups; both present classic examples of frightened ethnic behavior.

All of this is unfortunate, of course, because in addition to being members of one particular ethnic group, the intellectual elite are, by definition, the idea-shaping segment of the leadership of American society. For them to be alienated from the rest of society for reasons of presumed moral superiority or ignorance of what is going on in the rest of the society is a tragedy both for them and for the whole country. Curiously enough, members of the other ethnic groups have a great deal of respect for the intellectuals, though the respect is mixed with negative feelings. It would, one suspects, take relatively little in the way of sympathetic understanding on the part of the intellectual ethnics to begin to reestablish some kind of communication with the rest of America.

---

of other ethnic groups are saying something very important, however inelegantly, by their reaction to both the demonstration and the trial. However, it is much easier to dismiss other people as fascists than to try to understand them.

PART TWO

Identities in contemporary American society

A. THE METROPOLIS

In American society, the scene of the greatest impact of racial and ethnic groups has been the metropolis. No other single way of life has been so influenced by racial and ethnic group identities as urban life. No other areas of residence have retained racial and ethnic group identities as the urban scene. And nowhere can the interaction, confrontation, and conflict of racial and ethnic groups be seen more clearly than in the cities.

The city has been the focus of race and ethnicity for two reasons. First, most racial and ethnic groups migrated into the city in large waves, either related to migration from foreign countries, or in the case of the black people, to migration from another region of the United States.[1] Second, the groups created segregated settlements or neighborhoods within the city.[2] The attraction of the city for these groups was predominantly an economic one: the city offered both easy entry jobs

---

[1]On foreign immigration, see Arthur M. Schlesinger, *The Rise of the City, 1878-1898* (New York: The Macmillan Co., 1933), pp. 53-77; Oscar Handlin, *The American People in the Twentieth Century* (Cambridge, Mass.: Harvard University Press, 1954), pp. 47–85; Nathan Glazer and Daniel P. Moynihan, *Beyond the Melting Pot* (2d ed.; Cambridge, Mass.: The M.I.T. Press, 1970); and David Ward, *Cities and Immigrants* (New York: Oxford University Press, 1971). On black migration to the cities, see Charles Tilly, "Race and migration to the American city," in James Q. Wilson (ed.), *The Metropolitan Enigma* (Cambridge, Mass.: Harvard University Press, 1968), pp. 137–57; and Oscar Handlin, *The Newcomers: Negroes and Puerto Ricans in a Changing Metropolis* (Cambridge, Mass.: Harvard University Press, 1959).

[2]The degree of ethnic segregation has not been comprehensively assessed. However, there is considerable evidence of the existence of such segregation. See, for example, Otto Feinstein (ed.), *Ethnic Groups in the City* (Lexington, Mass.: D.C. Heath & Co., 1971); Nathan Kantrowitz, "Ethnic and racial segregation in the New York metropolis, 1960," *American Journal of Sociology,* May 1969, 74:685–95; and Herbert Gans, *The Urban Villagers* (Glencoe, Ill.: The Free Press, 1962). On racial segregation, see Karl E. Taeuber and Alma F. Taeuber, *Negroes in Cities* (Chicago: Aldine Publishing Co., 1965); and Norman M. Bradburn, Seymour Sudman, and Galen L. Gockel, *Side by Side: Integrated Neighborhoods in America* (Chicago: Quadrangle Books, Inc., 1971). On the relationship between ethnic composition and neighborhood social structure, see Maurice D. Van Arsdol, Jr., and Leo A. Schuerman, "Redistribution and assimilation of ethnic populations: The Los Angeles case," *Demography,* November 1971, 8:459–80.

and cheap housing located relatively near to the jobs. The attraction was also a cultural one, as the new migrant was more likely to find others of his own language and national background in the city, which meant being able to live with people having similar values and customs.

It also meant the development of various urban neighborhoods, most having some sense of turf or territoriality. Scholars have only recently given renewed attention to this sense of turf, especially as held by members of white ethnic groups.[3] The sense is perhaps most strongly evidenced by the desire to remain in one's neighborhood and to prevent attempts by outsiders (usually government) to change the neighborhood, whether by urban renewal, scatter-site housing, block-busting, or school busing. Territoriality was also maintained in those neighborhoods where several different ethnic groups lived in the same small area, with each group retaining its own separate identity. In the first article in this section (Selection 16), Caroline Ware describes the local life in an ethnically mixed neighborhood 50 years ago in New York City. For many of the country's large cities, this description is still relevant, although the specific ethnic groups and the times have changed.[4] Another topic related to ethnic neighborhoods is the question of the residential succession of one group by another. In recent years, much concern has arisen, for instance, over the change within a neighborhood from white to black residents, and in particular over such apparent stages of succession as invasion, tipping points, and consolidation. The reader is referred elsewhere for a selection of articles on this aspect of neighborhood change.[5]

Of all the racial and ethnic neighborhoods in the city, none has become more notorious than the ghetto. The word "ghetto" was originally used in the 16th century to identify the Jewish quarter of Italian cities, but it has since come to be linked with areas of American cities whose residents are of any distinct ethnic or racial group, generally of low-income.[6] Oscar Handlin has written the more traditional description of ghetto life in the U.S. city, with its overcrowding, poor housing, and

---

[3]Most prominent has been the work of Gerald Suttles (see his *The Social Construction of Communities* [Chicago: University of Chicago Press, 1972]). See also Andrew M. Greeley, *Why Can't They Be Like Us?* (New York: E. P. Dutton & Co., Inc., 1971), pp. 96 ff; and Marshall Sklare, "Jews, ethnics, and the American city," *Commentary,* April 1972, pp. 70–77.

[4]For an example of a contemporary situation, see Gerald D. Suttles, *The Social Order of the Slum: Ethnicity and Territory in the Inner City* (Chicago: University of Chicago Press, 1968).

[5]See Robert K. Yin (ed.), *The City in the Seventies* (Itasca, Ill.: F. E. Peacock Publishers, Inc., 1972), pp. 39–83. For other articles on the same subject, see Harvey Molotch, "Racial change in a stable community," *American Journal of Sociology,* September 1969, 75:226–38: Herbert J. Gans, "The white exodus to suburbia steps up," *The New York Times Magazine,* January 7, 1968; and Paul Wilkes, "As the blacks move in, the ethnics move out," *The New York Times Magazine,* January 24, 1971.

[6]For more on the early origins, see Louis Wirth, *The Ghetto* (Chicago: University of Chicago Press, 1928).

poor public health conditions.[7] It is interesting to note that Handlin's description already covered one form of ghetto behavior that many people have only linked with very recent ghetto life, the throwing of garbage out windows:

> Here is a woman. In the Old Country, she had lived much of her life, done most of her work, outdoors. In America, the flat confines her . . .
>
> The very simplest tasks become complex and disorganizing. Every day there is a family to feed. Assume she knows how to shop, and can manage the unfamiliar coal stove or gas range. But what does one do with rubbish who has never known the meaning of waste? It is not really so important to walk down the flight of narrow stairs each time there are some scraps to be disposed of. The windows offer an easier alternative. After all, the obnoxious wooden garbage boxes that adorn the littered fronts of the houses expose their contents unashamed through split sides and, rarely emptied, themselves become the nests of boldly foraging rodents.
>
> The filthy streets are seldom cleaned; the municipality is not particularly solicitious of these, the poorest quarters of the city. The alleys are altogether passed by and the larger thoroughfares receive only occasionally the services of the scavenger. The inaccessible alleys and rear yards are never touched and, to be sure, are redolent of the fact. In the hot summer months the stench of rotting things will mark these places and the stained snow of winter will not conceal what lies beneath. . . .[8]

Much of the recent attention to ghetto conditions has been concerned with the black ghetto and its rise in many cities.[9] Kenneth Clark, among others, has written about the more pathological consequences of life in the black ghetto, including the problem that many people have little hope of ever escaping the ghetto.[10] Joseph Boskin (Selection 17) contrasts the condition of the black ghetto with the increased prosperity of the general American society during the 1960s, the frustrations over the Civil Rights movement, and the effects of the mass media in presenting an exaggerated image of the wealthier society to the ghetto resident. He suggests that the combination had much to do with the urban riots of the mid-1960s.[11]

Life in the contemporary black ghetto has also led to a new interpretation of the role of the ghetto, one that is quite different from the tradi-

---

[7]Oscar Handlin, *The Uprooted: The Epic Story of the Great Migrations That Made the American People* (Boston: Little, Brown and Company, 1951), pp. 144–69.

[8]*Ibid.,* pp. 151–52.

[9]On the historical evolution of the black ghetto in two cities, see Gilbert Osofsky, *Harlem: The Making of a Ghetto, 1890-1930* (New York: Harper & Row, Publishers, 1966); and Allan H. Spear, *Black Chicago: The Making of a Negro Ghetto, 1890-1920* (Chicago: University of Chicago Press, 1967).

[10]Kenneth B. Clark, *Dark Ghetto* (New York: Harper & Row, Publishers, 1965). See also Bonnie Bullough, "Alienation in the ghetto," *American Journal of Sociology,* March 1967, 72:469–78; and Hyman Rodman, "Family and social pathology in the ghetto," *Science,* August 1968, 161:756–62.

tional descriptions by people like Handlin and Clark. The new interpretation is based on the fact that the black ghetto has had two characteristics distinguishing it from other ghettos: a high degree of involuntary segregation, and heavy ownership of ghetto enterprises by other than black (and predominantly Jewish) people. Thus several analysts have claimed that the black ghetto is actually another example of white American colonialism, in which the ghetto and its resources are deliberately exploited to serve the majority society.[12] To the casual observer who walks around an extremely poor neighborhood like Brownsville (New York City), and sees that the residents are all black and Puerto Rican, but that the firemen, policemen, teachers, construction workers, and store owners purporting to serve the neighborhood are predominantly white, the colonial analogy seems quite appropriate. If the ghetto is a colony from the vantage point of the white majority society, then from the vantage point of the blacks in the ghetto it might be something else. Roy Simon Bryce-LaPorte (Selection 18) suggests what that something else could be: a frontier. He views the ghetto as the battleground for the future of black Americans, and compares the white domination of the ghetto to the Indian domination of the old American West.

In addition to the ghetto, one other type of residential neighborhood has been prominent in the city: the bedroom suburb. In older cities, the bedroom suburb was not necessarily located outside of the city limits. For instance, Brooklyn was once considered the wealthy suburb of New York. Nowadays, some suburban areas are still within the city limits, but the newer suburbs have formed so far away from the central city that suburbs of different metropolitan areas almost seem to merge with each other.

Suburban life is generally marked by home ownership, a plot of land, and generally homogeneous levels of income within individual suburban communities. Because of this and the apparent homogeneity of suburban life-styles, the suburb has also been popularly depicted as a place where racial and ethnic identities have disappeared. But this image does little justice to the high degree of residential segregation in the suburbs (with Jews and blacks in particular usually forming separate communities), nor to the research evidence suggesting that racial and ethnic identities survive even among white ethnic groups.[13] Bennett Berger (Selection 19)

---

[11]A comprehensive review of the riots is the *Report of the National Advisory Commission on Civil Disorders* (New York: Bantam Books, Inc., 1968).

[12]See Robert Blauner, "Internal colonialism and ghetto revolt," *Social Problems,* Spring 1969, 16:393–408; and William K. Tabb, "Race relations models and social change," *Social Problems,* Spring 1971, 18:431–44. For comments in relation to another ethnic group, see Joan W. Moore, "Colonialism: The case of the Mexican-Americans," *Social Problems,* Spring 1970, 17:463–72.

[13]For example, see William M. Dobriner, *Class in Suburbia* (Englewood Cliffs, N.J.: Prentice-Hall, Inc., 1963), pp. 65–67, 118; Albert I. Gordon, *Jews in Suburbia* (Boston: Beacon Press, 1959); and Benjamin B. Ringer, *The Edge of Friendliness* (New York: Basic Books, Inc., 1967).

discusses the myth of the suburb as a latter-day melting pot, and suggests how racial and ethnic factors are still relevant in the suburb.

Aside from residential segregation and the peculiar characteristics of the ghetto and the suburb, race and ethnicity have played an important role in structuring city government and city politics. The most well-known relationship has been that between immigrant groups and the rise and decline of the political machine.[14] The ethnic governmental patterns are still very much evident in places like New York, where the Irish dominate the police and fire-fighting forces; the Italians, the sanitation department; the Jews, the teaching profession at all levels; and the blacks and Puerto Ricans, the health and social services.[15] At the same time, racial and ethnic factors have been important to the voting patterns of the urban populace. James Q. Wilson and Edward C. Banfield, for instance, have suggested that ethnic differences are reflected in the concern for local versus cosmopolitan (citywide) issues,[16] while others have examined ethnic voting as a major factor in the outcome of city elections.[17] The last two articles of this section cover the role of race and ethnicity in government and voting patterns. William Shannon (Selection 20) describes the function of the political arena as a career opportunity for Irish-Americans, a group that has dominated the urban political scene, while Raymond Wolfinger (Selection 21) analyzes voting patterns in New Haven and suggests a mobilization theory of ethnic voting patterns.

---

[14]Elmer E. Cornwell, Jr., "Bosses, machines, and ethnic groups," *The Annals,* May 1964, 353:27–39. See also Daniel N. Gordon, "Immigrants and urban governmental form in American cities, 1933-1960," *American Journal of Sociology,* September 1968, 74:158–71; and for a general review, see Lawrence H. Fuchs (ed.), *American Ethnic Politics* (New York: Harper & Row, Publishers, 1968).

[15]For instance, see Glazer and Moynihan, *Beyond the Melting Pot, op. cit.* For more on the role of the Irish as policemen, see James Q. Wilson, "Generational and ethnic differences among career police officers," *American Journal of Sociology,* March 1964, 69:522–28.

[16]James Q. Wilson and Edward C. Banfield, "Public regardingness as a value premise in voting behavior," *American Political Science Review,* December 1964, 58:876–87; and James Q. Wilson and Edward C. Banfield, "Political ethos revisited," *American Political Science Review,* December 1971, 65:1048–62.

[17]For example, see Michael Parenti, "Ethnic politics and the persistence of ethnic identification," *American Political Science Review,* September 1967, 61:717–26; Arthur M. Klebanoff, "Is there a Jewish vote?" *Commentary,* January 1970, pp. 43–47; and Daniel N. Gordon, "Immigrants and municipal voting turnout," *American Sociological Review,* August 1970, 35:665–81.

16. Ethnic groupings

CAROLINE F. WARE

Among the local people, the most fundamental social division was the ethnic one. More than economic barriers or geographic divisions, ethnic lines cut across the local population so firmly that for practically every aspect of local life the several ethnic groups had separate institutions and distinctive ways and were more or less firmly separated from each other by social barriers. Though these lines were not, and had never been, hard and fast, and though they varied in their intensity and inclusiveness for different ages, degrees of education and economic levels, they were inescapable.

The Italians, comprising over half of the population of the district, had come nearest to imposing upon the whole area their own social characteristics. The Irish were less ethnically distinguishable from the other English-speaking people at a similar economic level, but they, too, were conscious of themselves as a group and possessed distinctive habits. Though few in number, the Jews stood out clearly. The Spanish colony had so lost in membership as to have been almost eliminated, but it still supported its own institutions and had little to do with anybody else in the community. The scattered remnant of Germans had been cruelly reminded of their national origin during the War. Even the mere handful of families who survived from other groups were still distinguishable in 1930. The original old American families had retained enough sense of themselves as a group to be able to supply the names of the families who really "belonged." In 1920, three Negro blocks had been all that remained of what was once the principal Negro settlement in New York. By 1930, two "Negro houses," dilapidated tenements under the elevated, housed all the Negroes except janitors or seamen who were left. The Lithuanian settlement, which had been sufficiently strong and cohesive to organize a church in 1909, had nearly disappeared by 1930, but the church continued to function. The French settlement, which had been large enough around 1900 to furnish talent for French plays at Greenwich House, was reduced to a few houses containing some of the French

Abridged and edited from Caroline F. Ware, *Greenwich Village, 1920-1930: A Comment on American Civilization in the Post-War Years* (Boston: Houghton Mifflin, 1935), pp. 127–42. Copyright renewed 1963 by Caroline F. Ware. Reprinted by permission of the publisher.

waiters in the lower Fifth Avenue hotels. The scattering of Polish, Austrian, and Scandinavian families represented the remains of groups that had never had the coherence of the other ethnic elements in the community.

Ethnic-divisions among the local population in the community arose as a matter of historical development. Because each group represented an inroad into the area at a different time and under different conditions, the ethnic label carried more than a strictly ethnic implication. To the Irish the "Guineas" were not only "foreigners" but newcomers. They were the ones who "took their neighborhood away from them." Even in 1930, thirty years after the Italian mass invasion, the older Irish still regarded the Italians as intruders.

The original difference in economic status which distinguished the penniless immigrant at the time of his arrival from those already in the community survived as a social attitude even after the difference had factually disappeared. Although during these years the relative economic position of Italian and Irish was almost reversed by a combination of hard work, saving, and bootlegging on the part of Italians and the decline of the longshore trade and selective migration among the Irish, the latter continued to look upon the former as poor immigrants. When they recognized the economic realities of the situation, it was to comment, "You would be surprised how well off some of them are," or else, "No wonder they get ahead. They will grab anything."

The social origins of the immigrant groups still further reinforced the ethnic line. Because most of the Italians and Spaniards were peasants at home, they were accorded in this community the status of peasant immigrants, and the son of a professional Italian, as far as non-Italians were concerned, was tarred with the same brush as the rest of the group as long as he remained in it.

The passage of time had worn off the sharp edges of the ethnic groupings, but had not destroyed their basic relevance. No other division cut across so many lines and was, itself, cut by so few. To analyze the community in other than ethnic terms in 1930 would have been difficult, for each alternative category would have had to be broken down into ethnic subdivisions. To have done so in 1920 would have been virtually impossible. Though the cessation of immigration, the Americanization or standardizing influences of the schools, the tremendous growth of the popular press, and the widespread impact of radio and movies all tended to reduce differences and to destroy the rigidity of ethnic lines, the process of standardization had only touched the outer surface. Ethnic lines were blurred but not blotted out, ethnic differences lessened but not eliminated. Under all the veneer of movie-minded, ten-cent-store Americanism, ethnic groupings remained fundamental to the mass of the population of this area, still determining both the culture patterns and the social structure of the local community and producing those social habits which continually called attention to differences. The smell of Italian cooking was a constant reminder frequently commented upon by the Irish neighbor. A young man was not allowed to forget that the girl whom he wished to take out was Italian when he found that she could not come, or that he must deliver her home again by ten o'clock or earlier.

Between the principal ethnic groups which made up the local population, Italians and Irish, relations ranged from violent antagonism to indifference, with some little contact and a tendency over the years toward less bitterness at least, if not toward more cordiality. Far from living in a different world as did the Villagers, the Irish were very much of the Italians' world, occupying the same houses, the same jobs, and the same streets. In a very real sense the Irish community, rather than the world which the Villagers represented, was the "America" to which the immigrant Italians came. Their ways, in so far as the Italians could observe them, were "American" ways. They occupied a higher position on the same plane rather than an altogether different and distant plane.

In their first impact, the clash between Irish and Italians resulted from fundamental economic competition. When the Italians began to invade the Village, they were a direct menace to the homogeneity and the residential quality of the area. Some of the better-class Irish met the invasion by moving to other parts of the city, while the rest retreated gradually westward, slowly abandoning block after block to the newcomers.

In this situation, it was not surprising that active conflict between Italians and Irish should arise. In the first stages, the fight came mostly from the Irish side, in resistance to the invasion of foreigners. Gangs of Irish boys did their best to prevent Italian children from using the public library by lying in wait for them and destroying the books. Interblock fights with bricks and stones were not uncommon. The Italian boy knew which streets it was good for him to walk on and he also knew the consequence of walking on the side of the park which the Irish had set apart for themselves. One street was, for many years, the no man's land where the major fights between the "Wops" and the "Micks" were waged—fights not always confined to youngsters.

. . . . .

The years lessened the gap between these principal ethnic groups though they did not narrow the gulf between local people and Villagers. Though the Italians continued to regard the Irish as pig-headed drunkards who acted as if they owned the earth, and the latter still looked upon the Italians as dirty, foreign Guineas who had ruined a good neighborhood and were out for all they could get, they had enough in common to understand each other in at least some respects. Occupying a similar economic status and living in the same type of houses, their living habits were not unlike. Though the Church played a different role in the two groups, the fact that both were Catholic gave a primary basis for *rapprochement*. Most especially, the fact that many of the Italian ideas about Americans were drawn from the conduct of the Irish among whom they moved and who dominated the neighborhood gave them common standards to the extent that the Italians adopted Irish ways. Yet the fact remained that Irish-Italian relationships in this community rested on so precarious a foundation that sympathy was not easy to maintain in the face of the ever-present consciousness that the others were different, and not always desirably different.

From the beginning, Jews and Italians lived side by side in the district with comparatively little friction. To be sure, it was the code in the public schools for the Italian majority to pick on the Jewish boys, probably as much because they were likely to be good at their lessons and classifiable as "sissies" as because they were Jewish. They were free, also, to call "Jew boy" not only at the Jewish child, but, on at least one occasion, at a Jewish teacher who strayed onto an Italian block. A large proportion of the Italians questioned—70 per cent of the older and 49 per cent of the younger groups—said they objected to intermarriage with Jews, and family battles had arisen over such intermarriages when they did take place. Nevertheless, these differences did not prevent a sympathetic attitude and never led to the kind of open clashes that used to characterize difficulties between Italians and Irish—possibly for no other reason than that the Jews had always been few in number. A number of Italians interviewed gratuitously offered the generalization that Italians got along well with the Jews—better, in fact, than with the Irish or old Americans—and none were at pains to assert, or even ready to admit, the opposite proposition. Some pointed to the amicable relations between Jews and Italians at work; others mentioned the regard in which the local Jewish shopkeepers were held and the extent to which they were accepted on the street where they lived with Italians; others called attention to the Italian boys who went with Jewish girls. A number of Italians who had moved away selected a Jewish section of the Bronx in preference to an Italian or any other type of neighborhood.

Since the Jews of this district had always been a scattered minority living among the Italians, they necessarily occupied the same houses, attended the same public schools, their children played together, and they had dealings with each other. They were drawn together, too, by the treatment which both received from the dominant American and Irish elements. Latin and Semitic immigrant newcomers of the same period shared a position of inferiority in the face of entrenched "Nordic" domination. Years of common residence and of common experience in rebuff made them increasingly sympathetic. Together they were excluded from much in American life which they sought. Some few might have had contact with exclusive schools which "do not take Jews and Italians." More had applied for jobs where "Jews and Italians are not wanted." Still others had been members, or sought to be members, of trade unions where officials disliked "Jews and Italians," whom they regarded as bad workers, always out to get something for themselves. As the two largest minority groups in the city, the Jews and Italians found themselves coupled together and excluded by those who occupied desired positions or held the keys to social and economic advancement.

But for all the similarity of experience which brought Jews and Italians near together, their fundamental difference of religion and the racial separateness of the Jews kept them in some respects farther apart than Italians and Irish. The Jews, long acclimated to the position of a minority group living its own distinctive life within a larger community, never forgot the line which separated the Gentiles from them, or the fact that their neighbors, the Italians, belonged on the other side of that line. All Gentiles were inferior, but to the Jews of this district the Gentile population with which they came in contact was especially inferior. Traditionally devoted to education, the local Jews could not fail to look down upon the Italians and the low-class Irish, a large proportion of whom were indifferent to educational benefits. In the local schools the Jews were used to being the bright ones, making up the rapid advancement classes, going on to high school and continuing in college while most of their Italian friends dropped by the way. Taught to rely on their wits rather than on their brawn and not to fight back, the Jewish boys rated as sissies. Neither on the street nor in school, nor, more especially, at home, were they allowed to forget their difference. They must earn admission to street groups by their skill at ball; when they got home, it was again and again impressed upon them that they were not to be like the "Irish bums" or the "Wops." Rough language and conduct picked up on the street was described as "the way the Goys act," and condemned as unworthy of a Jew.

At an earlier age than the Italian or the Irish child, each of whom started his career in an environment predominantly composed of members of his own group, and much earlier than the Jew of a Jewish neighborhood, the Jewish child of Greenwich Village learned that to be a Jew was to be different. Instead of adhering closely to the pattern of behavior which he found about him, he was taught from the first that he must act differently, and as soon as he began to notice the conduct of his neighbors he realized that their rhythm of life differed from his—the Sabbath, food, Christmas which was nothing to him and the High Holidays which were nothing to them. Whatever his later experience, the Jew raised in this community had had impressed on him in his early years a consciousness of difference which the Jew of the Bronx did not have.

While to the Jews the Italians remained low "Goy," the latter in turn regarded the Jews as forever outside the pale. The highest compliment they could pay to the individual Jew whom they had taken into their group was, "You're one square Jew."

It was hard to distinguish any indications that this basic gap had been in any way actually lessened. The Jews among the local population of the Village were no less conscious of their Jewishness than they had been a decade before. Though they had dropped many of their observances, the Jewish families of the neighborhood still remained consciously and self-consciously Jewish. The slight decrease in Jew-baiting reported at school seemed to reflect a decrease in the roughness of the school rather than an increase in tolerance, and the Jewish youngsters in school in 1930 insisted that they had to face the same scorn and dislike as their older brothers had found. Jewish children joined in Irish and Italian play groups because they were too scattered to form block groups of their own, but the young people, with very few exceptions, either hung around together or spent their time in the Jewish neighborhoods of Brooklyn or the Bronx.

Between Jews and Irish there had always been less harmony than between Jews and Italians, for the former resented the superiority which the Irish maintained but the Italians could not assume. Only those who entered politics found it expedient to come to terms with the Irish. The most conspicuous of these went so far as to turn Catholic and to proclaim his political intentions by passing the contribution plate in the church attended by the leading Irish politicians. The parishioners understood and commented, "When I saw him going around with that plate, I knew which way he was headed!"

The Spanish colony on the extreme western edge of the district, though small, remained absolutely distinct, and hardly touched most of the elements in the locality closely enough to produce either conflict or contact. With their separate church, their own cafés, grocers, tailors, and barbers, the only institution that brought them into contact with others was the school. Relations with their Irish neighbors were far from cordial. These were currently described in what had plainly become a conventional phrase, "The Irishman fears the Spaniard's knife; the Spaniard fears the Irishman's fist." Active conflict existed on the waterfront, where the Irish had waged a losing fight to hold their own.

The Irish considered the Spanish dirty as well as dangerous, regarding them, even more than the Italians, as "foreigners" and lumping together all Spanish-speaking people of various complexions—"Cubans," Filipinos, Mexicans—as "niggers." The Spanish either disliked the Irish for being unfriendly, having "bad morals," or "thinking the world is theirs," or, more generally, they ignored them completely. Some who were questioned directly said they had never lived or worked among them, when actually there were Irish families in the immediate vicinity of their homes. Although the Spanish had occupied the same blocks for two decades, there had been no *rapprochement*. There was some intermingling on the part of the children. Spanish children were found in 1930 in one solidly Spanish-speaking street play group and in four mixed groups where they were in the minority.

The Italians had practically no contact with the Spanish because they lived at the opposite end of the district. Those few who had had any contact with them were much more ready to say a good word for them, however, than were the Irish. On the whole, the Spanish kept very strictly to themselves, the women never going out except to church and the men associating closely within their own group. They knew other Spanish people in upper Manhattan and Brooklyn rather than non-Spanish in the locality. They maintained an attitude of extreme suspicion toward all others. Whenever the interviewer who canvassed the district knocked, he was greeted from behind the closed door by the same question, "Who is there? Do you speak Spanish?" Although most had been in America for more than ten years, few of those interviewed could speak English. They had remained entirely isolated from the life of other elements in the community.

The only two ethnic groups in the locality which had really shown social amalgamation had been the Irish and Germans. It may have been the advent of the Italians, alien to both, which brought the Germans and Irish together and made relations between them seem closer than they actually had been. But even when discounted for this attitude, the evidence of such *rapprochement* was strong. Irish and Germans alike, in describing the old neighborhood of the early days of the century, offered the statement that the two groups always got along well together—lived together, "shared" the neighborhood, attended each other's church picnics in spite of differences of religion, and formed a harmonious community. Intermarriage between Irish and Germans was said to have been general, and those few German families who still remained in the neighborhood bore out this generalization. Among the eighteen German families interviewed, all stated that marriage between Germans and Irish was usual and two had Irish wives. Half of these, however, did not approve of such intermarriage, insisting "like should stick to like, otherwise there's always trouble." Although intermarriage with Protestants was strongly opposed among those Irish who remained, difference in religion appeared not to have been an insuperable barrier to the marriage of German boys with Irish girls a generation before.

The contrast between the close relationship among the earlier groups in the locality and the distance among the later groups clearly reflected the fundamental change in the character of the neighborhood. Thirty or more years before, when the neighborhood was a community with many of the characteristics of a small town, its assimilative powers were good. Whoever came into the community was, in due time, incorporated into it. In the community of the post-War period, no such assimilative powers remained. It had become merely an area, no longer a community.

· · · · ·

17. The revolt of the urban ghettos, 1964-1967

JOSEPH BOSKIN

· · · · ·

THE CITY: NEVER THE PROMISED LAND

One of the most poignant and enduring conflicts in our national life, frequently subtle, yet constantly gnawing, has been the antagonism between rural and urban America. This has been far more than a conflict between the political and power interests of divergent human locales; it has been a conflict in the American consciousness, and is implicit in the American value system. Since the early nineteenth century, millions of Americans have yielded to a seemingly fatal attraction to make the great migration from farm and village to the city. Whatever may have been the harsh imperatives which guided them, there was a persistent tendency to look back, with a degree of nostalgia and with a sense of irreparable loss, to an idyllic rural setting. In a nation in which the forces of urbanization were unrelenting, where urban living was clearly the shape of the future, there was a deep conviction, as Walter Lippmann wrote, that the city should not be acknowledged as the American ideal. This mood was not limited merely to those who had strayed from the intended ways, but was shared by those who were born in the city environs. The city has never been conceived as being the preferred place to inhabit permanently, nor has it been romanticized in the arts and mass media. It has rarely been regarded as a focus for creative living.

Abridged and edited from Joseph Boskin, "The revolt of the urban ghettos, 1964-1967," *The Annals,* March 1969, 382:1–14. Copyright © 1969 by The American Academy of Political and Social Science. Reprinted by permission.
The author is Professor of History, Boston University, Boston, Mass.

The burgeoning of industry, and the expansion of the middle class, with its increased financial and physical mobility, enabled the nostalgic rural life to be transplanted into suburbia and exurbia. Thus, for this group of urban dwellers, alternatives of living were possible. The actuality of choice, however, gave rise to an ambivalence in which the best and worst of feelings conjoined: the desire for the idealized rural life-style and a strong desire to partake in the activities of the city.

The movement into the cities in the past two centuries, then, was not accomplished without the creation of a basic paradox. The economic means to achieve a fuller life, though associated with the city, was not fulfilled within the city. The compromise of the suburban community seemed to provide a solution to the uncomfortable dilemma of rural versus urban life. Seemingly, one could have the best of both styles. Several difficulties, however, prevented the suburb from becoming the American middle-class nirvana. The magnitude of the march to the suburbs necessitated mass transportation to and from the central cities. The city administrators' choice, the freeway, soon became a strangulated contact with the city, bringing it not close enough, yet too far away. Yet, many who lived in suburbia were economically dependent upon the city, so that contact with the core city was never physically far removed. Ironically, too, transportation arteries made possible the invisibility of the ghettos.

The development of a sophisticated mass communications system, in the form of television, in the early 1950's reinforced the ambivalent antagonisms towards the city. Throughout the 1950's and 1960's, television portrayed the city as a violent, unhealthy, dirty, corrupt, lonely, unseemly place for people to live, develop, and grow. Survival appeared to be the main component dramatized in series after series. With the exceptions of such productions as were borrowed from earlier successful radio shows, the bulk of television performances were antiurban in substance. In such medical series as "Ben Casey," "The Young Interns," and "The Nurses," psychological maladies or life and death were constant themes. The decade of the 1920's, depicted in such series as "The Roaring Twenties" and "The Untouchables," consistently associated the city with gang violence. In such outstanding series as "Naked City," which dealt with some realistic problems of life in New York, and "East Side, West Side," a series based on the experiences of a social worker, the promise and potential of the city were lacking. Television largely reinforced the image of the city earlier perpetuated by literature and the movies. As Herbert Kosower has correctly noted: "Almost all of Hollywood's films deal with contemporary urban life on a superficial fantasy plane."[1] Even

---

[1]Herbert Kosower, King Vidor, and Joseph Boshur, "The Arts," *Psychology Today,* August 1968, 2(3):16.

Street Scene, On the Waterfront, The Naked City, The Pawnbroker, and *A Thousand Clowns* tended to reflect the harsh aspects of urban life.

Resistance to city living grew from several sources. The organization of the city was felt to be antagonistic to basic American values. It bred impersonality, detachment, and unhealthy conditions. Criticism stemmed from the conception of the city as being antiindividualistic. Groups of people were herded together in living and working conditions which placed a premium on co-operative and collectivistic solutions to social problems.

The city was further indicted for altering the landscape of America, for denying its past and playing havoc with its future. As Anselm Strauss has accurately written, the United States managed to develop an industrial economy without developing a thoroughly urbanized citizenry. Americans, he noted, entered upon the great urbanization of the nineteenth century "protestingly, metaphorically walking backward."[2]

The image of the city was capped in the catch phrase originally ascribed to New York City: "It's a nice place to visit but I wouldn't want to live there." Living was to be done in the suburbs, away from the source of corruptions. The "Promised Land," then, was to be sought outside the city.

Aided by affluence, millions fled from the city into the landscaped suburbs—leaving the core cities to the newer migrant and immigrant groups. Negro-, Puerto Rican-, Mexican-, and Japanese-Americans, and other smaller American minority groups with dark or nonwhite skins, filled the central cities. By the 1960's, all major and most smaller cities had sizable numbers of various ethnic groups in the downtown areas, living in slum ghettos, breathing the increasingly foul urban air, and becoming increasingly alienated. They gradually developed an urban consciousness—a consciousness of the entrapped underclass.

The sense of entrapment stemmed from the inability of the ethnic groups to break out of the urban ghetto and become part of the burgeoning middle classes. Alienation grew out of the anger of betrayal, a betrayal that began when the inner-city dwellers were made the inheritors of decaying cities. That they were being deserted, that the promised land in the North and West was drying up, as Langston Hughes caustically expressed it, "like a raisin in the sun," became increasingly clear in the decades of the 1950's and 1960's. Claude Brown, in his *Manchild in the Promised Land,* an affectionate portrayal of Harlem, began his sketch with this denial of the promise:

I want to talk about the first Northern urban generation of Negroes. I want to talk about the experiences of a misplaced generation, of a

---

[2]Anselm Strauss, *Images of the American City* (New York: The Free Press, 1961), p. 123.

misplaced people in an extremely complex, confused society. This is a story of their searching, their dreams, their sorrows, their small and futile rebellions, and their endless battle to establish their own place in America's greatest metropolis—and in America itself.

The characters are sons and daughters of former Southern sharecroppers. These were the poorest people of the South, who poured into New York City during the decade following the Great Depression. These migrants were told that unlimited opportunities for prosperity existed in New York and that there was no "color problem" there. They were told that Negroes lived in houses with bathrooms, electricity, running water, and indoor toilets. To them, this was the "promised land" that Mammy had been singing about in the cotton fields for many years. . . . It seems that Cousin Willie, in his lying haste, had neglected to tell the folks down home about one of the most important aspects of the promised land: it was a slum ghetto. There was a tremendous difference in the way life was lived up North. There were too many people full of hate and bitterness crowded into a dirty, stinky, uncared-for closet-size section of a great city.

Before the soreness of the cotton fields had left Mama's back, her knees were getting sore from scrubbing "Goldberg's" floor. Nevertheless, she was better off; she had gone from the fire into the frying pan.

The children of these disillusioned colored pioneers inherited the total lot of their parents—the disappointments, the anger. To add to their misery, they had little hope of deliverance. For where does one run to when he's already in the promised land?[3]

One runs to one's soul brother.

The significant consequences of the great migration along the hallelujah trail was the development of an urban consciousness in the ghettos of the industrial cities. Alain Locke, in his important book in the 1920's, *The New Negro,* took cognizance of the ecological forces at work in Harlem. Proscription and prejudice, he noted, had thrown dissimilar black elements into a common area of contact and interaction. Prior to the movement into Harlem, the Negro was "a race more in name than in fact, or to be exact, more in sentiment than in experience." The central experience between these groups, he continued, was that of "a common condition rather than a life in common. In Harlem, Negro life is seizing upon its first chances for group expression and self-determination."[4] The fusing of sentiment and experience in Harlem was repeated over and again in ghettos across the country. Indeed, ghetto experience became a common denominator, its lifestyle and language and conditions a similarity of experiences.

Had the ghetto become a viable environment within a dynamic city

---

[3]Claude Brown, *Manchild in the Promised Land* (New York: New American Library, 1965), pp. vii–viii.

[4]Alain Locke, *The New Negro* (New York: Albert and Charles Boni, 1925), pp. 6–7.

existence, the level of grievance-consciousness shared by Negroes would have been muted. But the opposite occurred. Instead, the ghetto became a dead-end to those who lived in it. It became an object of loathing, a mirror of a squalid existence. Feelings of hopelessness and isolation were recurrent themes in the testimony of the slum residents, wrote the United States Commission on Civil Rights in 1967. When asked what she would do if she had sufficient income, one resident declared, "The first thing I would do myself is move out of the neighborhood. I feel the entire neighborhood is more or less a trap."[5]

Compounding these antagonisms were, of course, the intensifying antiurban attitudes of whites. "The people in Harlem," wrote James Baldwin in *Nobody Knows My Name,* two years before the first protest riot, "know they are living there because white people do not think they are good enough to live elsewhere. No amount of 'improvement' can sweeten this fact. . . . A ghetto can be improved in one way only: out of existence."[6] These resentments were further exacerbated by the obvious disparity between the Caucasian and black neighborhoods. Said a young man to Budd Schulberg in the Watts Happening Coffee House immediately after the riots:

> The contrast: the spectacular growth of central and west L.A. vs. the stagnation of Watts. . . . You've conquered it, baby. You've got it made. Some nights on the roof of our rotten falling down buildings we can actually see your lights shining in the distance. So near and yet so far. We want to reach out and grab it and punch it on the nose.[7]

The mythical urban melting pot began to simmer and finally boiled over.

The protest riots which occurred in massive profusion were thus the consequence of a myriad of historical and ecological factors which fused in the 1960's. Their outstanding feature was a collective mode of attitude, behavior, and sense of power.

THE CRY: BURN, BABY, BURN

The sudden burst of rage which rent Harlem in July 1964 was the third mass outburst in that community in the twentieth century. On two previous occasions, the first time during the Great Depression and the second during World War II, blacks in one of the most highly concen-

---

[5]U.S., Commission on Civil Rights, *A Time to Listen . . . A Time to Act* (Washington, D.C.: U.S. Government Printing Office, 1967), p. 6.

[6]James Baldwin, *Nobody Knows My Name* (New York: Delta Books, 1962), p. 65.

[7]"Watts—End or beginning," *Los Angeles Times,* Calendar, May 15, 1966, p. 3, col. 2.

trated, racially, ethnic ghettos in the nation signified their protest in spontaneous rioting. Unlike the earlier uprisings which were confined to Harlem, however, the actions in 1964 proved to be the beginning of an urban black protest throughout the country. In city after city, summer after summer, blacks took vengeance by wrecking the hated symbols within their own ghetto areas.

The violent protest in Harlem was rapidly repeated in seven other urban Negro ghettos in the next two months: Bedford-Stuyvesant (Brooklyn), Rochester, Paterson, Jersey City, Elizabeth, Philadelphia, and Dixmoor (Chicago). In 1965, eruptions occurred in five cities, the major conflagrations taking place in Chicago and especially in Los Angeles. Large-scale rioting increased in intensity in the following year, when blacks took to the streets in twenty cities, including Cleveland, Chicago, Omaha, East Oakland, and San Francisco. The year 1967 began on a volatile note as disturbances occurred in the spring in the Southern cities of Nashville, Jackson, and Houston. As the heat of the summer increased, so did the temper for violence. There were mass assaults in Roxbury (Boston), Tampa, Dayton, Atlanta, Buffalo, and Cincinnati in the month of June. Within the next two months, Negroes swarmed through the ghettos of twenty-two cities in the North, Midwest, and South, with the largest riots taking place in Toledo, Grand Rapids, Plainfield (New Jersey), Milwaukee, and especially in Newark and Detroit. By 1968 the rioting had subsided, suggesting that the anger had been channeled into aggressive community programs.

The toll of the rioting over the four-year period was devastating. Between 1964 and 1967, approximately 130 civilians, mainly Negroes, and 12 civil personnel, mainly Caucasian, were killed. Approximately 4,700 Negroes and civil personnel were injured. Over 20,000 persons were arrested during the melees; property damages mounted into the hundreds of millions of dollars; many cities resembled the hollowed remnants of war-torn cities.[8]

Despite the disparity of distance, there was a consensus of attitudes and a similarity of actions among those urban blacks who revolted and those who supported the violent protest.[9] Significantly, the riots were largely unplanned, unorganized, and unscheduled. Ray Lewis, a Cleveland youth worker, explained the origins of the outbreak in that city:

It wasn't that people planned our riot so consciously. But take a Negro

---

[8]The rioting which occurred following the assassination of Dr. Martin Luther King in April 1968 is not covered in this paper. These actions were not specifically related to the origins and spread of the urban revolt.

[9]For a further analysis of the "consensus of attitudes and behavior," see Joseph Boskin. "Violence in the ghettos: A consensus of attitudes," in *Violence in Contemporary Society,* ed. Joseph Frank, *New Mexico Quarterly,* Winter 1968, 37(4):317–34.

ghetto where men sit around for years saying, "we gonna get whitey," and you build up a group knowledge of what to do.[10]

Taken together, the riots were the actions of a people, poor and dispossessed and crushed in huge numbers into large slum ghettos, who rose up in wrath against a society committed to democratic ideals. Their outburst was an expression of class antagonism, resentment against racial prejudice, anger at the unreachable affluence around them, and frustration at their sociopolitical powerlessness. "What are these people riotin' about in other cities?" exclaimed Efelka Brown, of the "Sons of Watts," an organization set up to train young males in trade skills. "They want *recognition* and the only way they goin' get it is to riot. We don't want to overthrow the country—we just want what we ain't got."[11]

The sense of betrayal of expectations brought about a focus on the grievances of the past and present. The visibility of an affluent, comfortable, middle-class life, made possible by a powerful mass communications system, was in itself enough to induce dual feelings of resentment and emulation. Pronouncements by the political establishment, however, served only to increase these emotions. Thus, enticed by advertising of the leisure life, excited by legislative programs such as the Civil Rights Acts and the War on Poverty, lured by television programs depicting middle-class life, and hopeful of change in their environment, the poor anticipated an imminent improvement in their socioeconomic position. The failure of society effectively to raise the status of those trapped in the cities contributed immensely to the smoldering resentments.

The urge to retaliate, to return the hurts and the injustices, played an integral part of the protest. By itself, the riot was not "a major thing," stated James Richards to the United States Commission on Civil Rights after the Hunter's Point riot in San Francisco in 1966:

> It was just an idea to strike out at something and someone. Even if you don't do anything but break a window or a chair or something like this, you feel that you are hurting a white man or something like this because the white man is the one that is doing everything to you that causes you to have all these problems on you now.[12]

Similar expressions of deep-welled anger were heard from Puerto Ricans in Spanish Harlem. Piri Thomas, author of *Down These Mean Streets,* in testimony before the National Advisory Commission on Civil Disorders, described the origins of the explosion in that area:

---

[10]John Allan Long, "After the midwest riots," *Christian Science Monitor,* November 10, 1966, p. 11.

[11]"The hard-core ghetto mood," *Newsweek,* Vol. LXX, No. 8, August 21, 1967, p. 21.

[12]*A Time to Listen . . . A Time to Act, op. cit.,* p. 5.

Did you ever stand on street corners and look the other way, at the world of muchos ricos and think, I ain't got a damn? Did you ever count the garbage that flowed down dirty streets, or dig in the back yards who in their glory were a garbage dumps dream? Did you ever stand on rooftops and watch night time cover the bad below? Did you ever put your hand around your throat and feel your pulse beat say, "I do belong and there's not gonna be nobody can tell me, I'm wrong?"[13]

Intense grievances vis-à-vis their inability to achieve even the basic promises of American life of work, status, and housing combined with other minor factors to make the cities highly combustible. The National Advisory Commission found in almost all the cities surveyed "the same major grievance topic among Negro communities."[14] The Commission ranked three levels of grievances among Negroes:

First Level of Intensity.
1. Police practices
2. Unemployment and underemployment
3. Inadequate housing
Second Level of Intensity:
1. Inadequate education
2. Poor recreational facilities and programs
3. Ineffectiveness of the political structure and grievance mechanisms
Third Level of Intensity:
1. Disrespectful white attitudes
2. Discriminatory administration of justice
3. Inadequacy of federal programs
4. Inadequacy of municipal services
5. Discriminatory consumer and credit practices
6. Inadequate welfare programs[15]

To strike out against the visible symbols of white society became a sign of brotherhood. In more than one instance, rock-throwing blacks placed missiles into the hands of residents of the community, saying, "You're either with us or against us, man." In the Watts riot, Mervin Dymally, a Negro assemblyman, was asked by one of the rioters to prove his loyalty by heaving an object at a police car. Dymally refused, saying, "No, man, I'm for peace." The boy quickly replied, "No, you're with the man."[16] Many residents of ghetto areas who did not participate in the actions shouted their approval to those on the streets.

That a general approval, a collective behavior, pervaded the ghettos

---

[13]Piri Thomas, in testimony before the National Advisory Commission on Civil Disorders, September 21, 1967.

[14]U.S., Riot Commission, *Report of the National Advisory Commission on Civil Disorders* (New York: Bantam Books, Inc., 1968), p. 143.

[15]*Ibid.,* pp. 143–144.

[16]*Report of the Governor's Commission on the Los Angeles Riot,* Vol. II (Sacramento, 1966), pp. 88–89.

can be borne out by analysis of the actions of blacks. The two groups singled out for attack were the police and Caucasian-owned businesses. Relations between the police and the minorities, particularly members of the dark-skinned ethnic groups, have always been volatile. As an institution, the police have reflected the attitudes of the majority. To have expected the police to act as a social agency oriented towards reform or conflict-amelioration is to misconstrue their primary function as they view it: namely, the maintenance of law and order. Thus, the police have practiced physical attacks and verbal harassment on minority-group members without interference. Though the public was generally unaware of the treatment accorded minority-ethnic-group members, a prejudicial attitude on its part sanctioned police actions. The language of the police vis-à-vis Negroes—"nigger," "monkey," "them," "boy"— were terms in general usage in American culture. For many years, blacks have attempted to bring to light the ample evidence of discriminatory beatings and humiliations. One such attempt in 1965, by furious blacks in the South-Central area of Los Angeles, compiled a listing of the discriminatory remarks of the then Los Angeles Chief of Police William H. Parker—which resulted in a fifteen-page report entitled "Police Chief William H. Parker Speaks"—and distributed it in the community.[17]

Yet, the police became a main focal point for attack not only because of their attitude toward and behavior with minority groups, but primarily because they came to symbolize the despised invisible white power structure. Of the institutional contacts with which ghetto-dwellers have intimate contact—schools, social welfare and employment agencies, medical facilities, business owners—the police embody the most crushing authority. For many blacks, the police had come to represent more than enforcement of law; they were viewed as members of an occupying army and as an oppressive force acting on behalf of those who rule their environment but who fled it for the greener pastures. "A policeman is an object of contempt," Ernie W. Chambers of Omaha bitterly stated in testimony given before the National Advisory Committee on Civil Disorders.[18] The system represented by the police has been oppressive, the method of rule has been heavy with force, and the phrase "maintain law and order" has been directed basically towards the control of Negroes. "Like why, man, should I get home?" angrily inquired a young black during the Watts riot. "These cops have been pushin' me 'round all my life. Kickin' my ——— and things like that. Whitey ain't no damn good, he talks 'bout law and order, it's his law and order, it ain't mine [word deleted by the Commission]."[19]

---

[17]William H. Parker, "Police Chief William H. Parker Speaks" (Los Angeles: Community Relations Conference of Southern California, 1965).

[18]Ernie W. Chambers, in testimony before the National Advisory Commission on Civil Disorders, September 23, 1967. The Commission described Chambers as a "grass-roots leader."

[19]*Report of the Governor's Commission on the Los Angeles Riot,* Vol. I (Sacramento, 1966), p. 43.

That a collective wrath directed against the police goaded ghetto residents is evident from an analysis of the early stages of the riots. It is significant that most revolts began as a consequence of an incident in which the police were, in some manner, involved. In several instances, the initiating episode was in the line of routine activity. In the Watts situation, for instance, police stopped two men who were driving in an intoxicated condition. Nevertheless, the significance of the specific event bore no relation to the more serious undercurrent of animosity which had been previously created. In other cases, verbal and physical actions by the police were instrumental in increasing a tense situation by inflaming the ghetto people, as happened in the Newark riot of 1967, which really began when the police charged out of the station house towards a large group of demonstrating and jeering Negroes.

Equally instructive is the fact that snipers, despite their numbers, hit extremely few policemen and firemen during the three years of rioting. The low number of deaths of law officials could hardly be ascribed to poor marksmanship. By 1967, especially in Detroit, the incidence of sniper fire had increased considerably; yet, only four law officers were killed, as compared to thirty-nine civilians. Indeed, of the eighty-three persons who died in seventy-five disorders analyzed by the Permanent Sub-committee on Investigations of the Senate Committee on Government Operations in 1967, approximately ten persons were public officials, primarily law officers and firemen, whereas the remainder were civilians, primarily Negroes.[20]

White businessmen were the second most exposed group singled out for attack. Resentment against the practices of exploitation, in the form of hidden and higher interest rates, shoddy goods and lower quality, higher prices and questionable service, had likewise been building for many years. The communications system in the community had long isolated such business establishments. Consequently, the majority of stores damaged and looted were those against which ill-feelings had developed. Negro stores frequently were protected by identifying signs: "Blood Brother," "Soul Brother," "Negro-owned." Not only were black businesses generally left untouched, but so, too, were libraries, schools, hospitals, clinics, and, surprisingly, governmental agencies. There were instances of bricks and sniper fire hitting these various buildings; however, no concerted attack was conducted. Many places burned down because of the refusal of the rioters to permit fire engines into the area.

Nevertheless, retail businesses suffered a much greater proportion of the damage during the violence than public institutions, industrial properties, or private residences. In Newark in 1967, 1,029 establishments listed damage to buildings or loss of inventory or both.[21] Those businesses which were hardest hit by rioters were those which were felt

[20] Report of the National Advisory Commission on Civil Disorders, op. cit., pp. 115–116.
[21] Ibid.

to be the most exploitative in their business practices: liquor, clothing, food, and furniture stores. Indeed, in at least nine of the riots studied by the President's National Advisory Commission on Civil Disorders, the damage was, in part, the result of "deliberate attacks on white-owned businesses characterized in the Negro community as unfair or disrespectful toward Negroes."[22]

. . . . .

In sum, the revolts in the mid-1960's—more than the nonviolent movement of Dr. Martin Luther King and the extraordinarily powerful civil rights movement of the early 1960's—directed attention to the anguished plights of millions of Negroes, Puerto Ricans, and Mexican-Americans living in the urban centers of the country. The spontaneous outbursts, the collective actions, and the consensual attitudes of blacks and browns highlighted the failure of American society to recognize the problems of the racial minority groups in the cities. The events stemmed not only from the tradition of racist mentality but also from the ambiguous attitudes towards the city itself. The enormity of the failure led to one of the most intense social crises in American society in the twentieth century.

18. The ghetto as legacy

ROY SIMON BRYCE-LA PORTE

The abolition of slavery and the disappearance of the slave plantation can be likened to the sudden destruction of any total institution by external sources. The afflicted are usually transferred to another total institution of the same type. That is, until their social definition or the larger society's attitudes toward the afflicted have changed, special institutions will be developed to quarantine and service them. In fact, whatever the emergency structure that is used to hold and treat them, it will then take on the identity of a specific total institutional type by virtue of its association with the afflicted; e.g., prisons for the bad, asylums for the mad,

---

[22] *Ibid.*

This excerpt from "The slave plantation: Background to present conditions of urban blacks," by Roy Simon Bryce-LaPorte is reprinted from *Race, Change, and Urban Society,* edited by Peter Orleans and William R. Ellis, Jr., 1971, pp. 257–84, by permission of the Publisher, Sage Publications, Inc.

The author is Associate Professor of Sociology, Yale University, New Haven, Conn.

reservations for the useless, concentration camps for the dangerous and disdained.

Accordingly we should not be surprised that blacks have increasingly been quarantined into urban ghettos, disproportionately to more conventional but negatively labeled total institutions, and continue to be deprived of frontier, property, power, or community. Nor should we be surprised at the structure of these new locales. These present forms of institutionalized racism are simply indications that blacks have not undergone, in the eyes of their former masters, what Peter Berger and Thomas Luckmann (1966: 157–167) call "successful alteration"; that is, sufficient rehabilitation to be accepted fully and treated as equals. But, as pointed out, the denial of rehabilitative opportunities is perhaps as old and institutionalized as the denial of a rehabilitated status. Slavery was intended as a self-sustaining system—a vicious circle of injustice. Military and moral pressures, perhaps economic ones, mitigated against the persistence of slavery, and urbanization mitigated against the prevalence of plantations today, but underlying those new urban forms is that lingering definition of blacks as contemptuous unequals. And, built into their operations and structures, are mechanisms for maintaining and reinforcing that inequality.

The ghetto then is not simply an expression of unequal urban development or black social disorganization. It is an expression of the racial legacy of slavery, an urban adaptation of a historically racist society. The phrase "to get Mr. Charlie [Whitey, the Man] off our backs" is at minimum a recognition of that legacy. It is obviously derived from the "ole Massa" tradition of slave plantation days. And while from an objective analytic stance the ghetto as an urban condition is much more complex and diffused than the plantation, it is sociologically fruitful to speculate on the similarities and differences between the two social forms. In fact, the concern should go further to inquire as to which blacks utter such phrases and when. It is already interesting to hear them uttered at times of anxiety and desperation, for it implies a visceral, deeply felt sentiment. To the extent that under such circumstances the range extends beyond just ghetto dwellers to the wider black population, it is suggested that as an utterance of purpose and a definition of a situation, this sentiment is widely shared as well.

Compared to a plantation, the proximity of the black ghetto to the model of a total institution is less obvious but, nevertheless, it shares a number of the anticommunal characteristics of the old estate, even though slavery as such is nonexistent in the United States today. The black ghetto is not owned or managed by a single individual, but from the eyes of the black residents it is often perceived to be owned and managed by one single, exclusive group—whites. "Mr. Charlie" or "the Man" is thus a label for a collective referent with little regard for sex, age, ethnicity, or number. It is a recognition that on certain structural levels the discrete stratification of people into white dominant and black subordinate within a given urban residential context is not a crucial break from the usually smaller and more simplified plantation structure but rather an elaboration. The extrinsic objectives of the ghetto may be multiple, diffused, and less clear, but its intrinsic function is quite similar to the plantation—to legitimize differences among men in terms of the superiority and acceptability of those who *can* live outside from those who *must* live within. Its specialized functions are not always as utilitarian as the plantation, but it shares the same universal functions as the plantation—to exercise custody over the different or unequal. Even though the physical boundaries are often less static than the plantation, they are always made salient in the minds of the populace. Police patrols, uncooperative taxi drivers and garbage collectors, unscrupulous real estate agents and merchants, and uninhibited black pedestrians by their activities give clues to the shift in boundary from time to time. The scope of confinement in the ghetto is felt particularly by those residents who are unemployed or for other reasons are forced to perform most of their daily activities within the local neighborhood. This saliency is even more sharply felt by those whose imaginative or intellectual faculties are not sufficiently developed to provide psychological escape from their physical confinement.

Even though urban power structures are generally viewed as more diffused and democratic than older agrarian forms, in the case of the black ghetto the power structure tends to be in fact unilaterally white and remote at its highest levels. This is still generally true notwithstanding the growing number of black mayors in American cities, particularly as it becomes clear that white suburban and rural populations, through state and county governments, maintain a stranglehold on urban development. The problems and priorities of the ghetto dwellers are often ignored or relegated to a secondary concern unless by implication the calamities they represent are thought to have far-reaching effects. Property and space are often owned by white absentee proprietors. And whether the loci of employment are local or not, unemployment tends to be high, various forms of social ills tend to prevail, and there is a proliferation of welfare and other forms of corrective or paternalistic agencies. In addition to many such agencies being nonrepresentative and substandard, they tend to be noneffective in that they neither improve the rehabilitative potential of their wards nor change the local conditions. They also tend to be ritualistic, repressive, or both. In fact, they often come to recruit, mortify, and stigmatize ghetto dwellers and, therefore, add to the justification of their continued segregation. With reference to their repressiveness, it takes various forms from outright police brutality to more subtle means of social control and cooptation. The institutional network of the ghetto thus represents a system of social control and sanction which is executed by way of coercion and control of crucial services, and is designed to stifle creative individuality, daring leadership, or viable local cooperative groupings which in any way seem likely to undermine the present relationship of the ghetto to the rest of the society, and by extension, blacks to whites.

The ghetto then represents many things not normally found in standard white or establishment-sociological literature. It is an arena of uneven confrontation of will, sentiments, and interests between two traditionally antagonistic forces—those who have achieved status, power, frontier, and community, and those whom they seek to prevent from acquiring such bases of equality (Clark, 1965). Surely it is also the arena of contest and simultaneously of communion (Kaplan, 1969: 164–176; Neuwirth, 1969: 148–165; Pitt, 1970) among blacks themselves, who, beyond the monolithic category imposed upon them by their white antagonists, comprise an array of different statuses, types, and stages of social development. But despite these internal differentiations there is a shared feeling among blacks of not having undergone a complete change of status in the eyes of white America, that their conditions have not completely changed *as a people,* even if as individuals. Thus, as *black* individuals, their acquired statuses are threatened and their individualities overlooked, especially in time of crisis.

It is this frustration, ending sometimes in futility, sometimes in a fighting mood, that such utterances express. It is a feeling of unfulfillment. For, while the ghetto has become the modern birthplace of some of the most ambitious and creative schemes for self-development and self-determination in black America, it has also been the scene of some of the most telling catastrophes and fiascos. The situation is complicated further by accumulated tensions. Tension converts into distress as the immediate causes seem not solely externally derived but also stem from internal frictions and disabilities within the black population (Comer, 1967: 21–27; Kramer, 1970: 213–253). Thus the utterances and actions of ghetto dwellers reflect not simply a style of life nor preoccupation with the present problems, but rather the burdensome baggage of bondage and oppression which antedates the contemporary and the urban.

The history of the United States has been described as that of the acquisition and development of the frontiers. Some historians have declared the frontier closed since the end of the nineteenth century (Turner, 1893). Elkins and McKitrick (1954: 321–353) have ably demonstrated that an important concomitant of frontier development has been local community development and participatory democracy. The history of the United States has also been described as a movement from rural to urban society. Urbanization, of which all of this is a part, is then a historical process, one that has been defined as an increase in the complexity or scale of social organization (Greer, 1962: 33–66). However, urbanization is not equally experienced or shared by all people or regions of a society at the same given time (Myrdal, 1957). That is just part of the complexity. Another aspect of that complexity has to do with a *masking* process which accompanies urbanization, so that old issues are constantly being replaced by new issues whether they have been solved or not. Given the inequality in the society, the problems of the powerful and articulate in-groups are often attended to and solutions sanctioned over those of less powerful, inarticulate groups. In fact, given the power and interest of those who constitute the "establishment" (and I use this term broadly to include even radical white groups in the United States, who are not in power or in conformity with government but nevertheless control resources and hold privileged positions, in terms of being heard, over nonwhites), the problems and priorities of black people are often submerged or redefined away from the uncomfortable and the threatening basic truths of American racism that predate and underlie urban arrangements.

It is a basic truth of American racism that blacks as a group in the United States have been deprived of frontier and its concomitants of community and participatory democracy in respectable proportions. The plantation may have had, as one of its original functions, the opening of the frontier (Gray, 1933; Lynd, 1967: 139), but while the slaves labored within the plantation to open that frontier, they were deprived access to that frontier and of the opportunity to establish communities in the Plantation South. On the other hand, the notion of frontier, a more symbolic phenomenon, a sense of having to achieve, acquire, and exercise domain over something of value, must have been cherished by them in their quest to be equals in the American context. Given the racialistically instigated lag between black and white political-economic developments, it is not difficult to understand that the notion of frontier persists among blacks when it may have died or even been transformed in meaning for whites. Given the power differentiation between whites and blacks today, it is not difficult to appreciate either, that the present urban institutions are not oriented to articulate or reinforce the notions of black people over those of whites. Hence the very notions of ethnic frontier and local neighborhood which are essential for providing impetus to the movement of black people at this particular moment in their history, are issued negative values or secondary priorities by urban agencies, in contrast to the thrust of the Black Muslims, CORE, Republic of New Africa, Black studies, the Black Academy of Arts and Letters, the Institute of the Black World, and other current expressions of nationalist domain.

The history of the United States has been described as that of waves of immigrants, each motivated by notions of frontier, which they eventually came to enjoy either as plural communities or as parts of an integrated political-economic arrangement or both (Gordon, 1964; Lewis, 1969). Blacks, one of the oldest immigrant groups, despite the coercive nature of their arrival to America and their brutalizing slave experience, rejected colonization as a scheme and instead chose the way of other Americans—integrated communities or homogeneous ones within a presumably larger integrated total society. Both efforts were frustrated by the two evil white twins of power and paternalism. They have been refused the alternative of equal participation in American democracy or that of establishing control over their own communities. Thus the frustration continues, and the fundamental fight for black frontier persists.

The scene of the struggle today is the ghetto—" getting Mr. Charlie off our back," "getting ourselves together," and "getting our own thing going." The very ordering of these phrases is suggestive of the mood, momentum, and direction of current black movement—from the earlier unorganized, tension-releasing rebellions of Watts, Newark, and Detroit, to the later organized community- and institution-building struggles at Ocean Hill-Brownsville, Newark, and Atlanta. The present can be history and black ghettos are the scene of the making of history by blacks in the interests of blacks.

The ghetto must be studied as frontierland which black people are trying to conquer, to develop as *their* community, to engage in participatory democracy as they seek to build and develop that community. The ghetto is not closed frontier, as establishment-historical literature would suggest. It is merely urban. It is claimed developed territory, defended by white interest groups, much more powerful and sophisticated than the red Indians of old. The drive for domain and the quest for community control by the "newly arrived" black people are repeatedly frustrated by the self-proclaimed new "natives." The contest of urban confrontation is so complex and dynamic that the underlying issues are constantly being masked by new overlays of cumulating epiphenomenal ones. The urban condition continues to be an overwhelmingly complex institutional arrangement which reflects interest intrinsically at odds with the desire of black people, but interests often distant and beyond "where black people are at."

The rhetoric of the ghetto must not be dismissed any more than the actions of its speakers. Cool talk, angry talk, crazy talk, jive. Whatever it may be called it must be looked upon with historical consciousness as existential and perceptive cues for new sociological insights on the meaning and nature of black urban behavior. The urban condition of most black people, the ghetto, must be studied for its retentions, parallels, and departures from the slave plantation. The particular behavioral and organizational nuances and limitations of ghetto people must be studied in comparison with slaves, as Malcolm X suggested. Likewise, the discriminatory and exploitative system of postbellum society must be studied against the background of the slave system of antebellum society. The complexity of ghetto culture must be studied in terms of a "bicultural underlife" of a people of whom most have been segregated and suppressed ever since their arrival in the continental USA (Blauner, 1970: 347–366; Valentine and Valentine, 1970). As such it is a set of behaviors and expectations too often unnoticed, misunderstood, and disregarded. It is pregnant with secondary adjustments and esoteric symbolism, which confound scholars and white citizens alike. The conception that white men hold today of black men and the institutionalized system by which it is expressed must be studied against the plantation past. It is only then we can begin to answer how far we have come, how much further we must go, and what means are necessary to get there. *Dig it? Then let's get with it.*

REFERENCES

Berger, P. and Luckmann, T. *The Social Construction of Reality.* Garden City, N.Y.: Doubleday, 1966.

Blauner, R. "Black culture: myth or reality?" in N. Whitten and J. Szwed (eds.) *Afro-American Anthropology.* New York: Free Press, 1970.

Clark, K. *The Dark Ghetto,* New York: Harper & Row, 1965.

Comer, J. "The social power of the Negro." *Scientific American,* April 1967, 216: 21–27.

Elkins, S. and McKitrick, E., Jr. "A meaning for Turner's frontier." Parts I and II. *Political Science Quarterly,* 1954, 69: 3 & 4.

Gordon, M. *Assimilation in American Life.* New York: Oxford University Press, 1964.

Gray, L. C. *History of Agriculture in the Southern United States to 1860,* Vol. 1. Washington, D.C.: Carnegie Institute, 1933.

Greer, S. *The Emerging City.* New York: Free Press, 1962.

Kaplan, H. M. "The Black Muslims and the Negro American quest for communion." *British Journal of Sociology,* June 1969, 20: 164–76.

Kramer, J. *The American Minority Community.* New York: Thomas Y. Crowell, 1970.

Lewis, Sir A. "Black power and the American university." *Princeton University Magazine.* Spring 1969, pp. 8-12.

Lynd, S., Jr. *Class Conflict, Slavery, and the United States Constitution.* New York: Bobbs-Merrill, 1967.

Myrdal, G. *Rich Lands and Poor Lands.* New York: Harper & Brothers, 1957.

Neuwirth, G. "A Weberian outline of a theory of community: Its application to the 'dark ghetto'." *British Journal of Sociology,* June 1969, 20: 148–63.

Pitt, J. P. "The meaning of black consciousness: Community or communion?" Paper given at 55th Annual Meeting of the Assn. for the Study of Negro Life and History. Philadelphia, 1970.

Turner, F. J. "The significance of the frontier in American history," in E. E. and F. M. (eds.), *The Early Writings of Frederick Jackson Turner.* Madison: University of Wisconsin Press, 1893.

Valentine, C. and Valentine, M. L. "Blackston." Progress report of a community study on Urban Afro-America. Unpublished manuscript, 1970.
Wish, H. *Antebellum*. New York: Capricorn Books, 1961.

19. Suburbia and the American dream

BENNETT M. BERGER

Americans have never been other than ambivalent in their commitment to cultural variety, as against their longing for cultural uniformity.
Today, this ambivalence is becoming a central concern of public policy.
For, as urban planning becomes an increasingly visible and legitimate
part of the activity of the public sector, its power will grow to support or
to undermine cultural diversity in the traditional seat of that diversity—
the cities. Like the myth of a homogeneous "suburbia," which for a long
time obscured, and to some extent still obscures, the actual variety of
suburban life, complacence about the cultural diversity of cities may
blind us to the conditions which sustain it. My aim in this essay is to
take what I and others have learned about the variety of suburban styles
of life, and to relate this knowledge, first to some of the more pervasive
pluralisms of American culture, and then to a few of the problems of
planning for urban diversity.

THE PERSISTENCE OF THE MYTH OF SUBURBIA

Some years back, I undertook a study (reported in *Working-Class
Suburb,* University of California Press, 1960) in order to observe the
transformation of a group of automobile assembly line workers into the
"suburbanites" who had become stock figures in American popular culture in the 1950's through the satirical and other efforts of a variety of
popular magazines. It seemed to me that, having found a working class
population more than two years settled in a new suburb, I was provided
with an almost natural experimental setting in which to document the
processes through which "suburbia" exercised its profound and diffuse

Abridged and edited from Bennett M. Berger, "Suburbia and the American
dream," *The Public Interest,* Winter 1966, No. 2, pp. 80–91. Copyright © 1966 by
National Affairs, Inc. Reprinted by permission.
The author is Professor of Sociology, University of California, Davis.

influence in transforming a group of poorly educated factory workers into those model middle-class Americans obsessed with the problems of crab-grass and "conformity."

Well, it is now a matter of public record that my basic assumption was wrong. As the interview evidence piled up, it became clearer and clearer that the lives of the suburbanites I was studying had not been profoundly affected in any statistically identifiable or sociologically interesting way. They were still overwhelmingly Democrats; they attended church as infrequently as they ever did; like most working class people, their informal contacts were limited largely to kin; they neither gave nor went to parties; on the whole they had no great hopes of getting ahead in their jobs; and instead of a transient psychology, most of them harbored a view of their new suburban homes as paradise permanently gained.

But (appropriately enough for a Ph.D. candidate) I was cautious in the general inferences I drew from that study. It was, after all, based only on a small sample, of one suburb, of one metropolitan area, in one region, and it suffered from all of the methodological limitations inherent in small case studies. None of my findings gave me any reason to doubt the truth of what William H. Whyte, for example, had said of his organization men; but it also seemed to me that there was little reason *not* to believe that my findings in San Jose would be repeatedly confirmed in many of the less expensive suburbs around the country whose houses were priced well within the means of unionized workers in heavy industry, and of lower white collar employees as well. I did, in short, question the right of others to generalize freely about suburbia on the basis of very few studies of selected suburbs which happened to be homogeneously middle or upper middle class in character—especially when it seemed apparent that suburban housing was increasingly available to all but the lowest income levels and status groups.

The considerable bulk of research that has been done on suburbs in the years since I did my work has given me no reason to alter the conclusions I drew then. Indeed, none of this research can be expected to give much comfort to those who find it convenient to believe that a suburb exercises some mysterious power over its residents, transforming them into replicas of Whyte's practitioners of "The Outgoing Life." There seems to be increasing consensus among students of suburbia that suburban development is simply the latest phase of a process of urban growth that has been going on for a long time, that the cultural character of suburbs varies widely in terms of the social make-up of its residents, and of the personal and group dispositions that led them to move to suburbs in the first place; that the variety of physical and demographic differences between cities and suburbs (and there *are* some) bears little significance for the way of life of their inhabitants, and that some of these differences, although statistically accurate, are sociologically spurious, since the appropriate comparisons are not between residential suburbs and cities as wholes, but between suburbs and urban residential neighborhoods. In general, the reported changes in the lives of suburbanites were not *caused* by the move to suburbia, but were reasons for moving there in the first place. In suburbs, as in city apartments, social class, the age-composition of residents, the age of the neighborhood, etc., are much more profound predictors of the style of life than is residential location with respect to the city limits. Analysis of national samples has provided confirmation neither of a trend to Republicanism in politics nor a return to religion. Suburbs, in short, seem—as Reissman and Ktsanes have characterized them—to be "new homes for old values."

It appears, then, that there are no grounds for believing that suburbia has created a distinctive style of life or a new social character for Americans. Yet the myth of suburbia persists, as is evident from the fact that it is still eminently discussable over the whole range of our cultural media, from comic books to learned journals. One should not be surprised at this, for myths are seldom dispelled by research; they have going for them something considerably more powerful than mere evidence. And though nothing I say here can change this fact, it may give us some comfort to understand the sources of the myth, the functions it performs for the groups by whom it is sustained, and the nature of its appeal to America's image of itself.

In my book, and then, again, later in an article, I undertook a functional explanation of the myth of suburbia. I pointed first to the fact that suburbs were rich with ready made visible symbols: patios and barbecues, lawnmowers and tricycles, shopping centers, station wagons, and so on, and that such symbols were readily organizable into an image of a way of life that could be marketed to the non-suburban public. I also pointed out that this marketing was facilitated by the odd fact that the myth of suburbia conveniently suited the ideological purposes of several influential groups who market social and political opinion—odd because these groups could usually be found disagreeing with each other, not only about matters of opinion, but about matters of fact as well. Realtor-chamber-of-commerce interests and the range of opinion represented by the Luce magazines could use the myth of suburbia to affirm the American Way of Life; city planners, architects, urban design people and so on could use the myth of suburbia to warn that those agglomerations of standardized, vulgarized, mass-produced cheerfulness which masqueraded as homes would be the slums of tomorrow. Liberal and left-wing culture-critics could (and did) use the myth of suburbia to launch an attack on complacency, conformity, and mass culture, and found in this myth an up-to-date polemical vocabulary with which to rebuke the whole slick tenor of American life: what used to be disdained as "bourgeois" was now simply designated as "suburban." In short, the *descriptive* accuracy of the myth of suburbia went largely unchallenged because it suited the *prescriptive* desires of such a wide variety of opinion, from the yea-sayers of the right to the agonizers of the center to the naysayers of the left.

But though I still think this analysis of the myth makes good sense, I think too that there is something more — something, if I may be permitted to say so, deeper, profounder, and which I was only dimly aware of then. I think now that the myth can be understood also as our society's most recent attempt to come to terms with the melting pot problem, a problem that goes straight to the heart of American ambivalence about cultural pluralism.

CULTURAL PLURALISM AND THE MELTING POT

America has never really come to terms with the legend of the melting pot. That legend, if I may quote the windy text of its original source, saw America as the place where "Celt and Latin, Slav and Teuton, Greek and Syrian, Black and Yellow, Jew and Gentile, the palm and the pine, the pole and the equator, the crescent and the cross" would together build "the Republic of Man and the Kingdom of God." Despite the hope that a unified American culture might emerge from the seething cauldron, it didn't happen; instead, the formation of ethnically homogeneous communities—ghettoes—helped the immigrants preserve large segments of their cultures, and the tendency to endogamy helped them preserve it beyond the first generation. But in spite of the evident facts of our cultural pluralism (by which I mean the persisting correlation of significant differences in values and behavior with ethnic, regional, and social class differences), attempts are continually made to create an image of *the* typical or representative or genuine American and his community. These attempts have usually succeeded only in creating stereotypes—most familiarly, perhaps, a caricature of one or another variety of Our Town: white, Anglo-Saxon, Protestant, and middle class. *Saturday Evening Post* covers, white picket fences, colonial houses, maple hutches and the like have historically played an important role in such attempts. *The myth of suburbia is the latest attempt to render America in this homogeneous manner,* to see in the highly visible and proliferating suburban developments a new melting pot which would receive the diverse elements of a new generation from a society fragmented by class, region, religion, and ethnicity, and from them create *the* American style of life. Suburbia as America is no more false a picture, probably, than Babbitt or Our Town as America; but it fails as a melting pot for the same reason that the original melting pot idea failed: like many other urban neighborhoods, specific suburbs developed a tendency to homogeneity, almost always in terms of social class and very often in terms of ethnicity.

The myth of American cultural homogeneity and the stubborn fact of heterogeneity reflect a persistent ambivalence in American society regarding cultural unity and diversity, between the melting pot idea and the pluralist idea. During and after the perod of rapid immigration into the "teeming cities," for example, free public education expressed the need for some minimum "Americanization," whereas the ghetto expressed the impulse to cultural self-preservation (both by the natives who excluded and the immigrants who segregated themselves). In the rest of the country, 4th of July style patriotic rhetoric expressed the gropings toward an elementary national identity, whereas provincial arrogance—and hostility to "the government" and to centers of cosmopolitan influence—expressed the affirmation of narrow local autonomies. The ambivalence was really a double ambivalence; each polar position was itself unstable: to be truly tenable, a pluralist ideology must accord intrinsic honor and value to a diversity of life styles, and this it has never completely done. The salient features of minority subcultural styles have more often than not been regarded as stigmata by dominant groups, tolerable so long as they were temporary, that is, *transitional* to something approaching the dominant cultural style. On the other hand, the attempts of provincial, nativist ("WASP") groups to secure their own style as the American style stopped short of supporting the emergence of broadly inclusive national institutions which would have facilitated that transition. The most enthusiastic celebrators of "Americanism" were precisely the groups who were most wary of integrating the varieties of the national life into a unified culture.

Indeed, a unified national culture has until quite recently been a most improbable prospect, since the United States has traditionally been a society without very powerful national institutions with which to promote that unity and pass it on down the generations. Without an established church or a powerful federal government, without national political parties or a standardized educational system, enormous distances and poor communications enabled local economies to breed a highly differentiated system of *native* subcultures—in addition to those created by the immigrants. Even today, there are probably dozens of distinctive American types, to some extent stereotypes, perhaps, but which nevertheless call attention to the wide variety of *native* styles: Vermont farmers and Boston Brahmins, Southern Bourbons and Tennessee hillbillies, Beatniks and organization men, Plainvillers, Middletowners, and cosmopolitan intellectuals, to say nothing of teenagers, the jet set, and many, many more, all American, all different, and none probably very eager to be integrated into an idea of *"the* American" at a level of complexity suitable for a *Time* cover story or a patriotic war movie.

It is not surprising, then, that when one tries to abstract from American life a system of values which can be called distinctively or representatively American, the task is immensely difficult. The most systematic attempt by a sociologist, that of Robin Williams in his book *American Society,* is foiled by the fact that important groups in American society do not share the 15 or 16 values which he offers as basically American. There is no question that values such as "achievement," "work," "efficiency," "equality," and the rest have played a significant role in creating the quality of American life, but important parts of the lower and working classes (important because of their numbers) do not share them, and important parts of the upper class (important because of their influence) do not share them—although they may affirm them when a journalist is nearby.

MYTHS AND STYLES OF LIFE

The persistent attempts to find some transcendent principles or values which define the unity of American culture have been defeated by the persistence of important class and ethnic differences. Even under natural or "organic" conditions, then, "American" patterns of culture are enormously difficult to describe with any accuracy. This difficulty is exacerbated when a society becomes sophisticated enough to be self conscious about its culture and rich enough to do something about it. The maturity and the luxury of our civilization constrain its elites to define an "American" style, and the miracle of our technology arms us to manufacture it. Our society is wealthy enough to support a substantial class of intellectuals devoted to staying on top of contemporary events to "spot the trend," "see the pattern," "find the meaning," "discover the style." And our media are such that these spottings and seeings are more or less instantaneously communicated to audiences of millions, whose demand upon the marketers of opinions and interpretations for sensible and coherent syntheses is greater than the available supply.

Under such conditions, we do not get serious historical interpretation of contemporary events; we do not even get responsible journalism; we get myths, which themselves become part of the forces shaping what is happening, and which hence function ideologically. The myth of suburbia fosters an image of a homogeneous and classless America without a trace of ethnicity but fully equipped for happiness by the marvelous productivity of American industry: the ranch house with the occupied two-car garage, the refrigerator and freezer, the washer and dryer, the garbage disposal and the built-in range and dishwasher, the color TV and the hi-fi stereo. Suburbia: its lawns trim, its driveways clean, its children happy on its curving streets and in its pastel schools. Suburbia, California style, is America.

. . . . .

But becoming aware of the myth of suburbia, and pointing to the disparities between it and what we actually know of suburbs we have closely studied, should not be confused with a *defense* of suburbia. Nor should anything I have said about the critics of suburbia be interpreted as an expression of my personal bias in favor of suburbia. As I suggested earlier, myths are potent enough to survive evidence; they are not disarmed by understanding. Quite the contrary. Once myths gain currency, once they go, as we say, "into the cultural air," they *become real,* and function frequently as self-fulfilling prophecies. Life copies literature; fact is affected by fiction; history is constrained by myth. "If a situation is defined as real," said William I. Thomas, "it is real in its consequences," and I have no doubt (though I have no data) that family decisions regarding whether to move to the suburbs have been affected (both pro and con) by the myth of suburbia. And despite everything reasonable I have said about suburbs, I *know* that the fact that I unreasonably dislike them has been conditioned, *beyond the possibility of redemption by mere research,* by the very myth of suburbia I have helped explode.

In the sense in which I have been speaking of them, myths are more or less noble fictions; fictions in that they are *made,* and noble depending on the art with which they are made, the extent to which one is in favor of the consequences they foster, and, most particularly, the forms of solidarity they promote. In the context of the debate over "suburbia," what is usually at stake is whose version of America shall become "American."

PLURALISM AND PLANNING

Whose shall? I want to suggest that the question is relevant to the way in which the future quality of urban life is planned. Like Emile Durkheim, who suggested that the punishment of crime was significant less as a deterrent or as simple revenge than as a collective reaffirmation of cultural values, I want to suggest that we look more closely at the images of solidarity which inform the proposals for dealing with social problems in general, and with urban problems in particular. For social problems, of course, have no objective existence—although the facts to which they refer may. It is objectively true that some people have always lived in dilapidated, unsafe, unheated, vermin-infested residences, but "slums" have not always been a social problem. Slums become a social problem when a large enough group of important people decide that poor people ought not to live in such places.

. . . . .

I see three broad alternatives for those who are confronted with the problem of planning the quality of urban life. First of all, planners can simply abdicate from any concern for the cultural consequences of what they do, and instead interpret their mandate narrowly—for example, the improvement of the physical environment for the poorly housed. To the extent that they have been planned at all, most new, inexpensive suburbs have been developed in this way—with occasional exceptions, as in the gestures by the Levittowns toward the provision of some institutional facilities. More centrally located urban residential development for the poor and the less-than-affluent has also been dominated by considerations such as square footage, hygiene, and domestic technology. Now to provide room, cleanliness, comfort, and convenience to people who have previously been without them is an important achievement; but it is not planning for the quality of urban life. Quite the contrary; the *quality* of urban life is precisely what is usually left out of consideration—perhaps as a luxury rendered expeddable by the need to bring large numbers of people up to some minimum physical standard. Under these conditions of planning, images of human solidarity seem limited exclusively to *households* within which *family* solidarity may be symbolized by culinary and recreational technology (refrigerators, freezers, barbecues, TVs, etc.), whereas solidarities beyond that of the family and household seem irrelevant, alien, or distant. There is a sense in which this alternative is evasive because such planning *does* engender a quality in urban life, but it is the quality that most cultivated foreign observers complain about in most American cities.

Planning's second alternative, it seems to me, is to make a conscious effort to alter the environments of certain groups, with the overt intention of bringing their culture closer to some monolithic or homogeneous ideal. Presumably, this would be some more advanced version of the melting pot idea, in which either a bureaucratic or entrepreneurial version of a middle class life-style would be given as an ideal toward which the poor should be encouraged to reach. Here the aim would be to make the society more monolithically what it already dominantly is. This alternative founders on its utopianism, on its assumption that a cultural consensus can be engineered or induced in a society in which conflict is endemic and which will remain so as long as the interests of groups and classes remain opposed. In the absence of any ability by planners to wipe out class differences, we must expect, in any multi-class community, controversy not only over the appropriate means to reach agreed-upon goals but over the goals themselves and the priorities to be assigned to them. This is the stuff of politics and culture, and where interests and norms are rooted in a class-based style of life, the attempt by one group to elicit the commitment of the entire community to a specific goal will very likely threaten another group and elicit its opposition. Moreover, these political and cultural diversities have a right to exist and persist. We can be reasonably sure that the vulnerable and dependent groups most readily affected by planning would gladly be rid of their slums, their poverty, and the discrimination against them. Beyond this it is difficult to assume anything with great assurance except, perhaps, that groups develop an attachment to those aspects of their culture which have not been imposed by necessity, an attachment made evident by their tendency to take the culture with them when they move from one environment to another, and to preserve whatever of it that circumstances permit. On the other hand, utopian planning dominated by visions of profound cultural changes is always interesting, and such planners might well devote more energy to making these visionary ideals manifest and rhetorically vivid, if only in order to help others to know whether to be for or against the form of solidarity they envision.

THE PLURALIST ALTERNATIVE

Finally, there is the pluralist alternative, an alternative perhaps best expressed in the recent work of Herbert Gans, and, to a lesser extent, of Jane Jacobs. Whatever reservations one may have about the work of either, each of them projects an unambiguous image of the kind of human solidarity they would like to see fostered by urban planning. This solidarity is loose and heterogeneous, composed of more or less autonomous groups and neighborhoods formed on the basis of ethnicity and social class; communities attached, perhaps, to the notion that good fences make good neighbors, but necessarily related to one another through those political and economic accommodations long characteristic of urban life. If they are open to criticism as "romanticists" (although it is not clear to me why a preference for dense street life, or an insistence that an ethnic working-class neighborhood is not necessarily a slum, renders one vulnerable to such criticism), it should at least be said in their defense that they obviously care enough about the *quality* of urban life to evoke a strong and clear image of it (something their critics do not always do)—strong enough in Mrs. Jacobs' case and clear enough in Professor Gans' case to make it easy for a reader to be for or against them.

I am mostly for them, since planning for pluralism seems to me not only the most sensible way of responding to the fact of persisting cultural diversities but the most honorable way as well. In making their assumptions, planners might first of all assume (it is the most reasonable assumption) that most groups which are displaced by planning *will take their culture with them* if they can. Planners would do well to anticipate this, and to modify their plans accordingly, to facilitate the preservation of those parts of their culture that the groups want preserved. This means that planning would have to be done for *specific types of people with distinctive cultural styles,* that is, for a variety of specific, known tastes rather than for faceless densities with a given amount of disposable income for housing. A working class group with a durable pattern of sexual segregation (husbands and wives living largely separate extra-familial lives) requires for its sustenance residential and community facilities different from those required by a middle class group with a culture pattern emphasizing companionable family togetherness.

If the strain put upon the middle class biases of professional planners by such considerations seems excessive, I ask only that you think of the problem of the Negro ghetto and the potential controversy about whether *its* subculture ought to be preserved. People as different as a sociologist like Lee Rainwater and a Negro leader like James Baldwin have remarked (without clearly deploring it) upon the Dyonisianism prevalent in the Negro ghetto. Now, this is a culture pattern which clearly is both at once an adaptation to the trapped character of ghetto life, and a means of providing compensatory satisfactions for that blocked access to middle class life. If the satisfactions are not only compensatory but real, planners might think about providing facilities for the nourishment of this psycho-cultural pattern—even as they think about eliminating the enforced segregation and demoralization which make it more attractive.

Even after discrimination on the basis of race disappears, however, we have no evidence to suggest that segregation will ever disappear. If the experience of other ethnic groups is any guide (and I know of no better guide), many Negroes will choose to live among their own "kind" even after they have formally free choice of housing. However "kind" may be defined in the future, there is no reason *not* to expect social class and ethnicity to continue to play an important role—although it is quite conceivable that color may eventually not have much to do with ethnicity. We know little enough about the nature of ethnicity—and even less, perhaps, about which members of an ethnic group *prefer* to live in ghettoes, or why, even after they can live almost wherever they please. But the *fact* that many of them do is beyond question. We have no reason *not* to expect this to be true of Negroes also, particularly of those whose views are represented by the most militant Negro leaders, insistent upon the acceptance of Negroes into American society *as Negroes*— with all that this historically implies.

I hope it is clear that these remarks are not the elaborate rationalizations of a conservative searching for an acceptable rhetoric to defend the *status quo.* Quite the contrary; they are the remarks of a sociologist who, being for the extension of the widest possible range of choice to all segments of the population, nevertheless knows that choices are hardly ever random, and that no man is so free that he is not constrained by the norms of the groups to which he belongs or would like to belong. This is as it should be; but the sense of choice rests on the existence of real alternatives. Cultural diversity has somehow been maintained in the suburbs without much help from planners. We may not be so lucky in the cities unless planners begin to understand the conditions of cultural distinctiveness and to design for it.

20. The Irish style in politics

WILLIAM V. SHANNON

In the decades after the Civil War, the Irish developed their characteristic style in American politics. The Irishman as politician is the member of the Irish community most familiar to other Americans. The Irish brought to American politics two advantages other immigrants did not have: a knowledge of the English language and an acquaintance with the dominant Anglo-American culture. In addition to a common language and a shared culture, they had gifts of organization and eloquence, a sense of cohesion, and the beginnings of a political tradition in the nationalist agitation in Ireland. Their antagonism toward England offended leaders of opinion along the eastern seaboard, but it did not upset most Americans since, in the nineteenth century, twisting the lion's tail was the national sport.

. . . . .

The Irish, the most numerous and advanced section of the immigrant community, took over the political party (usually the Democratic Party) at the local level and converted it into virtually a parallel system of government. The network of party clubhouses and the hierarchy of party committees with a citywide leader or "boss" at the apex constituted a "shadow government," a supplementary structure of power that performed some functions more vital than those of the nominal, legal government. The main objective of the party, of course, was to capture control of the city government, but even when the party was out of office, it could continue to function. It had revenue from the "tax" it levied upon saloons, houses of prostitution, gamblers, and contractors. Out of these

Adapted with permission of The Macmillan Company from *The American Irish: A Political and Social Portrait* by William V. Shannon, pp. 60–67. Copyright © William V. Shannon, 1963, 1966.
The author is a member of the editorial board of *The New York Times*.

funds, the party machine could provide the food and coal it gave to those who were destitute. It could finance the young lawyers who interceded in court for the delinquent, wrote letters home to the old country for the illiterate, and intervened at city hall for those bewildered by the regulations and intricacies of the government. It could pay for the torchlight parades, the children's picnics, and the one-day excursion trips up the river or to the beach which brought recreation and a touch of color to the lives of working-class families.

When the machine was in office, it could provide that most precious of all commodities: a job. Public construction work was one of the major sources of jobs and income. When reform administrations were in power, they cut back on construction to save money and reduce the tax rate. When the machine was in power, it expanded construction, building courthouses and schoolhouses, paving more streets, digging more subways, and erecting new bridges. The politicians at the top liked building programs because they could collect bribes from those who received the contract, make "a killing" on the sale of the land on the basis of their advance knowledge, profit by writing the insurance on the project, and sometimes organize a sand-and-gravel company and get cut into the actual construction as a subcontractor. This was "honest graft," sometimes known as "white graft" to distinguish it from the "dirty graft" collected via the police department from the underworld. The contractors liked this expansive attitude toward public works projects because it increased their business, and so did the carpenters, plumbers, plasterers, and other skilled craftsmen. But, most of all, the newest and least skilled of the immigrants were enthusiastic because these projects enabled them to find work as laborers. Since, at the outset of their life in America, they were fitted only to do pick-and-shovel work, they were peculiarly dependent upon the machine and its free-and-easy spending of public money. No number of exposés by citizens' committees and good government groups of graft, payroll padding, and excessive spending on public projects shook their loyalty to the machine. If there were no "corrupt machine," they reasoned, there might not be any building projects, and if there were no projects to work on, how would they earn enough to live? Padded payrolls were better than no payrolls. Since the city usually needed the building or public improvement, it was not easy for critics to demonstrate to working-class voters what harm had been done.

The political machines the Irish built in most of the major cities of the North and Midwest developed out of the block and the neighborhood. Family friendships and neighborhood loyalties were the basis of power. The boyhood gangs with their emphasis on loyalty and cohesiveness provided the morale and the habits of mind that were easily transmuted, in adult years, into the rationale of the machine. The city-wide leaders, the ward and precinct captains, and the rank-and-file members of the party machines developed a set of political ethics and an attitude toward politics and power that were strikingly different from those of the native middle-class code. The Irish viewed municipal politics not as a conflict over how to obtain the best government at the lowest cost but as a struggle for power among competing groups.

The earliest leaders organized the Irish voters as a battering ram to break the power of a hostile majority. They put an end to elementary forms of discrimination such as the exclusive use of the King James Bible in the schools and the assignment of Protestant chaplains to Catholic inmates of hospitals, jails, and charitable institutions. Next, they fought for the appointment of Irish as schoolteachers and as policemen and firemen. Finally, they sought to take all political power into their own hands.

In the course of this struggle for power, the Irish community evolved an attitude of tolerant acceptance of political corruption. This was neither cynicism nor hypocrisy; rather it was close to a straightforward acceptance of graft as necessary and inevitable. Graft was part of the operating compromise between the formal rules of the political system and the facts of life as it was actually lived. Corruption was often viewed as a primitive mechanism for redistributing the wealth because, as people said, "at least it keeps the money in circulation." The Irish and their allies among other immigrants had the attitude typical of those who comprise a client group and not a ruling class. For a long period, they were people who had stature without status, power without responsibility. Only gradually did the social discipline grow to match the power, and only when that happened did the majority detach themselves from the values of the political machine.

For individual Irish, politics was an attractive career. Since newly naturalized voters were usually more willing to give their votes to another "son of the old country" than to a native-born candidate, politics was the only major profession in which it was an asset rather than a drawback to be an immigrant. Politics, like baseball, prizefighting, and the Church, was a career open to talents, a path of social mobility for the ambitious sons of impoverished families.

This Irish concept of politics as another profession—practical, profitable, and pursued every day in the year—diverged sharply from the ordinary civic code that draped politics in the mantle of "public service." According to the genteel tradition, the holding of office was an ephemeral activity; it might be thought of as an accident comparable to a call for jury service that might befall any citizen. For those who regarded the main business of America as business, service in a political office represented a sacrifice. In the Irish community, there was no talk of duty or sacrifice. Nor did those who gave their time to politics regard the holding of public office as an interlude or an accident. Politics was their career. Like every other profession, it was expected to reward its practitioners with money, prestige and, if possible, security. It was generally expected that a politician would make money out of his office, collaterally if not directly, and that if he lost he would be "taken care of" in a sinecure.[1]

Since Irish politicians were of working-class origin, they entered public office trailing long strings of needy relatives. Because the public payroll was the politician's only resource, he was expected to use it to succor his family and dependents. The result was the nepotism so frequently and so futilely condemned by civic reformers. This nepotism was usually controlled by some sense of official responsibility. A halfwit or a drunkard would not be placed in a responsible job, but some other provision might be made for him. Indeed, some other provision had to be made for him. (What of his wife and children? If no one else would hire him, what politician would take the responsibility of sending "your own flesh-and-blood" to the relief rolls or the gutter?)

Nepotism had old-country roots. For generations, each immigrant who "went out to the States" had a fixed responsibility to send back money to pay for the subsequent passage of one of his brothers or sisters. In many families the oldest son came first, paid the fare of the next oldest who paid for the next, and so on. This recruitment practice was known as "sending for a greenhorn." The immigrant was also morally obligated to find jobs here for his relatives and for as many of his neighbors from the old country as he could. In this way, the kitchens of many a mansion and the police, fire, and streetcar departments of many a city were regularly staffed.

Conrad Arensberg, when he wrote his study *The Irish Countryman* in the 1930's, provided a graphic example of this process: "One little settlement called Cross, on the Loop Head peninsula which juts from Clare into the Atlantic at the Shannon's mouth, is said locally to be supported by the Shanghai police force. The first man to go is now Chief of Police in the International Settlement there, and many places in the Force have gone to men of Cross."

It is a short step from neighborliness to nepotism. However much such nepotism might be deplored, it could not be otherwise when men were bred from childhood to an urgent and overriding feeling of family duty and parochial loyalty.

Politics as a career not only required a minimum of education, preparation, and money; it also had the advantage over competing occupations that for the few who had the requisite talents it produced its

---

[1]Shortly after World War II, the author was walking in Boston with a well-known local politician. The politician exchanged greetings with a passerby, an aged, poorly dressed woman. "When her husband was in the City Council with me," he remarked, "he was called 'Honest John.' But I never took it seriously. I figured he had an angle somewhere. But then he died and it was true. He didn't leave her a cent. Now what do you think of a dumbbell like that who wouldn't take a buck when he could get one and now his wife has to go out and work?"

rewards relatively quickly. In this respect, politics had the same appeal as professional athletics. It is significant how many politicians achieved power at an early age. James Curley was a congressman at thirty-six and mayor of Boston at thirty-nine; Joseph Tumulty of Jersey City became President Wilson's chief aid at thirty-three; Alfred E. Smith and James J. Walker were floor leaders in the New York legislature while still in their thirties. Charm, boldness, energy, a quick mind and a fluent tongue brought young politicos to the top; unlike careers in business and the professions, politics required neither long years of saving and scrimping nor any exact training.

The swiftness of success was probably important in shaping the psychology of many of these political leaders. Because of family necessity, a youth would become a part-time wage earner—a newsboy or bootblack or messenger—and thereby be forced into a premature maturity. He found himself drawn out of his own neighborhood, which up until then had seemed exciting and satisfying, and into the larger world. Back on his home block, a dime had been a fortune, pot roast was a Sunday treat, and beer was his father's luxury after a ten- or twelve-hour shift. But in the brighter, faster-moving world in which he now entered, the youth encountered men who wore silk shirts, ate steak for lunch, and seemed to possess large sums of money. The ambitious adolescent went through several kinds of experience simultaneously. He became aware that, in material terms, there were ways of life better than that of his own family; he felt the first pangs of the adult desires for freedom, sex, and money; he felt the sharp twinges of class envy and personal hope. For many youths this accelerated coming of age in a materialistic society must have had permanently distorting effects. They could see that ordinary occupations—tending a machine or pounding a beat, pressing pants or making them, selling spools of thread or pecks of potatoes—were not going to bring quick success. For those with the right blend of imagination, audacity, and style, politics was the obvious answer.

A politician with this psychological background was obviously more vulnerable to the temptations to dishonesty in office than one who enjoyed a more secure and orderly transition through adolescence into adulthood. During the psychological crisis which shaped his personal sense of identity, certain material objects and a certain style of life obtained an excessive hold on his imagination. The keener his imagination and the better his mind, then the greater the potentiality for a certain kind of tragedy. The routine wardheeler may graft on a petty scale because the ethical code of his community condones it, but the abler and more ambitious politico grafts not only because it is permissible but also because he is subject to all the pressures and insecurities of the parvenu. Having entered politics to raise himself from the ranks of laborers and hodcarriers, he travels a long way vertically in a larger society which recognizes material success as its chief criterion. To move in the social circles and live in the manner which he desired took more money than the politician could possibly acquire honestly. This was true even though he remained within the orbit of the rich and successful of his own kind. The races at Saratoga, the summer house at the seashore, daughter's grand piano—all these and other tangibles of success cost money. One does not have to join the Four Hundred to live beyond one's means. An Alfred E. Smith or Joseph Tumulty would have a code of rigid personal honesty or develop a set of social ideals to protect himself against the grafter's temptation, but the more typical politician could not avoid giving the wrong answer to the uneasy question: If it was not to travel with these people and live this way, then why did he ring doorbells, run for alderman, or go into politics in the first place?

Those who entered politics as a means of rapid personal advancement were acting from a motive that neither the theory of the founders of the nation nor the theory of the late nineteenth century middle classes had taken into account or could accommodate. Moreover, Irish machine politics was carried on in an intellectual void. It was the intuitive response to practical necessities and unrelated to any comprehensive theory of politics and society. Until the emergence of Finley Peter Dunne's "Mr. Dooley" in the late 1890's and the realistic investigations of politics by Lincoln Steffens and other muckraking magazine writers early in this century, the code by which the Irish politicians and their mass of supporters lived and governed remained unarticulated and undefended. As a result, the larger society outside the Irish community looked upon the party bosses as grotesque; politics seemed a morality play in which, despite frequent scandals and exposures, vice always triumphed; and the gloomier observers despaired of democracy. But for the Irish, politics was a functioning system of power and not an exercise in moral judgment. While E. L. Godkin and Henry Adams despaired of the American experiment, the Irish took over City Hall.

21. The development and persistence of ethnic voting

RAYMOND E. WOLFINGER

Mass immigration ended fifty years ago, but national origins continue to be a salient dimension in many people's perceptions of themselves and of others. Where this salience is widespread, ethnicity plays a major

---

Abridged and edited from Raymond E. Wolfinger, "The development and persis-

role in politics. Ethnicity is often an important independent variable in voting behavior. "Ethnic voting" as I shall call it, has two manifestations. (1) Members of an ethnic group show an affinity for one party or the other which cannot be explained solely as a result of other demographic characteristics. Voters of Irish descent, to take a familiar example, are more likely than other voters of similar economic status to be Democrats. (2) Members of an ethnic group will cross party lines to vote for—or against—a candidate belonging to a particular ethnic group.

This article deals with the development and persistence of ethnic voting. The customary theory holds that ethnic voting is strongest during an ethnic group's earliest residence in this country and subsequently declines from this peak as the group's members make their way out of the working class. This might be called an "assimilation theory." It sees a direct relationship between the proportion of a nationality group in the working class and that group's political homogeneity. As more and more of the group join the middle class, its political unity is progressively eroded. Along with middle-class status, these group members are said to acquire different political interests and to identify more with the majority society and less with their nationality group: in short, they become assimilated. Presumably the end of the process is reached when group members are as occupationally differentiated as the whole population. At this point they are politically indistinguishable from the general population, or from a control group with similar non-ethnic characteristics, and ethnicity is no longer a factor in their voting behavior.

This is a plausible argument, but it is not consistent with voting patterns in New Haven, Connecticut. People of Italian descent there comprise about one-third of the city's population. Although the Italians are the poorest segment of the white population, they are also one of the strongest Republican voting blocs. If the assimilation theory held in New Haven, this Italian Republicanism would have been strongest some generations ago when Italians first settled there in numbers, and would have declined with the passage of time. But the overwhelming support that New Haven Italians give to the Republican party is a development of the past 25 years. It began when the first New Haven Italian candidate for a major city office won the Republican mayoralty nomination. Since then Italians have been the mainstay of Republican voting strength in New Haven, even in elections with no Italian candidates.

These events may not be as anomalous as they seem. They can be explained by a theory that may also be pertinent to many other places. I

tence of ethnic voting," *American Political Science Review,* December 1965, 59:896–908. Copyright © 1965 by the American Political Science Association. Reprinted by permission. Footnotes enlarging upon the author's text have been omitted.

The author is Professor of Political Science, University of California, Berkeley, Calif.

will discuss this alternate theory after a detailed description of the development of ethnic voting in New Haven. Finally, I will consider available evidence on the persistence of ethnic voting.

I. THE CONDITIONS OF ETHNIC POLITICS

The history of nationality group relations in New Haven is from all accounts typical of many industrial cities in the Northeastern states. In the course of the 19th and early 20th centuries the descendants of New Haven's original Anglo-Saxon Protestant settlers were out-numbered by waves of immigrants from Ireland and later from Southern and Eastern Europe. By 1910, according to the census data, two-thirds of the population were first- or second-generation Americans; in 1960 some 42 per cent of the population were in these categories. More detailed information on the ethnic composition of the population comes from a sample survey of 525 registered voters conducted in the summer of 1959. White Protestants comprised less than 20 per cent of this sample; 31 per cent of the respondents were born in Italy or were in the second or third generation of Italian immigrants. Eleven per cent were of similarly recent Irish origin, 9 per cent were Negroes; and 15 per cent were Jews.

Beginning with the first mass Irish immigration the old settlers met the non-Protestant newcomers with hostility, economic exploitation, and religious discrimination. The immigrants were usually penniless and could get only the least desirable jobs. The affronts of everyday life enhanced their ethnic consciousness; so did the obvious gap in well-being between them and the old settlers.

In addition to Yankee hostility, other forces tended to maintain ethnic solidarity. For European peasants trying to live in an American city, a familiar language, religion and culture were comforting when so much else was different. Members of any given nationality group usually settled in the same neighborhoods, lived together and married among their kind and not with Yankees or other immigrants, formed nationality associations, and worshipped in national churches.

Needless to say, the ethnics often responded to the Yankees with a hatred that has not yet vanished, while many Yankees continue to look down on the ethnics. Members of each of the major ethnic groups still regard the others with varying amounts of good will, of jealousy and suspicion. As the years have passed, the immigrants and their descendants have moved, in varying numbers, into the middle class. This economic mobility did not result in equivalent geographical dispersion, in part because some of the new prosperity came from neighborhood enterprises such as groceries and mortuaries, in part because of the continuing comforts of ethnic proximity.

One consequence of this history is a persistent emphasis on ethnic differences, which continue to be a major organizing principle in the city's social structure. There are, for example, no less than six Junior Leagues in New Haven, including one each for the not very numerous local young ladies of Swedish and Danish extraction. There are also Jewish organizations with similar functions but different names. The major Catholic ethnic groups have their own national churches.

Ethnic consciousness is an important and pronounced regional characteristic. It is difficult to suggest an objective measure for comparing ethnic salience, much less to find data on this subject, but on the basis of impressionistic evidence it appears that concern with national origins is much greater in the Northeast than in some other parts of the country. The reasons for this regional difference are not immediately apparent. The numerical prevalence of ethnics does not account for it, for the major cities of the West Coast have sizable ethnic populations. San Francisco has about the same proportion of first- and second-generation Americans as New Haven (43 as against 42 per cent) but there is no comparison between the two cities with respect to ethnic salience.

This regional difference may be due to the fact that in the Northeast the non-British immigrants came to settled communities with relatively stable class structures and systems of status ascription. Only menial jobs were open to them. The distribution of economic rewards and opportunities reinforced the unambiguous class system. On the other hand, immigrants came to the West at the same time as the Yankees, or on their heels. "The Forty-Niners came from all parts of the world, and foreign accents were as common in the mining camps as American ones." The two groups shared the same pioneering experiences and lived in communities with wildly fluctuating economies and unsettled social systems. Economic advantage was not so closely associated with ethnicity, and class distinctions were not so rigid.

The immigrants in New England were equal to the older settlers in only one relevant respect: they could vote. Little in their previous experience suggested that their opinions had much to do with government, and so their votes had no abstract value to them. But these votes mattered to American politicians, who solicited them with advice, favors, petty gifts, and jobs.

Two typical loci of immigrant politicization were the bosses of casual labor gangs on public works, who owed their positions to their ability to deliver their gangs' votes and their vote-delivering ability to their command of jobs; and the leaders of nationality associations, usually men who were the first to achieve some economic success. Such relationships set the pattern for ethnic politics. Each nationality group in a city had leaders who bargained with politicians, trading their followers' votes for money, favors, and jobs. For their part the politicians found it convenient and efficient to classify the electorate by ethnicity and to dispense rewards on this basis.

. . . . .

II. ETHNIC POLITICS IN NEW HAVEN

The first Irishman was elected to the New Haven Board of Aldermen in 1857. Henceforth Irishmen and other ethnics held municipal office in increasing numbers. Democratic mayoralty candidates continued for a while to be Yankee businessmen, demographically indistinguishable from their Republican opponents. The election of 1899 marked the end of Yankee dominance in local politics. Cornelius Driscoll, born in County Cork, was elected mayor on the Democratic ticket. As the Irish subsequently strengthened their hold on the party, some Yankee Democrats defected to the Republicans.

The Irish were not reluctant to take the spoils of victory. In the early 1930s first- and second-generation Irishmen comprised 13 per cent of a sample of 1600 family heads in New Haven, but they accounted for 49 per cent of all governmental jobs. The Italians suffered most of all from Irish chauvinism: there were *no* government employees among the 27 per cent of the sample who were Italian. These survey data exaggerate the Italians' exclusion from political rewards, but not by very much. In 1930 the proportion of Italians in low-paying municipal jobs was only a quarter of the proportion of Italians in the total population, and the ratio for better city jobs was much lower. By 1940 the Italians had attained half their "quota" of the poorer positions, and only about a fifth in white collar posts. Subsequently their representation in both appointive and elective positions has increased enormously.

The explanation of the New Haven Italians' Republicanism may then be thought to lie here: shut out of the Democratic party, they had no place to go but to the Republicans. This argument has two crippling limitations. (1) The Italians became more Republican during the period when they finally came closer to getting their "fair share" of municipal jobs. (2) Irish control of the local Democratic party is common in Northeastern industrial cities, but the level of Italian Republicanism found in New Haven is not. Allegations about the Republican inclinations of Italians abound in scholarly and journalistic literature, but concrete and systematic evidence for this general proposition is hard to find. Some Italians will split their ballots to vote for an Italian Republican, but the same is true for an Italian Democratic candidate. The best present source of data on this subject is the series of national election studies conducted over the past dozen years by the Survey Research Center of the University of Michigan. I have compared the party identification of the Italian and Irish respondents in the 1952, 1956 and 1958 studies who lived in the New England and Middle Atlantic states. As Table 1 shows, the Italians are a little more inclined than the Irish to consider themselves Democrats.

Since the level of Italian Republicanism found in New Haven is not common in the Northeast, local history is more likely to provide an ex-

Table 1*
Party identification of Italians and Irish in the Northeast, 1952, 1956, and 1958

Party identification	Irish	Italian
	(%)	(%)
Democratic	51	57
Independent	18	13
Republican	32	30
	101*	100
N	152	143

*Does not sum to 100 because of rounding.
Source: Inter-University Consortium for Political Research. I am indebted to Ralph Bisco and Richard T. Lane of the Consortium staff for their assistance.

planation than are more widespread political events. Two such local causes can be identified. The first was the determined courting of the Italian vote by Louis and Isaac Ullman, the leaders of the New Haven Republican party in the first part of the 20th century. The Ullman brothers realized that the large and hitherto passive Italian population was an untapped source of potential Republicans. They set out to capture the Italians, using the familar techniques of ethnic politics. They helped them take out citizenship papers, registered them as voters, found them jobs, used their considerable political influence to smooth over administrative and legal difficulties, subsidized Italian-American fraternal and political clubs, and so on.

It is not too much to say that the Ullman brothers' foresight and political skill kept the Republican party competitive in New Haven. Although the Italians were the poorest part of the population, they were, in the thirty years after 1910, less favorable to Democratic candidates than any other immigrant group, except perhaps the Jews. In the 10th Ward, with the city's heaviest concentration of Italians, the Democratic share of the presidential and mayoralty vote fluctuated around 50 per cent. In fact, the 10th voted much like the city as a whole, a remarkable similarity in view of its residents' modest economic position. The other wards in which Italians predominated were also less wholeheartedly Democratic than one would expect from their low income levels. It seems likely that this situation was due largely to the extent and intensity of the Ullmans' proselytizing.

III. CRITICAL ELECTIONS

The Ullman brothers' efforts gave the Republicans a certain advantage with Italian voters. Yet for some thirty years the result was no more than a stand-off; the Italians split their votes more or less evenly between the two parties until the end of the 1930s. Since then they have been very strongly Republican. The big shift in Italian voting habits came when William C. Celentano, a self-made mortician and son of a fruit peddler, won the Republican nomination for mayor in 1939. Celentano was the first New Haven Italian to win either party's nomination for a major city office. He cut 10,000 votes from the enormous majority that the incumbent Democrat, John W. Murphy, had won two years earlier, and came close to winning the election. The Second World War kept Celentano from getting the nomination again until 1945, for the city's Republican leaders did not think it prudent to nominate an Italian while Italy was fighting against the United States. But in that year he defeated Murphy by 6,000 votes.

Celentano's candidacy brought thousands of Italians into the Republican party, as the voting history of the heavily Italian 10th Ward illustrates. In 1937 Murphy received 52 per cent of the Tenth's vote. Two years later, running against Celentano for the first time, he got 22 per cent and fared almost as badly in other Italian neighborhoods. Matters improved somewhat for the Democrats during the war, but Celentano's second candidacy produced an even greater Republican swing; in 1945 Murphy won only 17 per cent of the 10th Ward's vote.

In 1947 the Democrats tried to match Celentano's appeal by giving the mayoralty nomination to an obscure Italian dentist. Thereby they recouped most of their losses in Italian neighborhoods—their share of the 10th Ward vote rose from 17 to 42 per cent and was about this high in the other Italian wards—but lost heavily elsewhere in the city. Furthermore, a Socialist candidate won a sixth of the total vote and made his best showing in middle-class neighborhoods. Since this was several times greater than any third-party vote in a generation, anti-Italian sentiment may have motivated many of these Socialist votes. The 1947 election was the only one in the city's history in which both major party candidates were Italians.

In every mayoralty election since 1947 the Democratic candidate has been Richard C. Lee, a Catholic of mixed English, Scottish, and Irish descent who, for obvious reasons, emphasizes his Irish side. Lee unseated Celentano in 1953 after two unsuccessful attempts. Celentano did not run for mayor again, preferring to bide his time until Lee left the scene. Since then Lee has defeated a series of Republican candidates, usually by sizable margins.

Although Celentano has not run for office for more than ten years, his impact on the political allegiance of New Haven's Italians appears to have been enduring. In a well known article some years ago the late V. O. Key suggested "the existence of a category of elections . . . in which the decisive results of the voting reveal a sharp alteration of the pre-existing cleavage within the electorate. Moreover, . . . the realignment made manifest in the voting in such elections seems to persist for several succeeding elections. Key called such contests "critical elections." As the following data show, Celentano's several mayoralty campaigns were critical elections with respect to the voting behavior of at least the Italians in New Haven.

Since 1947 the Italian wards have been the most Republican ones in the city. Table 2 shows the city-wide Democratic percentage of the vote in mayoralty elections from 1949 through 1961 and the deviations from this percentage of wards with the heaviest concentrations of Italians, Irish, and Negroes, respectively. As the table indicates, even a Yankee Republican will make his best showing in the Italian wards. In fact, the Tenth is the only ward that Lee has never carried. Since the Italian wards are among the poorest in town, their marked Republican inclinations can be attributed to ethnic voting.

Italian support for Republican candidates has been so lopsided that the customary relationship between Democratic voting and foreign birth is reversed in New Haven. The ward-by-ward correlation coefficient (Pearson's r) between percentage of foreign-born residents and percentage of the vote for Democratic mayoralty candidates has been *negative* for most elections since 1937.

While Italian Republicanism is a product of local politics, it is also expressed in state and national elections. The ethnic voting that resulted from Italian solidarity in New Haven is now manifested in elections where "recognition" of Italians is not an issue. . . . The 10th Ward (for example) has been considerably more Republican than the city as a whole in elections where neither candidate was Irish or Italian. For instance, ex-Governor Ribicoff barely carried the Tenth in 1958, while in the Irish 17th Ward, where the median family income was more than $600 higher, he won by a three-to-one ratio.

Most Italians not only vote for Republican candidates, but consider themselves Republicans. Their party identification was changed and fixed by Celentano's several campaigns. Comparing the percentages of blue-collar workers and of Democrats in various ethnic groups reveals that little more than a third of the Italians are Democrats, although they are second only to Negroes in proportion of manual workers.

These data show why New Haven politicians customarily explain the outcome of elections in terms of nationality groups rather than social classes: the most important lines of division in the electorate are ethnic rather than economic. In fact, ethnic cleavages wash out the usual relationships between socio-economic status and partisan preference. When New Haven wards are correlated by median income and Republican vote in the 1959 mayoralty election, the coefficient is —.02. Similarly, there is no relationship between the proportion of manual workers in an ethnic group and the percentage of the group's members who consider themselves Democrats. . . . The salience of ethnicity explains the apparent anomaly that the Republican party's stronghold is in the poorest parts of town, while the Democrats draw their strongest support from middle-class Jews and Irishmen as well as low-income Negroes. Since the two best examples of ethnic voting are the Republican inclinations of working-class Italians and the Democratic affiliation of middle-class Irishmen, the political correlates of ethnicity do not merely represent underlying economic differences.

Plainly, the assimilation theory does not fit the development of Italian bloc voting in New Haven. The New Haven case can be explained by a different view of ethnic voting that I will call a "mobilization theory." I will introduce it by reexamining in greater detail the assumptions of the assimilation theory.

IV. THE MOBILIZATION OF ETHNIC
POLITICAL RESOURCES

The assimilation theory is based on the assumption that the strength of ethnic voting depends on the intensity of the individual's identification with his ethnic group. The theory supposes that this identification is never stronger than in the early years of residence in this country and declines thereafter as the immigrants gain some measure of well being. There is another prerequisite to ethnic voting that the assimilation theory overlooks: no matter how salient an individual's ethnic identification may be, it will not influence his voting behavior unless he sees a connection between this identity and the choice he makes on election day. How does the Irishman know which candidate (if any) is friendlier to the Irish? The implications of this problem are worth further exploration.

Established politicians appealed to immigrants with tangible rewards and recognition. While one party may have been more vigorous in its efforts, both parties usually made some attempt to win their votes. These campaign efforts posed a twofold communication problem of pervasiveness and persuasion: how could the party get its message to every ethnic voter, and how could it make the message credible? Only some ethnics would get a job or favor, and only some would know of the recognition given by one party or the other; or, confusingly, by both. How did the ethnic know which party was friendlier to his people?

Precinct workers who talk directly to the individual voter are the most effective means of electioneering. There are no systematic data on precinct workers' activity at the peak of the immigrant era. Contemporary accounts indicate that, in at least some cities, few prospective voters could escape the attention of the political organizations. At present the level of precinct work is much lower. In northern cities with over 100,000 population less than 20 per cent of the adults reported contact with a party worker in a single presidential election. In New Haven, where both parties have very strong and active campaign organizations, 40 per cent of the registered voters have *never* been reached by a precinct worker.

Let us assume that precinct organizations were able to contact almost every potential voter fifty years ago. What if both parties sent workers around? What if both parties had won—or bought—the support of some ethnic leaders? No matter how fervently the ethnic might identify with his group, the appropriate political expression of this identification might not be clear to him.

First-generation ethnic groups seldom had many political resources aside from their votes. Many of their members were illiterate; except for the Irish, many could not speak English. At this stage it was easiest for the parties to compete for ethnic votes, for the enticements least in demand by party activists were most suitable for the immigrants. As time passed children went to school, men prospered, and the ethnic group produced representatives with the organizational and communications skills necessary for political leadership. There were greater demands on both parties for recognition and the men making the demands were more skilled at pressing their claims. Such demands raised the level of bidding between the parties, for now the ethnics were asking for rewards that were both scarcer and more highly prized by the people already established in the party organizations. The ethnics' ambitions were resisted by those who would be displaced. Because of this resistance and the time it took to develop political skills, a generation or more went by before members of the new nationality group found their way into positions of any visibility and influence.

Sooner or later some ethnics will occupy party positions. One party will nominate an ethnic for a minor office. Such positions are unimportant, and if the bid seems to pull votes the other party will soon match the offer. Most ethnic voters still have the problem of figuring out the "right" ticket to vote for, since it is still not evident which party is friendlier. The ethnic group may be given some unity if it has an unquestioned leader who can deliver its vote to the party with which he has made a deal, but this does not appear to have been a common phenomenon. Customarily, ethnic groups were fragmented, with several leaders, each telling his constituents about his exclusive inside track to the political bigwigs.

The day will come when an ethnic will win a party nomination for a major elective office. When this happens the problems of pervasiveness and persuasion will be solved for many of his fellow ethnics. They will all see his name on the ballot, and many will take this as proof that the party that nominated him is the right party for them because it has given the most recognition to their group. The bigotry that often accompanies a "first" candidacy is likely to enhance the political relevance of ethnicity for the members of the candidate's group.

It seems plausible that an ethnic group will get such a major nomination when adversity forces one party or the other to appeal to new sources of support. This seems to have been the case with Celentano's nomination. In the late 1930s the New Haven Republicans were in dire straits. Some of the state party's leading figures had been implicated in the spectacular "Waterbury scandals." In 1937 the local party had suffered its most crushing loss in any mayoralty election in a century. Coming on the heels of Roosevelt's overwhelming re-election victory, Murphy's 1937 landslide must have suggested the need for a new campaign strategy to the city's Republicans; they had little more to lose. It was in this desperate situation that a member of New Haven's most numerous voting bloc was first nominated for mayor.

Celentano was chosen for the 1939 nomination by leaders of the Republican organization. In 1941 and 1943 the party had come close to beating Murphy with non-Italian candidates and by the summer of 1945 the city administration had suffered such a decline in popularity that Republican leaders were confident of winning the election that fall. They did not then want to give the nomination to Celentano, preferring a non-Italian who would be more dependent on their support. Celentano had to wage a hard fight in ward primaries to win the nomination.

The Democrats had nominated Driscoll, their first Irish mayoralty candidate, under similar circumstances a half century earlier. The great controversy over free coinage of silver had split the party and given the 1897 mayoralty election to the Republicans. The defection of Gold Democrats may well have driven the Democratic leaders of that day to adopt a strategy of maximizing their party's appeal to the Irish.

The mobilization theory of ethnic voting states that: *The strength of ethnic voting depends on both the intensity of ethnic identification and the level of ethnic relevance in the election. The most powerful and visible sign of ethnic political relevance is a fellow-ethnic's name at the head of the ticket, evident to everyone who enters the voting booth. Middle-class status is a virtual prerequisite for candidacy for major office; an ethnic group's development of sufficient political skill and influence to secure such a nomination also requires the development of a middle class. Therefore ethnic voting will be greatest when the ethnic group has produced a middle class, i.e., in the second and third generations, not in the first. Furthermore, the shifts in party identification resulting from this first major candidacy will persist beyond the election in which they occurred.*

This is not to say that the growth of a middle class past the point of mobilization will necessarily produce increasing ethnic voting. Nor does the theory state that the resulting alignment is impervious to other political and social developments, or that more than one such shift cannot take place. But it does say that, in a given political arena and for a given nationality group, the development of voting solidarity is a product of leadership; that such leadership requires a middle class; and that such alignments are more durable than the political candidacies that produce them.

The mobilization theory seems to be more useful than the assimilation theory in explaining ethnic voting at the national level. Most members of ethnic groups in big cities are, by and large, strongly Democratic. It is often forgotten that this is a rather recent development. In the early part of the 20th century, when the foreign population of many big cities was predominantly first and second generation, these cities were carried by Republican presidential candidates as often as not. In 1920, shortly after the ending of unrestricted immigration, the Republicans carried most cities with big immigrant populations. Harding swept New York, Cleveland, Boston, Chicago, Philadelphia, Pittsburgh, and Detroit by an aggregate plurality of 1,330,000 votes. The Republicans did almost as well in 1924. But in 1928 the aggregate Democratic margin in these seven cities was 307,000, and since then they have gone Democratic in every election, usually by substantial margins.

Smith's candidacy seems to have been particularly important in its impact on partisan alignments in Southern New England. Connecticut, Massachusetts, and Rhode Island, with the highest ethnic populations in the country, were also, until 1928, stoutly Republican in state and national elections. Since then they have been in the Democratic column as often as not. Key's article on critical elections demonstrates this point more precisely. Cities which underwent a sharp and durable pro-Democratic change in 1928 had large Catholic, foreign-born populations; cities which reacted in the opposite way were largely Protestant and native-born. In short, the ethnic population of Southern New England has become more Democratic as the duration of its residence in this country has increased.

V. THE PERSISTENCE OF ETHNIC VOTING

I have argued that the importance of ethnicity in voting decisions does not steadily diminish from an initial peak, but instead increases during at least the first two generations. What next? While the assimilation theory may be inadequate for the first development of ethnic voting, what about succeeding generations? Does the importance of ethnicity diminish rapidly with more general acculturation and occupational differentiation? Or does it persist as a major independent variable, although perhaps declining somewhat in importance? It is commonly thought that the first alternative is more correct. I shall argue here for the second proposition and suggest some factors that seem to be associated with the persistence of ethnic voting.

Useful trend data on this subject are scarce. Data on Catholic voting patterns are suggestive since Catholicism is analogous to ethnicity as a variable in voting behavior. Catholics, too, tend to be more Democratic then Protestants, and this difference persists when income, occupation, or education is controlled—it is not simply an artifact of Protestants' higher status.

The passage of time by itself does not reduce ethnic salience: witness Quebec. Nationality groups seem to vary in their rates of assimilation. Few Irishmen have ancestors who came to the United States after the turn of the century, yet from all indications there are many places where Irish self-consciousness is still very strong—notably in New York City, for instance. But the Germans, who immigrated there in considerable numbers at about the same time as the Irish, no longer seem to be a self-conscious nationality group. Catholic preference for the Democratic party does not seem to be a result of the disproportionately heavy representation of Catholics among more recent arrivals to this country. When generation of American residence is controlled, Catholic-Protestant differences do not disappear nor even diminish significantly.

The passage of time is thought to be associated with weakening ethnic consciousness not just through attenuation of immigrant memories, but because members of any given ethnic group will get better jobs and, after two or three generations, be represented among all occupational levels, more or less in proportion to their numbers. Occupational mobility is believed to reduce the importance of ethnicity in voting decisions for two reasons: (1) it will produce economic interests inconsistent with ethnic voting; and (2) the mobile individuals will come into contact with a broader, socially heterogeneous environment that will dilute ethnic salience.

The extent to which social mobility alters the political expression of ethnic feelings undoubtedly varies with a number of other circumstances. The voting behavior of the New Haven Irish seems to have been relatively impervious to their changed social status. Although they are almost all in the middle class, their support of the Democratic party is so pronounced that it could not have declined very much as they went from manual labor to white collar jobs. Even when mobility does produce changes in political perspectives, these changes do not obliterate all hitherto existing predispositions. Social change begins from a "base point" of previous habits. Occupational mobility will change the politics of many of the immigrants' children, but it will do the same for old Americans. The net political difference between the two groups may be as great in the middle class as in the working class. This proposition is supported by the Elmira study, which found that differences between Catholics and Protestants in their support of the Republican presidential candidate were actually greater in the middle and upper than in the lower class. If anything, social mobility had heightened the importance of religion as an independent variable.

Upward-mobile members of the middle class have political characteristics intermediate between those typical of their old and their new status positions. While more Republican than their parents, they are considerably more likely to be Democrats than are status-stable members of their class. The voting behavior studies have established that as many as four-fifths of all voters identify with the same party as their parents. This is not just a reflection of similar life conditions; the authors of *Voting* report that most of their respondents whose vote was "inconsistent" with their social class were following parental political preferences.

The data in Table 2 indicate that ethnic voting has not declined in New Haven in the postwar period. Deviation from the city-wide vote by Italian and Irish wards was as great in 1959 as in the 1940s. The smaller Italian deviation in 1961 may be a sign of declining ethnic salience, but it may also reflect Italian coolness to a Yankee Republican candidate, or the first wave of population changes resulting from the Wooster Square Renewal Project. At least in New Haven, all the social changes of the 1940s and 1950s do not seem to have reduced the political importance of national origins.

One contemporary trend that may be relevant to ethnic voting has not been mentioned. Most of the data in this paper describe only those ethnics who have chosen to remain in the old core cities. Their neighborhoods tend to be ethnically homogeneous but economically diverse, with working-class and middle-class families intermingled. It is plausible that those ethnics who have decided to stay in such neighborhoods despite their financial ability to move to the suburbs have stronger ethnic identifications, whether as a consequence or as a cause of continued proximity. What about the ethnics who have moved to the suburbs? They should be less ethnically conscious. Suburbs tend to be economically homogeneous and ethnically diverse; in these respects they are the reverse of the old city neighborhoods. It seems likely that these new suburbanites break off the interpersonal and institutional relationships that sustain and transmit ethnic consciousness. Since group solidarity is maintained by personal contact, it is probable that geographical dispersion will dilute ethnic salience. At the same time, however, it will help to maintain the solidarity of the urban survivors by draining off those with the weakest ethnic identifications.

There are not many data relevant to these speculations. *The American Voter's* discussion of suburbanization is tentative and inconclusive, while an earlier analysis of some of the same data produced findings consistent with the line of argument in the preceding paragraph. The most useful evidence comes from Scott Greer's study of Catholic voting be-

Table 2

Deviations from New Haven city-wide Democratic vote by selected wards with concentrations of various ethnic groups—Mayoralty Elections, 1949-61

Year and ethnicity of Republican mayoralty candidate[a]	City-wide Democratic vote[b]	10th & 11th Wards (Italian)[c]	16th & 17th Wards (Irish)[d]	19th Ward (Negro)[e]
	(%)	(%)	(%)	(%)
1949—Italian	46.6	−21.9	8.5	7.9
1951—Italian	49.9	−24.3	8.0	4.3
1953—Italian	51.9	−27.3	9.0	8.3
1955—Italian	65.3	−21.3	8.1	13.4
1957—Yankee	64.8	−14.4	11.5	14.2
1959—Italian	61.8	−20.2	11.0	16.3
1961—Yankee	53.5	−10.7	15.9	24.3
1950 median family income	$3,301	$2,660 $2,318	$3,174 $3,280	$2,117

[a]In all these elections the Democratic candidate was Richard C. Lee.

[b]Percentages are of the total vote cast for mayor.

[c]In 1960 population shifts caused by an urban renewal project began to change the composition of the 10th and 11th Wards. By 1963 a substantial fraction of the old residents had been replaced by newcomers, most of whom were neither Italians nor Republicans.

[d]Since about 1958 these wards have had an influx of Negroes.

[e]Negroes comprised 72% of the 19th Ward in 1950. Increasing Democratic majorities there may be due in part to continued growth of the ward's Negro population.

Sources: Voting returns for 1949—57 are from official sources; for 1959—61, from newspapers. Choice of wards was based on a combination of Census data and political lore. (Census tracts do not coincide with wards. The 1950 Census data were matched with wards, but this was an expensive process and was not repeated for the 1960 Census.) One of the three wards with the highest proportion of Italian-born residents, the 12th, has a dissident Democratic organization and was excluded for this reason. Since the first sizeable numbers of Irish came to New Haven 120 years ago, Census data on the birthplace of present ward residents are an unreliable index of Irish predominance. I have followed the advice of New Haven politicians in choosing the 16th and 17th as the most Irish wards.

havior in and around St. Louis. He found that, with education and generation of American residence controlled, suburban Catholics were more likely than urban Catholics to defect to the Republicans.

Several political circumstances are also associated with the strength of ethnic voting. In general, it appears that ethnicity will be more important in the absence of other plain cues to guide voters' decisions. It is likely to play a greater role in non-partisan elections, where voters cannot rely on the party label. But, while party identification may impede the free play of ethnic salience, it also stabilizes and prolongs ethnic voting by providing a vehicle for continuing perception of ethnic relevance. Celentano's candidacy won Italian support not only for him, but also for the Republican party in subsequent elections because his association with the party led Italians to think that it gave them more recognition. Ethnic voting also seems to be less important when some great issue dominates political perspectives, as the Depression did in the 1930s. This may explain the unusually pro-Democratic voting of New Haven Italians in the 1932 and 1936 presidential elections.

The major proposition of this section is that ethnicity is still an important factor in voting behavior and is not eliminated by changes in the economic characteristics of the individuals affected. This is not to say that perspectives formed in the first generations of American residence will persist forever. Ethnic consciousness is fading; it is already faint in some parts of the country and for some ethnic groups. Continuing increases in education, geographical dispersion, intermarriage and intergroup contacts are all likely to reduce ethnic consciousness.

Even when ethnic salience has faded, however, its political effects will remain. One of the most remarkable tendencies in political behavior is the persistence of partisan affiliations for generations after the reasons for their formation have become irrelevant to contemporary society. Key and Munger's article on county voting patterns in Indiana is one of the best-known demonstrations of this proposition. Some Indiana counties were consistently Democratic while others, apparently identical in demographic characteristics, were consistently Republican. The roots of these variations seemed to be the origins of the counties' first settlers—New England or the South: "If one plots on the map of Indiana clusters of underground railroad stations and points at which Union authorities had difficulties in drafting troops, he separates, on the whole, Republican and Democratic counties." Key and Munger conclude that for many voters elections are merely "a reaffirmation of past decisions." It seems plausible that this will be the legacy of ethnic politics: when national origins are forgotten, the political allegiances formed in the old days of ethnic salience will be reflected in the partisan choices of totally assimilated descendants of the old immigrants.

B. INSTITUTIONAL DISCRIMINATION

In addition to their impact on the metropolis, racial and ethnic identities have been important in American society because of the differential treatment of racial and ethnic groups by American public and private institutions. As mentioned earlier,[1] much of the discrimination is of an institutional rather than individual nature, and the articles in this section attempt to trace the existing discriminatory effects in a variety of public institutions: federal government programs, criminal justice, health care, and education. While this selection only represents a sample of the institutions that could have been covered (other possibilities: employment, military service, labor unions, consumerism, and the mass media[2]), the examples should illustrate the contemporary nature of institutional discrimination.

In the first article, Leo Grebler et al. (Selection 22) describe some of the historic difficulties of the U.S. Census in determining the Mexican-American population. Since the census is the basis for much social science and many public policy decisions, the student of race and ethnicity should be aware that census definitions involve a certain degree of

---

[1]See p. xvii. See also Report of the Advisory Commission on Civil Disorders (New York: Bantam Books, Inc., 1968); Louis L. Knowles and Kenneth Prewitt (eds.), Institutional Racism in America (Englewood Cliffs, N.J.: Prentice-Hall, Inc., 1969); and Roger Daniels and Harry H. L. Kitano, American Racism: Exploration of the Nature of Prejudice (Englewood Cliffs, N.J.: Prentice-Hall, Inc., 1970).

[2]For a start in these other areas, the reader should refer on employment to Arthur M. Ross and Herbert Hill (eds.), Employment, Race, and Poverty (New York: Harcourt, Brace & World, 1967). On military service, see Charles C. Moskos, Jr., "Racial integration in the armed forces," American Journal of Sociology, July 1966, 72:132–48 (although the study is dated). On labor and the role of unions, see Julius Jacobson (ed.), The Negro and the American Labor Movement (Garden City, N.Y.: Doubleday & Co., Inc., 1968); Bayard Rustin, "The blacks and the unions," Harper's Magazine, May 1971; and Paul Good, "The bricks and mortar of racism," The New York Times Magazine, May 21, 1972. On consumerism, see S. Roxanne Hiltz, "Black and white in the consumer financial system," American Journal of Sociology, May 1971, 76:987–98, and on the media, see Report of the Advisory Commission, Chap. 15.

arbitrariness, and that the definitions can change in successive censuses. Grebler's article, for instance, describes the situation up through the 1960 census. In 1970, the Census Bureau again changed the definition of Mexican-Americans, this time to include persons of Spanish language as well as Spanish surname. In general, Grebler's article highlights the major difficulties involved in official definitions of racial and ethnic groups, difficulties that exist not only with the Mexican-Americans, but also with the blacks and other groups as well.

While the federal government has obviously played the critical role in expanding equal opportunities to members of all racial and ethnic groups, some of its own programs have ironically helped to produce the discriminatory nature of American institutions. Some of the discriminatory consequences may have been unintended; they nevertheless have had great impact, especially in the treatment of black people. Eunice and George Grier (Selection 23) summarize the effects of federal housing policies on the development of racially segregated residential patterns throughout the post-World War II period.[3] The article by Arthur M. Brazier (Selection 24) covers some of the problems of federally supported urban redevelopment programs. Brazier repeats the commonly held notion that renovation of the slums rarely leads to an improvement for the people in the slums; rather, the original residents are forced to move elsewhere as their original homes are demolished, and the slum sites are rebuilt for use by a newer and higher income clientele. Moreover, Brazier makes clear that such experiences have occurred repeatedly in spite of the fact that the ostensible goal of the federal programs has been to aid the slum resident. For this reason, he takes a much more suspicious and skeptical attitude toward programs like Model Cities, an attitude shared by many other urban residents.

A second area of institutional discrimination is the criminal justice system. The accusations against police agencies in the unfair persecution of black and other ethnic groups are well-known.[4] Less well-researched, but perhaps equally important, are the role of the courts and prisons in discriminating against blacks and other ethnic groups like the Puerto

---

[3]For a recent review of the impact of race on the housing market, see John Boston et al., "The impact of race on housing markets," *Social Problems,* Winter 1972, 19:382–93.

[4]See, for example, Paul Jacobs, *Prelude to Riot: A View of Urban American from the Bottom* (New York: Random House, Inc., 1966), pp. 13–60; *Report of the Advisory Commission,* Chap. 11; Stan Steiner, *La Raza: The Mexican-Americans* (New York: Harper & Row, Publishers, 1969), Chap. 12; Harlan Hahn, "Local variations in urban law enforcement," in Peter Orleans and William R. Ellis, Jr. (eds.), *Race, Change, and Urban Society* (Beverly Hills, Calif.: Sage, 1971), pp. 373–400; and Edward T. Rogowsky et al., "The police: The civilian review board controversy," in Jewel Bellush and Stephen David (eds.), *Race and Politics in New York City* (New York: Praeger Publishers, Inc., 1971), pp. 59–97.

Ricans and Mexican-Americans.[5] Marvin Wolfgang and Bernard Cohen (Selection 25) review the extent to which rates of reported crime differ, first for blacks and whites, and then for other ethnic groups. Their review shows again that such official records must be interpreted very cautiously. Haywood Burns (Selection 26) considers the degree of discrimination in the current legal system, and shows how the system has consistently produced a different justice for black people than for white people.

The American health care system is a third area where racial and ethnic groups receive discriminatory treatment. Different groups may begin with different physical needs for health care and different attitudes towards sickness and medical treatment.[6] In fact, the basic value differences among cultures and families are often nowhere more evident than when illness occurs. Rather than compensating for these conditions, however, the American health care system, i.e., medical personnel, medical schools, and hospitals, tend to aggravate them by favoring white patients with higher incomes. The discriminatory treatment is described briefly by Barbara and John Ehrenreich (Selection 27). They note not only the racial discrimination but also the differential treatment of women in the health care system. They also emphasize the attitudinal aspects of discrimination; while white patients are "customers," black patients are "teaching material," and women are "objects." Since health care will be of increasing concern to the American public, an important change in the future should be the development of new institutions capable of providing the best medical care for every individual, based both on his medical problem and his racial and ethnic background. Hospitals and medical personnel will have to become more sensitive, for instance, to the everyday linguistic, culinary, and life-style differences among patients of different race and ethnicity.[7]

Finally, the American educational system has consistently provided unequal education for racial and ethnic groups. The inequality has meant that blacks and foreign-speaking ethnic groups in particular have

[5]For example, see John Burma, *Spanish-Speaking Groups in the United States* (Durham, N.C.: Duke University Press, 1954), pp. 113–20; *Report of the Advisory Commission,* Chap. 13; and William R. Arnold, "Race and ethnicity relative to other factors in juvenile court dispositions," *American Journal of Sociology,* September 1971, 77:211–27.

[6]See Edward A. Suchman, "Sociomedical variations among ethnic groups," *American Journal of Sociology,* November 1964, 70:319–31; Jacobs, *Prelude to Riot, op. cit.,* pp. 171–204; and the several articles in "The elderly in minority groups," special issue of *The Gerontologist,* Spring 1971, 2(1), Part 2.

[7]These aspects of medical care are just beginning to be developed. See, for instance, Irving B. Wicker, Jr., "Overcoming cultural barriers," (in inservice training for nurses), *Hospitals, Journal of the American Hospital Association,* October 16, 1971, 45:77–80; and Joseph A. Gordon and Velma Kilgore, "Planning ethnic menus," *Hospitals, Journal of the American Hospital Association,* November 1, 1971, 45:87–91.

not been taught the basic skill: how to read. The magnitude of such a negative accomplishment should not be underestimated. As one observer poignantly describes the New York City school system,

> The average child in eighty-five percent of the Black and Puerto Rican schools is functionally illiterate after eight years of schooling in the richest city in the world.
> This is a massive accomplishment.
> It took the effort of 63,000 teachers, thousands more administrators, scholars, and social scientists, and the expenditure of billions of dollars to achieve. Alone, however, the "professional" educators could not have done it. They needed the active support of all the forces of business, real estate interests, trade unions, willing politicians, city officials, the police, and the courts.
> . . . How is it possible to fail to teach reading to the great majority of *any* population after eight years of trying? The strategies involved are complex.
> The curve of reading achievement by school in New York City is strange. It is bi-modal, a double-humped "normal" curve. It peaks at two-and-a-half years *below* grade level, falls nearly to zero *at* grade level, and then rises to a peak again at two-and-a-half years *above* grade level. Black and Puerto Rican schools lie on the below-grade half of the curve, continental white schools on the above-grade. There are, in effect, two independent curves, one for Blacks and Puerto Ricans, the other for whites. They are a graphic description of two school systems—one that fails and one that succeeds. Thus, the accomplishment of the school system is even more impressive. Their task is not only to succeed in failing the Black and Puerto Rican children; they must, at the same time, succeed in teaching the white children how to read well.[8]

In the final article of this section, Anthony Dworkin (Selection 28) discusses the treatment of Mexican-American students in public schools. He attempts to explain why the basic values of the Mexican-American family are at odds with the implicit values of the American school system and American school teachers. Dworkin's scenario perhaps also serves as a partial explanation for the failure of the schools to provide an acceptable level of education for certain racial and ethnic groups.[9]

---

[8]Annie Stein, "Strategies for failure," *Harvard Educational Review,* May 1971, 41:158–204.

[9]For other readings, see Kenneth B. Clark, *Dark Ghetto* (New York: Harper & Row, Publishers, 1965), Chap. 6; Jacobs, *Prelude to Riot, op. cit.,* pp. 205–36; Thomas F. Pettigrew, "Racial segregation and Negro education," in Daniel P. Moynihan (ed.), *Toward a National Urban Policy* (New York: Basic Books, Inc., 1970), pp. 167–77; and Stephen S. Baratz and Joan C. Baratz, "Early childhood intervention: The social science base of institutional racism," *Harvard Educational Review,* Winter 1970, 40:29–50. On higher education, see Fred E. Crossland, *Minority Access to College: A Ford Foundation Report* (New York: Schocken Books, Inc., 1971).

22. Mexican Americans and the U.S. Census

LEO GREBLER, JOAN W. MOORE and RALPH C. GUZMAN

Before 1930, the census data on persons of Mexican descent were limited to counts of those born in Mexico and those of Mexican or mixed parentage. This classification was consistent with the traditional attention in U.S. census statistics to the foreign stock in the white population, and it has been maintained to the present time.

The first effort to identify Mexican Americans more broadly to include the native born of native parentage as well as the foreign stock was made in 1930. The classification selected by the Census Bureau was "Mexican," and it was placed in the larger rubric "other races" which also included Indians, Negroes, and Orientals. This definition made clear that Mexicans were not considered whites. Census enumerators were instructed to classify as Mexicans all persons of Mexican origin, whether of old colonial stock or immigrants and their children, who were not definitely white, Negro, Indian, or Oriental.

Records in the United States Archives reveal that the 1930 census definition of Mexicans evoked "unfavorable reactions" from the Mexican government and the U.S. Department of State. Besides, the classification proved to be highly inadequate. Among other things, it resulted in a gross undercount of native persons of Mexican descent, especially in New Mexico. There is reason to believe that enumerators failed to include Mexican Americans of lighter complexion, especially when they had middle-class or upper-class status.

In 1940 the Bureau of the Census turned to mother tongue as a means of identification—the language other than English spoken in earliest childhood. This was part of a general attempt to obtain information on the spoken mother tongue from a sample of the entire population. However, the results turned out to be of dubious value for statistical identification of national minorities. For example, about seven percent of the native population of Mexican parentage in the United States reported English as their mother tongue in 1940, and this percentage was probably much higher for natives of native parentage.

When the 1950 census was prepared, the Bureau of the Census decided to use the "Spanish-surname" identification, and the same method was applied in 1960 with very minor modifications.

Adapted with permission of The Macmillan Company from *The Mexican-American People; The Nation's Second Largest Minority* by Leo Grebler, Joan W. Moore, and Ralph C. Guzman, pp. 601–04. Copyright © 1970 by The Free Press, a Division of the Macmillan Company.

The senior author is Professor Emeritus, School of Management, University of California at Los Angeles.

Significantly, Spanish-surname persons were now classified in principle as whites; they were called "white persons of Spanish surname." Thus, the statistical identification had run full circle from a subcategory of "other races" to a subgroup of the white population. How the Spanish-surname definition came to be developed is not entirely clear. But the record indicates that social scientists in the Southwest pressed for more adequate data on Mexican Americans and that Census Bureau statisticians had already used a surname technique informally for other purposes.[1] In any event, the changing classifications confine systematic comparisons of census data to the years 1950 and 1960.

THE SPANISH-SURNAME DEFINITION

The Spanish-surname definition is probably as good as any that can be devised for broad statistical purposes. The Bureau of the Census uses surnames based on a list of about 7,000 originally prepared by the U.S. Immigration and Naturalization Service in 1936. The census coders are instructed to classify a name as Spanish only if it appears in the list. Other names of apparent Spanish origin are referred to specialists trained to distinguish Spanish surnames from surnames in other Romance languages.[2]

There may be questions about the completeness and accuracy of any such list of surnames. On the other hand, this method has the considerable advantage that it can be applied to any non-census set of records which list surnames. For example, it was the basis for the compilation of statistics on intermarriages which are reported in this volume. The technique was also used as a screening device for the selection of Mexican-American households in our Los Angeles and San Antonio sample surveys. Its application is facilitated by the fact that the Bureau of the Census has prepared an abbreviated list of about 700 Spanish surnames that appear with greatest frequency—a source sufficient for statistical approximations.

---

[1]The surname technique had been helpful in distinguishing between French Canadians and other Canadians in the United States and in allocating persons in the United States to the several countries formed after the breakup of the Austrian empire in the aftermath of World War I. This account of changing census classification is based on the "Definitions and Explanations" provided in the 1950 and 1960 Census volumes on persons of Spanish Surname, on discussion with Census Bureau staff members, and on a review of minutes (in the United States Archives) of the meetings of the Census Bureau's Technical Advisory Committees. For a local survey designed to test the differences in results obtained from applying the Spanish-surname technique, the mother-tongue criterion, and the test of Spanish ancestry of household heads, see William W. Winnie, Jr., "The Spanish surname criterion for identifying Hispanos in the southwestern United States," *Social Forces,* May 1960, 38:363–66.

[2]See the "Definitions and explanations" in the census volumes referred to above.

The Spanish-surname method is certainly superior to most of the identification procedures employed by state and local government agencies for record-keeping purposes. Altogether too often receptionists or other clerks have been given the responsibility of defining a person as Mexican, and they do so on the basis of superficial impressions which, in turn, may reflect their own prejudices or the visitor's class status. The Spanish-surname technique, if properly applied, lends itself to far more accurate local investigations in such fields as health, welfare, education, and law enforcement. If these potentials are to be utilized, more methodological work is needed to identify Spanish surnames and their frequency in different areas and localities, and computer programs to extract Spanish surnames must be further developed.[3]

The Spanish-surname definition does not identify Mexican Americans directly. The following minimum adjustments are required for transforming the number of Spanish-surname people to the number of Mexican Americans: (1) Deduct persons of Spanish surname who are not of Mexican origin; (2) Add persons who are of Mexican origin but have surnames other than Spanish.

As for the first group, for example, persons of Spanish surname include immigrants from Spain and their descendants as well as individuals of Latin American stock other than Mexican, such as Cubans, Puerto Ricans, and people from Central or South America.

The second group is mainly composed of (*a*) persons who simply changed their name, say from Moreno to Brown or from Rey to King (which involves a relatively simple procedure in this country), and (*b*) Mexican-American females who married Anglos and the progeny of such unions. It seems that legal name changes have been relatively infrequent among Mexican Americans, but no substantial data are available on this point. However, the statistical disappearance of Mexican-American females from the Spanish-surname group through intermarriage has been quite significant, and it may become increasingly significant in the future. On the other hand, intermarriages of Spanish-surname males with Anglo females produce statistical increments to the Spanish-surname group. Census counts based on the surname identification of the household head include the wife and children.

As ethnic identification reaches back in time, one enters the never-never land of highly mixed origins which characterize so large a segment of our total population. The intermarriage in 1925 of a Spanish-surname male and an Anglo female may have produced a son who married an

---

[3]See, for example, Robert W. Buechley, "A reproducible method of counting persons of Spanish surname," *Journal of the American Statistical Association,* March 1961, 56:88–97. This article includes some suggestive ideas for using a highly abbreviated list of Spanish surnames. See also the same author's "Characteristic name sets of Spanish populations," *Names,* March 1967, 15:53–69.

Anglo girl of Italian stock, a daughter who married a Mexican American, another daughter who entered matrimony with a Jew, and so forth.

Some analysts have concluded that the census statistics understate the number of Spanish-surname persons in the Southwest, and they have more or less arbitrarily added 10 percent.[4] The assumption of an undercount is reinforced by the fact that the census has failed to enumerate Negroes as completely as whites. It is possible that some of the difficulties that account for this failure apply to Spanish-name persons as well. Besides, fear of governmental authority or dubious legality of residence status among Mexican Americans may have resulted in a disproportionate amount of statistical "slippage." Nevertheless, we abstain from making corrections for which there is no sufficient factual basis.[5] As was already indicated, any adjustment of the census data to allow for persons of non-Spanish surname must also exclude Spanish-surname people who are not of Mexican origin—if the objective is to arrive at an estimate of Mexican Americans. Moreover, the analysis here focuses on socioeconomic characteristics of this segment of our population in comparison to other population groups; and it would be impossible to assign any additional or reduced numbers to subgroups of Mexican Americans differentiated by age, sex, educational attainment, occupation, income, urban or rural residence, and so forth. For these purposes, one has no choice but to use the census data on Spanish-surname persons as they come.

However, the numerical differences between Spanish-surname people

---

[4]See, for example, Herschel T. Manuel, *Spanish-Speaking Children of the Southwest* (Austin, Tex.: University of Texas Press, 1965), pp. 21 and 22. One of the reasons given for the "correction" is the fact that Mexican Americans may not have Spanish surnames although they identify themselves historically and culturally with the Mexican-American population. This argument, however, ignores the Spanish-surname persons who are not of Mexican origin and do not identify themselves with Mexican Americans.

[5]Post-enumeration studies by the U.S. Bureau of the Census after the 1950 and 1960 censuses have revealed substantial underenumeration of the total population. Depending on the methods used, the estimates of "missed" persons range up to 4.7 percent of the total population in 1960. Of particular interest here is a greater-than-average underenumeration of people in slum areas and of nonwhites. By inference, one would expect underenumeration to be greater than average for Spanish-surname persons as well. However, the post-enumeration studies were not specifically addressed to this segment of the population. Since the census data in this volume are mainly used for comparing the socioeconomic characteristics of the Spanish-surname population with Anglos and nonwhites in the Southwest, the post-enumeration studies provide no sufficient basis for statistical corrections. For a technical discussion of census underenumeration, see the following papers delivered at the annual meeting of the American Statistical Association in 1966 (American Statistical Association, *Proceedings of the Social Statistics Section*): Eli S. Marks and Joseph Waksberg, "Evaluation of coverage in the 1960 Census of population through case-by-case checking," and Jacob S. Siegel and Melvin Zelnik, "An evaluation of the coverage in the 1960 Census of population by techniques of demographic analysis and by composite methods."

and Mexican Americans do complicate the analysis of socioeconomic characteristics. For example, if the Spanish-surname females who married Anglos and were therefore lost in the census count were typically more educated than other Spanish-surname females, had a higher labor-force participation rate, and were engaged in more skilled occupations, the socioeconomic position of Mexican-American females as shown in census data would be lower than otherwise. Or, if the socioeconomic status of Spanish-surname persons of other than Mexican origin was typically better than that of Mexican Americans, the census figures would paint a brighter picture than was warranted for Mexican Americans alone.

Another complicating factor is the inclusion of farm workers from Mexico in the census figures on Spanish-surname persons, despite the fact that they are not permanent residents. This procedure, rarely recognized in the literature, affects not only the numbers and the age and sex distributions but should tend to lower the socioeconomic status of the group as a whole.[6] It produces no serious distortions when large aggregates of people are involved, but it can create more substantial defects in data for certain age or sex groups or for small areas where temporary agricultural workers may represent a significant portion of the Spanish-surname population.[7]

It is generally recognized that the accuracy of census data can be affected by response errors. Whether response error is more frequent for Spanish-surname persons than for others is a moot question, but people

---

[6]According to the *Enumerators' Reference Manual* of the Bureau of the Census, the enumerators are instructed to include, among others, citizens of foreign countries living in the enumeration district who are employed in the United States even if they do not expect to remain here, as well as members of their families living with them in this country. Instructions pertaining to "persons with no usual residence" specify that persons in camps for migratory agricultural workers are to be enumerated. Our interpretation of these instructions was verified by the U.S. Bureau of the Census as follows: "You are correct in your assumption that *braceros* living in the United States when the 1960 Census was taken were to be enumerated and were counted as Spanish-surname persons when their surname so indicated. They were also included in the twenty-five percent sample." (From a letter to Leo Grebler, Director of the Mexican-American Study Project, dated June 22, 1966, by Howard G. Brunsman, U.S. Bureau of the Census.) The 25 percent sample covers most of the socioeconomic characteristics of the population.

[7]In April 1960, when the census was taken, nearly 70,000 Mexican contract workers were employed on farms, according to figures supplied by the U.S. Department of Labor (House Committee on the Judiciary, *Study of Population and Immigration Problems,* Special Series No. 11, 1963, table 7, p. 45). Of the 70,000 a little over 33,000 were in California, nearly 24,000 were in Texas, 10,000 were in Arizona, and 3,100 were in New Mexico. These numbers are quite low relative to the total Mexican-American population in the Southwest or the various states. However, when smaller statistical aggregates are involved, such as males in certain age groups or occupations, or when limited areas such as rural segments in Arizona and New Mexico are analyzed, the inclusion of migratory farm workers may affect the figures more significantly.

with an insufficient command of English and a low level of schooling may misunderstand census questions.

Finally, the 1960 census data on Spanish-surname persons are based on a 25 percent sample, whereas the general population count was designed to be complete. Most of the socioeconomic characteristics of both the general and the Spanish-name population are derived from a 25 percent sample. Although a sample of this size is adequate for most purposes, the errors resulting from sampling variability are greater the smaller the number of persons in a particular group or area. Altogether, the limitations of census data and procedures suggest caution in the interpretation of the results.

23. Equality and beyond: Housing segregation in the Great Society

EUNICE and GEORGE GRIER

Riots, racial protests, and rising waves of crime and violence in Los Angeles and other cities across the nation have focused attention upon a problem unique to America—and one which, if not dealt with decisively and soon, can wreak wholesale destruction upon the objectives of the "Great Society." The point at issue is the increasing dominance of Negro ghettos, with all their human problems, at the heart of the nation's metropolitan areas. While racial segregation is by no means new to this country, in recent years it has assumed new dimensions. And the long-smoldering difficulties and disillusionments of a suppressed Negro population have simultaneously taken on new and frightening forms of expression.

The newly emergent pattern of segregation is as simple to describe as it is ominous in its implications. Since the end of World War II, Negroes have rapidly been replacing whites as the dominant population of our greatest cities. Meanwhile, the vast new suburbs growing up around

Abridged and edited from Eunice and George Grier, "Equality and beyond: Housing segregation in the Great Society," *Daedalus,* Winter 1966, pp. 77–106. Reprinted by permission of *Daedalus,* Journal of the American Academy of Arts and Sciences, Boston, Mass. Winter 1966, *The Negro American -2.*

The senior author is Senior Associate, Washington Center for Metropolitan Studies, Washington, D.C.

these same urban centers—sharing most of the same problems and feeding upon a common economic base, but separated from the cities politically—have become the residence of an almost exclusively white population. Too many of the suburbanites disavow any concern or responsibility for the cities they have left behind.[1]

· · · · ·

How did this change occur so swiftly and so massively? Discrimination and prejudice are certainly among the causes, but they are not the only ones. America cannot escape responsibility for the many decades in which the rights of its Negro citizens were denied. Nonetheless, the present situation cannot be fully understood, nor can solutions to its perplexing aspects be found, without recognizing that it was produced and is maintained in significant part by forces that are both broader than and different from racial discrimination.

The background to all that has happened lies in certain facts concerning the rapid urbanization of America's people—facts racially neutral in themselves, but having profound racial effects. As the nation has grown more populous, its inhabitants have located increasingly within metropolitan centers. A century ago Americans numbered 31 million, about one-fifth of whom lived in urban areas. By 1920 the total population had risen to 106 million, and the urban proportion had grown to one-half—a ninefold jump in absolute numbers (from about 6 million to 54 million) in only sixty years.

After World War II, population growth accelerated sharply. The largest ten-year increase in the nation's history took place between 1950 and 1960. During that decade 28 million new citizens were added, a total nearly equal to the entire population of a century ago. About 85 per cent of this increase occurred within 212 metropolitan areas, making about two-thirds of the nation's people urban today.

In addition to increase through births and immigration during these fruitful years, the cities gained also from large-scale population movements from the center of the country toward its boundaries (especially to

---

[1]There is a vast literature on the implications for local government of the divergence between population patterns and political boundaries in today's metropolitan areas. For an overview of governmental efforts to cope with the resulting problems, see Roscoe C. Martin, *Metropolis in Transition: Local Government Adaptation to Changing Urban Needs* (Washington, D.C., Housing and Home Finance Agency, September 1963). This study contains an extensive bibliography. An early and prescient discussion of the racial implications of metropolitan population shifts will be found in Morton Grodzins, *The Metropolitan Area as a Racial Problem* (Pittsburgh, Pa., University of Pittsburgh Press, 1958). While Grodzins' prescriptions for solution sometimes seem a bit naive in retrospect, his dramatic presentation of the problem has been amply confirmed by later knowledge. A provocative discussion of the suburbanites' viewpoint toward metropolitan-area-wide cooperation toward solution of urban problems will be found in Charles R. Adrian, "Metropology: Folklore and field research," *Public Administration Review,* Summer 1961, 21:148–157.

the seacoasts and Great Lakes region) and from the South to the North. These streams of people, most experts agree, were both "pulled" toward the cities by job opportunities and other urban attractions (especially in the coastal areas) and "pushed" out of the rural areas by shrinking labor needs, especially in the depressed portions of the agricultural South. Negroes and whites shared in the migration—Negroes to a somewhat, but not drastically, greater degree in proportion to their share of the total population.

Migration to the cities helps explain why, after World War II, the nation turned to its suburbs in order to satisfy housing needs which had been accumulating during almost two decades of economic depression and world conflict. The previous growth of the cities had used up most of the land suitable for development within their boundaries. Yet the people had to be housed somewhere, and swiftly. The easiest place, requiring no costly and time-consuming demolition of existing buildings, was the suburbs.

How should the suburbs be developed? In answering this question certain key public policy decisions—involving racial implications which were probably neither foreseen nor intended—joined with private actions to help produce the present situation. Primary among these was the critical decision to allow the private-enterprise system to meet the housing shortage on its own terms. Most of the government mechanisms mobilized to aid in the task, especially the mortgage guarantee provisions of the Federal Housing Administration and the Veterans Administration, served to support and encourage the efforts of private enterprise.[2]

Such a decision was completely in accord with America's social philosophy and economic structure. And, in light of the inherent dynamism of the private-enterprise system, it is not surprising that the home-building industry was able to provide usable physical shelter. Indeed, this success can be counted as one of the major achievements of a nation which has never been satisfied with small accomplishments. Almost every year following World War II more than one million dwelling units were constructed and occupied, a figure which is double the rate at which new families were formed. And, despite rapid population growth during the fifties, the 1960 Census showed that Americans were far better housed than ever before. Overcrowding and "doubling up" (two or more families in one dwelling) had been considerably reduced. So had

---

[2]The indirect racial effects of federal housing policies are discussed in Bertram Weissbourd, *Segregation, Subsidies and Megalopolis* (Santa Barbara, Calif., Center for the Study of Democratic Institutions, 1964). Also, in more detail, in an unpublished paper by Eunice and George Grier, "Federal powers in housing affecting race relations," prepared for the Potomac Institute and the Washington Center for Metropolitan Studies in September 1962.

dilapidated and otherwise substandard housing. To a greater or lesser degree, the entire population benefited from this widespread improvement—even Negroes, though they continued to be less adequately housed than whites.[3]

Nonetheless, the decision to let private enterprise satisfy the housing need carried with it unfortunate consequences for future residential patterns. It meant that the great majority of the new postwar suburban housing was built for those who could afford to pay the full economic price. Thus the basic mechanisms of the private enterprise system, successful as they were in meeting overall housing needs, selectively operated to reinforce existing trends which concentrated low-income families in the cities. At the same time, they encouraged the centrifugal movement of those who were more wealthy to the outskirts of the cities.

Most Negro families were among those with low incomes, the result of generations of discrimination in employment and education. Quite apart from direct racial discrimination, in which the private housing industry also indulged whenever it felt necessary, economics posed a giant barrier to the free dispersal of the growing Negro populations. The findings of a market analysis conducted by Chester Rapkin and others at the University of Pennsylvania's Institute for Urban Studies at the peak of the postwar housing boom in the mid-1950's were quite typical. At that time, only 0.5 per cent of all dwellings costing $12,000 or more in Philadelphia had been purchased by Negroes—a fact which the authors laid mainly to economic incapacity. This was about the minimum cost of a modest new house in Philadelphia's suburbs.[4]

But this is only part of the story. Federal policies and practices in housing reinforced and increased the separation between the "Negro" cities and the white suburbs. In part, this was intentional. From 1935 to 1950—a period in which about 15 million new dwellings were constructed—the power of the national government was explicitly used to prevent integrated housing. Federal policies were based upon the premise that economic and social stability could best be achieved through keeping neighborhood populations as homogeneous as possible. Thus, the *Underwriting Manual* of the Federal Housing Administration (oldest and largest of the federal housing agencies, established by the Housing Act of 1934) warned that "if a neighborhood is to retain stability, it is necessary that properties shall continue to be occupied by the same social and racial group." It advised appraisers to lower their valuation of properties in mixed neighborhoods, "often to the point of rejec-

---

[3]*Our Non-white Population and Its Housing: The Changes between 1950 and 1960* (Washington, D.C., Housing and Home Finance Agency, July 1963).

[4]Chester Rapkin and William G. Grigsby, *The Demand for Housing in Eartwick*, prepared under contract for the Redevelopment Agency of the City of Philadelphia by the Institute for Urban Studies, University of Pennsylvania, Philadelphia, 1960.

tion." FHA actually drove out of business some developers who insisted upon open policies.[5]

More recently, a number of studies by competent real-estate economists have thrown serious doubt upon the thesis that Negro entry lowers property values. Laurenti, in his thorough analysis entitled *Property Values and Race,* found that prices *rose* in 44 per cent of those areas which Negroes entered, were unchanged in another 41 per cent, and declined in only 15 per cent. These were long-term trends, and they were measured *relative* to trends in carefully-matched neighborhoods which remained all white—thus obviating any possibly misleading effects of generally rising prices.[6]

Surveying the literature, Laurenti noted similar results from other studies in various cities extending back as far as 1930. But erroneous though the allegation of nonwhite destruction of property values may have been, it nonetheless provided "justification" for widespread discriminatory practices, as well as active encouragement of private discrimination, by agencies of the federal government during a period of critical importance in determining present residential patterns.

However, discrimination *per se* was only a small factor in the impact of federal policies and practices upon racial patterns during this crucial period. Much more important were more basic aspects of the structure and functioning of federal housing programs. Three major programs have dominated the field. The largest and most significant has been the Federal Housing Administration's mortgage insurance program, with its post-World War II counterpart for veterans, the Veterans Administration's loan guarantee program. Both granted their benefits chiefly to the "modal" family recently embarked upon married life, with children already born or on the way, and willing to commit itself to the responsibilities of home ownership with a mortgage. For such families, down-payment requirements were minimal, repayment periods lengthy, and credit restrictions lenient. A certain minimum of present earnings and good prospects for future income were paramount, as well as some evidence of faithful repayment of past obligations. Households which did not fit these criteria—smaller families, older couples, single persons, people with low or precarious earnings, families who sought dwellings for rent rather than for sale, even families dependent upon the wife's employment for an adequate income—all were required to satisfy their

[5]The federal role in enforcing housing discrimination is documented in Charles Abrams, *Forbidden Neighbors* (New York, 1955). Also in Eunice and George Grier, *Privately Developed Interracial Housing* (Berkeley, Calif., 1960). The latter volume contains, in Chapter VIII, detailed case histories of two post-World War II developments intended for interracial occupancy which were driven to financial ruin by FHA opposition despite powerful private support.

[6]Luigi Laurenti, *Property Values and Race* (Berkeley, Calif.: University of California Press, 1960).

needs chiefly through the older housing left vacant by people moving to new homes in the suburbs.

Prominent among those left behind, of course, were Negroes. The federal programs permitted them to "inherit" the cities, along with an assortment of whites who did not meet the conditions for access to the new suburbs: the old, the poor, the physically and mentally handicapped, the single and divorced, together with some persons of wealth and influence who preferred the convenience of living in the central city. The significance of the housing programs for residential patterns, however, lay also in their tendency to pull young and upwardly mobile white families away from the cities and out toward the suburbs.

It may be that a large number of these families, given free choice, would have preferred to remain within the cities, close to work and to older relatives. But the FHA and VA programs generally did not provide nearly so liberal terms on the mortgages of older homes in the cities. Down payments were usually larger; repayment periods shorter, monthly payments higher. For most young families, therefore, the suburbs were the only practical areas in which to solve their housing needs. In this way, the FHA and VA programs, essentially independent of any direct racial bias in their decisions on applications, enhanced the tendency toward white dominance in the suburbs.

The second of the federal government's major housing programs is subsidized low-income public housing, administered by the Public Housing Administration through local housing authorities. Its criteria for admission are based upon *maximum* rather than minimum income levels. Under these conditions relatively small numbers of whites can qualify because their earnings exceed the required standard. In many areas, even where conscious efforts are made to attract an interracial clientele, the great majority of residents are Negro. In further contrast to the FHA and VA programs, most public housing projects have been constructed in the central cities rather than in the suburbs—since one of their objectives is to reduce the incidence of blighted housing.

The differences between the two programs thus reinforce each other in their effects upon patterns of residence. While the FHA and VA have helped promote white dominance in the suburbs, public housing has helped enhance Negro dominance in the cities.

The third of the major federal housing programs is urban renewal. Established by the Housing Act of 1949, its chief goal is to combat physical decay in the central cities. In a sense, urban renewal has worked against FHA and VA programs, since, among other things, it attempts to draw back to the cities the more prosperous of the families who have left it. Until recently, the renewal program has usually cleared off blighted sections and replaced them with housing units priced in the middle-to upper income brackets. Most often, as might be expected, the occupants of the site before renewal have been low-income members of a racial minority. They have been displaced by housing which, for economic reasons alone, was available mainly to whites and to very few Negroes. Some civil rights groups therefore have dubbed urban renewal "Negro removal."[7]

Renewal agencies are required by law to relocate displaced families into "decent, safe and sanitary" housing. Relocation procedures have recently received a great deal of criticism throughout the nation. Whether or not all of it is valid, it is an undeniable fact that most relocatees move only a short distance from their former homes. One study found, for example, that two-thirds of them relocated within a radius of twelve city blocks. As a result, displaced low-income minorities ring the renewal site.

Sometimes this movement appears to set off a chain reaction. Whites in the neighborhoods to which the displacees move take up residence elsewhere—as do some of the more secure Negroes. The ultimate effect too often is to touch off spreading waves of racial change, which in the end only produce a broader extension of segregated living patterns. Thus, if the FHA, VA, and public housing programs have helped produce metropolitan areas which increasingly resemble black bullseyes with white outer rings, urban renewal has too often created small white or largely white areas in the center of the bullseyes—simultaneously causing the black ghettos to expand outward even further.

Combined with rapid population growth in the metropolitan areas, the interacting effects of federal policies and practices in the postwar era did much to produce the present segregated patterns. But they were not the only factors. Clear discrimination by private individuals and groups —including the mortgage, real-estate, and home-building industries— has also played its part. The activities of the "blockbuster" provide a good focus for examining the way this works.

The *modus operandi* of the blockbuster is to turn over whole blocks of homes from white to Negro occupancy—the quicker the better for his own profits, if not for neighborhood stability. Once one Negro family has entered a block, the speculator preys on the racial fears and

---

[7]The impact of race upon urban renewal, and vice versa, has been touched upon in many places. Among them: Robert C. Weaver, "Class, race and urban renewal," *Land Economics,* August 1960, 36(3). Also L. K. Northwood, "The threat and potential of urban renewal," *Journal of Intergroup Relations,* Spring 1961, 2:101–114; and Mel J. Ravitz, "Effects of urban renewal on community racial patterns," *Journal of Social Issues,* 1957, 13(4):38–49. For an optimistic view on the consequences of renewal for displaced families see *The Housing of Relocated Families,* a summary of a Bureau of the Census survey of families recently displaced from urban renewal sites published by the Housing and Home Finance Agency, Washington, D.C. in March 1965. The "pro-renewal" viewpoint is also presented in *New Patterns in Urban Housing,* Experience Report 104, published by the U.S. Conference of Mayors, Community Relations Service, Washington, D.C., May 15, 1965.

prejudices of the whites in order to purchase their homes at prices as low as possible—often considerably below fair market value. He then plays upon the pent-up housing needs of Negroes and resells the same houses at prices often well *above* their value in a free market situation. Often he makes a profit of several thousand dollars within a period of a few days. Studies have indicated that skillful blockbusters frequently double their investments in a brief interval. They can do this only because tight residential restrictions have "dammed up" the Negro need for housing to such a point that its sudden release can change the racial composition of a neighborhood within a matter of weeks or months. Apart from the damage done to both sellers and buyers and to the structure of the neighborhoods themselves, blockbusters have a far wider negative impact. By funneling Negro housing demand into limited sections of the city (usually around the edges of the Negro slums, since these neighborhoods are easier to throw into panic), the blockbusters relieve much of the pressure which might otherwise have encouraged the dispersion of Negroes throughout the metropolitan areas.[8]

Technically speaking blockbusters represent an unscrupulous minority of the real estate industry—"outlaws" in a moral if not a legal sense. However, their activities would not prove profitable if racial restrictions on place of residence were not accepted and enforced by the large majority of builders, brokers, and lenders, backed by the supporting opinion of large segments of the white public.

By restraining the Negro market and permitting its housing needs to be satisfied only on a waiting-list basis, "reputable" members of the banking and housing industries have helped perpetuate the conditions under which their less-scrupulous colleagues can flourish. For reasons they consider entirely justifiable, they guard assiduously against the entry of Negroes into white areas. In recent testimony before the Commissioners of the District of Columbia, the President of the Mortgage Bankers Association of Metropolitan Washington stated bluntly that "applications from minority groups are not generally considered in areas that are not recognized as being racially mixed." A study by the Chicago Commission on Human Relations found that such a policy was pursued by almost all lending sources in that city. Voluminous evidence from

---

[8]Probably the most thorough and telling analysis of the economics involved in racial turnover mediated by real-estate speculators was published by the Chicago Commission on Human Relations, a municipal agency, in 1962. In a single block which had changed from all-white to virtually all-Negro with heavy involvement by speculators, the differential between the price paid by the speculator and that paid by the Negro buyer upon purchase under an installment contract ranged from 35 to 115 per cent, with an average of 73 per cent. The installment contract itself is a financing device which yields higher-than-average returns to the entrepreneur, so the profiteering only began with the sale. For a graphic description of the activities of these speculators, see Norris Vitchek (as told to Alfred Balk). "Confessions of a blockbuster," *Saturday Evening Post,* July 14, 1962.

both social research surveys and testimony before legislative and executive bodies indicates that the same is true of most real-estate boards in cities throughout the country.

Supporting this activity is the subjective equivalent of the ostensibly objective economic argument that underlay federal housing policy for years: the belief in neighborhood homogeneity—that is, neighborhood exclusiveness. The general attitude of much of the public (or the most vocal) has been that neighborhoods were better off when the people within them all belonged to the same broad socioeconomic groups and had the same ethnic or racial origins. In practice, of course, this commitment to neighborhood homogeneity has tended to exclude individuals who fell below a certain status level, not those who were above it. The latter, however, usually have "excluded" themselves in neighborhoods restricted to occupants of their own status.

After 1948, when the Supreme Court ruled that racial and religious convenants were unenforceable in the courts, minority groups began to find it somewhat less difficult to obtain access to neighborhoods on the basis of financial status and preference. Still, neighborhood exclusiveness remained a commonly accepted value, widely enforced by the real-estate, home-building, and lending industries. It served as the final factor in the constellation which created the nation's new patterns of residential segregation.

24. What kind of Model Cities?

ARTHUR M. BRAZIER

I shall address my comments to what I consider is the major prerequisite for a successful Model Cities program in Woodlawn. But first, let me make it clear that when I refer to a "successful" program, I mean successful from the point of view of the people of Woodlawn, the people who are to participate in and be served by this program. I must make that point clear at the very outset of my remarks, because black Americans have learned through many years of bitter disillusionment that we no longer can permit others—however friendly they may be—to define our needs, nor can we permit others to solely determine how these needs should be administered or satisfied. While we welcome the help of our friends—and everybody needs somebody—we cannot abdicate our responsibility to ourselves.

Therefore, I shall not speak to the technical requirements of this program. I shall confine my remarks to questions of the relationships of powerful components, their basic postures, their underlying attitudes, their primary motivations, and, if you will permit me to sound a bit paranoid, I shall allude to ulterior motives that could destroy the program in its infancy.

The Model Cities concept—in general terms—is a beautiful and timely projection. A bit late, but still a great idea. What black man could be against its multifaceted community services? What black man could reject the idea of a concentrated attack on poverty, inferior education, unemployment and slum housing? Who among us could oppose more legal aid for the defenseless, better health services for the poor—just to mention a few ingredients of the Model Cities idea. I say again, no one is against such a program *in principle*.

However, we are concerned with the application of these programs; how and by whom these programs are going to be administered; the extent and depth of the financial commitment to these programs; and who will have the determining, ultimate voice in the structuring and in the crucial decision-making processes involved.

Why do I raise these questions at this time? Why sound suspicious? Why speak of certain ulterior motives? Why bring up that sore spot—community control—at this point? I would imagine that there are some people—even black people—who would advise us to go ahead and get some of that government money moving in Woodlawn. Things couldn't be much worse, they may say. Furthermore, the city has experts available. That could be the logic adopted by some anxious souls, but not those who comprise The Woodlawn Organization.

In the first place, money alone will not answer our needs; and secondly, some experts lose their expertise when the question of race appears on the drawing board. All plausible arguments to the contrary notwithstanding, now, right now, is the time to settle all the questions that I have raised.

The present Model Cities concept is not the first noble idea presented supposedly to help the disadvantaged. The history of modern urban society is replete with the failures of ideas of equal worth and urgency. Some of these failures represented the best thinking of prominent names, experts in their particular fields; some represented great wealth; some immense political skill and influence; while others were well-known for their sympathy for the poor and the powerless. But most of them had one thing in common: they thought that they, and only they, were capable of working out the solutions to our needs.

A "Delivery System" to them meant for black people to sit quietly by while they, with alternatingly warm and stern paternalism, delivered to us what they thought we needed. To them, our advice and consent was not needed, and when volunteered, it was not heeded.

At this moment my mind goes back to the 1930's, when the concept of public housing became a reality. The only people who opposed public housing AT THAT TIME were the conservatives who were either frightened by the spectre of socialism or who just didn't want to see the government spending much money on any poor people—black or white. Many people remember the completion of Ida B. Wells Homes. It provided a sort of model public housing program for that decade. It received much public approval throughout the land. And it was a truly great, humane idea. It took thousands of overcrowded blacks out of intolerable conditions and provided them with neat, new apartments with rents to match their incomes.

But witness what happened later. Witness what our experts, so-called friends, and sympathizers did with this noble idea. Public housing was converted into a compound for poor, powerless, and politically exploited black people. You've seen State Street, from 22nd Street to Garfield Boulevard, that endless reservation for the black disadvantaged, who, by the very structure of their physical environment ALONE, remain disadvantaged. But to large numbers of white Chicagoans, public housing is a success. It keeps large numbers of overcrowded blacks from spilling over into lily white neighborhoods. But to the people who must live in these compounds, public housing is a failure when it crams 27,000 poor people within the confines of a Robert Taylor Homes.

Public housing is a dismal failure if you are a mother trying to rear small children from a highrise apartment. Public housing is a failure when its stultifying social climate turns blacks against blacks in daily outbursts of violence. It is significant that some of the most violent of racial explosions of the past four years occurred in or around some of these public housing compounds.

Yes, when we look back at public housing we must raise the questions of goal orientation and the ulterior motives that I spoke of earlier. And from the vantage point of the present, it is candidly clear that the powers who finally determined the character and course of public housing in this city gave little thought to the plight of the people who would occupy those buildings. They were preoccupied with other overriding considerations, to wit: the maintenance of segregated housing in Chicago; and, of course, the city fathers had other very practical goals in mind, too; however, none of their goals gave priority to the crying needs of the people who would live out their lives and bring up their children in a public housing project.

The same can be said of slum clearance and urban renewal. Everybody is against slums, and who could oppose the renewal of our cities? We were introduced to the concept of urban renewal in the late 1940's. It was hailed by some of our best minds as a savior of the cities. In 1948, we got a chance to see urban renewal in action in the communities adjacent to Michael Reese Hospital. Even then, many blacks suspected that this was not urban renewal but "Negro Removal." But they were drowned out and overridden by the establishment. Some of our white friends accused the black protester of being too sensitive, biased and shortsighted.

It is now 1969, 21 years later—and we don't have to guess any more. The people with the power, the people who determined the character of urban renewal in the Michael Reese–Illinois Institute of Technology area, were not concerned with the plight of the black people who lived there before renewal. They were primarily concerned with maintaining the hospital and school as viable institutions and making the surrounding communities compatible with the growth plans of those institutions. They were concerned with reclaiming valuable land in close proximity to the Loop and the Lake. They were concerned with the low tax yield of the property in the community, and they were alarmed about another white problem common to nearly all big cities: the flight of white residents to the suburbs. In the midst of all these concerns, the powerless black population was not merely pushed to the back of the bus; it was pushed off and left to its own devices. In 1948, to have suggested that this would happen would have meant that you were paranoid.

But witness this headline in the April 19, 1969, edition of the *Chicago Daily Defender,* page 11. The headline says, "South Commons Luring Many Families Back from the Suburbs." For your information, South Commons is located on 30 acres of land on South Michigan Avenue, between 31st and 26th Streets, the front yard of Illinois Tech. It is a $20 million community developed on urban renewal land. The community's management is simply overjoyed by the so-called success of their program. According to Edward N. Kelly, vice-president, the managing agent, Baird & Warner, "It's gratifying" to see that a growing number of suburban families are making a trek back to the city.

According to Mr. Kelly, the suburbs already represented at South Commons are Park Ridge, Morton Grove, Des Plaines, Highland Park, Evanston, Downers Grove, Glenview, and St. Charles. Need I remind you that the overwhelming number of new residents in this old black community will be white with a sprinkling of blacks just for the record.

Yes, urban renewal at South Commons is a *success* for those whose primary motivation is to make the world nice and comfortable for the middle classes. But what about the blacks who once lived there, the blacks who had no voice in the development of their community?

The same can be said of another wonderful idea—the F.H.A. home loan. Initially, blacks thought that this would be a boon to black ownership, since F.H.A. was designed to help people purchase homes with small down payments, reasonable rates of interest and long-term amortization. Thanks to F.H.A., we would be able to purchase adequate housing throughout the city, anywhere, because we no longer would be at the complete mercy of loan sharks and prejudiced mortgage institutions.

Need I tell you that didn't happen. Our federal government, through F.H.A., simply made it easier for whites to flee the city to the suburbs—extending segregation to the countrysides—and now through urban renewal and black removal it is making it easier for these same people to return to the city and live in communities taken from blacks.

There is one discernable thread woven through all of this: It is the fact that the people who determined the structure and administration of all these programs were thinking only of what is good for white people. *The black community determined nothing and controlled nothing.* The fact that a few of us blacks may live in South Commons, Lake Meadows or Prairie Shores fades into insignificance.

That is why I must speak today as I do. That is why I must tell you that regardless of the individual sincerity of many of you fine people here today, the Model Cities program is looked upon with suspicion by thoughtful black people in Chicago.

Yes, suspicion was and still is a part of the climate whenever we hear of any program involving government funds or powerful white institutions. When the highly laudable War on Poverty program was announced, once again we were suspicious. Out of habit we asked, does white America really intend to do something about hunger? Or does it merely intend to do a snow job? Is its main purpose to issue a few tranquilizers to restless, riot-prone black communities?

If you read the article on hunger in the *Chicago Sun-Times* and the *Chicago Daily News* and that shocking front page story in the *New York Times,* you will understand that our suspicions were justified. According to the *New York Times,* thousands of black children are still suffering brain damage because of a lack of proteins. These children will be damaged PERMANENTLY. And while we have reached the moon we haven't reached their homes with a full meal. And in another article, the *Times* reports a survey on the effectiveness of Operation Head Start. That survey shows that most children under the program are hardly any better off than before. Now I don't believe everything that I read in the newspapers, but I certainly take a second look when they say something that I have suspected all the time.

And right here I must again ask, did that noble idea of a national War on Poverty become more concerned with protecting the political status quo than with the hunger of the poor?

I recognize that many poor people have been helped by all of these programs, but I suspect that they represent only a fraction of a fraction of the needy.

I have declined to address myself to the technicalities and specifics of the Model Cities program because I am certain that regardless of how much money is available now and how qualified our technical advisors are, this program can become just another failure in a long chain of failures. . . . As I have stated, this program is clouded with suspicion marks, and the burden of removing that suspicion must be placed on the shoulders of the governmental agencies involved and the major private institutions.

The governmental agencies must convincingly show that they are concerned with the community's people rather than with politics. And by the same token, the powerful institutions must convincingly demonstrate that they, too, are primarily concerned with the people who are their neighbors as well as the long-range goals of the institutions. That overall climate of trust does not exist today.

We need a fresh start, and by a fresh start I do not mean new clichés, new rhetoric about maximum feasible public participation, etc., etc., etc. I mean a beginning based on tangible, visible, permanent, sincere examples of respect and concern for the people of Woodlawn, Lawndale, Uptown, Kenwood-Oakland, Grand Boulevard, and any other community where Model Cities programs are contemplated.

First, all of us must recognize that we need each other, that we have something to offer each other, and that we can work together if we try.

The Woodlawn community deserves and is in dire need of ample government funds. At the same time, The University of Chicago has unduplicated technical know-how that should be made available to the Woodlawn community. On the other hand, neither the government nor the University can fulfill the hopes embraced in the Model Cities concept without the first-hand knowledge and experience of a self-determining Woodlawn community.

I am exceedingly happy to report that The University of Chicago and the Woodlawn community have taken the first step in the direction of mutual understanding and cooperation. Over the past few years, T.W.O. and the University specialists in law, urban planning, social welfare, medicine, economic development, and education have been working together in the development of a meaningful Model Cities program, and

I should stress here that the University has worked under the direction of the Woodlawn community. This is how it should be, in fact, this is the only way it can be.

Lest anyone should misunderstand, it should be clearly pointed out that within the Woodlawn community there remains a certain amount of hostility and suspicion toward the University. The long years of conflict and confrontation between The University of Chicago and the Woodlawn community have not been forgotten by many of its residents. There are many who believe that the University's ultimate goal is clearance of Woodlawn and a rebuilding designed for middle class white and black residents. It is incumbent upon the University to so function that it will dispel this lingering suspicion and hostility.

What I have discussed is to me a prerequisite for the success of our Model Cities program. And again, the people in the community must also share in the definition of "success."

What I am calling for is in reality a Model Cities program in which the organized communities play a meaningful and determining role, a program designed for the people of our communities, a program that meets the requirements of God and men made in the image of God.

25. The convergence of race and crime

MARVIN E. WOLFGANG and BERNARD COHEN

We are at that point in our analysis where we must determine the extent of overlap between two poorly conceived terms—namely, "race" and "crime."

Man, as we have seen, is so genetically blended that it is virtually impossible to determine the extent of genetic variations or, more particularly, the extent to which genetic variations operate to produce certain conduct. Many of the traits commonly considered "racial" are the product of cultural environment. Thus, as we also have noted, when we classify individuals by race simply according to color, these classifications often have relatively little genetic validity.

Abridged and edited from Marvin E. Wolfgang and Bernard Cohen, *Crime and Race: Conceptions and Misconceptions* (New York: Institute of Human Relations Press, 1970), pp. 28–39. Copyright © 1970 by The American Jewish Committee. Reprinted by permission.

The senior author is Chairman, Department of Sociology, University of Pennsylvania, Philadelphia, Pa.

Crime, too, is a word charged with uncertain meaning, ranging from murder to disturbing the peace. Thus, when we use terms like black, white, or Puerto Rican as if they were racially clear-cut, and when we also speak of crime as if that term meant the same thing to everyone who uses it, we are compounding confusion by faulty assumptions.

STATISTICAL GAPS

Studies of self-reporting of crime by persons who were never arrested have shown a more even distribution by social class than do official crime statistics. Mabel A. Elliott, in referring to a study of college students, suggests an explanation: "The major distinction between the delinquent behavior of college students and the cases brought into court seemed to lie in the relative immunity accorded the students because they belonged to a more favored group. College students represented a higher economic and social level, their family backgrounds were more stable, and their post-delinquent behavior was not followed by social ostracism which seems to incline the institutionalized offender to further delinquencies and misconduct."[1]

That proportionately fewer Negroes than whites are college students or come from stable family backgrounds is obvious to any observer. The fact that social-class differences begin to decline in studies of committed but non-recorded offenses, raises serious questions about interpreting the racial distribution of offenders arrested by the police.

Moreover, official data in *Uniform Crime Reports* do not include Federal offenses nor, more importantly for our purposes, what Edwin H. Sutherland called "white collar crime"—mainly offenses committed by businessmen in the pursuit of their occupations. Long before the famous "electrical conspiracy" of 1961, and other, more recently publicized cases of stock fraud, price fixing and bid rigging,[2] Sutherland analyzed a number of corporations and said that all our statistics on crime were incomplete and misleading because they almost completely ignored the high rate of lawbreaking among the leading business and professional groups.[3] He argued that arrests, convictions and punishments had been reserved principally for the lower economic and social classes.

Sutherland examined 70 of the 200 largest manufacturing, mining and mercantile corporations in America, and 15 power and light corporations. The findings revealed an amazing picture of lawlessness in big

---

[1]Mabel A. Elliott, *Crime in Modern Society* (New York: Harper & Brothers, 1952), p. 36.

[2]Richard A. Smith, "The incredible electrical conspiracy," *Fortune,* April 1961, pp. 132–80; May 1961, pp. 161–224.

[3]Edwin H. Sutherland, *White Collar Crime* (New York: The Dryden Press, Inc., 1949).

business, such as restraint of trade and misrepresentation in advertising, infringement of patents, trademarks and copyrights, unfair labor practice, financial fraud and violation of trust. The 70 corporations had received 980 decisions against them for illegal activities, with the number of violations ranging from one to 50. The average for all corporations was 14. Most (84 per cent) were not brought to the criminal courts, but Sutherland maintained that all of the cases tried by the civil courts or other agencies were truly criminal.

We cannot recount here the character of all these criminal violations. Suffice to say that the social harm to the community, the amount of corporate theft and loss to the consumers, the actual damage to life and health through violations of food and drug laws, the volume of financial fraud suffered by society, all amounted to many times the loss incurred by common law offenses such as burglary, robbery or larceny. Yet these white collar crimes are not recorded in the national crime index.

These facts have led some writers to suggest that the man who steals a wallet lands in jail; but if he steals a railroad, he may become not only wealthy but respected for his business acumen, and politically powerful enough to retain his immunity. That the victims of most white collar crime, as compared to common law offenses, are impersonal and diffused, and that we have a social system in which corporate crime can function, partially explain the absence of such crime from official statistics.

Neither Sutherland nor other criminologists indict our whole economic structure, nor do they ignore the concerted efforts of business to regulate itself and of government to enforce restrictions. The point is, however, that most corporate crime reflects not only the color of the collar but of the skin as well, and neither becomes part of the arrest statistics available for analysis by race.

CRIME RATE OF NEGROES

In *Uniform Crime Reports* there is no definition of race. Breakdowns are presented under the headings of white, Negro, Indian, Chinese, Japanese, all others (including unknown). Our presumption is that the designation of race is similar to that used by the Bureau of the Census. . . . Now, if a careful, detached scholar knew nothing about crime rates but was aware of the social, economic and political disparities between whites and Negroes in the United States, and if this diligent researcher had prior knowledge of the historical status of the American Negro, what would be the most plausible hypothesis our scholar could make about the crime rate of Negroes? Even this small amount of relevant knowledge would justify the expectation that Negroes would be found to have a higher crime rate than whites. And the data at hand readily confirm this hypothesis.

The *Uniform Crime Reports* statistics reveal that, generally and proportionately, black Americans are arrested between three and four times more frequently than whites. While blacks in 1967 comprised only one-tenth of the population, they constituted nearly one-third of persons arrested for all offenses (computed from UCR 1967, p. 126, using total population arrest figures). Comparing the arrest rates of blacks and whites for a variety of offenses, as reported in the 1967 *Uniform Crime Reports,* the rates for blacks are consistently higher than those for whites, ranging from twice as high, in the case of embezzlement, to 24 times as high, in the case of gambling.

These types of data are reproducible in most local, state and national arrest statistics, from the old study of the Chicago Commission on Race Relations in 1919[4] up to reports in the late sixties. An examination of many studies in cities throughout the country, over time spans and by specific offenses, by age, sex and race, shows consistently that black adult crime and juvenile delinquency rates, measured by arrests, are higher than white rates.[5]

The President's Crime Commission Report pointed out that though many more whites than blacks were arrested in 1965, there was a significantly higher rate of Negro arrests in every offense category except certain crimes against public order and morals.[6]

The Commission added that the disparity of rates for offenses of violence was much greater than comparable differences between the races for offenses against property. The black arrest rate for homicide, for instance, was 24.1 compared to 2.5 for whites, or almost 10 times as high. This was significantly greater than the difference between blacks and whites for crimes against property. For example, the black arrest rate for burglary (378) was about 3½ times as high as that for whites (107).

The most recent comprehensive analysis of crimes of violence committed by different racial groups was conducted by the National Commission on the Causes and Prevention of Violence.[7] Examining UCR arrest data and U.S. Census statistics on populations, the Violence Commission found that, for the period 1964-1967, Negro rates per 100,000

---

[4]Chicago Commission on Race Relations, *The Negro in Chicago: A Study of Race Relations and a Race Riot* (Chicago: University of Chicago Press, 1922).

[5]For a comprehensive bibliography of 402 titles on Negro criminality, see Leonard Savitz, "The Negro and Crime: A Bibliography," Department of Sociology, University of Pennsylvania, 1958, mimeographed, 25 pp.

[6]National Commission on the Causes and Prevention of Violence, *Commission Statement on Violent Crime* (Washington, D.C.: U.S. Government Printing Office, 1969), p. 44.

[7]*Task Force Report of the National Commission on the Causes and Prevention of Violence: Crimes of Violence, 1969.*

for the four major violent crimes of homicide, rape, robbery and aggravated assault, were higher than the corresponding rates for whites. The statistics for 1967, a typical year, disclosed that the Negro arrest rate for homicide was about 17 times greater than the corresponding white rate, while the rate for forcible rape was approximately 12 times the rate for whites. The black rate for robbery was 16 times higher than the corresponding rate for whites; the rate for aggravated assault, 10 times higher. Similar differences appear between black and white juvenile delinquency rates. A typical example is in homicide, committed 17 times more frequently by Negro youths aged 10-17 than by white juveniles.

The Violence Commission also reported that the Negro rate for crimes of violence had increased dramatically during the past few years, and at a greater pace than white rates. Thus, during the four-year period 1964-1967 the homicide and robbery rates for blacks increased 40 and 52 per cent, respectively, while white rates during this same period rose about 10 per cent.[8]

An ongoing study of crime and delinquency in Philadelphia has been tracing the educational and delinquent histories of approximately 10,000 males born in 1945 who resided in Philadelphia at least between ages 10 and 17.[9] Because the statistics reflect the accumulated delinquency history of this group over a period of 11 years, they make possible long-term comparison of delinquent white and Negro youth.

The study found that more than half of the Negroes, compared to only a third of the whites, had at one time or another been taken into police custody. In addition, the records of the black youths included more violence: 14 homicides, as against none for the whites, and a forcible rape rate 13 times higher than that of the white boys. Their rate for robbery was 21 times higher, and for aggravated assault 11 times higher.

These statistics show that Negroes are arrested proportionally more often than whites. The same conclusion may be drawn from judicial and prisoner statistics, which show Negroes with much higher rates of conviction and imprisonment than whites. We have had no satisfactory national judicial statistics in the United States, but according to individual studies, mostly localized, convictions of Negroes come to three to four times their proportion in the population. From reports in *National Prison Statistics,* Negroes comprise about one-third of all prisoners, although they form only one-tenth of the U.S. population.[10]

With monotonous regularity in methodologically well-designed studies

---

[8]*Ibid.*

[9]Marvin E. Wolfgang et al., *Delinquency in a Birth Cohort* (Chicago: University of Chicago Press, 1972).

[10]*National Prisoner Statistics, 1951:* "Prisoners released from state and federal institutions, 1951," (Washington, D.C.: Federal Bureau of Prisons, 1955).

of delinquency, from Shaw and McKay in Chicago to Lander in Baltimore,[11-12] and in many less capably performed analyses, the disparity between white and Negro rates of juvenile delinquency has been duly spread before scholars and citizens. It should be kept in mind, however, that none of these figures demonstrates that Negroes as a race are more prone to crime. They do demonstrate that the average black citizen is more likely than the average white citizen to be exposed to a plethora of conditions that result in his being arrested, convicted and imprisoned. Most of these conditions are inherent in the social structure and are not subject to control by an individual.

CRIME RATES OF OTHER GROUPS

Much has been said, but very little research has been done, about Mexican Americans in Southern California and Puerto Ricans, especially in New York City. Lemert and Rosberg found, in studying the figures for convictions, that the felony rates per 100,000 Mexicans (356) in Los Angeles County were somewhat higher than the white rate (248) but lower than the Negro rate (835). But when corrections were made for age and sex, the Mexican rate was proportionately lowered (843 per 100,000 males aged 18-39 years), so that it approximated the white rate (716). Indians (2,540) had a rate three times that of Negroes (when computed per 100,000 male population); Japanese consistently had the lowest rate of all ethnic groups included in the study.[13]

In a study of 8,615 juveniles referred to the Los Angeles County Probation Department for delinquent acts in 1956, Eaton and Polk reported that the rate for Mexican-American boys (2,941) was only slightly higher than for Negro boys (2,594) and over three times that for Anglo-white boys (851). In many respects, including socio-economic status, the Mexican-American juveniles were overrepresented in drug violations compared to both Negroes and whites. Nearly 50 per cent of Mexican-American offenses were petty violations.[14] Using probation and conviction rates as a measure of criminal deviation is, however, invalid procedure. These rates are, more accurately, a measure of how often members of ethnic groups become involved in the law enforcement machinery.

Reports on delinquency among Puerto Rican juveniles in New York

[11]Clifford R. Shaw and Henry D. McKay, *Juvenile Delinquency and Urban Areas* (Chicago: University of Chicago Press, 1942).

[12]Bernard Lander, *Towards an Understanding of Juvenile Delinquency* (New York: Columbia University Press, 1954).

[13]Edwin M. Lemert and Judy Rosberg, *The Administration of Justice to Minority Groups in Los Angeles County* (Berkeley: University of California Press, 1948), pp. 4–5. Data are for 1938.

[14]Joseph Eaton and Kenneth Polk, *Measuring Delinquency* (Pittsburgh: University of Pittsburgh Press, 1961) pp. 20, 28.

City do not confirm a widespread assumption of high rates. Clarence O. Senior, a leading authority on the Puerto Rican population on the mainland and in Puerto Rico, has reported that "Puerto Ricans form 8 per cent of the population and their share of the crime rate is only slightly more than 8 per cent."[15] Moreover, in a comparison between the proportion of the Manhattan juvenile population which was Puerto Rican (25 per cent) and the proportion given in the 20th Annual Report of the Children's Court of New York City (27 per cent), it appeared that the Puerto Rican juvenile was not overrepresented.[16] Puerto Rican delinquency was described as "of a milder type," such as ungovernability or truancy, while burglary and gang activities involving felonious assault and homicide were much less frequent than among non-Puerto Ricans.

Finally, a study in two Manhattan school districts in New York City found that the court appearances for Puerto Rican children was 12 per 1,000 pupils, compared with 14 per 1,000 for non-Puerto Ricans. "Like other children," the report concluded, "Puerto Rican children tend to become about as good or about as bad as the children or youth with whom they associate."[17]

BENEATH THE FINDINGS

Our task for the moment is neither to recount nor review, nor even to appraise these reports. We are interested in analyzing what may be some of the factors which underlie the uniform findings, and in determining what the statistics tell beyond the fact of the differential rates.

What can be said beyond the oft-repeated assertion that white bias by the community, the police, prosecutors, judges and juries accounts for most of the higher rate of Negroes in criminal statistics? The assertion may very well be true, but despite the many documented individual cases of such discrimination, there are only a few verified, methodologically adequate scientific studies which suggest but do not prove that this kind of bias actually causes the disparity in rates. While the unbroken sequence of untoward experiences in the life history of American Negroes, Puerto Ricans and Mexicans supports the assumption that bias affects disparity, more research on the topic, while admittedly difficult to perform, is sorely needed.

In their provocative discussion of race and crime, Korn and McCorkle refer . . . to Herskovits' estimates of the frequency distribution of mixed

---

[15]Clarence O. Senior, *Strangers—Then Neighbors* (New York: Anti-Defamation League of B'nai B'rith, 1961), p. 30. Senior cites *Time,* June 30, 1958.

[16]*Ibid.,* p. 31.

[17]*The Puerto Rican Study: 1953-1957,* New York City Board of Education, 1958, p. 120; see also: "Fact sheet on Puerto Ricans in the United States," New York: Migration Division, Department of Labor, Commission of Puerto Rico, May 31, 1961.

and pure Negroes in the United States. On the basis of these estimates and the fact that race is quantitative and relative rather than qualitative and absolute, they make a suggestion that is theoretically compelling but impossible in practice because the data are unattainable. Racially mixed persons in the United States, they remind us, include some who are almost totally white (seven-eighths white ancestry), some predominantly white, and some one-half white. These authors contend that "any valid racial study of criminality should apportion the criminality of these groups under both white and Negro categories. Thus, in figuring the totals of white and Negro offenders, unmixed whites and unmixed Negroes would count as one (1.0) for each racial category; every person seven-eighths white would add 0.875 to the white and 0.125 to the Negro categories; each person three-quarters white would add 0.75 to the white and 0.25 to the Negro categories; the equally mixed, 0.5 to each category, etc."[18]

Recalling that, according to Herskovits, about 40 per cent of persons classified as Negroes are more white than Negro or at least half white, and claiming there is no evidence that Negro criminals are more or less mixed than Negroes in the general population,[19] Korn and McCorkle suggest that almost 40 per cent of the offenders contributing to the total of "Negro" crime are either half or more than half white. "Any correction," they conclude, "of the totals of Negro offenders toward greater conformity with this genetic distribution would have the effect of redistributing a very considerable number of criminals from the Negro to the white side of the ledger. The percentage 'transferred' by this procedure would be large enough to reduce the presently 'unfavorable' picture of Negro crime drastically."[20]

Such a procedure would be genetically more valid than the present system of attributing white and Negro racial factors to criminal behavior. But we are still faced with the social definition, which classifies anyone with any known Negro ancestry or apparent Negro characteristics as black. To paraphrase W. I. Thomas, a social group defined as Negro is Negro in its consequences.

One of the consequences, as we have noted, is the greater probability of being arrested. No one really knows whether blacks, as socially defined, commit more crime than whites; but we do know that, according to official police statistics, more persons with the designated status of Negro than with the status of white are arrested. The validity of

[18]Richard R. Korn and Lloyd W. McCorkle, *Criminology and Penology* (New York: Henry Holt, 1959), p. 231.

[19]Ernest A. Hooton, *Crime and the Man* (Cambridge, Mass.: Harvard University Press, 1939) concluded that only about 19 per cent of Negro prisoners examined were classified as unmixed Negroes.

[20]Korn and McCorkle, *Criminology and Penology, op. cit.*, p. 232.

the data is open to question on grounds we have mentioned; but if arrest statistics are poor indicators of the amount or kinds of crime generally, they are probably even more unreliable for determining the amount of Negro crime.

One of the reasons is that arrest statistics understate crime rates of both whites and blacks, but most probably more for whites. To understand why, recall that in 1967, 92 per cent of the crime index offenses in *Uniform Crime Reports* were property offenses, and only 8 per cent were offenses against the person. These distributions are consistent over time. Yet, as we have seen, only 22 per cent of the property offenses were cleared by arrest, so more than three-fourths of these crimes never resulted in identification of the offender's race. Offenses against the person, however, have relatively high clearance rates of around 75 per cent. Hence, because the Negro arrest rate is much higher for crimes against the person, the likelihood that the offender's race will be known is higher among those very offenses which Negroes are more likely to commit.[21]

In the case of criminal homicide, about nine out of every 10 offenses are cleared by arrest and we can feel reasonably secure about our knowledge of the race distribution. In cases of burglary, larceny and auto theft, less than three out of 10 yield information about the offender's race, our sample is more highly select and smaller, and it is very doubtful that we can assume the same race distribution. It is among the much larger number of uncleared property offenses that a hypothesis suggesting a higher proportion and rate of white than Negro offenders would be most plausible.

26. Can a black man get a fair trial in this country?

HAYWOOD BURNS

I am appalled and ashamed that things should have come to such a pass that I am skeptical of the ability of black revolutionaries to achieve a fair trial anywhere in the United States.

[21]See also Korn and McCorkle, *Criminology and Penology op. cit.*, pp. 235-236, on this point.

Reprinted from Haywood Burns, "Can a black man get a fair trial in this country?" *The New York Times Magazine,* July 12, 1970. Copyright © 1970 by The New York Times Company. Reprinted by permission.

The author is National Director, National Conference of Black Lawyers, New York, N.Y.

In large part the atmosphere has been created by police actions and prosecutions against the Panthers in many parts of the country. It is also one more inheritance from centuries of racial discrimination and oppression.

When Yale president Kingman Brewster recently expressed these doubts about the possibility of a black revolutionary receiving a fair trial in the United State, today, there was an immediate outcry. The judge in the New Haven Black Panther trial took Brewster to task for his statement, and the Vice President of the United States had some rather unkind comments for the Yale president. There are, however, more and more persons who not only share Brewster's doubts as they apply to revolutionaries but also wonder whether *any* black man in American can receive a fair trial.

Given the special relationship blacks have had to the law since they were brought to this country, such doubts are more than reasonable. Whereas white Americans are accustomed to viewing the law as an historic vehicle through which liberties have been progressively expanded, black Americans have experienced law in quite another fashion. From the very first, American law has been the handmaiden of American racism. It has been the means by which the generalized racism in the society has been made specific and converted into the particularized policies and standards of social control.

So many of the milestones in the early history of liberty in this country are emblazoned with the exception: "But not for blacks." Thus, black people cannot view the Declaration of Independence, the Constitution or Jacksonian democracy in the same lofty manner as many who see them as triumphs of liberty; for the early Americans who sought freedom so assiduously for themselves, at the same time so cruelly denied it to others in their midst.

For so much of the past, the law rather than being a tool for expanding liberty, has been an implement for constricting, downgrading and narrowing the possibilities for blacks. It was the law which institutionalized American chattel slavery (by making black bondage life-long and later hereditary). It was the law which provided the onerous slave codes to govern in oppressive detail the lives of millions of blacks until their emancipation, and which returned to perform the same function through the notorious Black Codes after emancipation. It was with the law that the architects of segregation built a Jim Crow society which is still intact a decade and a half after *Brown* v. *Board of Education* and more than a century after the Emancipation Proclamation.

For long stretches of American history in many parts of the country, black people lacked any legal personality whatsoever. By law they were excluded from bringing lawsuits to protect their rights. There was no legal recourse for injury to themselves or their property. They were not even allowed to take the witness stand to testify in cases where the interests of white persons were involved. Nor were they permitted to serve on juries. In the criminal area—it is the criminal case that I shall concentrate on in this article—the penalties the law prescribed for blacks were often different from those prescribed for whites for the same offense.

Perhaps the most striking example of the latter disparity is the way in which certain jurisdictions reserved the penalty of sexual mutilation for blacks and Indians accused of interracial sex crimes. A reading of the statutes provides insights into the psychosocial pathology of white America—of its fear of letting black men be men; of its need to deprive them of their manhood; of its artfulness in employing the law in this base service. As recently as the mid-nineteenth century, white men sat in the Kansas Legislature and introduced, debated and passed legislation which provided that the penalty for any black convicted of attempting to compel a white woman to marry should be castration "by some skillful person," the cost of such a procedure to be charged to the convicted person. The penalty for corresponding acts by white persons was "confinement and hard labor not less than five years."

The Agnews and the present-day guardians of the American judicial system often have little patience with such discussions of the past. References to past legal unpleasantness, at best, are seen as irrelevant diversions from the present point, and at worst, as inflammatory devices which hinder a cool, contemporary and pragmatic approach to the closing of what are seen as minor gaps in the legal system. The fact that the explicit racial distinctions have for the most part been removed from the statute books, and that, in a formal sense, race has ceased to be an articulated ground for judicial decision, is for many sufficient proof that our avowedly neutral system of justice is both neutral and just.

This impatience with history would be justified if America had, in fact, somehow accomplished the impossible task of severing the past and completely exorcising the demons of old. However, in truth, the past of the American legal system is inextricably bound up with its present. Many of the same forces which kept blacks out of the courts or imposed harsher penalties on them in the past are at work today, militating against any black man receiving full justice in an American court.

The barriers to fairness are basically of two kinds: (1) personal—those related to the racial views and attitudes of persons responsible for the day-to-day administration of justice; and (2) structural—those related to the nature of our legal system itself, its procedural rules and substantive doctrines. Sometimes the barriers are a hybrid combination of both.

The manifestations of racism in the legal system today may be more subtle than many of those of the past, but they are not necessarily less pernicious. As their cases make their way through the courts, black lawyers and litigants must still often sustain personal indignities from biased judges and other court personnel. Despite United States Supreme Court disapproval of the practice, it is still not uncommon to find judges and prosecutors who fail to use the courtesy titles "Mr.," "Mrs." or "Miss" when addressing black defendants, and in some cases when addressing black lawyers. Similarly, normally expected courtesies often fall away when court attendants, clerks, bailiffs and marshals find themselves dealing with blacks.

Recently, I appeared with two other black lawyers before a Federal judge in the South, challenging employment discrimination against our black clients. Early in the legal proceedings, much to his consternation, we had taken exception to the judge referring to our clients as "nigras." At the very beginning of the trial itself, the judge told us in no uncertain terms that "nigra" was listed in his dictionary as a regional pronunciation for "Negro" (he did not point out that it is a *white* "regional pronunciation"), and that for the balance of the proceedings he and anyone else in the courtroom could use the term. By instant judicial decree we then had become nigra lawyers pressing the claims of nigra clients in a white man's court. A corollary of the judge's pronouncement was that we were not to use the term "black" in referring to our clients and the racial community from which they came, since it was not the term traditionally used in "our jurisprudence."

This is by no means to suggest that what we are contending with is exclusively a Southern phenomenon. Daily, in courts throughout the country, black and poor defendants suffer the humiliations of a legal system which refuses to accord them full recognition of their dignity as human beings. In February of this year, Judge John M. Murtagh, presiding at the New York Panther conspiracy trial, ordered the pretrial hearings recessed and the defendants remanded to jail until all of them gave him a promise that they would deport themselves at the hearings in a manner in keeping with his standards of "good conduct."

A group of lawyers from the National Conference of Black Lawyers challenged the constitutionality of Judge Murtagh's action by petitioning for a writ of *habeas corpus* in the Supreme Court of Queens County, the area where the defendants were being held. When the defendants refused to comply with Judge Murtagh's demand, it appeared that they would be jailed indefinitely, awaiting trial. The *habeas corpus* action of the black lawyers on their behalf was something of a psychological victory for the Panther defendants because it enabled them to get back into court—in another jurisdiction—to carry on their struggle without having had to comply with the demands of the New York County trial judge.

However, when the 11 defendants were led into the courtroom for the argument on the petition they found that no chairs had been provided for them next to the counsel table. They were told to sit on the floor. They did so slowly, reluctantly; only the tensing of their bodies and their facial expressions betrayed their controlled fury. All this was demeaning for the proud young black men, but no less so for the "the dignity of the court." Eleven might be considerably more than the average number of defendants in a criminal case, but not so many more that the largesse of New York State was incapable of providing seats for them.

Outside courtrooms the clerk's office is an area where personal attitudes can impair fairness. Lower-level clerks are often extremely powerful persons in the bureaucratic machinery of justice and they can use this power in an obstructionist and hostile manner when they do not like the people or the issue involved. This is seldom blatant, but can be seen in differences in flexibility and cooperativeness, and in the way normally straightforward matters can suddenly become complicated—as, for example, with the simple act of incorporating an organization or group when that group happens to have the word "black" in its title.

Biased judges use procedural devices and their judicial discretion to avoid ruling in favor of blacks when the legal mandate in their favor is clear. This is true in a wide variety of areas, but perhaps most obviously with many Southern judges in civil-rights cases. In general, judicial or administrative discretion can be used to cloak racism in sentencing, parole and probation.

Unexpressed racial bias creeps in to pollute the process—North and South—without fear of being exposed or proved. While it may not always be possible to show the bias in an individual case, an examination of statistical patterns demonstrates the disparity in treatment received by black and white persons convicted of crime. It is impossible to determine to what extent disparities are related to individual bias and to what extent they flow from a built-in systemic inequity, but there can be no argument with the fact of the disparity.

Blacks usually receive longer prison sentences than whites for most criminal offenses. A study of persons convicted of burglary and auto theft in Los Angeles County, most of them first offenders and unskilled laborers, revealed that on the average whites were treated much less severely than blacks. Forty-five per cent of the whites and 27 per cent of the blacks were given sentences for these crimes of four months' imprisonment or less, or probation; 42 per cent of the whites and 47 per cent of the blacks received four to nine months; and 13 per cent of the whites and 27 per cent of the blacks got 10 to 20 months.

A 1951 study showed that the average number of months served before release in all the states was 25 for blacks and 20 for whites. The disparity was greatest in the West and the Northeast. Proportionately about 10 to 14 per cent more whites than blacks are annually "released conditionally" or granted some kind of parole. This racial disparity in the granting of parole helps to keep the percentage of blacks in the prison population high. According to reports in National Prison Statistics, blacks comprise about one-third of all prisoners, though they make up only about 11 per cent of the general population.

Some of the most glaring disparities occur in sentences imposed for capital crimes. According to the Bureau of Prisons, 3,857 persons were executed in the United States between 1930 and 1966; 53.5 per cent of these were black, 45.4 per cent were white and 1.1 per cent were members of other minority groups. Not only is it less likely that a white person will be sentenced to the electric chair, gas chamber, gallows or firing squad, but the workings of executive and administrative discretion are such that, once condemned to die, a white person is more likely to have his sentence commuted to life imprisonment by a governmental executive, board of pardons or similar agency. Marvin E. Wolfgang, the noted criminologist, reports that among those condemned to die, between 10 and 20 per cent more blacks than whites are actually executed.

White America still reserves special penalties for blacks convicted of sex crimes—especially interracial sex crimes. National Prison Statistics shows that of the 19 jurisdictions that have executed men for rape since 1930, almost one-third of them—six states—have executed *only* blacks. There have been some years in which everyone who was executed for rape in this country was black. Detailed state-by-state analysis has shown that the discrepancy in death sentences for rape is related to the race of the victim.

Blacks raping blacks is apparently less serious than whites raping whites, and certainly less serious than whites raping blacks. But the black man today convicted of raping a white woman can be as certain of receiving the harshest treatment as was a Kansas black convicted of an interracial sex crime in 1855. For example, in Florida between 1960 and 1964, of the 125 white males who raped white females, six—or about 5 per cent—received death sentences (four of these involved attacks on children). Of the 68 black males in the same period who were convicted in Florida of raping black females, three—or about 4 per cent —received death sentences; and this when in two cases the victims were children. However, of the 84 blacks (same period, same state) convicted of raping white women, 45—or 54 per cent—received the death sentence; only one of these cases involved an attack on a juvenile. *None* of the eight white men who raped black women was sentenced to death.

Although there have not been sufficient detailed statistical analyses, available evidence indicates that black youths are more likely to be condemned to death and executed than the children of white parents. One study has shown that between 1950 and 1953, nine teen-agers were executed in the United States—seven black, two white. In 1954, 10 teen-agers were executed—seven in Georgia, two in New York, and one in Florida. All were black.

Just as with their elders, black youths can expect a difference in what the system of justice metes out to them and to others. The President's Commission on Law Enforcement and the Administration of Justice found that almost *all* youths committed acts for which they could be arrested and taken to court. However, the commission also found that the likelihood of a youth being arrested and taken to court varied according to where he lived. Juveniles from the nation's ghettos were much more likely to be arrested as delinquents than youths from white suburbia.

Of course, a good deal of the difference may be attributed to the cold sociological fact that certain kinds of conditions of economic deprivation breed more so-called "antisocial" acts. But it must also be attributed to the differences in the way the police and the courts perform. If a suburban youth is arrested, it is more likely that some disposition will be worked out which will not involve incarceration. A ghetto youth will seldom find a policeman cautious about making an arrest merely because the youth is the son of a community leader, any more than in court will his parents be able to provide private counsel, private psychiatrists or to make an impression with personal prestige of their own as their child's fate is weighed in the balance.

Black people distrust the judicial system not only because of what happens to them when they are caught up in its machinery, but because of the failings of the legal system they witness when blacks are the victims. Black people wonder why no arrest was made last winter in Indiana when guards at the Pendleton Reformatory systematically shot unarmed black prisoners engaging in a sit-down demonstration. Black people wonder why there were no arrests in Brooklyn recently when a group of off-duty policemen fell upon and savagely beat Black Panther party members in the halls of the courthouse. Black people wonder why in Chicago—particularly after the Federal grand jury report—no one was arrested for the murderous late-night submachine-gun assault upon nine young Black Panthers. Black people wonder why in Mississippi there was never a murder prosecution of the men charged with snuffing out the lives of James Chaney, Andrew Goodman and Michael Schwerner (the Federal prosecution for violating the civil rights of the three was hardly a sufficient response for so heinous a crime).

Black people wonder why in November, 1969, white radicals charged with bombing several New York buildings could have their bail reduced by 80 per cent to a reasonable amount in two days, while Black Panthers have languished in jail under unreasonable bail for 15 months for allegedly *plotting* to blow up the Botanical Garden.

Black people wonder why white men's juries in Michigan or Mississippi cannot find it in the evidence—or perhaps, even with the evidence, in their hearts—to convict white men for killing unknown blacks in the Algiers Motel in Detroit, or Medgar Evers in front of his home in Jackson. Black people wonder.

Blacks are no longer barred, because they are black, from bringing lawsuits or giving testimony in American courts. They have the legal capacity to give testimony no matter whose rights are involved. However, the weight that testimony is accorded is another matter. British barrister Anthony Lester conducted a study of state courts in the Deep South in 1964 and reported in his "Justice in the American South" that "whenever there was a conflict of evidence between Negro and white, the judge appeared automatically to believe the white man. On no occasion was a policeman's evidence challenged."

Though this situation may have changed somewhat since Lester made his study, it is the general experience of lawyers who represent blacks—North, South, East and West—that judges and juries seldom accord the testimony of nonwhites the same weight as that of whites. When the issue is one of credibility, one white witness on one side of a lawsuit often cancels out several nonwhite witnesses on the other.

I recently represented some young black defendants who had been stopped by the police in the Bronx, allegedly for an infraction of the traffic laws. Prompted by a racial remark from one of the officers, a verbal duel between the young men and the officers ensued, in which the officers were outfenced. The result was that the young men were jailed on a long string of charges, including resisting arrest and inciting to riot. The defendants, though disturbed by the treatment they received, were not overly concerned about their trial since there had been so many people at the site of the incident who had seen the most that had occurred was an argument between the police and the defendants.

By way of defense, I put on a large group of these witnesses—all black or Puerto Rican—most of whom did not know the defendants and who had no personal interest in testifying. Despite the disinterestedness of our witnesses and their number, the court chose to believe the policemen, on all but the most serious of the charges, and convicted the defendants. The impact of this lesson in credibility was strong, both on the defendants and on some of the spectators.

One of the defendants indicated to me that some of his worst notions about the workings of American justice had been confirmed and that the lesson he took away from the experience was in the future to resist unwarranted police action directed at himself, since he would probably be charged with doing so anyway. One boy of 11 or 12 who had seen the arrest and been at the trial blurted out to me at its conclusion, "Wow, if that's what happens to you in courts, I ain't gonna stop if a cop ever tells me to stop. I'm gonna run. Those guys didn't do nuthin'!"

It has long been the law that systematic exclusion of blacks from grand and petit juries is unconstitutional. In 1880 in *Strauder* v. *West Virginia,* the Supreme Court overturned a state statute which explicitly limited jury service to whites. Nonetheless, jury selection procedures are still such that it is difficult for blacks to obtain juries on which members of their race are fairly represented. Jury-qualification rules, the discretion left to jury commissioners and the lists selected as the source of prospective jurors have resulted in gross underrepresentation of the young, the black and the poor. Legal scholar Michael O. Finkelstein has recently documented the fact of racial exclusion in several Northern communities. His analysis of venire records of persons selected for grand juries in Manhattan, the Bronx and Westchester revealed that Harlem districts with heavy black populations contributed *less* than 1 per cent of the Manhattan veniremen, although they comprised 11 per cent of the voting population.

If there had been a random selection of jurors, it would have been virtually impossible for discrepancies this large to occur. According to Wolfgang and Cohen in their study "Crime and Race," the mathematical probability that the Manhattan grand jury venires in 1967 would have had the racial composition they did have through chance was smaller than the probability of being dealt 24 consecutive royal flushes in an honest game of five-card draw poker. Finkelstein also showed that in Westchester towns with large black populations—Mount Vernon, New Rochelle and Yonkers—blacks were represented almost not at all on the jury rolls.

It is not enough, however, to get blacks on the rolls as prospective jurors, for there still remain means of assuring that they do not serve. Throughout the country in cases involving black defendants, prosecutors use their allotted peremptory strikes to make sure that, so far as possible, the outcome will be determined by a white jury. Thus, legions of black men must still have their fates decided by juries from which members of their own race have been systematically excluded. A prosecutor is not required to give any reason when he uses his peremptory strikes to remove prospective jurors from the jury panel. The Supreme Court, while continuing to hold explicit exclusion invalid, in *Swain* v. *Alabama* (1965) has sustained this use of the peremptory strike.

Some of the greatest barriers to blacks receiving fair treatment in the courts today rise not so much from direct racial antipathies as from the structure of the law itself. It is here that the link from the past to the present is most clearly revealed. Historically, the men who made the laws were for the most part explicitly hostile to the interests of the poor and the nonwhite, or at least ignored them. This historic hostility and neglect have brought about a structural inequality through which the law, by its substantive doctrines and procedural rules, works invidious discriminations against the poor and the nonwhite.

Intent is not necessary. Institutionalized bias need never make reference to race or class to remain in its operation and impact highly discriminatory. The structural inequality represents a confluence of caste and class bias in the law in which poor whites are deeply affected, too.

On its face, the structural inequality relates largely to differences in the economic status of individuals, but it has a peculiarly racial dimension since such a widely disproportionate number of the poor in this country is nonwhite. Even without bad motives on the part of those who administer the system of justice, the continued application of the legal system in this way is racist because of the way in which it perpetuates past racial wrongs. It battens upon blacks' depressed condition, for which racial injustices were largely responsible in the first place.

A prime example of the structural inequality in the law, and one which results in massive systemic unfairness to the typical nonwhite brought before the courts, is the operation of the money-bail system. Two accused persons can be in otherwise comparable situations—length of time in the community, length of time steadily employed, number of dependents and family obligations—except that one has money and the other does not. Upon arraignment on a criminal charge, one will walk free until the time of trial, the other will be locked up—though both are equally presumed innocent.

The city jails across the country are filled to overcrowding with the poor and nonwhite who must serve weeks, months, and sometimes more than a year in jail before coming to trial. In many cases the amount of bail is nominal—but even $25 is a considerable sum if you have not got it.

Statistically, the jailed defendant has much less chance of being acquitted than the bailed defendant. The defendant who comes to trial from the streets will have had greater access to his lawyer in preparing his defense, and having been at liberty will be able to arrive in court with a demeanor that will not cause those trying him to associate him readily with criminality. Jail in lieu of fines for indigents, creditor-biased consumer law, landlord-biased tenant law, lack of due process before administrative agencies which deal with the poor are but a few further examples of the law's structural inequality.

Many of the revolutionaries of whom Kingman Brewster spoke have identified some or all of these impediments to fairness endemic to the present legal system. They have no expectation of an acquittal when charged with crimes in connection with their political activity, for they know that they face not only the institutional bias against black defendants, but the political animus as well that is reserved for those that are perceived as a serious threat to things as they are.

As far as the legal system is concerned, the question becomes, as it did with Debs and with Sacco and Vanzetti and other unpopular defendants, not so much whether the defendants are guilty or innocent, in the sense of having committed or not committed certain acts, but whether in the present political climate such a determination can be made fairly.

Brewster and persons both in and outside the legal community admit to skepticism on this point. Many black revolutionaries have answered the question firmly in the negative. Having made this assessment of the legal system and their chances within it, many revolutionary defendants have ceased to look upon the courtroom as an arena in which a contest for and against their exoneration is waged, but rather as a platform to expose the failings of the legal system, to educate and politicize a larger public—to indict the system. What has so often been characterized as disruption is often less a calculated attempt to impede the progress of their trial than it is a refusal to sit silent when being subjected to personal affronts.

If such defendants believe someone is lying about them, they say so. If they believe their constitutional rights are being abridged, they say so. If they believe the judge is behaving in a racist fashion, they say so—and in their own terms. This refusal to accept the rules of the judicial game stems from a judgment on their part that the game is fixed.

In their minds there is no reason to sit passively by or to participate cooperatively in a process that is designed for their own destruction. As revolutionaries they believe it is their obligation to behave as revolutionaries wherever they find themselves—in the streets, in the courtroom, in jail. If this conduct is calculated at all, it is calculated to make manifest the latent bias which these defendants believe is rife in the legal system, to bring to the surface the vicious antipathies that would otherwise be masked by the niceties of legal rules.

This approach sometimes results in something of a self-fulfilling prophecy. It has, in fact, often provoked extreme judicial responses which were subversive of the rights of the defendants and in violation of the accepted legal standards of a fair trial.

What is the role of the black lawyer in this whole process? If there is structural inequality in the machinery of justice in this country, is not the lawyer guilty of complicity when he participates in this process? Is he not, in fact, an agent of the system?

The answer has to be that of course he is, but as one activist black lawyer recently said, "The lawyer must be a double agent." He participates in the process, but he can do so in such a way as to maximize the protection and the gains that are possible for oppressed persons under the existing order. He can use the rules of the very system that many of the oppressed are challenging to insulate them so that they can continue to go about the business of challenge.

The legal system has so far proved unable to eradicate racism from American society, in large part because it is itself so severely tainted with racism. But the law is much too valuable a weapon in the struggle for major social change to be discarded for this reason. Not only can it serve as an insulator of the activist, but experience has shown that through test-case litigation it is possible to correct at least some of its structural inequality.

It is unrealistic, however, to speak of major structural change and fairness to blacks in the legal system without examining the social context in which law operates. In many ways, the law merely reflects the larger society. It is unreasonable to think that in a racist society the law, or any institution, can completely transcend that racism. Changing the law involves changing America. In a nation of inverted priorities, misallocated resources and inhumane, materialistic values, it is too much to expect that the law will provide the fairness and justice to the poor and the nonwhite that is being denied them in every other sector of society.

There will not be institutional fairness for blacks in the courts until there is fairness for blacks in America. This relates not only to the structure of the law in terms of its procedural and substantive rules, but to the personal level as well. It is folly to say that ours is a government of laws, not men. Laws are made, interpreted and applied by men—and in America's case by men in a racist society. Ultimately, there is the simple and obvious truth that the judicial system is run by people, mostly by white people and that most white people are racially biased.

The likelihood of the legal process being entirely uncontaminated by bias in any given case is small. Individual blacks can and do win civil suits and individual blacks can and are acquitted of criminal charges, but in an institutional sense in almost all instances the law functions in a discriminatory and unfair manner when blacks (and poor people) are involved.

Can a black man get a fair trial in the United States? If by fair one means free of bias, the answer has to be generally NO.

27. Overcoming the built-in racism and male chauvinism of doctors and hospitals

BARBARA and JOHN EHRENREICH

In the ways that it irritates, exhausts, and occasionally injures patients, the American medical system is not egalitarian. Everything that is bad about American medicine is especially so for Americans who are not male or white. Blacks, and in some areas Indians, Puerto Ricans, or Mexicans, face unique problems of access to medical care, and not just because they are poor. Many hospitals in the south are still unofficially segregated, or at least highly selective. For instance, in towns outside of Orangeburg, South Carolina, blacks claim they are admitted to the hospital only on the recommendation of a (white) employer or other white "reference."

In the big cities of the North, health facilities are available on a more equal footing to blacks, browns, and poor whites. But for the nonwhite patient, the medical experience is more likely to be something he will not look forward to repeating. The first thing he notices about the large hospital—he is more likely to be at a hospital clinic than at a private doctor's office—is that the doctors are almost uniformly white; the nonskilled workers are almost entirely brown or black. Thus the nonwhite patient enters the hospital at the bottom end of its social scale, quite aside from any personal racial prejudices the staff may harbor. And, in medicine, these prejudices take a particularly insulting form. Black and Puerto Rican patients complain again and again of literally being "treated like animals" by everyone from the clerks to the M.D.'s. Since blacks are assumed to be less sensitive than white patients, they get less privacy. Since blacks are assumed to be more ignorant than whites, they get less by way of explanation of what is happening to them. And since they are assumed to be irresponsible and forgetful, they are more likely to be given a drastic, one-shot treatment, instead of a prolonged regimen of drugs, or a restricted diet.

Only a part of this medical racism is due to the racist attitudes of individual medical personnel. The rest is "institutional racism," a built-in feature of the way medicine is learned and practiced in the United States. As interns and residents, young doctors get their training by practicing on the hospital ward and clinic patients—generally nonwhite. Later they make their money by practicing for a paying clientele —generally white. White patients are "customers"; black patients are "teaching material." White patients pay for care with their money; black patients pay with their dignity and their comfort. Clinic patients at the hospital affiliated with Columbia University's medical school recently learned this distinction in a particularly painful way. They had complained that anesthesia was never available in the dental clinic. Finally, a leak from one of the dental interns showed that this was an official policy: the patient's pain is a good guide to the dentist-in-training—it teaches him not to drill too deep. Anesthesia would deaden the pain and dull the intern's learning experience.

Hospitals' institutional racism clearly serves the needs of the medical system, but it is also an instrument of the racist, repressive impulses of the society at large. Black community organizations in New York have charged hospitals with "genocidal" policies towards the black community. Harlem residents tell of medical atrocities—cases where patients have unwittingly given their lives or their organs in the cause of medical research. A more common charge is that, to public hospital doctors, "the birth control method of choice for black women is the hysterectomy." Even some doctors admit that hysterectomies are often performed with pretty slim justification in ghetto hospitals. (After all, they can't be expected to take a pill every day, can they? And one less black baby is one less baby on welfare, isn't it?) If deaths from sloppy abortions run highest in the ghetto, it is partly because black women are afraid to go to the hospital for an abortion or for treatment following a sloppy abortion, fearing that an involuntary sterilization—all for "medical" reasons —will be the likely result. Aside from their medical policies, ghetto hospitals have a reputation as racist because they serve as police strongholds in the community. In the emergency room, cops often outnumber doctors. They interrogate the wounded—often before the doctor does, and pick up any vagrants, police brutality victims, drunks or addicts who have mistakenly come in for help. In fact, during the 1964 riots in New York, the police used Harlem Hospital as a launching pad for their pacification measures.

Women are the other major group of Americans singled out for special treatment by the medical system. Just as blacks face a medical hierarchy dominated by whites, women entering a hospital or doctor's office encounter a hierarchy headed by men, with women as nurses and aides playing subservient, hand-maid roles. And in the medical system, women face all the male supremacist attitudes and superstitions that characterize American society in general—they are the victims of sexism, as blacks are of racism. Women are assumed to be incapable of understanding complex technological explanations, so they are not given any. Women are assumed to be emotional and "difficult," so they are often classified as neurotic well before physical illness has been ruled out. (Note how many tranquilizer ads in medical journals depict women, rather than men, as likely customers.) And women are assumed to be vain, so they are the special prey of the paramedical dieting, cosmetics, and plastic surgery businesses.

Everyone who enters the medical system in search of care quickly finds himself transformed into an object, a mass of organs and pathology. Women have a special handicap—they start out as "objects." Physicians, despite their supposed objectivity and clinical impersonality, share all the sexual hangups of other American men. The sick person who enters the gynecology clinic is the same sex as the sexual "object" who sells cars in the magazine ads. What makes matters worse is that a high proportion of routine medical care for women centers on the most superstitious and fantasy-ridden aspect of female physiology—the reproductive system. Women of all classes almost uniformly hate or fear their gynecologists. The gynecologist plays a controlling role in that aspect of their lives society values most, the sexual aspect—and he knows it. Middle-class women find a man who is either patronizingly jolly, or cold and condescending. Poorer women, using clinics, are more likely to encounter outright brutality and sadism. Of course, black women have it worst of all. A shy teenager from a New York ghetto reports going to the clinic for her first prenatal check-up, and being used as teaching material for an entire class of young, male medical students learning to give pelvic examinations.

Doctors and hospitals treat pregnancy and childbirth, which are probably among the healthier things that women experience, as diseases—to be supervised by doctors and confined to hospitals. Women in other economically advanced countries, such as Holland, receive their prenatal care at home, from nurses, and, if all goes well, are delivered at home by trained midwives. (The Netherlands ranks third lowest in infant mortality rate; the U.S. ranks fourteenth!) But for American women, pregnancy and childbirth are just another harrowing, expensive medical procedure. The doctor does it; the woman is essentially passive. Even in large cities, women often have to go from one obstetrician to another before they find one who approves of natural childbirth. Otherwise, childbirth is handled as if it were a surgical operation, even to the point of "scheduling" the event to suit the obstetrician's convenience through the use of possibly dangerous labor-inducing drugs.

Most people who have set out to look for medical care eventually have to conclude that there *is* no American medical system—at least there is no systematic way in America of getting medical help when you need it, without being financially ruined, humiliated, or injured in the process. What system there is—the three hundred thousand doctors, seven thousand hospitals and supporting insurance plans—was clearly not designed to deal with the sick. In fact the one thing you need most in order to qualify for care financially and to survive the process of obtaining it is *health,* plus, of course, a good deal of cunning and resourcefulness. The trouble is that it's almost impossible to stay healthy and strong enough to be able to tackle the medical system. Preventive health care (regular check-ups, chest X-rays, pap tests, etc.) is not a specialty or even an interest of the American medical system.

The price of this double bind—having to be healthy just to stay healthy—is not just consumer frustration and discomfort. The price is lives. The United States ranks fourteenth among the nations of the world in infant mortality, which means that approximately 33,000 American babies under one year old die unnecessarily every year. (Our infant mortality statistics are not, as often asserted, so high because they are "spoiled" by the death rates for blacks. The statistics for white America alone compare unfavorably to those for countries such as Sweden, the Netherlands, Norway, etc.) Mothers also stand a better chance of dying in the United States, where the maternal mortality rate ranks twelfth among the world's nations. The average American man lives five years less than the Swedish man, and his life expectancy is shorter than for males in seventeen other nations. Many American men never live out their already relatively short lifetime, since the chance of dying between ages forty and fifty is twice as high for an American as it is for a Scandinavian. What is perhaps most alarming about these statistics is that they are, in a relative sense, getting worse. The statistics improve a little each year, but at a rate far slower than that for other advanced countries. Gradually, the United States is slipping behind most of the European nations, and even some non-European nations, in its ability to keep its citizens alive.

28. "But they're just different"

ANTHONY GARY DWORKIN

The educational level of the Mexican-American in the ghetto is lower than in the more disadvantaged Negro ghetto of Watts, because the Mexican value system is so much more at odds with the school system than is that of the Negro. In this section we shall discuss the cultural factors which make the Mexican seem so strange to the Anglo teachers.

There is a sharp split between the Anglo's and Mexican's culture. The Anglo is secular, practical, objective, competitive, materialistic, and future-oriented. Traditionally the Mexican was not.[2] The new Mexican-

---

From *Our Children's Burden*, edited by Raymond W. Mack. Copyright © 1968 by Raymond W. Mack. Reprinted by permission of Random House, Inc.

[1] A frequently heard statement among Anglo teachers in the Mexican-American ghetto in Los Angeles. One teacher elaborated on the statement by pointing out that "the reason Mexican kids get into so much trouble is that they are born Mexican."

[2] Of the sociological models available to explain the differences between the Mexican and Anglo societies, the most frequently used among researchers in Mexican-Anglo relations is that of the Folk-Urban asymptotic dichotomy. Born in the nineteenth-century tradition of Tönnies, Maine, and Durkheim, the distinction was tested empirically by Redfield, with data from villages in Mexico. Redfield characterized the ideal-typical folk society as follows: "Such a society is small, isolated,

Americans are changing, but a viable culture, reinforced by generations of ghetto life and discrimination, and centuries of life in Mexico does not die easily. A conglomeration of Spanish, Indian, and Roman Catholic in origin, the Mexican-American culture has served as a defense against the exploitation by the Anglo. One Mexican-American teacher, who feared that busing Mexican children from the ghetto to Anglo schools out of the ghetto would cause the children to lose their grasp of the Mexican culture, proclaimed:

[The Mexican American] has a culture upon which he can fall back. . . . The actual fact is that the Mexican-American individual, the Spanish-speaking individual, would much rather stay within his own realms of his own neighborhood because he speaks Spanish, he is at home there, why should he want otherwise?[3]

Since there is time to touch upon only a few aspects of Mexican culture, our concern shall be with those aspects which are of maximal importance to the Mexican-American in Los Angeles with respect to his educational opportunities. As such, our discussion shall touch upon the mystical belief in *La Raza* (the race), the Mexican world view; the dominance of *machismo,* or the male-oriented society; the importance of one's parents and extended family; and the cohesion-producing effect of speaking only Spanish in a society whose language is English.

In his discussion of the *Mexican-Americans of South Texas,*[4] William Madsen stated that:

The Mexican-American thinks of himself as both a citizen of the United States and a member of *La Raza* (the Race). This term refers to all Latin-Americans who are united by cultural and spiritual bonds derived from God. The spiritual aspect is perhaps more important than the cultural. . . . The spirit of the Spanish-speaking people, however, is taken to be divine and infinite. As one Latin expressed it, "We are bound together by the common destiny of our souls."

---

nonliterate, and homogeneous, with a strong sense of group solidarity. The ways of living are conventionalized into that coherent system which we call 'a culture.' Behavior is traditional, spontaneous, uncritical, and personal; there is no legislation or habit of experiment and reflection for intellectual ends. Kinship, its relationships and institutions, are the type categories of experience, and the familial group is the unit of action. The sacred prevails over the secular; the economy is one of status rather than of market." (Robert Redfield, "The folk society," *American Journal of Sociology,* 1947, 52: 294.)

[3]From the transcript of "Human relations—Yesterday, today, and tomorrow," Part 1-B (Education), aired on KNBC/television, Channel 4, Los Angeles, Sunday, October 4, 1964, 11:15–11:55 P.M.

[4]William Madsen, *Mexican-Americans of South Texas* (New York: Holt, Rinehart and Winston, 1964).

In Mexico, the concept of *La Raza* carries the idea of a splendid and glorious destiny. Mexicans see their greatest national strength in the spiritual vigor of *La Raza*. In Texas, the history of discrimination and economic subordination has modified the concept of the ultimate destiny of *La Raza*. Many Spanish-speaking Texans would say that God had originally planned a glorious future for the Mexican-American, but it probably will never be attained. The failure of *La Raza,* he would continue, is due to the sins of individual Latins. Some believe that *La Raza* is held back by the sins of all Mexican-Americans. . . . Other Latins think that only the worst sinners are holding back *La Raza*. . . . I once asked a Latin if he thought the Anglos were in any way responsible for holding back the Mexican-Americans from their God-given destiny. "Of course not," he replied. "If we lived by God's commands we would be so strong that no one could block us. Of course, the Anglos take advantage of our weakness but it is we who make ourselves weak, not the Anglos."

Not all Mexican-Americans believe that *La Raza* has failed. The militant members of the Mexican-American middle class, most of whom have escaped from the Los Angeles ghetto to Anglo neighborhoods, often speak with pride of their Mexican heritage. One Mexican-American businessman who is a member of that category maintained:

If you show the prejudiced Anglos what an advanced culture the Mayans and Aztecs had and prove to them that the Mexican has a great cultural heritage, they will wish that they were Mexicans and respect us. In fact many will want to leave the North and move to Mexico to live.

He is so confident that the Anglo would prefer to live in Mexico once he learned about the culture and history of the land that he has begun to manufacture phonograph records which tell of the Mexican heritage and contain guitar renditions of popular Mexican songs. He sells these at cost to the Anglos who can afford the two dollars, and gives them free to Anglos who are in economic straits.

A second component of Mexican-American culture is *machismo,* the cult of masculinity. The Mexican family, like the Catholic Church, is patriarchal and authoritarian. There is a double standard in which the restrictions upon the male are significantly less. Education is for the man, sexual liberties are for the man, material comforts are for the man, and politics are for the man. The woman is subordinate. She must be faithful to her husband and her children. She is controlled by her parents until she marries; then she is dominated by her husband. In theory and in practice the woman's role in life is one of wife and mother—and nothing more.

The cult of masculinity is at odds with the egalitarian material relationship of the Anglo. Within the ghetto, which is isolated from the

Anglo community, strains are less apparent. Still, *machismo* affects female participation and support of such Anglo-operated activities as the school and P.T.A. As the East Central Area Director of the Los Angeles Region Welfare Planning Council observed:

> In the United States the two sexes are on a fairly equal basis. In the culture of Mexico the man is head of the household. The term *machismo* is oftentimes attributed to that trait in the Mexican male where he is the dominant figure in the family. When this characteristic exists, it is the man—the husband—who generally decides if the wife is to attend a P.T.A. meeting, or if she is to participate in a community or civic activity. Thus, because of his own indifference or aloofness, neither he, nor she, becomes actively involved in the community.[5]

When, however, the Mexican-American moves from the ghetto into areas more heavily populated by Anglos, the cultural factor of *machismo* becomes dysfunctional. Mexican-American women compare their relationship with their husbands to that of their Anglo neighbors, and marital unrest often results. As we noted previously, divorces are on the increase and *machismo* is declining. A Mexican-American social worker whose specialty is marriage counseling pointed out that:

> An American middle-class tradition is rough on Mexican husbands. The de-emphasis of *machismo* goes against the strong cultural traditions. Husbands feel the pressure and often leave their wives. For the women the situation is better. It is the first time that they are independent. But both conditions affect the parent-child relationship. Many Mexican kids came to this country when they were very young. They never learned to speak either proper Spanish or proper English. They can't communicate with their parents or their teachers, and vice versa. They feel alienated at home and thus turn to gang life. Only here can they find a peer group that understands them and their problems.

It is in the area of family relations that the dichotomy between the Anglo and Mexican value systems is most apparent, and where its effects upon Mexican educational opportunities are most devastating. The Anglo family is child-centered, while the Mexican family is family-centered. This presents problems with the schools. The social worker continued:

> The schools can't understand why a mother would keep her kid home to tend her brothers and sisters and her cousins while her mother takes her

---

[5]Martin Ortiz, "Mexican Americans in the Los Angeles region," unpublished report, 1965.

aunt to the hospital. The middle-class parent defines his child's education as the most important thing. But the Mexican parent says that it is the family welfare and family solidarity, including the extended family, that is most important. School is less important than family life, but the middle-class schoolteacher would not understand this.

Couple this with the belief that the woman's place is in the home and that *machismo* is of great importance, and one can understand why there are so few Mexican-Americans in public education. Out of the eight thousand teachers in the in-service training program in Los Angeles, only seventy-five are Mexican-Americans. Public school teaching is not a masculine occupation in the ghetto, and women are not encouraged to become professionals.

In addition, the school is a symbol of Anglo authority. It is the force which Mexicans see as trying to dissolve family ties. The school demands that the parents obey its wishes. If Juanita's mother wants to have her stay home from school and tend her twelve siblings, the school can seek an injunction against her. The school demands that the child forsake his familial obligations for the needs of the larger society—a demand that rubs against the values of the culture. This is one of the factors which contribute to the high dropout rate among Mexican-American youth. As one Anglo social scientist with an extensive knowledge of the Mexican-American commented:

Actually you are not going to affect dropout rates as long as the school stands as a symbol of Anglo-Saxon superiority. The Mexican community doesn't trust the schools. The schools threaten to take away the patriarchal rule in the families. A father cannot decide the fate of his children, because the women teachers do so. There is a good deal of paternal pressure on the kids to drop out of school.

Unlike the Anglo-American family, which puts a premium only upon loyalty to the nuclear family, the Mexican family ties extend to all relatives and even close friends. In a report to a group of public school teachers one sociologist noted:

[In the Mexican-American community] there is the extended family, not just parents, grandparents, children, uncles, aunts, cousins, but also other formal ties with close friends. You may be asked to officiate at the baptism of a child of your friend. I guess the closest role Anglos have to it is a godparent. Of course this is a great honor. It means that you will be a foster parent, *Padrino* or *Madrina* to the child and *compadre* or *comadre* to its parents. It means that the two families are very closely tied. The *compadre* is technically responsible for the religious instruction and for the vocational or professional training of the child. If there is any kind of trouble, he is considered to be a substitute parent. We do not have this relationship in the Anglo family system. I recall talking about a certain judge with a man who is prominent in the Los Angeles Mexican-American community. He said proudly, "I am *compadre* to him." That means he is a godfather to his children and has a formal relationship to the father. These are extensive family ties where everybody is close to everybody else.[6]

There is little question that the symbols which maintain a culture are best communicated through language, both written and spoken. Buttressing the culture of the ghetto is the Spanish language. The predominant number of members of the older generation of Mexican-Americans speak no English. Nearly 20 per cent of the entire population of the ghetto is functionally illiterate.[7] Among the school-age generation many are barely literate and barely fluent in either English or Spanish. In some sections of the ghetto it is not necessary to be able to speak English. A Mexican-American newspaperwoman observed:

Did you know that many Mexicans live and die in the East LA ghetto without ever learning English or even leaving the ghetto? Many have never even seen downtown Los Angeles, which is about five miles away. They don't realize that the rest of the world is not a run-down dilapidated slum. I think that if they realized that things were better in other areas, they might get even more militant and would demand their rights. What is keeping the Mexican from overcoming his problems partly is the fact that he doesn't know that things are any different anywhere else.

Because many Mexicans speak little or no English, they have little opportunity to interact with the dominant society. Instead, they seek the security of the ghetto.

Anglos ask why the Mexican-American insists on speaking Spanish. One Anglo teacher observed:

Mexican-Americans want to be different. They don't want to be American. They insist on speaking Spanish in school. Don't they think that American is good enough for them? If you ask me, it's too good for them!

This is not the issue; rather there is security in speaking Spanish. Ruth Tuck once observed that because Spanish is often the language spoken in the Mexican-American home, lapsing into this language often makes the Mexican-American feel more at ease. Besides, many idioms

---

[6]Paul M. Sheldon, "Mexican Americans and the public schools: Some contrasts in culture and social class," in the report of the Conference on Understanding and Teaching Mexican-American Children and Youth, California State Department of Education, 1964, p. 8.

[7]This, of course, does not mean that all members of this segment cannot read or communicate. Rather, it means that they cannot read English; however, an unknown percentage of this segment can read neither English, nor Spanish.

and turns of the tongue lose their meaning and significance when translated into English.[8]

In addition, there is considerable pressure within the community among the older generation to retain the Spanish language. As Madsen points out:

> From the Anglo viewpoint, Spanish is the primary symbol of "foreignness" of the Mexican-American. For the Latin, Spanish is the primary symbol of loyalty to *La Raza*. The Mexican-American who speaks English in a gathering of conservative Latins is mocked and regarded as a traitor to *La Raza*. Among members of the lower class such linguistic disloyalty is forgiven only when a man is drunk.[9]

Furthermore, Spanish allows the culture to flourish. Spanish permits the Mexican-American to maintain cultural pluralism and ties with his family in Mexico. There is reluctance to learn English, the language of the Anglo conquerors, the language of the Yankees who took Mexican land and forced the Mexican into the ghetto, stripping him of everything but his culture—his defense mechanism. As Sheldon notes:

> ... Among a large part of the Spanish-speaking community English has always been labelled the language of authority spoken by the cop on the beat. English is spoken by the sheriff's deputies. English is spoken by the social worker who controls the mother's allotment. English is spoken by the Anglo teacher.
> ... There is a carry-over of the Mexican image of the teacher. The *maestro* is much more a disciplinarian and authority figure than American figures. He is also a government figure in Mexican culture. Especially among new arrivals from Mexico, the teacher is held in awe, an attitude which, in a nation of almost universal literacy, is difficult to understand.[10]

We may thus conclude that the explanation for the difference between the educational level of the Negro and the Mexican-American can in part be accounted for by the fact that (1) because of the cult of masculinity, *machismo,* the father of the household determines whether or not his children will go to school, and girls are not encouraged to attend classes; (2) the school, being child-oriented, demands that the child forsake his family at times in order to attend classes, while the Mexican family is family-centered, and insists that the child not go to school if there are too many chores at home to do; and (3) that English, which has been the only language spoken in schools, is the language of the Anglo, the language of the person who conquered the Mexican, attempting to rob him of his culture.

. . . . .

---

[8]Ruth Tuck, *Not with the Fist* (New York: Harcourt, Brace, 1946).
[9]William Madsen, *The Mexican-Americans of South Texas, op. cit.*, p. 106.
[10]Sheldon, "Mexican Americans and the public schools", *op. cit.*, p. 7.

C. EVOLVING ISSUES

Many interesting people have grown up in New York City. But two in particular became well-known among college students in the 1950s and 1960s. The first one was Holden Caulfield, described by J.D. Salinger as a naive white adolescent, independently confronting the adult role for the first time.[1] Salinger traced Caulfield's encounters with the more cosmopolitan society as well as his disillusions with it. Caulfield's reactions, however, remained relatively passive, and indeed, *The Catcher in the Rye* has come to represent the "silent" generation of the 1950s. In the 1960s, Claude Brown wrote of his own experiences as a black youth who had migrated from the South to New York City.[2] Brown's story was a compassionate rendition of the trauma, disillusionment, and the despair that confronted the urban black, and indeed, *Manchild in the Promised Land* has come to represent the concern with racial injustice and social change in the 1960s.

It is not yet clear who the symbolic adolescent of the 1970s will be. Nevertheless, the changes in the last decade have been just as dramatic as the transition from J. D. Salinger to Claude Brown. The initial fervor of the civil rights movement and of the black nationalist movement, as embodied in the writings of Malcolm X, Eldridge Cleaver, and Stokely Carmichael,[3] has subsided. In addition, we are beginning to see the outcome of the social conflicts and public actions of the last few years.

In one sense, the outcome has been favorable for certain racial and ethnic groups: American society is becoming more egalitarian and representative than before. Through legislation, executive order, and reform, institutions have had to create more opportunities for blacks, Chicanos, and other disadvantaged ethnic groups. Employers have actively

---

[1]J. D. Salinger, *The Catcher in the Rye* (Boston: Little, Brown & Co., 1945).

[2]Claude Brown, *Manchild in the Promised Land* (New York: The Macmillan Co., 1965). A similar story, but from the point of view of a Puerto Rican, is Piri Thomas, *Down These Mean Streets* (New York: Alfred A. Knopf, Inc., 1967).

[3]See *The Autobiography of Malcolm X* (New York: Grove Press, Inc., 1964); Eldridge Cleaver, *Soul on Ice* (New York: Delta, 1968); and Stokely Carmichael and Charles V. Hamilton, *Black Power: The Politics of Liberation in America* (New York: Random House, Inc., 1967).

recruited not only the minorities traditionally regarded as oppressed, but also women and people under 30 years of age (the inclusion of one black woman under 30 can raise an employer's pluralism index considerably). This type of "reverse" discrimination may eventually offset some of the institutional discrimination traced in the previous section of this reader. Paul Seabury (Selection 29) describes how the federal government continues to press for more proportionate representation in large institutions, in this case focusing on the lack of equal opportunities in the university hierarchy. Although Seabury takes a critical view of the role of the federal government, the very existence of his account suggests the degree to which governmental action has already been effective.

In another sense, the outcome has been unfavorable for these same groups: The quality of life has not dramatically improved. Some cities have already gone one complete round, for instance, in decentralizing their schools and giving more power to parents and neighborhood groups. (The community control of schools, it is to be remembered, became a widespread demand when integration efforts appeared to have failed, and the quality of education remained unacceptably low in many neighborhoods.[4]) Yet in few cases has decentralized authority led to any improvement in the achievement of the students, at least as measured by conventional tests.[5] In addition, the research of Arthur Jensen has raised anew an old question: Could it be that genetic factors, and not environmental ones, account for the persistent differences in educational performance between blacks and whites?[6] The question goes as far back as the 19th century, when Sir Francis Galton first studied the apparent role of heredity in explaining the basis for genius and feeblemindedness.[7] Lee Edson (Selection 30), writing for *The New York Times,* carefully describes Jensen, his research, and his conclusions. The research has stirred a massive controversy among educators, and of course has led to renewed accusations concerning the white racist nature of social science.[8]

---

[4]For descriptions of the evolution of community control, see Mario Fantini, Marilyn Gittell, and Richard Magat, *Community Control and the Urban School* (New York: Praeger Publishers, Inc., 1970); and Alan A. Altshuler, *Community Control* (New York: Pegasus, 1970). For a brief discussion of the outcome of district elections, see George R. LaNoue and Bruce L. R. Smith, "The political evolution of school decentralization," *American Behavioral Scientist,* September-October 1971, 15:73–93.

[5]For instance, see Diane Ravitch, "Community control revisited," *Commentary,* February 1972, pp. 69–74.

[6]Arthur R. Jensen, "How much can we boost IQ and scholastic achievement?" *Harvard Educational Review,* Winter 1969, 39:1–123.

[7]Francis Galton, *Hereditary Genius: An Inquiry into Its Laws and Consequences* (London: The Macmillan Co., Ltd., 1869).

[8]For a start, see the several articles in the *Harvard Educational Review,* Spring 1969, 39(2) and Summer 1969, 39(3); Richard Herrnstein, "I.Q.," *The Atlantic,* September 1971, pp. 43-64; Sandra Scarr-Salapatek, "Race, social class, and IQ," *Science,* December 1971, 174:1285–95; Frank L. Morris, "The Jensen hypothesis,"

The lack of improvement in the quality of life has shown up on the economic side as well. The 1970 Census confirmed that the dollar income gap, for instance, between blacks and whites *increased* from 1960 to 1970, in spite of all the attempts to provide blacks with better economic opportunities.[9] Thomas Cook (Selection 31) shows how easily various income statistics can be misused and misinterpreted. He then elaborates on one of the most serious aspects of the income gap: Blacks receive a lower income than whites even when individuals are matched for the level of their education.

Yet a third outcome, not clearly favorable or unfavorable, has also emerged: There has been an increased polarization of American society along racial and ethnic lines. Typically, the older white immigrant groups, e.g., the Italians, the Irish, and the Jews, have become more self-conscious of their own identities. The reemergence of these older ethnic identities is described by Nathan Glazer and Daniel Moynihan (Selection 32) and by Nicholas Pileggi (Selection 33).[10] Both articles emphasize ethnicity in New York, but both point to changes that are noticeable across the country.

The reemergence of these older identities has occurred partly as a result of the increased attention given to blacks and the newer immigrant groups like the Puerto Ricans and the Mexican-Americans.[11] In addition, it has taken a conservative flavor, with the older immigrant groups often supporting a slowdown in the pace of social change. The conservative flavor may be quite understandable. As summarized by Andrew Greeley,

> We must remember that these [older] groups are but a generation or two away from the Old World; to be told that they are responsible or ought to feel guilty over the plight of the Negroes puzzles them, when it does not make them angry. It was not their ancestors who brought the black slaves to this country; it was not their ancestors who kept them enslaved until a

Journal of Black Studies, March 1972, 5:371–86; and Ken Richardson and David Spears (eds.), *Race and Intelligence: The Fallacies behind the Race-IQ Controversy* (Baltimore: Penguin Books Inc., 1972). For the standard position of the environmentalist view regarding race in general, see UNESCO, *Race and Science* (New York: Columbia University Press, 1961).

[9]U.S. Census Bureau, *General Social and Economic Characteristics: United States Summary, 1970 Census of Population* (Washington, D.C.: Government Printing Office, 1972).

[10]For more on the older ethnic groups, see also Andrew M. Greeley, *Why Can't They Be Like Us? America's White Ethnic Groups* (New York: E. P. Dutton & Co., Inc., 1971); Pete Hamill, "Notes on the new Irish," *New York Magazine* March 13, 1972; Richard Gambino, "Twenty million Italian-Americans can't be wrong," *The New York Times Magazine,* April 30, 1972; Marshall Sklare, "Jews, ethnics, and the American city," *Commentary,* April 1972, pp. 70–77; and Joseph L. Vigilante, "Ethnic affirmation, or kiss me, I'm Italian," *Social Work,* May 1972, 17:10–20.

[11]See Nathan Glazer, "Interethnic conflict," *Social Work,* May 1972, 17:3–9.

century ago; . . . They may not like the blacks, . . . but it seems to them that they are being asked to pay the heaviest price for social wrongs for which they have relatively little responsibility.[12]

How American society deals with the racial and ethnic polarity must be seen as one of the most pressing issues for the future. The polarity is complex, and not always simply limited to racial and ethnic issues. For instance, some interethnic conflicts can be related to differences in economic class, with the blacks and newer immigrant groups comprising the bulk of the nation's poor, and with the older immigrant groups constituting the middle and lower middle classes.[13] Moreover, the polarity can be quite subtle. For instance, two analysts of national voting patterns have claimed that the end of the 1960s saw the development of a new political issue, the "social" issue, which included concern over neighborhood change, public safety, and other social problems.[14] Voting on the "social" issue has often followed racial and ethnic lines. At the same time, the nature of the polarity will continue to change as new racial and ethnic identities appear, drawing attention to yet different social groups. This has been the case with women's liberation, a movement to create equal rights for women.[15] In the last article of this reader, Elizabeth Duncan Koontz (Selection 34) reviews the status of women in American society, and the implicit discrimination that exists against women.

In the final analysis, American society has moved farther away from the sense of national community that scholars have frequently sought.[16] But neither have racial and ethnic groups embraced the revolutionary movement that the urban and campus crises were supposed to ignite.[17]

---

[12]Greeley, *Why Can't They Be Like Us, op. cit.,* p. 156.

[13]For a brief appraisal of the current status of the white working class, see Louise Kapp Howe (ed.), *The White Majority: Between Poverty and Affluence* (New York: Random House, Inc., 1970). Interestingly, university groups tend to align themselves with the interests of the poor and disadvantaged, sometimes disregarding the interests of the white working class. See, for instance, Michael Lerner, "Respectable bigotry," *The American Scholar,* Autumn 1969, 38:606–17.

[14]Richard Scammon and Ben Wattenberg, *The Real Majority* (New York: Coward-McCann, Inc., 1970).

[15]For more on women's liberation, see Robert Sherrill, "That equal-rights amendment: What, exactly, does it mean?" *The New York Times Magazine,* September 20, 1970; and Joan D. Mandle, "Women's liberation: Humanizing rather than polarizing," *The Annals,* September 1971, 397:118–28.

[16]See, for example, Robert A. Nisbet, *The Quest for Community* (New York: Oxford Book Co., Inc., 1953, reissued as *Community and Power* in 1962); and Arthur M. Schlesinger, Jr., *The Crisis of Confidence* (Boston: Houghton Mifflin Co., 1969), especially Chap. 6.

[17]For observers anticipating revolution, see for example H. Rap Brown, *Die Nigger Die* (New York: Dial Press, 1969); Martin Oppenheimer, *The Urban Guerilla* (Chicago: Quadrangle Books, 1969); and Gary R. Weaver and James H. Weaver (eds.), *The University and Revolution* (Englewood Cliffs, N.J.: Prentice-Hall, Inc., 1969).

Instead, America appears to be slipping into a period of local isolationism, with neighborhoods perhaps to play a more important role in the future. Whether this trend is desirable, or whether it means the fragmentation of society into conflicting groups that cannot live with each other, remains for the future to determine.

29. HEW and the universities

PAUL SEABURY

Old Howard Smith, Virginia swamp fox of the House Rules Committee, was a clever tactical fighter. When Dixiecrats in 1964 unsuccessfully tried to obstruct passage of the Civil Rights bill, Smith in a fit of inspired raillery devised a perverse stratagem. He proposed an amendment to the bill, to include women as an object of federal protection in employment, by adding sex to the other criteria of race, color, national origin, and religion as illegitimate grounds for discrimination in hiring. This tactical maneuver had far-reaching effects; calculated to rouse at least some Northern masculine ire against the whole bill, it backfired by eliciting a chivalrous rather than (as we now call it) sexist response: the amendment actually passed!

Smith, however, had greater things in mind for women's rights. As a fall-back strategy, they would distract federal bureaucrats from the principal object of the bill, namely, to rectify employment inequities for Negroes. In this, at least in higher education, Smith's stratagem is paying off according to expectations. The middle-range bureaucrats staffing the HEW Civil Rights office, under its Director, J. Stanley Pottinger, now scent sexism more easily than racism in the crusade to purify university hiring practices. Minority-group spokesmen grumble when this powerful feminine competitor appears, to horn in. In the dynamics of competition between race and sex for scarce places on university faculties, a new hidden crisis of higher education is brewing. As universities climb out of the rubble of campus disorders of the 1960's, beset by harsh budgetary

Abridged and edited from Paul Seabury, "HEW and the universities," *Commentary,* February 1972, pp. 38–44. Reprinted from *Commentary,* by permission; Copyright © 1972 by The American Jewish Committee.

The author is Professor of Political Science, University of California, Berkeley, Calif.

reverses, they now are required to redress national social injustices within their walls at their own expense. Compliance with demands from the federal government to do this would compel a stark remodeling of their criteria of recruitment, their ethos of professionalism, and their standards of excellence. Refusal to comply satisfactorily would risk their destruction.

The story of how this came about, and what it portends, is a complex one, so complex that it is hard to know where to begin. It is also an unpleasant tale. Only its first chapters can be written.

Let us begin the story, then, with a brief history of the Civil Rights Act of 1964. This act, in the view of its principal sponsors, purposed (among other things) to engage the force of the federal government in battle to diminish or to rectify discriminatory hiring practices in firms and institutions having or seeking contracts with the federal government. Title VII of the act expressly forbids discrimination by employers on grounds of race, color, religion, and national origin, either in the form of preferential hiring or advancement, or in the form of differential compensation. Contracting institutions deemed negligent in complying with these provisions could be deemed ineligible for such contracts, or their contracts could be suspended, terminated, or not renewed.

When Title VII was debated in the Senate, some opponents of it, asserting (in the words of a Washington *Star* editorial) that it was a "draftsman's nightmare," voiced alarm that it might be used for discriminatory purposes, and employers might be coerced into hiring practices which might, in fact, violate the equal-protection doctrine of the Constitution, thus perversely reversing the stated purposes of the bill. In one significant interchange, this alarm, raised by Florida's Senator Smathers, was genially dismissed by Senator Humphrey, in words which bear recalling:

> MR. HUMPHREY: [T]he Senator from Florida is so convincing that when he speaks, as he does, with the ring of sincerity in his voice and heart, and says that an employee should be hired on the basis of his ability—
>
> MR. SMATHERS: Correct.
>
> MR. HUMPHREY: And that an employer should not be denied the right to hire on the basis of ability and should not take into consideration race— how right the Senator is. . . .
>
> But the trouble is that these idealistic pleadings are not followed by some sinful mortals. There are some who do not hire solely on the basis of ability. Doors are closed; positions are closed; unions are closed to people of color. That situation does not help America. . . .
>
> I know that the Senator from Florida desires to help America, industry

and enterprise. We ought to adopt the Smathers doctrine, which is contained in Title VII. I never realized that I would hear such an appropriate description of the philosophy behind Title VII as I have heard today.

MR. SMATHERS: Mr. President, the Senator from Minnesota has expressed my doctrine completely. . . .

The first steps in implementing the new act were based on executive orders of the President corresponding to Humphrey's Smathers Doctrine. President Johnson's Executive Order No. 11375 (1967) stated that

> The contractor will not discriminate against any employee or applicant because of race, color, religion, sex, or national origin. The contractor *will take affirmative action* [italics added] to ensure that employees are treated during employment, without regard to their race, color, religion, sex, or national origin.

Under such plausible auspices, "affirmative action" was born, and with a huge federal endowment to guarantee its success in life. Since 1967, however, this child prodigy—like Charles Addams's famous nursery boy with the test tubes—has been experimenting with novel brews, so as to change both his appearance and his behavior. And it is curious to see how the singleminded pursuers of an ideal of equity can overrun and trample the ideal itself, while injuring innocent bystanders as well.

Affirmative action was altered by a Labor Department order (based not on the Civil Rights Act but on revised Presidential directives) only months after the Johnson order was announced. This order reshaped it into a weapon for discriminatory hiring practices. If the reader will bear with a further recitation of federal prose, let me introduce Order No. 4, Department of Labor:

> An affirmative-action program is a set of specific and result-oriented procedures to which a contractor commits himself to apply every good faith effort. The objective of these procedures plus such efforts is equal employment opportunity. Procedures without effort to make them work are meaningless; and effort, undirected by specific and meaningful procedures, is inadequate. An acceptable affirmative-action program must include an analysis of areas within which the contractor is deficient in the utilization of minority groups and women, and further, *goals and timetables to which the contractor's good faith efforts must be directed to correct the deficiencies and thus, to increase materially the utilization of minorities and women, at all levels and in all segments of his work force where deficiencies exist.*

This directive is now applicable through HEW enforcement

procedures to universities by delegation of authority from the Labor Department. By late 1971, something of a brushfire, fanned by hard-working HEW compliance officers, had spread through American higher education, the cause of it being the demand that universities, as a condition of obtaining or retaining their federal contracts, establish hiring goals based upon race and sex.

Universities, for a variety of singular reasons, are extremely vulnerable to this novel attack. As President McGill of Columbia remarked recently, "We are no longer in all respects an independent private university." As early as 1967, the federal government was annually disbursing contract funds to universities at the rate of three-and-a-half billion dollars a year; recently the Carnegie Commission suggested that federal contract funding be increased by 1978 to thirteen billion dollars, if universities are to meet their educational objectives. Individual institutions, notably great and distinguished ones, already are extraordinarily dependent on continuing receipt of federal support. The University of California, for instance, currently (1970-71) depends upon federal contract funds for approximately $72 million. The University of Michigan, periodically harassed by HEW threats of contract suspension, cancellation, or non-renewal, would stand to lose as much as $60 million per annum. The threat of permanent disqualification, if consummated, could wholly wreck a university's prospects for the future.

In November 1971, HEW's Office for Civil Rights announced its intent to institute proceedings for Columbia's permanent debarment—*even though no charges or findings of discrimination had been made*: Columbia had simply not come up with an acceptable affirmative-action program to redress inequities which had not even been found to exist. When minor officials act like Alice in Wonderland's Red Queen, using threats of decapitation for frivolous purposes; when they act as investigator, prosecutor, and judge rolled into one, there may be no cause for surprise. But one can certainly wonder how even they would dare pronounce sentence—and a sentence of death at that—even before completion of the investigatory phase. Such, however, appears to be the deadly logic of HEW procedures. As J. Stanley Pottinger, chief of HEW's office, said at a West Coast press conference recently, "We have a whale of a lot of power and we're prepared to use it if necessary." In known circumstances of its recent use, the threat resembles the deployment of MIRV missiles to apprehend a suspected embezzler.

· · · · ·

To remain eligible for federal contracts under the new procedures, universities must devise package proposals, containing stated targets for preferential hiring on grounds of race and sex. HEW may reject these goals, giving the university thirty-day notice for swift rectification, even though no charges of discrimination have been brought. Innocence must either be quickly proved, or acceptable means of rectification devised. But how does one *prove* innocence?

"Hiring practices" (i.e., faculty recruitment procedures) are decentralized; they devolve chiefly upon departments. At Columbia, for instance, 77 units generate proposals for recruitment. Faculties resent (most of the time quite properly) attempts of administrators to tell them whom to hire, and whom not. Departments rarely keep records of the communications and transactions which precede the making of an employment offer, except as these records pertain to the individual finally selected. Still, the procedure is time-consuming and expensive. The Department of Economics of the San Diego campus of the University of California estimates that it costs twenty to forty man hours, plus three to five hundred dollars, to screen *one* candidate sufficiently to make an offer. Typically, dozens of candidates are reviewed in earlier stages.

Compliance data thus tend to be scanty and incomplete. "Columbia's problem," President McGill recently observed, "is that it is difficult to prove what we do because it is exceedingly difficult to develop the data base on which to show, in the depth and detail demanded [by HEW], what the University's personnel activities in fact are." Yet HEW demands such data from universities on thirty-day deadlines, with contract suspension threatened. Moreover, on its finding of discrimination (usually based on statistical, not qualitative, evidence), it may demand plans for rectification which oblige the university to commit itself to abstract preferential goals without regard to the issue of individual merit.

The best universities, which also happen to be those upon which HEW has chiefly worked its knout, habitually and commonsensically recruit from other best institutions. The top universities hire the top 5 per cent of graduate students in the top ten universities. This is the "skill pool" they rely upon. Some may now deem such practices archaic but they have definitely served to maintain quality. Just as definitely they have not served to obtain "equality of results" in terms of the proportional representation of sociological categories. Such equality assumes that faculties somehow must "represent" designated categories of people on grounds other than those of professional qualification. As Labor Department Order No. 4 states, special attention "should be given to academic, experience and skill requirements, to ensure that the requirements in themselves do not constitute inadvertent discrimination." Indeed, according to four professors at Cornell writing in the *Times* (Letters to the Editor, January 6), deans and department chairmen have been informed by that university's president that HEW policy means the " 'hiring of additional minority persons and females' even if 'in many instances, it may be necessary to hire unqualified or marginally qualified people.' "

If departments abandon the practice of looking to the best pools from which they can hope to draw, then quality must in fact be jeopardized. To comply with HEW orders, every department must come up not with the *best* candidate, but with the best-qualified *woman* or *non-white* candidate. For when a male or a white candidate is actually selected or recommended, it is now incumbent on both department and university to *prove* that no qualified woman or non-white was found available. Some universities already have gone so far in emulating the federal bureaucracy as to have installed their own bureaucratic monitors, in the form of affirmative-action coordinators, to screen recommendations for faculty appointments before final action is taken.

A striking contradiction exists between HEW's insistence that faculties prove they do not discriminate and its demand for goals and timetables which require discrimination to occur. For there is no reason to suppose that equitable processes in individual cases will automatically produce results which are set in the timetables and statistical goals universities are now required to develop. If all that HEW wishes is evidence that universities are bending over backward to be fair, why should it require them to have statistical goals at all? Do they know something no one else knows, about where fairness inevitably leads?

Yet another facet of HEW's procedures goes to the very heart of faculty due process: its demand of the right of access to faculty files, when searching for evidence of discrimination. Such files have always been the most sacrosanct documents of academia, and for good reason: it has been assumed that candor in the evaluation of candidates and personnel is best guaranteed by confidentiality of comment; and that evasiveness, caution, smoke-screening, and grandstanding—which would be the principal consequences of open files—would debase standards of judgment. In the past, universities have denied federal authorities—the FBI for instance—access to these files. Now HEW demands access. And it is the recent reluctance of the Berkeley campus of the University of California to render unto this agent of Caesar what was denied to previous agents, which occasioned the HEW ultimatum of possible contract suspension: $72 million. One might imagine the faculty would be in an uproar, what with Nixon's men ransacking the inner temple. But no. In this as in other aspects of this curious story, the faculty is silent.

"In respect of civil rights, common to all citizens, the Constitution of the United States does not, I think, permit any public authority to know the race of those entitled to be protected in the enjoyment of such rights. . . . Our Constitution is color-blind, and neither knows nor tolerates classes among citizens." This is Justice Harlan, dissenting in Plessy *v*. Ferguson in 1896, when the Supreme Court endorsed the "separate but equal" doctrine.

Some of us in the league of lost liberals are still wont to say that the Constitution is color-blind. Yet now under the watchful eye of federal functionaries, academic administrators are compelled to be as acutely sensitive as Kodachrome to the outward physical appearance of their faculty members and of proposed candidates for employment. Forms supplying such information are now fed into data-processing machines; print-outs supply ethnic profiles of departments, colleges, and schools, from which compliance reports may be sent to HEW, and university affirmative-action goals are approved or rejected.[1]

All of this is done in some uneasiness of mind, to put it mildly. In many states, Harlan-like blue-laws of a recent innocent epoch still expressly prohibit employers from collecting and maintaining data on prospective employees with respect to race, religion, and national origin. The crafty practices contrived to elude the intention of such laws while at the same time complying with HEW, vary from campus to campus. At the University of Michigan, the procedure entails what is known as "self-designation"—the employee indicates on a form the race or ethnic group of which he considers himself a part.[2] These forms are collected and grouped according to job-classifications, departments, etc., and then they are burned, so as to disappear without a trace. Other universities, less anxious to cover their traces, simply file the forms separately from regular personnel files, without the names of the individuals concerned. In New York, the CUNY system resorts to a quite different practice invented and perfected by South African Boers: "visual identification." Affirmative-action coordinators are told to proceed as follows: "The affirmative-action inventory is to be done by a *visual* survey [italics in original]. There *should not be a notation of any kind* as to ethnic background in either personnel records or permanent files. This is against the law. . . . Identification of Italian Americans will be done visually and by name. . . . Please remember, however, that each individual is to be listed in only one ethnic group."

The number of categories established on behalf of affirmative action, though at present finite, already betrays accordion-like expansibility. The affirmative-action program at San Francisco State College, typical of most, is now confined to six racial groups: Negroes; Orientals; other

---

[1]Since HEW has divulged no reliable standards of its own, the well-intentioned administrator is like a worshiper of Baal, propitiating a god who may punish or reward, but who is silent.

[2]Self-designation is not always reliable. At Michigan, the amused or disgusted members of one of the university's maintenance crews all self-designated themselves as American Indians (bureaucratese: Native American); their supervisor was quietly asked to redesignate them accurately.

Non-White; persons of Mexican, Central or South American ancestry ("except those who have physical characteristics of Negro, Oriental, or other Non-White races"); Native American (American Indian); and All Others, ". . . including those commonly designated as Caucasian or White." All but the last category are eligible for discriminatory preference.[3]

As the above CUNY memorandum signals, however, this last category of "those commonly designated as Caucasian or White" is a Pandora's box inside a Pandora's box. Now that the Italians have escaped from it in New York, the lid is open for others—all the many different groups now fashionably known as "ethnics"—to do likewise. A farseeing administrator, even as under HEW's gun he hastily devises future-oriented hiring quotas ("goals") to muffle the noise of one or two squeaky wheels, might wonder how he will be able to gratify subsequent claimants on the dwindling capital of reserved quotas still at his disposal.

Yet the administrator in practice has no choice but to act on the "sufficient unto the day is the evil thereof" principle. HEW ultimata, when they come, are imperious and immediate. Thirty-day rectifications are in order. At Johns Hopkins, MIT, Columbia, Michigan, and the University of California, an acute agony arises from no such philosophical long-range speculations, but from how to put together attractive compliance reports fast enough to avoid the threatened withholding of vast funds, the closing-down of whole facilities, the dismissal of thousands of staff workers, and the irreparable damage done to important ongoing research, especially to laboratory experiments. Crocodile tears do flow, from the gimlet-eyes of HEW investigators, who observe these sufferings from distant federal offices. Even J. Stanley Pottinger recently noted, in appropriate Pentagonese, that the act of contract suspension at Berkeley, for instance, might constitute "overkill." Yet no sooner had he voiced this note of sadness than his regional compliance director recommended to Washington precisely such action.

While deans, chancellors, and personnel officials struggle with these momentous matters, faculties and graduate students with few exceptions are silent. HEW is acting in the name of social justice. Who in the prevailing campus atmosphere would openly challenge anything done in that name? Tenured faculty perhaps consult their private interests and conclude that whatever damage the storm may do to less-protected colleagues or to their job-seeking students, prudence suggests a posture of silence. Others perhaps, refusing to admit that contending interests are involved, believe that affirmative action is cost-free, and that all will

---

[3]One object of current discriminatory hiring practices at San Francisco State is to make the institution's non-academic personnel ethnically mirror the population of the Bay Area.

benefit from it in the Keynesian long run. But someone *will* pay: namely very large numbers of white males who are among those distinguishable as "best qualified" and who will be shunted aside in the frantic quest for "disadvantaged qualifiables."

The inequities implied in affirmative action, and the concealed but real costs to individuals, would probably have had less damaging effects upon such highly-skilled graduate students had they been imposed in the early 1960's. Then, the sky was the limit on the growth and the affluence of higher education. If a pie gets bigger, so may its slices enlarge; nobody *seems* to lose. Such is today not the case. The pie now shrinks. One West Coast state college, for example, last year alone lost nearly 70 budgeted faculty positions due to financial stringency. Yet this same college has just announced ths boldest affirmative-action program in California higher education. "Decided educational advantages can accrue to the college," it said, "by having its faculty as well as its student body be more representative of the minority population of the area. *It is therefore expected that a substantial majority of all new faculty appointments during the immediate academic years will be from minorities, including women, until the underutilization no longer exists."* (Italics added.) Departments which refuse to play the game will have their budgets reviewed by university officials.

It is hard to say how widely such pernicious practices have been institutionalized in other colleges and universities. But were they to be generalized across the nation, one thing is certain: either large numbers of highly-qualified scholars will pay with their careers simply because they are male and white, *or,* affirmative action will have failed in its benevolent purposes.

It seems superfluous to end this chronicle of woe with mention of another heavy cost—one not so immediately visible—in the forceful administration of affirmative-action hiring goals. This is that men will be less able to know, much less sustain, the professional standards by which they and others judge and are judged. An enthusiastic affirmative-action administrator recently in argument with a skeptical college president said, "Let's face it—you and I know there are a lot of lousy programs and a lot of shoddiness around here. Why object to this?" By such logic, one bad turn deserves another. Since more and more less and less qualified students may enter universities, why bother too much about the quality of the new faculty hired to teach them? It is an interesting reflex habit of some federal bureaucrats and politicians (when confronted with objections that affirmative action might, for instance, discriminate against well- or better-qualified persons) to draw rhetorical analogies to confute their critics on this score. Told that affirmative action might actually discriminate against white males, J. Stanley Pottinger of HEW simply replied, "That is balderdash. That is the biggest crock I have ever heard. It is the kind of argument one expects to hear from a backwoods cracker farmer."

Indeed, backwoods cracker farmers *are* making this argument—though for reasons other than those Pottinger had in mind, and which have much to do with the things great universities require in order to survive in their greatness. Consider what a white third-year law student at a Southern university (self-designating himself disadvantaged but according to no currently approved norms) had to say with respect to his personal situation:

> The ability to think in the abstract is hard for a person with my cultural background and economic background. My parents were Wasps whose income barely exceeded the poverty level. My father is a Southern Baptist with a third-grade education.... My mother is a Southern Baptist also.... She can read and write but my father is illiterate.
>
> In the public schools I attended, memorization was always emphasized. At—— University ... during my first eight quarters at this law school no one has emphasized the ability to think in abstract terms.... I do not know if this type of education is good or bad, but I do know that all your time is spent taking notes and that there is no time for thought.... Regardless, the course has made me acutely aware of how fortunate I am to be an American. In no other country would I have been able to complete the requirements for a J.D. degree. My cultural and economic background would have prevent it.... My background also prevents me from answering a test like this in the manner you desire. But if I must answer, then I will....
>
> There is another form of discrimination of which, I believe, I am a victim. As a non-member of a minority group I feel that I ... [am] discriminated against constantly. The same admissions standards are not applied because a certain percentage of minority students must be admitted in each class regardless of their qualifications. My test score, undergraduate record, and my family (poor white) deny me admittance to Harvard because I am white. I do not say this in bitterness, but in observation of the current status of admission practices as I perceive them....

Somebody, then, has to pay, when the principle of merit is compromised or replaced by preferential ethnic and sex criteria.

Who then wins? The beneficiaries of preference? The particular institution involved? Society as a whole? One may debate the answer to each of those questions, but one thing is certain: HEW wins. It wins, as Aaron Wildavsky has pointed out, because winning can be defined by internal norms. The box-score is of its own devising. To the extent that its goals are met, and the body-count proves this, it wins. But then, where have we heard *that* before?

30. Jensenism, *n.*—The theory that I.Q. is largely determined by the genes

LEE EDSON

For most of the last 10 years Prof. Arthur Robert Jensen of the University of California, one of the nation's leading educational psychologists, has lived the generally quiet, cloistered existence of a scholar, burying himself in statistics, standards and students. If the Free Speech Movement, the People's Park confrontation or any of the other well-publicized blowoffs of Berkeley student unrest penetrated the Education Building on the west corner of the campus (where such egg-yolk institutions as Agricultural Extension, Life Sciences and Home Economics are clustered), it was hard to tell it from Jensen. A tall, almost somber figure, addicted to dark attire, he strode through the corridors with aloof dignity. He seldom cracked a smile, fraternized with colleagues or engaged in small talk. He was a very involved, very serious professor's professor who had no time for hanky-panky and insisted on keeping himself free of the academic maelstrom. "It's incredible," a colleague once remarked after leaving his office. "Jensen is so absorbed he doesn't realize he's on top of a volcano."

Then on Feb. 15 the volcano erupted. The *Harvard Educational Review,* a 30-year-old scholarly journal published by Harvard graduate students, came out with an article by Jensen entitled: "How Much Can We Boost I.Q. and Scholastic Achievement?"[1] The detailed scientific paper, the longest ever printed in the review, begins with an appraisal of the alleged failure of compensatory education programs such as Head Start, a project to help preschool ghetto youngsters overcome years of cultural deprivation in order to catch up with middle-class youngsters in school readiness. The article goes on to state that these programs seek, in effect, to raise children's academic achievement by increasing their I.Q.'s. Jensen then examines the entire concept of the I.Q.: "what makes it vary from one individual to another; what can change it, and by what amount." In the process he says that Negroes as a group—as opposed to any single individual Negro—test out poorly compared with whites or Orientals on that aspect of general intelligence that involves abstract reasoning and problem-solving. And he adds that this ability (which he equates with the ability measured by I.Q. tests) is largely inherited, a

Abridged and edited from Lee Edson, "Jensenism, *n.*—The Theory that I.Q. is largely determined by the genes," *The New York Times Magazine,* August 31, 1969. Copyright © 1969 by The New York Times Company. Reprinted by permission.
[1] *Harvard Educational Review,* Winter 1969, 39:1–123.

matter of genes and brain structure, and therefore no amount of compensatory education or forced exposure to culture is going to improve it substantially.

Jensen emphasizes in his article, that the "particular constellation of abilities we call 'intelligence,' and which we can measure by means of 'intelligence' tests," is only a part of the whole spectrum of human abilities—and that it "has been singled out from the total galaxy of mental abilities as being especially important in our society mainly because of the nature of our traditional system of formal education and the occupational structure with which it is coordinated." He points out that, "as far as we know, the full range of human talents is represented in all the major races of man." But such statements did little to lessen the impact of the article's conclusions about I.Q. and race. The magazine had hardly hit the academic mailboxes when a sound truck manned by members of the Students for a Democratic Society roared through the Berkeley campus, blaring: "Fight racism. Fire Jensen." Jensen's normally sparse scholarly mail grew fat with hate literature. He was accused of being a fascist, a white supremacist, of having black ancestry and hating it. He received postcards emblazoned with the Nazi swastika; one had a single hand-scrawled word: "Death." A group of aroused left-wing students invaded his classroom and he had to lecture in secret locations; crank callers engaged him on the phone, and he was forced to summon the Berkeley campus security forces to protect his files from being raided. At night the lights burned bright in his office to discourage looters. One fearful assistant quit her job.

In the academic and political worlds the furor has become ever more intense. Not since Darwin's theory of evolution, as one writer put it, has so much fiery discussion and violent opposition been generated over a treatise. A Congressman put all 123 pages of the article into the *Congressional Record,* and segregationists took to citing the article in court as the word of science. Lengthy reviews of the article were printed almost everywhere in intellectual circles. At Columbia University's Teachers College the article became required reading in some classes, and at the University of Minnesota a psychology professor, in as irrelevant a reaction as one could find, offered $100 to anyone who could predict a man's intelligence by looking at his features.

· · · · ·

Jensen says his case is based, "not on a single definitive study but on a preponderance of evidence pointing in a single direction, like the theory of evolution." Geneticists have long agreed, for instance, that intelligence has a genetic base. Studies of matings between cousins of normal I.Q. reveal that they produce larger numbers of retarded off-

spring than are produced in nonfamily, random matings. The link between retardation and heredity is very direct.

Jensen's most telling argument, he believes, and the easiest to grasp,
proceeds from studies of identical twins—siblings whose genetic inheritance is precisely the same, since they have developed from a single
fertilized egg. Psychologist Sir Cyril Burt and geneticist J. A. Shields
studied 100 pairs of identical twins in England who were reared apart
from each other. It was found that the separated twins were, on the
average, only six points apart in I.Q. By contrast, any two people in the
total population, chosen at random, will be on the average 18 points
apart. Nonidentical siblings reared in the same household are on the
average 12 I.Q. points apart.

"If you look at studies of adopted children," Jensen says, "you find
that their intelligence relates more closely to their natural parents than
to their adoptive parents. And if you add this to 100 other twin and
kinship studies over the last 25 years over four continents and a wide
range of environmental conditions, you have a strong body of evidence
for the heritability of I.Q. In short, the closer people are related, the
more similar are their I.Q.'s."

The second line of evidence of the heritability of intelligence, Jensen
says, comes from the studies of the relationship between intelligence and
socioeconomic status dating back to the work of Alfred Binet 70 years
ago. We know that people in the upper classes generally have higher
I.Q.'s than those in lower classes. Some people like to read an environmental cause into this. But, in fact, studies indicate otherwise. Regardless of the social class in which an adopted child is reared, for example,
the child's I.Q. will correlate better with that of his natural parents than
that of his adoptive parents. If a child's natural parents have high I.Q.'s,
it is most likely that he will also have a high I.Q. even if he is raised by
low-I.Q., lower-class adoptive parents. The environment is not the
deciding factor.

How does all this evidence tie up with racial differences? "First,"
Jensen says, "it should be noted that race is not an abstract Platonic essence—it is actually a 'breeding population,' as the geneticists term it;
the population is not closed, but there is a well-known probability of
greater mating within this population than outside it. As a result, the
frequency of genes for white skin or dark skin differs in the different
groups. It is true that there are extremely few if any Negroes of pure African descent in the United States today; but this doesn't change the
genetic analysis of a particular population or affect the opportunity to
study it by methods that have worked in other genetic fields."

Social scientists have been studying racial differences for many years,
Jensen says, citing some 400 major studies. "All of them point out—
unhappily perhaps—that in the standard distribution of I.Q. throughout

the population the Negro is 15 points lower than the white. Only 3 per cent of the Negro population exceed an I.Q. of 115; in the white population 16 per cent exceed 115. In the white population 1 per cent exceed 140; a sixth of that exceed 140 in the Negro population. A similar percentage prevails at the lower end of the distribution. In fact it may even be worse in the retarded area. A long-term study by researchers at Johns Hopkins, conducted in one rural county of Maryland, showed that 31 per cent of the Negro males tested between the ages of 40 and 44 were mentally retarded—that is, they had I.Q.'s under 70. This was true of only 1.5 per cent of the tested white males of the same age."

Jensen asks:

> Is this genetic in origin or caused by environment? I think it must be genetic to a very large extent. When you control samples of white and black population for social class differences, you still have major differences in I.Q. between them—from 15 points on the average to 11 points over the various social classes. In other words, across the same occupational category and income bracket, you still find this striking fact—children of Negroes in the highest income class of our society will average lower in I.Q. than white children of the lowest class; this is backed up by a great deal of data, including that obtained in studies conducted by the Federal Government. You couldn't predict such results from purely environmental theory, and it would be highly improbable to assume that the entire influence was due to subtle factors of early prenatal and postnatal environment. It is more likely—though speculative of course—that Negroes brought here as slaves were selected for docility and strength rather than mental ability, and that through selective mating the mental qualities never had a chance to flourish.
>
> In the famous Coleman study, the American Indians come out lower on all environmental indices than do American Negroes; yet the Indians score higher on I.Q. and scholastic achievement. So do disadvantaged children of the island of Taiwan. In fact, they do as well as children of white middle-class parents in the United States.
>
> Remember—we're talking of populations here, not of individuals. There are Negro geniuses, and certainly many greatly talented figures among Negroes, and race should not stand in the way of hiring, promotions or providing awards. But in large groups, one is compelled to say that on the basis of these studies improved environment is not likely to change the fundamental intelligence of large groups of individuals to a substantial extent—no matter how romantic the environmentalists want to be.

Jensen grants that some extremely deprived children can have their I.Q.'s raised by markedly changing their environment. He mentions the classic and dramatic case of Isabel, studied by Kingsley Davis of the University of California. An illegitimate child, she was reared for her first six years in a dark attic by a deaf-mute mother. When found, she was unable to speak, and tests showed that she had an idiot's mentality. But in two years in a good home with lots of attention her mental age jumped up to the average of her age group, and she could perform normally in school. But, as Jensen points out, her I.Q. didn't increase further than this average value. "You can boost an I.Q. in an enriched environment, but once its genetic potential is achieved—once the threshold environment capacity is reached—you cannot improve I.Q. any further. I am afraid there is nothing you can do to create an Einstein without the right kind of genes."

Against this skein of evidence the more rational critics of Jensen in anthropology, sociology and psychology have retaliated with a barrage of their own evidence and argument, picking their targets in virtually every aspect of the Jensen case. The I.Q. test, on which Jensen relies for a good deal of his data, has, for instance, come under probably the severest attack in the last few years. New York and Washington, anticipating pressure from minority groups, withdrew I.Q. testing from their school systems some years ago, but as a result of the Jensen article, the momentum of antipathy to testing has increased. This year, under pressure from Negro groups, the Los Angeles City Council voted to eliminate I.Q. tests from the early grades of the public school system; in Philadelphia, a similar change is being considered. One of the ironies of this movement is that the uneasiness that I.Q. testing generates among ethnic groups is shared by ardent right wingers such as the Birchites, who regard such testing as an instrument for Big Government brainwashing.

Many social scientists who once accepted I.Q. tests as predictive tools of school success and never thought more about it now slip into silence and leave the field to those who question whether there is even a definable quantity known as "g," or general intelligence, separate from interaction with environment. Some in fact argue that I.Q. tests are culturally unfair—loaded with factual material that only certain groups in our society could know or respond to.

Then there are those who attack the reliability of the tests on other grounds. In the case of the highly tested Sirhan Sirhan, for instance, his first test score was 89, and a second test score some months later was 109. Did his intelligence increase or was there something wrong with the tests? Teacher expectations are also said to contribute to scores. An experiment performed by Harvard's Robert Rosenthal and Lenore Jacobson showed that if the teacher persuaded a random group of subjects to believe they were superior, they actually did better than a group not told anything. "If all this is so," the argument runs, "then intelligence tests tell us nothing. They're even dangerous because they lead one to believe that mental ability is fixed at birth and nothing can be done about it."

Jensen is not convinced. "I am afraid," he says, "that the long history of the I.Q. test cannot be overcome by these bursts of criticism. The reliability of the Stanford-Binet test is 95 per cent, with a 5 per cent error, due to such things as the subject's not being up to par when he took the test. This test is more reliable than TB diagnosis based on chest X-rays.

"I.Q. predicts scholastic performance better than any single factor or personality trait. The higher the I.Q., the higher the performance. Below 75 he will not get a high-school education (though he might get a diploma), and below 90 it is doubtful. A good I.Q. is necessary for school success, and this in turn stands at the heart of our technological civilization, which in its simplest terms depends on the ability to manipulate symbols and reason abstractly from them. Not all people with high I.Q.'s succeed in school or in life, of course; other qualities are also needed. The I.Q., however, as a thermometer, explains why children differ in school, and there is no better measure, when used properly, to indicate the factors involved in these differences.

"As for the argument that the I.Q. is culturally unfair, psychologists have tested children in a variety of cultures and have eliminated as many items that relate to one culture and not to another as they can. While you probably can't make an entirely culture-fair test, we do find that in these specially devised, cross-culture tests, Negro youngsters score lower on abstract questions.

"As to teacher expectations, I am afraid that too much publicity in the popular press has been given to the book by Rosenthal and Jacobson, 'Pygmalion in the Classroom.' As a study, it is not regarded highly by professionals. Drs. Robert L. Thorndike and Richard Snow, for example, two psychologists who reviewed the book recently, state categorically that the book does nothing to raise standards of educational research. 'If there is such a bias as teacher expectation, the authors have not demonstrated it,' says Thorndike, and Snow adds that 'by publishing prematurely and inadequately they have performed a disservice to teachers and schools, to users and developers of mental tests, and perhaps worst of all to parents and children whose newly gained expectation may not prove quite so self-fulfilling.' "

CRITICS: Bruno Bettelheim and Benjamin Bloom argue that environment does have an effect on children's I.Q.'s, citing studies in Israel. They found that deprived Oriental Jewish youngsters from the desert raised in the kibbutzim showed higher I.Q.'s than those raised by their parents. And what about the Army qualification tests which showed that the scores of draftees in World War II were higher than those in World War I? Wasn't this caused by the general improvement in education—an environmental factor?

JENSEN: "Bloom's and Bettelheim's argument would be more convincing if Negroes were to be raised in kibbutzim (as Bettelheim suggested recently to Congress) to see whether they improved greatly. In any case some deprived youngsters would get adequate nutrition and possibly the right adult models to identify with. This is a study worth pursuing. But as it stands conclusions drawn from the Israeli work are rather wishful.

"Social scientists who raise the environmentalist flag over the Army Alpha tests are also drawing too much from the data. After all, an Army Alpha test is not an I.Q. test; it is a knowledge test. The Army wanted mainly to know what the draftees knew, and thus the test correlates highly with the number of years of schooling. Moreover, to clinch this argument, a national survey in Scotland in which all the youngsters were given the I.Q. test a generation apart shows that the gain was a mere two to four points."

CRITICS: Could the I.Q. be determined at a very early stage of life, before or soon after birth, when it might be affected by a lack of proper nutrition? Perhaps many Negroes are shortchanged in intelligence because of inadequate diets.

JENSEN: "Nutrition is undoubtedly important in early development. But one would have to prove malnutrition in a majority of Negro youngsters who have taken the I.Q. tests. Herbert Birch of Albert Einstein Medical School, one of the leading researchers in this area, says he cannot find malnutrition in marked degree in Harlem and had to go for his studies of deprivation to Mexico and other Latin-American countries. The Indian youngsters, who came out higher on the I.Q. tests than the Negro, are much more malnourished than American Negro youngsters. So are the children of the poorest untouchables in India, but they got approximately the same I.Q. scores as the Negro youngsters in California public schools.

"I am in favor of studies of early environment, particularly the prenatal environment, and I have been analyzing data from California school children in this regard. I am studying two groups of half-brothers and half-sisters. The brother and sister live in the same home, so the environment is a common factor. However, they have different parentage. The members of one group have the same fathers but different mothers. Those of the second group have the same mother. The question is, are the children with different mothers less alike in I.Q. than those with the same mother? In other words, will the difference in their prenatal environments affect their I.Q.'s? I think the answer could help reduce the heredity-environment uncertainty, at least insofar as the prenatal aspect of environment is concerned."

CRITICS: The argument has been raised in the *Harvard Educational Review* and elsewhere that you cannot separate black genes from white genes, so how can you tell which produce high or low intelligence?

JENSEN: "That is a silly question. There are no 'black' genes or 'white' genes; there are intelligence genes, which are found in populations in different proportions, somewhat like the distribution of blood types. The number of intelligence genes seems to be lower, over-all, in the black population than in the white.

"As to the effect of racial mixing, nobody has yet performed experiments that reveal its relative effect on I.Q. If the racial mixture weren't there, it is possible that the I.Q. difference between blacks and whites would be even greater. I think such studies should be done to lay this uncertainty to rest once and for all."

CRITICS: Even if the evidence suggests a genetic difference in racial intelligence distribution, is science really in a position to separate experimentally the effects of environment from heredity? Surely the factors are too complex, our tools too imprecise, and it would take generations to work out the interactions.

(The National Academy of Sciences underscored this viewpoint in their reaction to William Shockley, the Nobel physicist, who called for research into the genetic aspects of Negro intelligence. The Academy declared that "there is no scientific basis for the statement that there are or are not substantial hereditary differences in intelligence between Negro and white populations. In the absence of some unforeseen way of equalizing all aspects of environment, answers to this question can hardly be more than reasonable guesses.")

JENSEN: "This is true of a good deal of science. Take air turbulence, for instance—my engineering friends tell me that we don't really know all the factors in it, and we have no precise law of turbulence, but engineers design many devices to take it into account.

"I think we can set up experiments to decrease the heredity-environment uncertainties. I referred earlier to Bettelheim's suggestion —place disadvantaged Negro children in kibbutz-like setups and see what happens. I think this is preferable to throwing money into the entire school system, hoping for the best. I believe science is capable of creating techniques to cut through the complexities, if given a chance. Social scientists should be scientists, not ideologists."

CRITICS: Isn't it terrible and self-defeating to make people think they can never break the bonds of their genes? Why raise the specter of invisible disadvantage to an already disadvantaged group? Right now the Negro is coming into his own. Why allow others to use a weapon against him at such a critical time in history when he needs everything to give him a sense of uplift?

JENSEN: "I don't think one gets uplift from hiding from truths. Social scientists are annoyed because I am showing them that they must be loyal either to their science or their longings."

. . . . .

31. Benign neglect: Minimum feasible understanding

THOMAS J. COOK

The term frustration has become common to the discussion of the Negro's dilemma in America today. It has been defined (Lockard, 1968:4-5) as a feeling of futility resulting from a realization that obtained rights may be lost or that expected goals will not be achieved. The common cycle for the Negro in America has been that of promises in the form of legislation, leading to expectations of changes in his life condition, ultimately followed by frustration when the expected changes are not realized.

Harrington (1962:72-73) summarizes this condition as follows:

> If all the discriminatory laws in the United States were immediately repealed, race would still remain as one of the most pressing moral and political problems in the nation. Negroes and other minorities are not simply the victims of a series of iniquitous statutes. The American economy, the American society, the American unconscious are all racist. If all the laws were framed to provide equal opportunity, a majority of the Negroes would not be able to take full advantage of the change. There would still be a vast, silent, and automatic system directed against men and women of color . . . In a sense, the Negro is classically the "other" American, degraded and frustrated at every turn and not just because of laws.

The thrust of Harrington's statement was the principal indictment issued by the Kerner Commission in its urgent plea for the elimination of white racism as the basic solution to America's recent history of civil disorders. In the words of the Commission (1968:1) ". . . our nation is moving toward two societies, one black, one white—separate and unequal."

Contrary to the recommendations of the Kerner Commission Report, Daniel P. Moynihan, Special Assistant to President Nixon, has recently called for a period of "benign neglect." Moynihan (1969:8-9) stated that "the time may have come when the issue of race could benefit from a period of benign neglect." He seems to be saying that if we ignore the race question, i.e., de-emphasize the problem of race in the United

Reprinted from Thomas J. Cook, "Benign neglect: Minimum feasible understanding," *Social Problems,* Fall 1970, 18:145–152. Copyright © 1970 by The Society for the Study of Social Problems. Reprinted by permission.

The author is Assistant Professor of Political Science and Public Administration, Pennsylvania State University, University Park, Pa.

States, maybe it will either disappear or solve itself. He went on to say that "in quantitative terms, which are reliable, the Negro American is making extraordinary progress." Moynihan asserts that the "economic gap" between blacks and whites has significantly narrowed during the period 1959-1968. This assertion was supported by a selection of the most optimistic data from the latest census reports. For example, Moynihan (1969:8-9) stated that:

> The 1960's saw a great breakthrough for the blacks. A third (32 percent) of all families of Negro and other races earned $8,000 or more in 1968, compared, in contrast, in constant dollars with 15 percent in 1960. The South is still a problem. Slightly more than half (52 percent) of the Negro population lived in the South in 1969. There, only 19 percent of families of Negro and other races earned over $8,000. Young Negro families are achieving income parity with young white families outside the South. Outside the South, young husband-wife Negro families have 99 percent of the income of whites.

A conclusion of the type suggested by Moynihan requires close examination of the interpretation of data. The first question concerns the relationship between the data reported and conclusions reached. The emphasis in Moynihan's report is on the Northern black who, as Moynihan states, is a minority (48 percent) of the total Negro population. The increase from 15 percent to 32 percent of families with income of $8,000 or more for Negro and other races is mainly a function of the increase for the regions of the north and west, which is 43 percent. For the South, which represents a majority (52 percent) of the black population, the comparable figure is 19 percent (U.S. Bureau of the Census, 1969:17).

Moynihan's assertion is further weakened by comparison of blacks and whites over the time period 1960-1968, relative to the particular statistic cited. In 1960 there was a 24 percent differential (39 percent-15 percent) between whites and "Negroes and other races" in the proportion of families with income of $8,000 or more. The same figure for 1968 was 26 percent (58 percent-32 percent). The differential for the South in 1968 was even more pronounced, 31 percent (50 percent-19 percent) (U.S. Bureau of the Census, 1969:17). The increase from 15 percent to 32 percent cited by Moynihan does not represent a narrowing of black-white income differentials. Instead it reflects a general increase in income above $8,000 for both blacks and whites. The economic gap has actually widened during the time period covered and is found in its most pronounced condition in that region of the country containing a majority of the black population.

The distortion of the nation-wide Negro economic condition caused by the de-emphasis of the Southern black is further evidenced by an analysis of Negro income as a percent of white income in 1968. The income of Negro families as a percent of white family income in 1968 was 60 percent. However, if this same figure is noted on a regional basis, the results are not quite as clear-cut. Considering only the northeast, north-central, and western regions, Negro income as a percent of white income is approximately 74 percent. The relative contributions of these regions to the 74 percent figure are 69 percent, 75 percent, and 80 percent. These three regions comprise 19 percent, 21 percent, and seven percent, respectively, of the total black population in the United States. In the case of the South, which represents 52 percent of the black population, Negro income represents 54 percent of white income. This is approximately the same figure as reported for Negro and other races taken a whole in 1950. Thus, elimination of the Southern Negro has decreased the differential between black and white incomes by approximately 14 percent (74 percent-60 percent) (U.S. Bureau of the Census, 1969:15).

Moynihan's assertions become even less clear when we look at the distribution of persons below the poverty level ($3,553 for non-farm families in 1968) during the period from 1959-1968. While the proportion of both whites and Negroes below the poverty level decreased between 1959 and 1968, the decline was greater for whites than for Negroes. The number of whites below the poverty level dropped approximately 39 percent, compared with a 23 percent reduction in the number of Negroes. In 1968, one-tenth of the white population and approximately one-third of the Negro population was below the poverty level (U.S. Bureau of the Census, 1969:24). If anything, the gap has widened in terms of poverty incidence as a measure of economic progress.

The above data serve to illustrate the following at this point: Moynihan's conclusion regarding the closing of the economic gap between blacks and whites is a function of (1) the data he chose to report and (2) the method of analysis utilized in the reporting procedure. His treatment of the Negro's economic condition in a selective manner failed to reveal the regional differences necessary for an over-all assessment. The citation of economic gains for the northeast provides, at best, an incomplete assessment of the Negro economic condition as a nation-wide phenomenon. De-emphasis of the Southern black as a separate category of analysis resulted in a misrepresentation of the American Negro's total economic condition. The data reported on Negro income as a percent of white income underscored the amount of distortion that may be obtained through a procedure of this type. The failure to consider the gain in Negro family incomes above $8,000 relative to comparable increases for white families did not accurately reflect this gain as a general condition in the total population. The widening economic gap was not revealed and a misleading conclusion was reported.

As the data indicate, some statistics can be found which support a claim that the Negro has made economic progress. There is also a body of data which indicates that this is not true and that for a large proportion of the black population (especially the 52 percent in the South) the last ten years has been mainly a period of economic stagnation. Although a closer examination of regional differences casts some doubt on the generality of Moynihan's over-all assertion, the point about frustration raised at the outset is more directly addressed when we consider data not reported by Moynihan.

Following the Civil Rights Act in 1964, two books were written concerning the Negro's economic status up to that point. *Toward Equal Opportunity* by Duane Lockard (1968) claimed that despite the sweeping legislation of recent civil rights acts guaranteeing the Negro an equal place in the economic mainstream of America, the actual fulfillment of these promises has been agonizingly slow. Robert O. Blood, Jr. (1968) made the same claim through an examination of Lockard's general thesis in a particular locality—Minneapolis. The argument made in both of these books is that the economic condition of the Negro is not improved or significantly changed by simply passing legislative acts. Actual improvement is realized only in the concrete implementation of these programs. One need only consider the history of school desegregation since the 1954 Brown decision to realize the significance of this statement. Lockard (1968:6) emphasizes this point when he states that ". . . frustration varies directly with anticipation; the never-promised and unexpected gain is less likely to cause an outbreak than an often-promised but still denied right or opportunity."

The argument is not that Negroes with lower educational levels or at lower job levels than whites should make the same or more money than whites occupying higher positions. Rather the argument is that Negroes and whites at the same occupational and educational levels should make approximately the same amount of money for the work they are performing. If there has been a closing of the gap between blacks and whites, we should not expect to find blacks and whites at the same educational and occupational levels making significantly different money for the work they do. If, on the other hand, the type of income differentials reported by Lockard for 1959 still exist in 1968 then Moynihan's assertion that the Negro has made extraordinary economic progress is misleading.

Table 1-A displays the data reported by Lockard (1968:13) for 1959, and indicates that the earnings of whites and non-whites with identical education attainment are markedly different even when the non-whites can find employment. It can be seen that a white male with an eighth grade education earns more on the average than a Negro with some college education. When one considers non-white income as a percent of white income, a clear-cut pattern is present. An inverse relationship appears between non-white income as a percent of white income and educational level. The higher the educational level of the non-white, the less his income represents as a percent of the white income. Thus, in 1959 educational advancement for the non-white resulted in a greater discrepancy between his earning power and that of the white person at the same educational level. In view of these findings it is not surprising that the authors of *Black Rage* (Grier & Cobbs, 1968:113) made the statement that "in spite of the yammering of naive observers, education has never offered a significant solution to the Negro's dilemma in America."

Table 1*

A. Comparison of average earnings of whites and non-whites with equal educational attainment, 1959

Education	Average earnings		Non-white as % of white
	White	Non-White	
Elementary, 0-7 years	$ 4,440	$3,584	80.7
Elementary, 8 years	4,992	3,863	77.3
High School, 4 years	6,352	4,480	70.5
College, 1-3 years	7,647	4,769	62.3
College, 4 years or more	10,389	6,244	60.1

B. Comparison of whites and non-whites with equal educational attainment, 1968

Education	Average earnings		Non-white as % of white
	White	Non-white	
Elementary, 0-7 years	$ 4,349	$ 3,438	79
Elementary, 8-11 years	6,447	4,221	65
High School Graduate	9,843	6,155	62.5
College, 1-3 years	10,141	7,852	77
College Graduate	13,094	11,388	87

*Note: The author recognizes the slight difference in the category sub-headings between the 1959 and 1968 comparisons. It is felt that the data exhibit sufficient similarity to allow the type of comparison presented.

Source: 1959 Data (Lockard, 1968:74), 1968 Data (Survey Research Center, 1968).

Is Lockard's assertion regarding the differential earning power of blacks and whites at the same educational level valid for 1968? For approximately 90 percent of the black sample the answer is *yes.* The data in Table 1-B for 1968 (Survey Research Center, 1968) indicate clearly that at all educational levels whites consistently earn more money than blacks. One can also see that for an overwhelming majority of the blacks (approximately 90 percent of those represented in the total black population of the table) the trend reported for 1959 appears in more pronounced form in 1968. It is only when the black goes to college and graduates that the economic gap between black and white earning power begins to narrow. Even in the case of college grads, it should be noted that a 13 percent gap still remains in 1968. The optimism that may be gained from the data reported for the college and college grad educational levels should not obfuscate the fact that for the overwhelming majority of blacks in the United States, educational advancement through high school graduations has offered false hope for improvement of economic conditions relative to white earning power. At the lower educational levels, the economic gap between blacks and whites during the period 1959-1968 has widened; and for the black population represented at these levels, educational advancement has not resulted in comparative economic progress.

Lockard argued (1968:74) that the income differential observed for 1959 relative to education was partly due to the lack of black opportunity to enter the more remunerative occupations. Proportionately, one-half as many blacks as whites were employed in professional, technical, clerical and craft positions. The differential was larger for the classification of managers, officials, and proprietors, in which only one quarter as many blacks as whites were employed at this level. Conversely, he found that Negro employment was approximately twice as high as white employment at occupational levels such as service work, laborers, and household workers. Table 2 indicates that the situation described by Lockard for 1959 exists in almost identical form in 1968. With the exception of the job classification of clerical, sales, and kindred workers, there is a clearly discernible pattern of occupational location for blacks and whites. Blacks continued to be over-represented at the low paying occupational levels relative to their proportion of the labor force (approximately 11 percent) (Lockard, 1968:75).

Table 2
Percent white and non-white at different occupational levels, 1968

	Race	
Occupation	White	Non-white
Professional, technical, and kindred workers	18.4	8.7
Managers, officials, and proprietors (except farm)	16.2	4.6
Clerical, sales and kindred workers	12.9	9.1
Craftsmen, foremen, and kindred workers	21.7	9.6
Operatives and kindred	4.0	22.8
Service workers (including private household)	17.7	25.1

Source: (Survey Research Center, 1968).

The more disturbing argument presented by Lockard concerns the differential earning power of blacks and whites at the same occupational level. Lockard (1968:75) pointed out that when blacks and whites are at the same occupational level, the average income of the black is lower than that of the white. The data in Table 3 support his assertion, indicating clearly the gap between black and white earning power at the same occupational levels. It should be remembered that the data for this table come from those areas of the United States where fair employment practice laws are present (Lockard, 1968:73). It may well be that the differentials observed here would exist in more pronounced form in those parts of the United States where either fair employment practices do not exist or are present in form only (e.g., the South).

Table 3
Comparison of white and non-white incomes at
different occupational levels, 1959-1968

Occupation	Average Income—1959*		Average income—1968	
	White	Non-white	White	Non-White
Professional, technical, and kindred	$8,983	$6,198	$11,861	$9,920
Managers, officials, and proprietors (except farms)	9,916	5,532	12,779	9,899
Clerical, sales, and kindred workers	6,455	4,584	8,616	6,025
Craftsmen, foremen, and kindred workers	5,949	4,546	8,729	6,451
Operatives and kindred workers	5,115	4,175	4,907	4,508
Service workers, including private household	4,423	3,374	7,351	6,628

*Note: For comparative purposes the two categories—"clerical and kindred workers," and "sales workers"—originally contained in the 1959 data were combined to form the "clerical, sales, and kindred" category. The figure reported for this category in the 1959 comparison represents the mean of the incomes for the original categories.

Source: 1959 Data (Lockard, 1959:75), 1968 Data (Survey Research Center, 1968).

When Lockard's assertion is re-evaluated in 1968, the income differentials for whites and Negroes occupying the same occupational levels are still present. Table 3 shows that whites consistently earn more money than Negroes across all occupational categories. It is only in occupational categories such as operatives and service workers that the gap between black and white earning power is reduced to any degree. In the more remunerative occupational categories, an income differential of 20 to 30 percent between black and white earning power is evident. It is clear that occupational advancement for the black person is no guarantee that he will attain equal earning power with the white worker. Coupled with the data on education, the findings on occupation reinforce the conclusion reached by the Kerner Commission (National Advisory Commission, 1968:256):

Even given similar employment, Negro workers with the same education as white workers are paid less. This results to some extent to some training in segregated schools, and also from the fact that large numbers of Negroes are now entering certain occupations for the first time. However, the differentials are so large and so universal at all educational levels that they clearly reflect the practice of discrimination which characterizes hiring and promotion practices in many segments of the economy.

This conclusion strongly suggests the practice of "tokenism," in which the attempt is to employ one Negro per job category as a representative of his group. According to Blood (1968:21), the "employer's motive is to put up a good front to Negro and liberal white publics and to appease pressure groups." The Kerner Commission conclusion implies that white attitudes toward Negro economic advancement, rather than ability, explain the inequality between black and white earning power. Blood conducted a survey of Minneapolis-St. Paul managers to discern the attitudes of those in a position to hire blacks towards national fair employment practice legislation. He (Blood, 1968:122) found that 47 percent of those interviewed were against a national fair employment practice commission. An analysis of data from the 1968 presidential election conducted by the Survey Research Center at the University of Michigan focused on white attitudes towards a similar type of question. White respondents classified as managers, officials, and proprietors were selected on the assumption that these individuals were most likely to be responsible for hiring practices. The results obtained lend rather strong indirect support to the conclusion reached by the Kerner Commission. A majority (59.7 percent) of the whites expressed opposition towards national action to implement fair employment practices. Only 31.8 percent agreed with the statement that the federal government ". . . should see to it that Negroes get fair treatment in jobs." Conversely, 80 percent of the Negroes at the same occupational level expressed support for federal action. It is apparent that blacks and whites in this important occupational category differ sharply on the question posed by the survey. It can only be concluded that either the white respondents are ignorant of the indictment issued by the Kerner Commission on this point or aware of the conditions of discrimination and yet willing to condone their continuation. The implications of this type of attitude distribution for black economic advancement are clear. Gradual progress (relative to selected statistics) may suggest economic advancement for the Negro, as Moynihan asserts; but full equity appears as only a dim possibility in the near future.

CONCLUSION

As Lockard points out, frustration is a function of two related factors. The first is the perception that secured rights may be lost in the future.

The second is the perception that future advancement (be it economic, social, or political) is artificially limited by factors other than a man's ability or skill. This condition is the crux of the Kerner Commission's indictment of white America and forms the basis for the continuing frustration and alienation of the black man in America today. Moynihan's assertion of economic gains for certain selected sub-groups of the black population revealed a disturbing insensitivity to this fundamental aspect of the Negro condition. The fact that blacks occupying the same educational and occupational levels as whites earn less money for the work that they do is not negated by the mere recitation of selected census figures. The fact that the majority of the white managers expressed negative attitudes toward fair employment practice legislation is equally disturbing.

Fair employment practices may affect hiring practices, but they lack the authority to affect changes in question, of job promotion and salary advancement. Until the attitude distribution of the white managers approximates that of the blacks occupying these positions, such concepts as job ceilings and "tokenism" will remain a reality for Negroes seeking employment and job advancement. The problem is not addressed, much less resolved, by citation of optimistic statistics which provide a false sense of Negro progress. Progress will only result when the sense of black frustration is ameliorated through narrowing the gap between expectation and fulfillment.

REFERENCES

Blood, R. O., Jr. *Northern Breakthrough.* Belmont, Calif.: Wadsworth Publishing Company, 1968.

Bureau of the Census. "The Social and Economic Status of Negroes in the United States, 1969." Current Population Reports, Series P-23, No. 29, p. 17. Washington, D.C.: U.S. Government Printing Office, 1969.

Grier, William H., and Price M. Cobbs, *Black Rage.* New York: Bantam Books, 1968.

Harrington, M. *The Other America.* Baltimore, Md.: Penguin Books, 1962.

Lockard, D. *Toward Equal Opportunity.* New York: The Macmillan Company, 1968.

Moynihan, D. P. "Toward a National Urban Policy." The Public Interest, Fall 1969, pp. 8–9.

National Advisory Commission. *Report of the National Advisory Commission on Civil Disorders.* New York: Bantam Books, 1968.

Survey Research Center. 1968 Presidential Election Study. Michigan: University of Michigan, 1968. (SRC-S523). The average income was obtained by computing the group mean for each educational and occupational category. See: John E. Freund, *Modern Elementary Statistics,* (3rd ed.; Englewood Cliffs, N. J.: Prentice-Hall, Inc., 1967), p. 35. The South was eliminated from the data set to facilitate comparison with Lockard's.

32. A resurgence of ethnicity?

NATHAN GLAZER and DANIEL P. MOYNIHAN

The over-all ethnic pattern of New York City has not changed since 1960, though the proportions have. There are still six major, fairly well-defined groups. The most visible is the Negro, which is rapidly increasing its proportion of the city's population, and has risen from 14 per cent in 1960 to an estimated 20 per cent today. The second most visible and sharply defined group is the Puerto Rican, whose proportion within the city population has increased since 1960 from 8 to 11 per cent. Substantial numbers of Latin Americans—Cubans and others—have come into the city since 1960 and tend to be lumped in public identification with Puerto Ricans, though they resist this. The largest single ethnic group in the city is the Jewish. Our data on their numbers are very poor. We guess they are declining from the quarter of the city's population they have long formed, to more like a fifth, but they are still probably more numerous than the Negroes. The next largest white group is the Italian. The Italian-born and their children alone formed 11 per cent of the city's population in 1960, leaving out the entire third generation and beyond. Perhaps they form one-seventh of the city's population. The Irish are a steadily declining part of the city's population, owing to heavy movements to the suburbs (also true, but in lesser degree, of Jews and Italians). They form probably some 7 per cent of the city.[1]

White Anglo-Saxon Protestants form the sixth most important social segment of the city in ethnic terms. If Irish identity becomes questionable in the later generations, WASP identity is even less of a tangible and specific identity. It is a created identity, and largely forged in New York City in order to identify those who are not otherwise ethnically identified and who, while a small minority in the city, represent what is felt to be the "majority" for the rest of the country.

Even in New York they bear the prestige of representing the "majority," whatever that may be, and, more significantly, they dominate the large banks, the large insurance companies, the large corporations that make their headquarters in the city. Young people flock to the city to

Abridged and edited from Nathan Glazer and Daniel P. Moynihan, *Beyond the Melting Pot* (Cambridge: The M.I.T. Press, 1970, 2d edition), pp. xxxi–xli. Copyright © 1970 by The M.I.T. Press. Reprinted by permission.

The senior author is Professor of Education and Social Structure, Harvard University, Cambridge, Mass.

[1]The estimates of Negroes and Puerto Ricans in the city have some official standing; they are from the City Planning Commission. The others are based on sample surveys conducted for the 1969 election. These are rather contradictory, and we have simply made some educated guesses.

work in its communications industries, advertising agencies, in the corporate office buildings, and discover they have become WASPs. This odd term includes descendants of early Dutch settlers (there are still a few), of early English and Scottish settlers (there are still some of these, too), immigrants and descendants of immigrants to the city from Great Britain, and migrants to the city from parts of the country which have had substantial proportions of settlers of British, English-speaking background. Merged into this mix may be persons of German background who no longer feel ethnically identified as German-Americans. The Germans, who formed along with the Irish the dominant ethnic group of the late nineteenth and early twentieth century in the city, have not maintained, as a group, a prominence in the city proportionate to their numbers. (And yet in the 1960's the Steuben Day parade became a major event, at which the attendance of city officeholders was obligatory.)

Beyond the six major defined segments that are crucial to politics, to self-awareness, and also to the social description of the city, there are numerous others, but they tend to have a more local significance. In any given area, one must be aware of Poles, Russians, Greeks, Armenians, Chinese, Cubans, Norwegians, Swedes, Hungarians, Czechs, and so on, but even the largest of these groups forms no more than a few per cent of the city's population.

The Chinese community has grown, owing to the revision of the immigration laws in 1965, which eliminated the last references to race and national origin. The Cuban community is the largest new addition to the city's ethnic array. The over-all pattern, however, remains the familiar one of the early 1960's, with the trends then noted continuing: the growth of the Negro and Puerto Rican populations; the decline of the older ethnic groups, Irish and German; the continued significance of the two major groups of the "new immigration" of 1880 to 1924, the Jews and the Italians. This is the statistical pattern. Politically, economically, and culturally, however, two groups have outdistanced all others in the sixties: Jews and White Anglo-Saxon Protestants. The life of the city in the late sixties reflected nothing so much as an alliance between these groups, or parts of them, and the growing Negro group, against the remaining white, largely Catholic, groups. . . .

Have ethnic identity and the significance of ethnic identity declined in the city since the early 1960's? The long-expected and predicted decline of ethnicity, the fuller acculturation and the assimilation of the white ethnic groups, seems once again delayed—as it was by World War I, World War II, and the cold war—and by now one suspects, if something expected keeps on failing to happen, that there may be more reasons than accident that explain why ethnicity and ethnic identity continue to persist. In *Beyond the Melting Pot,* we suggested that ethnic groups, owing to their distinctive historical experiences, their cultures and skills, the times of their arrival and the economic situation they met, developed distinctive economic, political, and cultural patterns. As the old culture fell away—and it did rapidly enough—a new one, shaped by the distinctive experiences of life in America, was formed and a new identity was created. Italian-Americans might share precious little with Italians in Italy, but in America they were a distinctive group that maintained itself, was identifiable, and gave something to those who were identified with it, just as it also gave burdens that those in the group had to bear.

Beyond the accidents of history, one suspects, is the reality that human groups endure, that they provide some satisfaction to their members, and that the adoption of a totally new ethnic identity, by dropping whatever one is to become simply American, is inhibited by strong elements in the social structure of the United States. It is inhibited by a subtle system of identifying, which ranges from brutal discrimination and prejudice to merely naming. It is inhibited by the unavailability of a simple "American" identity. One is a New Englander, or a Southerner, or a Midwesterner, and all these things mean something too concrete for the ethnic to adopt completely, while excluding his ethnic identity.

In any case, whatever the underlying fault lines in American society that seem to maintain or permit the maintenance of ethnic identity beyond the point of cultural assimilation, the fact is ethnic identity continued in the sixties.

We have precious few studies of ethnic identity, despite the increasing prominence of its role in the mass media in recent years, and we speak consequently quite hypothetically. Yet we would like to suggest three hypotheses on the changing position of ethnic identity in recent years.

First: ethnic identities have taken over some of the task in self-definition and in definition by others that occupational identities, particularly working-class occupational identities, have generally played. The status of the worker has been downgraded; as a result, apparently, the status of being an ethnic, a member of an ethnic group, has been upgraded.

There is no question that many occupational identities have lost a good deal of their merit and virtue, not to say glamour, in the eyes of those who hold them, and in the eyes of those in positions of significance in communications and the mass media who do so much to dispense ideas of merit, virtue, and glamour. The unions, the organizations of the working class, have certainly lost much of their glamour. What young bright man coming out of college would think that the most attractive, personally satisfying, and useful job he could hold would be to work for a union, as the authors did in 1944? Indeed, the intelligentsia has been quietly departing from unions and moving into government and the universities for ten years and more. But more significant has been the downgrading of working-class occupations. In the depression, in World War II, even after the war, the worker held an honored and important position. Radicals fought over his allegiance, the Democratic party was happy in his support, one could even see workers portrayed in the movies by men such as Humphrey Bogart, John Garfield, Clark Gable, and these heroes portrayed occupations, whether as truck drivers or oilfield workers or even produce marketmen, that had some reputation and value.

Similarly, to be a homeowner after the war, and many workers became homeowners, was meritorious. It indicated rise in status, setting down roots, becoming a part of the community. Today, if one were to test associations to the word "worker" and "homeowner" among television newscasters and young college graduates, one is afraid one of the chief associations would be "racist" and "Wallaceite." It is hard to recall any movie of the late sixties, aside from *Pretty Poison,* in which a factory worker was a leading character, and in *Pretty Poison* the factory spewed chemical filth into the countryside, and the worker himself was half mad.[2]

Lower-middle-class statuses have also suffered, but the clerk or teacher or salesman never did do well in the mass media. The worker did; he formed part of that long-sustained and peculiar alliance that has always seemed to link those of higher status, in particular aristocrats and intellectuals, with lower-class people, leaving the middle classes in the middle to suffer the disdain of both. What has happened in recent years is that the lower pole of the alliance has shifted downward, leaving out the working class, and now hooking up the intellectuals and the upper-middle-class youth with the Negro lower class.

The Wallace movement and the Procaccino campaign [for Mayor of New York in 1969] were in part efforts to take political advantage of the declining sense of being valued in the working- and lower-middle class, and to ascribe to these groups a greater measure of credit and respect, as against both the more prosperous and better educated, who have supported measures designed to assist Negroes and the poor, and the Negroes and the poor themselves. If these class and occupational statuses have been downgraded, by that token alone ethnic identity seems somewhat more desirable. Today, it may be better to be an Italian than a worker. Twenty years ago, it was the other way around.

Thus, one reason we would suggest for the maintenance of ethnic identities is the fact that working-class identities and perhaps some other occupational identities have lost status and respect.

---

[2] See William Simon, John H. Gagnon, and Donald Carns, "Working-class youth: Alienation without an Image," *New Generation,* Spring 1969, 51:15–21.

Let us suggest a second hypothesis as to changes in ethnic identity in this decade: international events have declined as a source of feelings of ethnic identity, except for Jews; domestic events have become more important. The rise of Hitler and World War II led to an enormous rise in feelings of ethnic identification. Nor was there much decline after the war, as the descendants of East European immigrants who had been aroused by Hitler's conquests now saw their homelands become Russian satellites, and as other nations were threatened. But aside from Jews, no group now sees its homeland in danger. (Israel barely qualifies as a "homeland," but the emotional identification is the same.) Even the resurgence of conflict between Catholics and Protestants in Northern Ireland has evoked only a sluggish response among American Irish. By this very token, as involvement with and concern for the homelands decline, the sources of ethnic identification more and more are to be found in American experiences, on American soil. This is not to say that identification with homelands in danger or in conflict cannot rise again. But for the first time a wave of ethnic feeling in this country has been evoked not primarily by foreign affairs but by domestic developments. This is a striking and important development—it attests to the long-lived character of ethnic identification and raises the curtain somewhat on the future history of ethnic identity in this country.

A third hypothesis: along with occupation and homeland, religion has declined as a focus of ethnic identification. Just as ethnicity and occupation overlap, so do ethnicity and religion. For some time, it seemed as if new identities based on religion were taking over from ethnic identities. This was the hypothesis of Will Herberg.[3] The Jews remained Jews, with a subtle shift from an ethnic identification in the first and second generation to more of a religious identification in the third; the Irish became ever more Catholic in their self-image, and so did the Italians. Even the P in WASP stands for Protestant, as part of the identity. Only for Negroes did racial identity seem clearly far more significant than religion. In *Beyond the Melting Pot,* we argued that religion and race seemed to be taking over from ethnicity. Yet in the last few years, the role of religion as a primary identity for Americans has weakened. Particularly in the case of Catholics, confusion and uncertainty have entered what was only a few years ago a very firm and clear identity. Thus, for Irish and Italians alike, Catholicism once confirmed a basic conservatism; it was not only anti-Communist, obviously, but, more significantly, it took conservative positions on issues of family, sex, culture, education. Catholics formed the core of the Democratic party in New York, which, alongside its pronounced and decisive liberalism in social policy,

---

[3]Will Herberg, *Protestant, Catholic, Jew* (Garden City, N.Y.: Doubleday & Company, 1955).

remained conservative on issues of family and culture. The revolution in the Catholic Church has shaken this monolithic institution, and the identity of Catholic is no longer self-evident, to those holding it or to those outside the Church. The change is symbolized by the radical changes in ritual, in this most conservative of institutions, and in the possibility of changes in such ancient patterns as the celibacy of the clergy.

For the purposes of race relations, the most striking development is the divergence between clergy and laity (some clergy and some laity) on the issue of Negro militancy. When priests marched with Martin Luther King in Chicago, it was reported that Catholic workers who opposed the move of Negroes into their neighborhoods said, "Now even they are with them, and we are alone." Nothing as striking as this has happened in New York, where the laity are not as conservative as in Chicago (with its strong Polish and Lithuanian representation), and where the priests have not come up with a prominent radical leader. But if there is no equivalent of Father Groppi in New York, there are many smaller versions of Father Groppi. Catholicism no longer confirms as fully as it did some years ago the conservative tendencies of Italians and Irish.

We have suggested three aspects of the current prominence of ethnicity: that it is related to the declining merit of certain occupational identifications, that it increasingly finds its sources in domestic rather than foreign crises, and that the revolution in the Catholic Church means that, for the first time, it does not complement the conservative tendencies of Catholic ethnic groups. Now we come to a fourth aspect. In a word, is the resurgence of ethnicity simply a matter of the resurgence of racism, as is now often asserted? Is the reaction of whites, of ethnic groups and the working and middle class, to the increasingly militant demands of Negroes a matter of defense of ethnic and occupational turfs and privileges or is it a matter of racial antipathy, and more of racism, that large and ill-used term, which means, if it means anything, that those afflicted with it see the world primarily in racial categories, in black and white, and insist that black should be down and white up?

In the fifties, Herberg argued that religion was rising, not because of any interest really in its doctrines, but because religion was a more respectable way of maintaining ethnic primary groups than ethnicity itself. To be Italian or Jewish (ethnic rather than religious) was somehow not reputable and raised the issue of conflict with the demands of American citizenship, a potential conflict that became particularly sharp in World War II and that has remained alive for American Jews since the establishment of the State of Israel. Now, it is argued, religion, owing to the liberalism of the clergy, cannot serve to keep the Negroes out—of neighborhoods, schools, jobs. But ethnicity can still serve that function. So, by emphasizing ethnicity and ethnic attachment, the argument goes, one can cover one's racism and yet be racist.

Thus, it may be argued, just as religion in the 1950's covered for ethnicity, ethnicity in the 1960's covers for racism. The issue remains simply one of white against black, and to speak of Jews, Italians, Irish, is merely to obfuscate it. We disagree with this point of view and argue that ethnicity is a real and felt basis of political and social action.

. . . . .

. . . much of the answer to the question we have posed—ethnicity or racism?—is a matter of definition and self-definition, and much of the future of race relations in the city and the country depends on what designations and definitions we use. For just as a "nigger" can be made by treating him like a "nigger" and calling him a "nigger," just as a black can be made by educating him to a new, proud, black image— and this education is carried on in words and images, as well as in deeds —so can racists be made, by calling them racists and treating them like racists. And we have to ask ourselves, as we react to the myriad cases of group conflict in the city, what words shall we use, what images shall we present, with what effect? If a group of housewives insists that it does not want its children bussed to black schools because it fears for the safety of its children, or it does not want blacks bussed in because it fears for the academic quality of the schools, do we denounce this as "racism" or do we recognize that these fears have a base in reality and deal seriously with the issues? When a union insists that it has nothing against blacks but it must protect its jobs for its members and their children, do we deal with those fears directly, or do we denounce them as racists? When a neighborhood insists that it wants to maintain its character and its institutions, do we take this seriously or do we cry racism again?

We believe the conflicts we deal with in the city involve a mixture of *interests:* the defense of specific occupations, jobs, income, property; of *ethnicity:* the attachment to a specific group and its patterns; and of *racism:* the American (though not only American) dislike and fear of the racial other, in America's case in particular compounded by the heritage of slavery and the forcible placing of Negroes into a less than human position. We believe we must deal with all these sources of conflict, but to ignore the ethnic source, or the interest source, in an exclusive fixation on the racist source, will undoubtedly encourage the final tearing apart of the community and the country between groups that see each other as different species rather than as valued variants of a common humanity.

. . . . .

33. Risorgimento: The red, white and greening of New York

NICHOLAS PILEGGI

No one can be certain just when the Italian-American revolution began. It could have been September 21, 1969, when Mario Puzo's *Godfather* nudged *Portnoy* off the top of the *Times'* bestseller list; or maybe June 29, 1970, when a real godfather, in the name of unity, gathered 50,000 people around him at Columbus Circle. Perhaps it was last July, in time for the 1970 ethnic vote, when Attorney General John Mitchell ordered FBI agents to stop using the words "Mafia" and "Cosa Nostra" in their press releases; or maybe it will not begin until June 28 [1971] and the second Columbus Circle Unity Day rally, at which police expect a crowd of at least 150,000.

Whatever uncertainty there may be over the exact day, there is no uncertainty over the fact that sometime within the last two years New York's Italians, after 75 years of benign residence in their own neighborhoods, have become restive. In the suburbs, while conservative, vowel-voting Italians have begun to take over the political apparatus of Nassau, Suffolk and Westchester counties, their children have been reading *The Greening of America,* just like the rest of their college friends, and have brought the middle-class Italian family its first taste of pot and filial estrangement. Those heartwarming stories in the *New York Times* about Tony the elevator operator who was given an "honorary doctor of transportation" degree upon retiring from Baruch College, are not sitting so well with the current generation as they did with the last.

In the city, meanwhile, where prominent judges, ex-congressmen and daybed manufacturers have traditionally watched over working-class immigrants and their heirs like benevolent Sicilian landowners, a 47-year-old Brooklyn-born real-estate salesman, identified by the FBI as a Mafia boss, has suddenly taken over. In New York today, it is Joseph Colombo of the Italian-American Civil Rights League—not Surrogate S. Samuel DiFalco, ex-Congressman Alfred E. Santangelo or sofa-king Bernard Castro—who is appearing on the *Dick Cavett Show.* It is Colombo who is being taken seriously by the *New York Times,* being interviewed by Walter Cronkite, discussed at the Leonard Bernsteins'. And it is Colombo's son who now meets with officials at City Hall while the sons of the *prominenti* cool their heels.

Abridged and edited from Nicholas Pileggi, "Risorgimento: The red, white, and greening of New York," *New York Magazine,* June 7, 1971. Copyright © 1971 by the NYM Corporation. Reprinted by permission of Curtis Brown, Ltd.

Like most of the city's Jewish leaders who have been embarrassed by Meir Kahane's street-brawling Jews, Italian leaders, too, have begun to feel threatened by their own roots. All those rowdy truck drivers, embittered cabbies and boisterous construction workers, abandoned by the middle class in Throgs Neck and Canarsie less than a generation ago, have suddenly and noisily arisen. Beckoned by Colombo and his Civil Rights League, working-class Italians have come out of their tenement apartments and backyards in unprecedented numbers to shout "Italian Power" in front of FBI headquarters and march past Bonwit's to Saint Patrick's wearing KISS ME I'M ITALIAN buttons. Recently, when Colombo's league publicly formed an alliance with Kahane's JDL, the *Times* editorial writers and most of the city's ethnic establishment were shocked. They shouldn't have been. Colombo and Kahane had been sharing picket lines, membership and one attorney, Barry Slotnick, for months. Their followers had signed each other up during lunch breaks in the garment factories where they work. They had shared neighborhood candy stores and the elevated stops of Borough Park and Bensonhurst with each other for generations. They had played stoop-ball, three-man basketball and Dyker Park hardball together as kids. Today, they drive for the same cab companies, pay off the same loans to First National City and bet with the same neighborhood bookmakers, who are always Italians or Jews.

The alliance between Kahane's Jews and Colombo's Italians was the result of more than ethnic ego-building. Both men have, perhaps unwittingly, stepped into a leadership vacuum that has long existed among New York's low-income white working classes. They are providing a vehicle of outrage for all those borough-bound neighborhood people, most of whose kids are not getting draft deferments by going to college, whose already low incomes (63.2 per cent of all white ethnic families in New York earn less than $9,400) are being shrunk even further by inflation and who have grown bitterly resentful of even the token assistance doled out to black and Puerto Rican communities to deal with many of the same problems.

In spite of their dubious backgrounds, Colombo and Kahane speak to the two-job sons of immigrants who must compete with blacks and Puerto Ricans for that bottom third of the city's job market, the 1.3 million New York jobs that pay less than $100 a week. It is their children who battle with black and Puerto Rican youngsters for school playgrounds and Coney Island beaches. While Kahane's young men are fighting blacks for lunchroom space at Brooklyn College, Colombo's Italian families are reporting the highest white drug addiction rate in the city and, next to the Puerto Ricans, the highest dropout rate in the city's school system. It is in Italian neighborhoods, despite the anti-welfare ballyhoo of their own representatives, that welfare cases have increased by 16 per cent in the last two years, as compared with a 10 per cent rise in predominantly black and Puerto Rican neighborhoods. And it is in Italian neighborhoods, too, that old-age benefits have jumped 87.3 per cent in the last two years because the heads of families, no matter what old-world traditions dictate, can no longer afford to support their own parents.

While New York's Little Italys have helped make the urban scene more livable for the occasional visitor, it is their permanent occupants who have had to pay the price. And it is in precisely these neighborhoods, from Bensonhurst, Canarsie, Coney Island, Sheepshead Bay, Ridgewood, Elmont, Corona, Wakefield, Williamsbridge, Soundview, Fordham, Greenwich Village, East Harlem and the increasingly troubled working-class surburban ghettos of Nassau and Westchester, that Joe Colombo's chartered buses are being filled. When the congregation of Fifth Avenue's Temple Emanu-el snubbed Kahane and Fortune Pope barred Colombo from the Columbus Day parade, and the *Times'* editorial writer found their alliance "unlikely," "unsavory" and "a matter of public revulsion," New York's establishment had failed to see the greater significance of their appeal.

Politicians claim they first felt the rumblings of Italian discontent back in the late 1960s when Vito Battista initiated his taxpayer's revolt among small homeowners. When John Marchi beat John Lindsay for the Republican Party mayoral nomination in the spring of 1969, it was apparent to some that great numbers of traditionally Democratic Italians were, most uncharacteristically, registering Republican. When Marchi and Mario Procaccino, even in defeat, showed they could poll 58 per cent of the city's vote, almost all the city's politicians began watching the returns from Italian election districts. And, after Arthur Goldberg's resounding defeat last November, it was apparent that no candidate could again disregard the Italian vote with impunity. In that election, though neither party listed an Italian on the ticket, Rockefeller romanced Italians just as assiduously as Goldberg avoided them. Rockefeller ate pizza, attended street fairs and organized the "Columbia Coalition," which listed as his supporters almost every prominent Italian-American politician in the state. Goldberg, meanwhile, not only avoided Italian neighborhoods, but, supported by three Jewish running mates and innumerable Jewish organizations, publicly scolded one of his few Italian audiences for demanding that he stoop to ethnic politics.

The district-by-district analysis of the vote after Goldberg's defeat stunned political experts. They found, for instance, that Italians rarely moved. They found that long after the city's Irish and Jewish neighborhoods had been abandoned, Italians were still living in large numbers in the same borough-wide communities they had occupied in the 1920s. They read polls that showed that 40 per cent of Italians continued to live in the same neighborhoods as their parents, compared with 14 per cent of the Jews and 17 per cent of the Irish. Italian-Americans, now well into their third and fourth generations, were approaching 20 per cent of the city's population while there had been a noticeable decline in the populations of other white ethnic groups. There were, for instance, as many Italians in the northeast Bronx as there were blacks in Harlem, but somehow they had gone unseen by the media and unacknowledged by liberal politicians. Italian-American children were now almost 18 per cent of the city's public-school population, 25 per cent of the current freshman class at City University and more than half of the Fordham student body. They found that it was the Brooklyn piers, controlled by Italian locals, that now dominated the New York waterfront, not the traditionally Irish longshoremen's locals of the moribund West Side docks. The predominantly Irish New York Archdiocese found that Italian-Americans were now the majority of their parishioners and their children made up the bulk of parochial school students. Italian-American lobbyists, after years of watching Irishmen and Jews roam through the corridors of the statehouse in Albany, began demanding state aid to parochial schools and coaxing construction contracts for their own builders. Italian-Americans were not only the largest nationality bloc in the state, but as a result of the last election, now accounted for 40 per cent of the Albany legislators.

The political effect of all this has been immediate. Within a month of Goldberg's defeat, and after four years of bitter wrangling, the city suddenly reversed its condemnation proceedings against 69 Corona homes owned by Italian-Americans and decided to move them, shingle, stucco and stone, to what had previously been considered municipally sanctified Parks Department land. After two years and 180 attempts, the Congress of Italian-American Organizations, one of the city's only social-action Italian coalitions, received city approval to sponsor day-care centers and after-school and senior-citizen programs in predominantly low-income Italian neighborhoods. For the first time in CIAO's five years, Mayor John Lindsay attended its annual dinner-dance in Brooklyn. When introduced by its president, Mary Sansone, who like many of the 500 attending the dinner had supported Procaccino in the last campaign, Lindsay was surprised to hear himself being cheered.

. . . . .

Despite all the political scurrying and scholarship, however, it is still Joseph Colombo's Civil Rights League that has been most responsible for focusing attention on New York's Italians. Led by an extremely vulnerable Italian, the League has succeeded in attracting the media where other Italian organizations have failed. The League has filled Madison Square Garden, raised close to $2 million, opened chapters around the country, enrolled 50,000 members and pinned everyone from Nelson Rockefeller to William Kunstler as honorary members. The size of the League's rally in Columbus Circle last year was so impressive that the city has been forced to give the League permission to use the area again this year, despite the fact that environmentalists within the administration had earlier been turned down for the site because their plans were considered too disruptive. The League's success in silencing the FBI has spread to other kinds of Mafia-watching. It got "Mafia" and "Cosa Nostra" deleted from the *Godfather* script, but the real victory was forcing Paramount to agree to this demand on the front page of the *New York Times*. Since then, the League has also dealt with what it considers gratuitous slights and insults in television commercials. It has threatened to boycott Alka-Seltzer because of its "Datsa soma spicy meatball" commercial; a canned tomato sauce for which Enzo Stuarti intones "Datsa nice," and Ford automobiles because they sponsor *The FBI* TV series. As a result of the League's actions most magazines and newspapers stopped using the terms "Mafia" and "Cosa Nostra" immediately, and even the *New York Times,* after several bitter internal policy battles, began covering organized crime with greater restraint than it had during the booming Valachi years. In fact, Nicholas Gage, hired to replace retiring Charles Grutzner as the newspaper's Mafia expert, has not found the same kind of editorial enthusiasm for Mafia stories as his predecessor did.

In private, officials of the League admit that they have been astonished by their own success. Most of them believe the cachet of Mafia power attached to the man who leads them has lent the organization credibility among the neighborhood rank and file. They have been more astounded to see that his mob credentials carry some weight with the establishment too. The publisher of the *Daily News*, for instance, apparently conditioned by his own paper's rhetoric, became extremely agitated recently when he received a form letter from the League asking the paper to cease publication on June 28 in honor of Italian-American Unity Day. Rather than dispose of the request with a polite but perfunctory reply, the nervous publisher passed the letter on to his managing editor and the managing editor raced with it to the city desk and the city desk discussed it, photographed it and ran it through a copying machine. Finally, William Federici, a *News* crime expert, was ordered to devote a day to calling his contacts in the League and pacifying them in advance.

On other occasions, however, the League has taken matters into its own hands. During preparations for last year's Columbus Circle rally, for instance, the city was confused as to whether the Department of Water Supply, Cultural Affairs, Parks or the mayor's office had the authority to order the monument's fountain turned off to make way for the stage. When the city did not move quickly enough to suit the League, unidentified plumbers, armed with blueprints of their own, turned off all the proper nozzles and valves themselves. "Sure we were impressed," one city official said. "Most of our own guys wouldn't know how to turn that thing off."

This year, city officials are even more concerned. At the end of a series of meetings between the Department of Parks and officials of the League about the use of the southwest corner of Central Park, a Colombo representative said:

"Oh, by the way, could we chop down those three trees near the wall? They block the view of the stage."

"What!" the Parks representative screamed. "Those trees are 80-year-old maples. They're landmarks."

"That's okay," the League representative winked. "We could send somebody over late at night. Nobody would know."

. . . . .

Italian-Americans have always been a puzzle to outsiders. Even State Senator John Marchi, who has often emphasized his northern Italian ancestry, is confused by them. It is clear to Marchi, as it is to many other Italian-Americans, that Joe Colombo is essentially repeating in twentieth-century New York what the Honored Society has been pulling in Sicily since the seventeenth century. Colombo has managed to convince thousands of honest men and women that whoever defames the Honored Society also defames them. Marchi has very clearly pointed to the hole in Joe Colombo's boat, but he has offered nothing to the men and women on board by way of alternatives. Obviously Colombo and Kahane speak for a segment of the city's working population that has never felt comfortable with Marchi's Florentine style, or the kind of social activism represented by B'nai B'rith's princely Jews or John W. Gardner's most *un*Common Cause. It is Colombo's League, no matter how disreputable its leader, that has activated New York's traditionally disenfranchised working-class Italians.

Patrick Moynihan and Nathan Glazer, in their second edition of *Beyond the Melting Pot,* were only the latest in a series of social scientists who have wondered why Italians have failed to make a larger impact on the city. Since the 1960 census, Italians have been the largest ethnic group in the city next to the Jews, yet they have remained almost leaderless. There is no large or powerful upper-class Italian group or professional middle class that has taken on leadership in education, the media, politics or even the church. There was, for instance, only one Italian name among the 100 prominent businessmen organized last February by Loew's Corporation President Robert Tisch to help deal with municipal problems. (He was Joseph Grotto, a nearly anonymous real estate executive with Brown, Harris, Stevens.) Lindsay aides, who have been on an Italian-American talent hunt since the Goldberg defeat, have reported that most of their first choices want no part of the round-the-clock City Hall routine Lindsay people seem to enjoy. "Look around your own office," one of the Italians they approached explained in rejecting an offer. "Most of you are divorced or splitting up, your kids never see you and your parents read about you in the papers. That's no life for a family man."

Sociologists have repeatedly laid the blame for Italians' being of less social, economic and political importance than their numbers would indicate to their overly developed sense of family. Theirs is a cultural style that has preserved the life of the old-world village but also prevented Italian-Americans from thrusting themselves into municipal and national prominence. This social backwardness is so basic a characteristic that today, while almost one-quarter of the freshman class at City University is Italian, neither the chancellor, deputy-chancellor, four vice-chancellors, four university deans, nor any of the 20 college presidents is Italian. In fact, only 14 out of 165 of the university deans, and less than 6 per cent of the city's college-level teachers, are Italian. Of the 90 high school principals in the city's system, only one is Italian, and he is on leave, and less than 10 per cent of the city's 60,000 schoolteachers are of Italian ancestry.

"For most Italian-Americans it's a big thing to get elected to some office, like the State Legislature," said former Assembly Speaker Joseph Carlino. "A young, attractive Italian-American thinks he's reached the millenium when he becomes an assemblyman. And what does he want next? What does he dream of ? A judgeship!

"Why don't they seek higher office?" he said. "Well, first of all it's a hard thing for an assemblyman to get to higher office. It's difficult to get money from Italians. I guess it comes from their working hard to get where they got. But they don't give to the average campaign, just as they don't give to charities. Italians save everything. They work at home. Become conservative. They are the ideal suburbanites."

In addition, 90 per cent of New York's Italian-Americans are descended from the impoverished Italian provinces of Calabria, Apulia and Sicily, and many are burdened with a deadly regional Italian fatalism. They are the heirs of Italians who have been convinced, by hundreds of years of unrelieved woe, that nothing good is ever going to happen. Mothers prepare their daughters for the worst, fathers advise their sons against aiming too high, and proverbs always tell of the unhappiness that awaits the overly ambitious. For those who have not escaped the tenements the dour parents often proved right.

There is just no way to deal with Italian-Americans in New York without also dealing with the phenomenon of organized crime, the Mafia, Camorra, Unione Siciliana, mob or whatever one wants to call it. Although it has been inflated and promoted by the press and law-enforcement agencies beyond reason as far as its national influence, profits and wiles are concerned, it still has extraordinary power in the city's ghetto Italian communities and in some of the commercial areas in which Italians work. It cannot be discounted. In working-class Italian communities, it is probably the single most important form of local government. Dr. Irving Spergel, currently a professor at the University of Chicago, has spent years detailing and attempting to classify certain delinquent groups in New York. In a number of his books he has characterized Italian neighborhoods as "racket subcultures," identifying them as:

"Any community in which there exists lots of money and in which rackets are rife and an inherent part of the family structure. A neighborhood in which a dozen stores are converted into social clubs or meeting places for bookmakers, policymen and loan sharks. A neighborhood in which racketeers and the rackets are considered a local way of life. A neighborhood in which candy stores and luncheonettes have little equipment, almost no supplies and, except for male adults hanging around, no business whatever . . .

"In an area where the racket subculture predominates, delinquent groups tend to be organized as an outgrowth of juvenile play groups. Members have known each other for many years. Their families have lived in the same neighborhood and even on the same block for one or more generations; the youngsters have gone to school together and attend the same church. Brothers and cousins may be members of the same group, and its ethnic composition tends to be homogeneous."

Italians came to their homogenous tenement communities in the greatest numbers between 1890 and 1920, and they immediately set about recreating in New York's slums the same densely packed, overwhelmingly insular southern Italian towns and villages they had just escaped. They brought with them their own kinds of food, the apparatus to make their own wines and a form of southern Italian Catholicism much too superstitious and saint-burdened to be tolerated by the Irish Catholics of that day. The southern Italian also brought a healthy skepticism for any form of government. On the early Calabrian and Sicilian immigrants, the Italian government had practiced a form of regional genocide not much different from the kind it practices today. But southern Italian émigrés today can at least be assured passports. At the turn of the century, millions of southerners immigrated to the U.S. bearing a slip of paper with the name of the *padrone* or work foreman to whom they had been assigned and through whom they would be indentured to railroad gangs and factories. It was on these slips of paper that immigration officials rubber-stamped "W O P" (With Out Passport) for Calabrians and Sicilians.

The distrust of southern Italians for the Italian government had affected every aspect of their lives, and when they arrived in a strange land they brought their suspicions with them. They remained in their own enclaves, hiding from the alien society that surrounded them, very much as their ancestors had hidden from Saracens, Bourbons, Visigoths and Greeks. They moved into specific tenement buildings and onto certain blocks already filled with relatives and friends from not only their own provinces, but from their own villages and towns. In these extraordinarily insular communities Italians adhered to their own rules. They lived according to their own standards and old-world habits, resisting public housing, overhead expressways, indoor pushcart markets, compulsory education, the English language and American food. Differences were adjudicated by their own judges, not by strange men who mistook Anglo-Saxon law for justice. It was these men, these elderly gentlemen of respect, who sipped black coffee in the social clubs of New York's Italian ghettos and watched over their streets like vengeful shepherds, from whom advice was, and very often still is, sought.

It was the local Mafia boss who was the most savvy man on the block in matters of marginal morality. It was through him that payoffs to policemen were arranged by the newly arrived resident who wished to make wine in his basement, play cards on the street in front of his tenement or live with his family in the rear of his tiny shoe repair shop. It was to these local Mafia bosses that the fathers of compromised girls went for marriage or revenge, where the insulted were mollified and business contracts were sworn to or dissolved. The local priest might advise, but the local Don could *order*.

Francis A. J. Ianni, of Columbia University's Teachers College, recently wrote of these men in *The Public Interest*:

"The base of Mafia power is the personal relationship, for the Mafioso reduces every social relationship to a personal level, a level in which he can feel and perform in a manner superior to that of other men. The Mafioso operates as a middle man in a vacuum of political values, structures and organizations. He is a broker—although not always an honest one—who operates as a network builder and monitor between and among elements in an unstable system."

It has not been for the residents of Italian communities alone that these men have administered local affairs. The city of New York itself has repeatedly reached out to them for assistance with particularly sticky problems involving Italian-Americans. The police, during the Wagner administration, went to the old men and asked them to keep Mulberry Street youngsters from assaulting demonstrators who were picketing an official building that happened to be in Little Italy.

"After three nights of rioting and the pleas of priests, teachers and parents, we went to a couple of the clubs and explained that the whole thing was bad for business," one high police official recalled. "The next night there wasn't an Italian kid to be seen."

In the Lindsay administration, former Relocation Commissioner Frank Arricale managed to defuse a potentially disastrous confrontation between black and Italian youngsters that started over the integration of a predominantly white high school in Brooklyn. Hundreds of police had been assigned to the area for days, thousands of youngsters roamed the streets brawling, looting and burning whatever they considered enemy territory. In a final effort to end the madness, Arricale contacted the Gallo brothers, through their attorney, and made arrangements for them to get through police lines and, hopefully, to convince the young Italian-American toughs to go home. Larry Gallo, who with his brothers was involved in a widely publicized gangland war at the time, arrived at the intersection that had served as headquarters for the Italian-American gangs in a black Riviera. To youngsters and policemen alike, he was a genuine celebrity. Only the mayor's arrival the day before had aroused equal excitement. Gallo approached the young men he knew had influence with the white gangs and told them to go home. To stop.

"But the niggers are . . . " one young white began, and suddenly, Gallo smashed his fist into the youngster's face, sending him to the ground. The disturbances ended that night.

For their services to the communities in which they live, the gentlemen of respect have always exacted some kind of tribute—from a few dollars handed an elder for adjudicating a business matter to a whole community's conspiracy of silence to guard him and his friends from prying strangers and hostile cops. The Mafioso has always been, if not welcome, at least at home, in New York's Little Italys and he has been far more at home in the U.S. than he ever was in the impoverished villages he came from. He is, in a sense, ideally suited to New York's eat-thy-neighbor business morality. He has become the perfect conduit for the kinds of vice America's law-abiding citizens insist upon enjoying. His success in New York today, after all, depends not only on the reliability of his bread-and-butter services (sports betting and usury), but upon the loyalty of his satisfied non-Italian customers. He has filled the gap between the letter and the spirit of unrealistic, unenforceable and unpopular laws, and to consider him an aberration, rather than a reflection of America today, is like blaming congenital obesity on an ice-cream manufacturer. Neighborhood Italian-Americans have understood this viscerally for many years; therefore when Joseph Colombo went out to picket the FBI in 1970, the day his son was seized, they were not surprised at a Mafia boss' expressing moral outrage, but at the fact that he had come from behind the traditional cloak of secrecy and had stepped before the public and the press for the first time.

Andrew Greeley, the sociologist, has cited six major steps in the American acculturation process. They include the first cultural shock of a new group, when survival is really the only practical issue. This is followed by the beginnings of organization and an emerging self-consciousness. The newly arrived become semi-skilled workers, develop key community figures and grow unmistakably American while preserving old-world customs and traits. The third process Greeley calls the assimilation of the elite—those who have reached the middle class and shun their ethnic past. Militancy follows when the group is fully middle class, has its own sources of power and becomes excessively patriotic. This is the time, Greeley pointed out, when Irish Catholic Fordham men began investigating the loyalty of Wasps at Harvard. When a group develops a substantial economic upper middle class, however, that Yankee Doodle militancy dissolves and young professionals, economically integrated into the rest of American society, deplore the narrow provincialism of the past. It is at this point that the most devastating criticism is aimed at every aspect of an ethnic tradition and every institution that strives to keep the old-world culture alive. This period of self-hatred, Greeley says, is followed by an emerging adjustment.

The Italian-Americans in New York today, using Greeley's scale, are spread in disproportionate numbers across the third, fourth and fifth stages of acculturation. Their paranoid elite has been partially assimiliated, their emerging middle class has decorated its automobiles with American and Italian flag decals, and the sons of the middle class grow increasingly resistant to that kind of ethnic aggression.

"It is not a static situation," the former Lindsay commissioner, Frank Arricale, explained. "Italian-Americans right now are almost our last hope for making New York a truly pluralistic community. Their numbers are large enough to make a discernible impact. Their defense agencies, like the League, have shown them that they can be Italian and still American, psychologically. The reform movement, which destroyed the neighborhood clubs, the only real avenue Italians had to enter politics, must now provide an alternative without trauma.

"Otherwise," said Arricale, "Italian-Americans could be seduced into what is already discernible as a neo-fascist, black-shirt, law-and-order puritanism."

. . . . .

34. Women as a minority group

ELIZABETH DUNCAN KOONTZ

. . . . .

The title "Women as a Minority Group" immediately raises the question, "Are women a minority group?" Many people think not.

Numerically, women are not in the minority; they comprise 51 per cent of the population.

Abridged and edited from Elizabeth Duncan Koontz, "Women as a minority group," in Mary Lou Thompson (ed.), *Voices of the New Feminism* (Boston: Beacon Press, 1970), pp. 77–86. Copyright © Elizabeth Duncan Koontz. Reprinted by permission.

The author is Director, Women's Bureau, U.S. Department of Labor, Washington, D.C.

As potential voters they outnumber men. In 1968, there were 62,071,000 women of voting age in the population as against 54,464,000 men. And, had women voted as a bloc in that year, they could have controlled the election, since those who voted outnumbered men by 2,938,000.

They also make up 51 per cent of individual shareholders owning stocks. However, this figure loses some of its significance when you consider that these holdings are usually managed by men. Consider also the volume of holdings of mutual funds, corporations, husband and wife joint accounts, and other owners of stock. Women account for only 18 per cent of the total ownership of stock.

The fact of the matter is that while women are not, in the overall picture, a minority group, they do constitute a minority in some facets of our society—in the work force, in labor unions, in the professions, and in public office.

And, of course, they are in many instances treated like a minority group. For example, women are not always equal with men before the law. In seven of the eight community property states in 1969 community property was generally under the control of the husband; in five states a married woman's freedom to venture into separate business is limited; and in nearly all states a wife does not have the same rights as her husband to establish a separate domicile.

The very fact that there is a debate as to whether or not women are equal under the Constitution implies minority status. One school of thought has held that women are guaranteed equality under the law in the Fifth and Fourteenth Amendments. The Supreme Court has thus far not dealt with any cases which raise this point.

Many feel that in order to adequately protect women we must have an Equal Rights Amendment to the Constitution. This proposed amendment states: "Equality of rights under the law shall not be denied or abridged by the United States or by any State on account of sex." As of March 11, 1970, it had been sponsored by 225 members of the House and 75 Senators, but for years has been held up in the Judiciary Committees of the House and Senate.

Education is another area in which women encounter discrimination. Not only are they discouraged from considering careers in fields generally considered "men's work," they are actually denied equal access to education. A few cases make the headlines, but I suspect those are only the top of the iceberg and the great bulk of injustice lies below the surface.

In one case a thirteen-year-old Brooklyn girl had to threaten court action to get into all-male Stuyvesant High School where she could get the kind of scientific education to fulfill the promise of a brilliant record.

The further such a brilliant girl goes up the academic ladder, the more difficult it may become for her. An example may illustrate what I mean.

Not long ago I read that one department of a large midwest university had awarded fellowships over the years at a rate of 513 for men, 121 for women. It was the department of sociology, a field usually thought to be as open to women as to men.

Graduate schools, too, tend to give preference to male applicants. According to the United States Office of Education, women do well on entrance examinations in law and medicine, but their admission into those graduate schools is held down. Indeed, the percentage of women graduates in some fields is so constant over the years—7 per cent for women physicians, for example—that one suspects the existence of a quota system.

And once a woman has been through graduate school, how does she fare if she seeks a teaching career? A couple of examples suggest the answer. In that sociology department I mentioned, there have been exactly four tenured women since 1892. An unspoken doctrine of "No women need apply here" seems to prevail.

In another university it takes an average of three years for a male Ph.D. to move from assistant to associate professor. It takes a woman Ph.D. an average of nine years to achieve that rank.

Outside the women's colleges, how many women attain the rank of full professor? Such a woman is an exception, and it is a good guess that her road was harder, her qualifications superior to those of her male colleagues. Outside the women's colleges, how many women have become presidents, vice presidents, or deans, except deans of women? And we are not talking of a field like nuclear physics where one might expect men to dominate, but education, where women have traditionally played a strong role.

Is it any wonder, then, that the number of women in some professions is small, especially small when compared with some other industrialized nations today? Compared to our seven per cent for women physicians, the British have sixteen per cent and the Soviet Union 75 per cent. Only three per cent of our lawyers are women. In Germany nearly a third of the lawyers are women; in Denmark nearly half. Both France and Sweden have more women dentists and pharmacists than the United States. Women make up only nine per cent of our scientists, nine per cent of our professors, one per cent of our engineers.

Women one meets abroad and foreign women who visit this country usually ask the same question sooner or later: "In a country where women have so much freedom and where their voluntary organizations are so influential, why are there so few women in the Congress and in top government jobs?" Both India and Israel have women heads of government. Denmark has a woman on its highest court. How long will it be before a woman sits on the bench of our Supreme Court? When will we again have a woman cabinet member?

One obvious answer, of course, might be that the prospects are improving. The decade of the sixties has brought real changes in the prospects for women—changes in Federal Government hiring policy, as well as great advances in legislation. It helps us gain perspective if we recall that until 1962 it was the policy of Federal agencies to allow a hiring officer to specify a particular sex for a job if he chose to, regardless of the duties and without advancing any reasons.

Contrast that with government policy now: hire on the basis of merit alone, without regard to race, color, religion, national origin—or sex. The change has created a much more hospitable atmosphere for women, especially professional women. Between 1963 and 1968 the proportion of women among persons hired by the Federal Government from professional registers has doubled.

The change was set in motion in December 1961, when President Kennedy established the Commission on the Status of Women. One of his intentions was to make the Federal career service free of discrimination based on sex. The recommendations of the Commission laid the groundwork for legislation that followed, legislation rooted in the principle of equality. Because it was enforced, it altered the character of Federal hiring and will have, I believe, an even greater effect on the nation at large.

The first Federal legislative attack was on wage differentials based on sex. The Equal Pay Act of 1963 established in law the principle that men and women have a right to equal pay for equal work. " 'A fair day's work for a fair day's wages'; it is as just a demand as governed men ever made of governing. It is the everlasting right of man," said Thomas Carlyle in 1843. It took 120 years more to see that it was the everlasting right of women, too.

Enactment of Title VII of the Civil Rights Act of 1964 advanced still further the principle that men and women workers should be treated as equals, for it prohibited discrimination on the basis of sex in all phases of employment. Guidelines laid down for the interpretation of this law have established, for example, that a job cannot be limited to members of only one sex unless sex is a bona fide occupational qualification for that job; that help-wanted ads classified on the basis of sex, such as columns headed "Male" or "Female," constitute discrimination based on sex; that employers can no longer maintain separate lists for men and women for the purpose of deciding lines of progression for promotion or seniority; and that employers cannot discriminate in such areas as retirement and insurance plans.

The Equal Employment Opportunity Commission has issued a new guideline which provides that state labor laws applying to women, such as those regulating hours of work and weightlifting, may not be used by an employer as a defense to a charge of sex discrimination in failing to hire women. This has the effect of a ruling that Title VII supersedes a state's so-called protective labor laws.

The principle of equal opportunity was reinforced in 1967 when President Johnson amended Executive Order 11246 to outlaw discrimination on the basis of sex in Federal employment, in employment by Federal contractors and subcontractors, and in employment under federally assisted construction contracts. This order is a real boon to women workers in the private sector, since an employer who refuses to comply can lose existing contracts and be denied future contracts.

President Nixon has strengthened the position of women in Federal employment by issuing Executive Order 11478 in which he directs Federal agencies, under the leadership and guidance of the Civil Service Commission, to follow an affirmative program of equal employment opportunity which includes, of course, elimination of discrimination on the basis of sex. His order supersedes those sections of the amended Executive Order 11246 relating to Federal Government employment.

But it is not the legislative accomplishments alone that have changed the outlook on employment for women. What may have equal effect in the long run are the standards the government itself has adopted; for it is becoming a showcase of model employment practices.

I have been pointing to hopeful signs that all is getting better; and it is. But no one believes that all is well. We know, for example, that discrimination against women still manifests itself in two major ways—the kind of salaries they receive, and the kind of work they do. What women won in the Equal Pay Act of 1963 was the right; we have yet to win the reality. There are still many ways around the law and still many situations in which it does not apply. It is not always easy to prove that jobs are virtually equal, and many intangibles are involved the higher up the scale one goes. As a result there are often great differences between what a man is paid to do a job and what a woman is paid to do the same job.

. . . . .

While the salary gap affects the lower-income woman's pocketbook, women all along the line feel it. It injures the morale of the woman with a Ph.D. in chemistry who finds she earns less than a man with an undergraduate degree. Women near the top are constantly bumping their heads against an unseen ceiling. We know it's there even though some women break through it, and we suspect that the motto engraved on it is: "So far you may go and no farther." Its existence is confirmed in the statistics: less than three per cent of the fully employed working women have passed the $10,000 salary limit. Exactly 2.9 per cent are in that wage bracket. The proportion of men in that bracket is 28 per cent.

When it comes to the jobs women do, we feel discrimination is practiced here, too; sometimes obvious, sometimes subtle. We know that women are crowded disproportionately into the menial, low-paying jobs. A majority become service workers, clerks, salesgirls, factory workers, perhaps secretaries. There is nothing wrong with these jobs. But there *is* something wrong in having so little choice. There are many other jobs that women could do, and do very well. They would be well-suited, for example, as upholsterers, optical mechanics, tool-and-die makers, or as repairmen for small electrical appliances, watches, office machines, computers, radios, and television sets. This is just a fraction of the occupations that should be open to young women and for which we should make the necessary training available. The horizons for young women today are needlessly narrow; and we have not done nearly enough to broaden them.

The same story of limited horizons applies to women in professional or technical fields. We educate a great many women; then we simply do not give them jobs in which they can use their real abilities. One statistic that has always distressed me is: of employed women in 1968 who had completed five or more years of college, 7 per cent had taken jobs as unskilled or semi-skilled workers. That represents as astonishing waste of the real abilities of highly educated women.

People call attention to the fact that women have penetrated almost every occupational field, and this, of course, is true. But the fact disguises the reality. For the educated woman, as for the uneducated, certain fields are considered women's work; other fields are considered unsuitable. Of the entire women's work force, only 14 per cent of the workers could be classified as professional or technical, and of these, almost two thirds are either teachers or nurses and other health workers. The question is not whether it is possible for a woman to enter almost any field she chooses; obviously it is possible. But she must have a lot more drive to succeed. She must at a comparatively early age have encouragement, self-confidence, and commitment to a goal to go her own way against the full weight of society's opinion and expectations. That is asking much more of a young woman than we ask of a young man. Not many of us can do it at any age.

In the final analysis, the most difficult barriers facing women are the invisible ones. All but unreachable by legislation, these are the barriers that will be lowered only when we have educated the human heart. For the real enemy lies within. It expresses itself in all those unadmitted prejudices, unthinking assumptions, and outworn myths which, often so subtly, oppose the full development of a woman as an individual. The grandmother of all these myths is: "A woman's place is in the home." But there are many, many more. To sample a few common myths:

A woman must choose between home and a job; she cannot do both well.
When a woman works, the chances are increased that her children will become neurotic or troubled.
Women are overly emotional; they couldn't be cool under pressure.
Women have a great deal of intuition but men have the logical, analytical minds.

Women are practical and down-to-earth, but only a man can think abstractly, take the larger, long-range view.
Women just don't have what it takes.

These are the kinds of prejudices women absorb from the world around them from the time they are little girls. From them a girl learns what is expected of her: that she may do things, but not too well; that she may aspire, but not too high. These are some of the myths which condition a woman to put limitations upon her own expectations, to narrow her vision of the world and what she might do in it. The really pernicious aspect of these myths is not that men believe them, but that women do. If *you* do, then ask yourself: "How can we really change the thinking of the world unless we change our own thinking first?" Perhaps the freedom we seek must begin in our own hearts.

Finally, let us be clear in our own minds about what we really want. Is it equal pay, equal job opportunities, equal rights? Or are these just victories along the way to some larger goal? I believe there is a larger goal that we pursue. I believe that what women must have is freedom—the freedom to choose different life styles, the freedom to fulfill the best that is in them. A philosopher once said: "The great law of culture is: Let each become all that he was created capable of being." I do not think we ask for more than that. I am convinced we cannot settle for less.

NAME INDEX

SUBJECT INDEX

Acculturation, 42; of family, 73
Achievement: relation to family size, 94
Affirmative action: and discrimination, 245; and hiring practices, 249; and hiring policies, 251, 252
Alien Act of 1798, 15; and residential requirement for naturalization, 15
Alienation: and feeling of betrayal, 140
Americanization, 36; during WWI, 36; and literacy tests, 36; rejection of theory of, 40; and free public education, 159; and national identity, 159
American: ethnic stock, 23; idea of, 24; three levels of meaning, 24; time orientation of, 76, 77; activity orientation of, 77; middle class family values, 80; "other-directedness" of character, 104; system of values, 160; patterns of culture, 160
Anglo-conformity, 35, 36, 38
Apartheid: in U.S., universal vs. selective, 68
Asians: increasing immigration of, 3
Assimilation: and assimilationist doctrine, xi, xii; and American frontier, xi; of blacks, xiii; of groups vs. individuals, xvi, xvii; cultural vs. structural, xvii; models of, 4; methods, 33; three ideologies, 34; and immigration, 35; and attitudes, 35; melting pot, 36–39; and cultural pluralism, 39; as multitude of subprocesses, 41,

42; behavioral vs. structural, 42; and intermarriage, 42; and theory of voting behavior, 171

Bail system and blacks, 226
Baltimore: juvenile delinquency rates among blacks, 214
Banks: lending policies regarding minority groups, 202
Belgium: one minority vs. one majority group, 52
Black Academy of Arts and Letters, 152
Black Codes, 218
Black culture: reexamination of, xiv
Black ghetto, 128; and involuntary segregation, 129; and non-black enterprise, 129; and American colonialism, 129; as frontier, 129
Black Muslims, 70, 71, 152
Black nationalism: and black ethnocentrism, 70
Black Panthers, 123, 218, 223; conspiracy trial in New York, 220
Black power: and integration, 69; conception of, 71; as organized minority, 71
Black separatists: remedies for conditions, 28
Black studies, 152
Blacks: *see also* Negroes
Blacks: family life reexamination of, xiv; voting rights, xviii; in Jamestown (1619), 2; percentage in colonies (1776), 2; segregation of as an American institution, 2; migration from South into cities, 4; racial or ethnic group, 46; American heritage of, 47;

301